Dante's Christian Astrology

University of Pennsylvania Press
MIDDLE AGES SERIES
Edited by
Edward Peters
Henry Charles Lea Professor
of Medieval History
University of Pennsylvania

A listing of the available books
in the series appears at the
back of this volume

Dante's Christian Astrology

Richard Kay

University of Pennsylvania Press
Philadelphia

Kay, Richard, 1931–
    Dante's christian astrology / Richard Kay.
       p.   cm.—(Middle Ages series)
    Includes bibliographical references and index.
    ISBN 0-8122-3233-X
    1. Dante Alighieri, 1265–1321. Divina commedia. 2. Dante
Alighieri, 1265–1321—Knowledge—Astronomy. 3. Astronomy, Medieval,
in literature. 4. Planets in literature. I. Title. II. Series.
    PQ4401.K39 1994
    851′.1—dc20   93-33923
                                                                          CIP

Dedicated to my mother
CAROLYN KAY

Contents

List of Abbreviations

For a list of the astrologers cited, see p. 14, with further details in Appendix 1. The books of the Bible are cited according to the Latin Vulgate version; the principal difference is that Vulgate 1–2 Reg. = AV 1–2 Samuel and Vulgate 3–4 Reg. = AV 1–2 Kings. Other frequently cited works have been abbreviated as follows:

Busnelli-Vandelli	Dante, *Il Convivio*, ed. G. Busnelli and G. Vandelli, in *Opere di Dante*, ed. V. Branca et al., vols. 4 and 5, 2nd ed., rev. A. E. Quaglio (Florence: Le Monnier, 1964).
Caramello	Thomas Aquinas, *Summa theologiae*, ed. P. Caramello, 3 vols. (Turin: Marietti, 1952–56).
Grandgent	*La "Divina Commedia" di Dante Alighieri*, ed. C. H. Grandgent, rev. ed. (Boston: Heath, 1933).
Jackson	*Dante's "Convivio" Translated into English* by William Walrond Jackson (Oxford: Clarendon Press, 1909).
Musa	Dante, *The Divine Comedy*, trans. Mark Musa, 3 vols. (New York: Penguin Books, 1984–86).
Nicholl	Dante, *"Monarchy" and Three Political Letters*, trans. Donald Nicholl (New York: Noonday Press, 1954).
Petrocchi	Dante, *La "Commedia" secondo l'antica vulgata*, ed. G. Petrocchi, Edizione nazionale 7.1–4 (Milan: Mondadori, 1966–67).
Ryan	Dante, *The Banquet*, trans. Christopher Ryan, Stanford French and Italian Studies, vol. 61 (Saratoga, Calif.: ANMA Libri, 1989).

Sapegno   Dante, *La Divina Commedia*, ed. N. Sapegno, Let-
                            teratura italiana: Storia e testi, vol. 4 (Milan:
                            Ricciardi, 1957).

Singleton   Dante, *The Divine Comedy*, trans. Charles S.
                            Singleton, Bollingen Series 80, 6 vols. (Princeton,
                            N.J.: Princeton University Press, 1970–75).

Toynbee-Singleton   *A Dictionary of Proper Names and Notable Matters
                            in the Works of Dante*, by Paget Toynbee, rev.
                            Charles S. Singleton (Oxford: Clarendon Press,
                            1968).

Preface

In this study I seek to establish that Dante filled the planetary heavens of his *Paradiso* with allusions to astrology. As far as I know, this is the first systematic attempt to identify astrological allusions in the *Commedia*. A novel proposal such as this is only likely to find general acceptance if it is based on a mass of evidence that can be readily followed by a nonspecialist. Consequently I have concentrated on only one isolated type of astrological evidence, namely the properties of planets, because above all I wish to convince the reader that Dante did make use of astrology. By linking Dante and astrology, then, the title of this book—*Dante's Christian Astrology*—conveys the main thrust of the study; moreover, by adding the qualification "Christian," it emphasizes Dante's departures from traditional astrology, which will gradually become apparent in the course of the book. An alternate title, which describes this monograph with cumbersome precision, would be "Dante's use of the astrological properties of planets in *Paradiso* 1–22."

In terms of literary theory, this is an old-fashioned book that relies on comparison of texts, which is a conventional method of traditional philological and historical criticism. I have assumed that my reader is already familiar with Dante and his work but not with astrology. I have not, however, attempted to sketch either the history or the technique of medieval astrology, since excellent accounts of each are now available: S. J. Tester, *A History of Western Astrology* (Woodbridge, Suffolk: Boydell Press, 1987) and J. D. North, *Chaucer's Universe* (New York: Oxford University Press, 1988). Since both my sources and their authors are not well known, I have described them at length in a biobibliographical appendix. Because this study relies on astrological sources that are difficult of access, I have quoted the texts extensively in the notes. In the text itself I have tried to ease the reader's way by providing an English translation or paraphrase of passages in Latin or Italian. For the *Commedia*, I have used Charles Singleton's prose translation, *The Divine Comedy* (Princeton, N.J.: Princeton University Press, 1970–1975) but have occasionally altered it when greater precision was desirable. The Italian text of the *Comedy* is that of

G. Petrocchi, *La Commedia secondo l'antica vulgata* (Milan: Mondadori, 1966–1967), which conveniently accompanies Singleton's translation.

This book could not have been written without the generous financial support of the University of Kansas, which gave me two sabbatical leaves and a grant from the General Research Fund. And I have had more than a little help from my friends and fellow scholars, to whom I am grateful not only for instruction and bibliography, but also for their advice, encouragement, enthusiasm, sympathetic interest, and moral support: Patrick Boyde, Anthony K. Cassell, Charles T. Davis, Ernst S. Dick, Glenn M. Edwards, Thomas E. Hart, Robert B. Hollander, Jr., Amilcare Iannucci, Christopher Kleinhenz, Maristella Lorch, Denise Low, John F. McGovern, Edward Peters, Oliver C. Phillips, Sesto Prete, Nancy G. Siraisi, Jerry Stannard, and Patricia Zupan. Special thanks are due to my wife, Sherry, and to Richard R. Ring, for reading the entire manuscript with vigilance, and also to James Helyar, for drawing the figure in Appendix 2. I also profited from the criticism of participants in five International Congresses on Medieval Studies at Western Michigan University (1983–1989) and in the annual meeting of the American Association for Italian Studies at the University of Virginia (1990), where samples of my results were presented. The first half of the Introduction appeared in *The "Divine Comedy" and the Encyclopedia of Arts and Sciences: Acta of the International Dante Symposium, 13–16 November 1983, Hunter College, New York*, edited by Giuseppe Di Scipio and Aldo Scaglione (Amsterdam and Philadelphia: John Benjamins, 1988), as "Astrology and Astronomy" (pp. 147–162). For permission to reproduce Frederick Goldin's translation of Folquet de Marseille from *Lyrics of the Troubadours and Trouvères*, I am indebted to Doubleday, A Division of Bantam, Doubleday, Dell Publishing Group, Inc.

Introduction

Astronomy and astrology. In the Middle Ages, the two terms were synonymous, but today they designate two distinct and seemingly irreconcilable disciplines. In modern usage, the term astronomy is reserved for the scientific study of the physical universe, while astrology is restricted to attempts to discern the occult influence of heavenly bodies on terrestrial, and especially human, events. The distinction dates from the Scientific Revolution of the seventeenth century, which discredited the Aristotelian doctrine of the four elements and thereby deprived astrology of its physical basis in Greek natural science. To be sure, astrologers continued to discern astral influences, as they had done before the Greeks, but they could only claim that these influences existed without being able to provide any rational explanation of how they worked. The few cases in which the stars clearly did influence earthly affairs, most notably the heat and light of the Sun, had stood at the core of ancient astrology, but such physical phenomena have ceased to be stressed by modern astrologers, who for the most part have been content to operate in terms of hidden or occult phenomena. Thus astronomy and astrology are distinguished today by their concern, respectively, for the natural and the supernatural.

This distinction, so obvious to us, was unknown in the university culture of the Latin Middle Ages. For the scholastics, the seventh liberal art was a single science that embraced both astronomy and astrology, to use modern nomenclature. The unity of that discipline in their view is perhaps best indicated by the fact that it was designated by a single name, though not always the same one. Some, like Dante, called it *astrologia*,[1] while others, like Albertus Magnus, preferred to call it *astronomia*,[2] and yet others, like Aquinas, used the two terms interchangeably.[3] Whatever the name, the content of the subject was, like all medieval university disciplines, best defined by the textbooks and commentaries from which it was taught in the schools. At Bologna, for example, the earliest statutes, of 1404, provided for a professor of *astrologia* who offered a four-year degree program consisting of fifteen courses. By modern standards, four of them are exclusively mathematical, seven more are strictly astronomical, and only four courses are devoted to astrological texts: Alcabitius's *Isago-gicus*, Ptolemy's *Centiloquium* and *Quadripartitum*, and the *De urina non visa* by William of England.[4] Astrology and astronomy, then, were regularly combined in a single curriculum.

Although this science of *astrologia* was a distinct branch of study, it was not monolithic, for the schoolmen subdivided it, as they did any subject, by making rational distinctions. Here Albertus Magnus, as one of Dante's favorite authorities in scientific matters, is probably our best guide. In his *Speculum astronomiae*, Albertus begins by dividing the subject into theoretical and practical astronomy.[5] Theoretical astronomy, he explains, seeks to describe the motions of the heavenly bodies in mathematical terms, whereas practical, applied, or judicial astronomy "teaches us how things on earth are changed to this or to that by the change of heavenly bodies."[6] Since Albertus's two parts of astronomy do roughly correspond to our modern distinction between astronomy and astrology, it is convenient to designate them by these anachronistic terms, but it must be stressed that the correspondence is only approximate and that for medieval men both kinds of star science were serious and respectable academic disciplines.

The point I have been making is no doubt a truism, for it is a common (and correct) opinion widely held by our culture that in the Middle Ages even the most highly educated men believed in astrology, whereas the subject today lacks academic respectability. But it is nonetheless worth insisting on the difference between the medieval and modern attitudes towards astrology because it may well be that the modern prejudice against astrology has inclined scholars to neglect this aspect of Dante's medieval culture. Every serious student of the *Divine Comedy* is of course aware that Dante believed in astrology. To mention only the most memorable passages, in *Paradiso* 8.97–148 Carlo Martello explains how the influence of the stars can override heredity so that children often do not resemble their parents, and in *Purgatorio* 16.67–81 Marco Lombardo allows that people are influenced by the heavens to some extent but insists that nevertheless they have free will and therefore are morally responsible for their actions. In addition to these two conspicuous landmarks, there are over thirty less memorable but equally unmistakable references to astrology in Dante's works—two-thirds of them in the *Comedy* itself. A brief systematic survey of them is perhaps the best way to grasp the extent of Dante's commitment to astrology.

His fundamental premise is that the heavens are God's "instruments" for producing goodness on earth. Goodness originates as an idea in the divine mind, which uses the heaven as "the organ of the divine art" to impose form on matter. Thus the heavens are synonymous with universal Nature, which gives each individual thing its specific nature (*Mon.* 2.2.2–3; cf. *Par.* 2.121). They make each thing as perfect as it can be, given the state of the material, and hence Dante says that all philosophers are agreed that the heavens are the cause of perfection (*Conv.* 2.13.5).

Dante recognized that various theories had been proposed to explain how the heavens impart their influence. At one point in the *Convivio* (2.13.5) he lists three solutions without indicating his preference; later, however, he adopts the view of Aristotle and his school as apparently closest to the truth, but he does not refute the alternate explanations (4.21.2–3), which in fact reappear in his works without ever being quite reconciled to the Aristotelian position. (1) The first explanation, which following Albertus Magnus[7] he attributes to Plato, Avicenna, and Algazel, held that the influence of the heavens is due to the spirits that move them, namely the intelligences or angels. This view provided Dante with the fiction or conceit on which he based his *canzone* "Voi che intendendo il terzo ciel movete" (*Conv.* 2.4; cf. 2.15.1), and in *Paradiso* 28 Beatrice assures the Pilgrim that each heaven does indeed correspond to one order of the angelic hierarchy. (2) The second explanation ascribes the influence of the heavens to the stars themselves, from which, according to Platonist doctrine, all living souls had descended to earth. In the *Commedia*, the poet has Beatrice dismiss this view as an error if it is taken literally, but she allows that it may conceal some truth "if he [Plato's Timaeus] means that the honor of their influence and the blame returns to these wheels" (*Par.* 4.49–57; cf. 9.95–96). (3) Thus Plato's view is effectively assimilated to the third position, which is that of Aristotle and the astrologers. In this view, the heavens, and more particularly the stars themselves, possess what Dante calls "celestial virtue," which they radiate in the form of light (*Conv.* 2.6.9). Like the astrologers, Dante attributed such virtues, or powers, not only to the seven planets but also to the fixed stars, as it is most evident when he writes of Saturn mixing its power with that of the brightest star in the zodiacal constellation of Leo (*Par.* 21.14–15; cf. *Quest.* 65–71). Unlike the astrologers, Dante rarely describes the particular virtue or power of a given star, but when he does, he agrees with them. For example, Mars "dries up and burns everything because its heat is like that of fire" (*Conv.* 2.13.21).

For the most part, however, Dante is more concerned with what the planets can do rather than how they do it, and of all their effects he is most concerned with generation. The scope of the generative process is most broadly defined by the character Thomas Aquinas in *Paradiso* 13.64–66 as "the generated things which the moving heavens produce with seed and without it." An example of generation produced without seed is the emergence of the hemisphere of land, which Dante argues in the *Questio de aqua et terra* was caused by the heaven, and in particular by the heaven of the fixed stars (65–69). Except for this isolated case, Dante usually concerns himself with the role of the heavens in the generation of animate, rather than inanimate, things. "Our life," he asserts, "and also the life of every living thing here below is caused by the heaven" (*Conv.* 4.23.6; cf. 2.14.17). Not only do the heavens give life; they also "direct every seed to some end according as the stars are its companions" (*Purg.* 31.109–111).

While thus acknowledging the power of the heavens over minerals, vegetables, and animals, Dante far more often considers astral influence in a specifically human context. His account of prenatal development, for example, recognizes three factors that determine the quality of the embryo before it receives the rational soul, or possible intellect, directly from God: the disposition of the parents, of the elements, and of the heavens. "The disposition of the heavens for this effect," he explains, "may be good, better, or best, for this varies on account of the constellations, which are always changing" (*Conv.* 4.21.4, 7). Thus for Dante the moment of conception is astrologically more important than that of birth, and accordingly in the *Vita nuova* Beatrice's affinity for the number nine is explained in these terms: "at her generation the relationship between all the nine moving heavens was most perfect" (*Vita nuova* 29.2).

In the *Commedia* Dante repeatedly refers to the role of the stars in shaping human character, but one passage is the key to all the others. In the heaven of Venus, Carlo Martello explains that although heredity is the basic influence that shapes human character, a second factor is often more influential, for the heavens can override heredity (*Par.* 8.133–135). Between them, these two factors account for the differences in human character, and the reason for this modification of heredity, Carlo explains, is because through it God provides the diversity of talents that are required by organized human society, which is based on specialization and exchange of services. "Therefore the roots of your works must needs be diverse, so that one is born Solon and another Xerxes, one Melchizedek and another he [Daedalus] who flew through the air and lost his son" (*Par.* 8.124–126).

These four examples are usually taken to represent four different professions, namely the legislator or politician, the general, the priest, and the mechanical inventor,[8] as, to be sure, they are; but they are also something more, for the examples are paired, each pair presenting a contrast between the right and wrong use of talent. Thus Solon was a wise political leader who promoted the welfare of his people by improving the laws, whereas Xerxes was not only an unsuccessful warrior but also a foolish king, whom Dante elsewhere reproaches for his pride, which led him to bridge the Hellespont and attempt the conquest of the rest of the world (*Mon.* 2.8.7; *Purg.* 28.71–72). Melchizedek and Daedalus are contrasted in the second pair: the one was the pious, priestly king of (Jeru)Salem, who is chiefly distinguished in the Bible because he gave both God and his victorious servant Abram their due (Gen. 14.18–20), and the other, who impiously, and ultimately to his sorrow, used his ingenuity to improve on God's creation by devising artificial wings whereby men, contrary to nature, could fly through the air. By these contrasts, the poet suggests that there is yet another factor that determines human character, namely free will, which enables each person to use or abuse the talents conferred on him by heredity and/or by the heavens.

This last point is more explicitly developed by Dante in connection with his own use of genius. Three times in the course of the *Commedia* the poet attributes his own *ingegno* to astral influence, most unmistakably in the constellation of Gemini under which he was born: "O glorious stars, O light impregnated with mighty power, from which I derive all my genius, whatsoever it may be" (*Par.* 22.112–117; cf. *Inf.* 15.55–59 and 26.21–24). (This, I believe, is the only astral endowment that is identified by name in the poem. True, in *Paradiso* 9, Cunizza says that she was conquered by the light of the planet Venus [32–33], and Folco later states that he was imprinted by the same light, but the reader is left to discover what the intended effect was in each case.) Why Dante chose to stress the astrological origin of his own *ingenium* is by no means clear, but one advantage is that in his use of this talent he can exemplify for the reader the proper relationship between astral influence and free will. This he does in an aside just before he describes his encounter with Ulysses; he says that he is restraining his genius here more than he usually does because its use should always be guided by virtue; to do otherwise would be to abuse a good gift that has been given to him, perhaps by a beneficent star or even by God's grace itself.

> e più lo 'ngegno affreno ch'i' non soglio,
> perché non corra che virtù nol guidi;
>   sì che, se stella bona o miglior cosa
>   m'ha dato 'l ben, ch'io stessi nol m'invidi.   (*Inf.* 26.21–24)

Thus it appears that Dante is endowed with a certain character, but it can used for either good or evil, and the moral responsibility is his alone.

The recognition that individuals are morally responsible for the use they make of their respective natural endowments stands in sharp contrast to the attitude of the souls who, as they assemble inside the gate of Hell, "curse God, their parents, the human race, the place, the time, the seed of their begetting and of their birth" (*Inf.* 3.103–105). This list amounts to a comprehensive catalogue of all the factors natural and supernatural that enter into Dante's account of human generation, so the lost souls are assuming that their fate was determined by something beyond their control; they do not recognize that they also had the gift of free will.

Again, the same point is made, most clearly of all, by Marco Lombardo in *Purgatorio* 16. Having declared that no one these days tries to be virtuous (47–48), Marco is asked by the Pilgrim whether this lack of moral purpose is caused by the heavens or by something on earth (58–63), and he begins his answer by ruling out astral determinism in the most explicit terms:

> You who are living refer every cause upward to the heavens alone, as if they of necessity moved all things with them. If this were so, free will would be destroyed in you, and there would be no justice in happiness for good or grief for evil. The heavens initiate your movements: I do not say all of them, but supposing I did say so, a light is given you to know good and evil, and free will, which if it endure fatigue in its first battles with the heavens, afterwards, if it is well nurtured, it conquers completely. You lie subject, in your freedom, to a greater power and to a better nature, and that creates the mind in you which the heavens have not in their charge. (*Purg.* 16.67–81)

Marco, in his trenchant manner, represents free will as fighting battles ("battaglie") with the heavens, which can be misleading if we take him to mean that the stars impel people to do evil, and therefore that their influence must be resisted. It would be more accurate to say that people receive certain capacities from the stars, or if you will, from Nature, and these talents are basically good at least, while some are better and others are best (*Conv.* 4.21.7); but, like Dante's genius, they can all be misused unless free will constantly guides them along the paths of virtue. The battle, then, is that between a spirited horse and its rider: potentially it is a good thing to have a horse, but in actuality its value depends on how it is trained. If broken to bit and bridle ("affreno," *Inf.* 26.21), a horse can be guided by its rider; otherwise it can be a liability. Marco's battle between the heavens and the will, then, refers to the breaking-in period, when the will struggles to gain mastery over the amoral powers of human nature that are the result of astral influence.[9]

In the essentially ethical context of Purgatory, there is considerable practical value in assuming that human nature is an adversary to be conquered, but in Paradise astral influence appears in a different, more positive light. There Carlo Martello urges us to accept the nature that the stars have conferred on us because it is part of God's plan, and specifically he would have each person follow a career that fits its talents (*Par.* 8.139–148). Although Carlo does not recommend recourse to astrology in so many words, he does insist that people should pay attention "to the foundation which Nature lays" (143), which is what medieval astrology professed to teach. We need not hesitate to include Dante himself among those who believed in the efficacy of a science of astrology, for he declared his convictions on the subject with remarkable vigor: "it is without doubt within the capacity of human understanding to comprehend the mover of the heaven, and his will, through the motion thereof."[10] Thus for Dante, astrology is a rational alternative to revelation, for it permits humans to discover the will of God by closely observing the heavens, which act on earthly things as agents of divine providence.

The talents conferred on humans *in utero* are not the only way in which God, working through the stars, indicates his will; a person continues to be subject to their influence throughout his life. A relatively simple example of the way in which humanity is thus subject to the influence of Nature is the annual cycle of seasonal change. Thus at the beginning of the *Inferno* we find the Pilgrim hopeful because the Sun "was with the stars that were with it when divine love first set those beautiful things in motion" (*Inf.* 1.37–40); and the narrator elaborates at the beginning of the *Paradiso*, explaining that after the Sun passes the point of the vernal equinox, it has "a better course and [is] conjoined with better stars, and tempers and stamps the wax of the world more after its own fashion" (*Par.* 1.37–42). At the winter solstice, on the other hand, the Sun's course makes the season cold and bitter, an effect that at times is enhanced by the placement of the other planets, as was the case in December 1296, when

Dante took such a configuration as the occasion for his *canzone* "Io son venuto."[11]

These seasonal variations are obvious, because familiar, examples of divine providence operating through the stars, but Nature imposes God's will on man in less evident ways as well. In addition to short-term, seasonal changes, the stars also produce long-term, secular trends by altering the irrational preferences of mankind. This truth is revealed in Paradise by Adam, who uses it to explain why not even man's first language was immutable: "for never was any product of reason durable forever, because of human liking (*lo piacere uman*), which is renewed, following the heavens" (*Par.* 26.127–129). Moreover, the influence of particular planets can bring about major political upheavals, for example "the death of kings and the transfer of kingdoms," which Dante, citing the astrologer Albumasar, says "are the effect of the lordship of Mars" (*Conv.* 2.13.22).[12] But the importance Dante attached to such influences can best be appreciated from the conclusion of the *Monarchia*, where, in a passage that has often been misinterpreted,[13] he argues that the emperor must be selected and confirmed directly by God:

> And since the disposition of this world follows the disposition of the heavens, which changes as they revolve, it is necessary that this caretaker [of the world, i.e., the emperor] be appointed by one [i.e., God] who contemplates the entire disposition of the heaven [throughout time] as immediately present, so that the advantageous principles of liberty and peace can be applied suitably to [different] places and times. (*Mon.* 3.15.12)

In other words, God, working through the stars, not only produces new political and social conditions, but also provides a ruler with the character required to deal with these changing circumstances. Thus, Dante reasons, the emperor is really appointed by God directly, not indirectly through the pope or the German electors, who are merely his spokesmen, proclaiming the divine will. That the emperor derives his authority directly from God is the final and politically most significant conclusion of the *Monarchia*, and to reach it Dante relied on astrology.

The emperor, of course, is only a special case of the process that Carlo Martello described, by which the heavens provide talented specialists adapted to the needs of society at a given time. For Dante, the most important of all these heaven-sent specialists was to be the Veltro, the hound who he expected would eventually appear and expel from human society the old wolf of Greed—or is it Fraud? (*Inf.* 1.101–111). By addressing his expectations directly to the heavens, the narrator indicates that he considered the appearance of this mysterious reformer to be governed by the stars: "O heaven, in whose revolution it seems conditions here below are thought to be changed, when will he come through whom she shall depart?" (*Purg.* 20.13). Similarly, Beatrice predicts that sometime in the next seventy centuries or so, "before January be all unwintered," a reforming governor will appear when "these lofty circles shall so shine forth" (*Par.* 27.139–148). Whatever these prophecies meant—and I am not at all sure that Dante himself could be precise about them—it is clear that they depend on the action of the stars, and consequently they are most probably derived from astrology.

Beyond prophecy, there is God's plan for the salvation of mankind, which is only imperfectly known to men, but Dante is sure that the stars play an essential role in this as well. When the Pilgrim is shown the souls that have been saved, Beatrice exclaims: "Behold the hosts of Christ's triumph and all the fruit garnered from the circling of these spheres" (*Par.* 23.21).

To sum up Dante's views on astrology, then, we can say that he believed that the stars were God's instruments for expressing his will through Nature. Moreover, a science of astrology is possible because through study man can understand God's will as it is manifested in the movements of the heavens. Although such a science can be useful in explaining the generation of minerals and plants, its chief practical value lies in discovering the innate strengths and weaknesses of human character that fit individuals for particular social functions. Because people have free will, however, astrology cannot predict how they are going to use the talents with which they were endowed by the stars. Finally, because whatever the stars have impressed with their influence continues to be subject to them, everything on earth is constantly responding to the ebb and flow of astral impulses, which God uses to regulate human affairs. Thus God's will concerning mankind as a whole, as well as his will in particular cases, can be ascertained from the stars. In short, astrology is for Dante the highest and most useful study of nature.

Dante's commitment to astrology has long been recognized and will come as no surprise to scholars. The *Enciclopedia dantesca*, for example, devoted seven columns to a summary not dissimilar to the one given above.[14] What is surprising is that Dante's astrology has attracted so little scholarly attention, particularly in comparison with his astronomy. The extent of the disproportion can be roughly gauged in an essay by Edward Moore, who took over a hundred pages to discuss Dante's astronomy but covered his astrology in less than two.[15] Or again, to offer a more recent example, Patrick Boyde's survey of Dante's views on man in the cosmos allots four pages to astrology and forty to astronomy.[16] The impression gained from counting pages is borne out by the bibliography of the two allied subjects. Dante's astronomy has given rise to a whole library of scholarship, so that today the student seeking comprehensive treatment of Dante's astronomy can consult, in addition to the works just mentioned, five book-length surveys by Orr,[17] Capasso,[18] Gizzi,[19] Pecoraro,[20] and, best of all, by Buti and Bertagni,[21] not to mention the scores of articles, monographs, and older works on which these syntheses are based. By contrast, Dante's astrology has never been studied, even once, with the intensity of any of these works. As far as I can discover, there are but two slender books and one article that profess in their titles to treat Dante's astrology,[22]—the most recent of them published in 1930—and I know of only one contemporary scholar, Robert Durling, who is using astrology to explicate the works of Dante (n. 11, above).

Given Dante's obvious commitment to astrology, it seems strange that this aspect of his thought has not attracted more attention, but there are good reasons for the disparity between interest in Dante's astrology and in his astronomy. Astronomy is certainly more to the modern taste, and some of the best work on Dante's astronomy has been done by scientists like Angelitti and Orr. Moreover, relatively more is known about medieval astronomy because historians of science, with some few notable exceptions, have generally tended to trace back the roots of modern science rather than to trouble themselves with what appears to be the endless elaboration of superstition; so the literary historian who is interested in astrology must work in a field that has not been as intensively cultivated as have most aspects of medieval university culture. Still, lack of popular interest and difficulty of access would not suffice to deter scholars if the need for research were manifest. The *Commedia* bristles with obscure astronomical passages that plainly call for explication, and the need is all the more urgent because they in turn promise to provide a secure chronological framework for the poem: Capasso, for example, has singled out for astronomical commentary almost a hundred passages of the *Comedy*. In contrast, there are only about two dozen passages in the poem that make overt reference to astrology, and almost every one seems intelligible without any special technical expertise.

This situation of course does not rule out the possibility that Dante used astrology in less obvious ways throughout the poem. For it is hardly possible to conceal an allusion to astronomy, which by its nature must refer plainly to the stars, their motions, or the effects thereof, such as time; astrology, on the other hand, lends itself to veiled allusions, since its effects are largely psychological. For example, a reference to war or violence implies the influence of Mars, just as Venus would be indicated in a context of sensual love. These examples are the commonplaces of popular astrology, and they do, of course, occur in the appropriate heavens of the *Paradiso*, but by using the elaborate lists of planetary properties found in most introductions to astrology, one can discover less obvious allusions that would be apparent only to one familiar with the technical literature of astrology. Indeed, Dante's abundant allusions to biblical, philosophical, and literary texts make it highly probable that he made similar use of astrology. And just as one must necessarily be familiar with the Bible, Aristotle, Virgil, Ovid, or Boethius in order to detect the poet's echoes from these authors, so one would have to be equally conversant with his astrological authorities in order to perceive whether he used them.

If Dante had indicated without ambiguity that he approved of any work on astrology, no doubt it would have been thoroughly examined by Dantists long ago. But in fact the astrological authors who appear in the *Comedy* either are better known for other works or else are rendered suspect by the circumstances of their damnation. In the first class, that of authors who were not primarily astrologers, the most trustworthy must be Albertus Magnus in the heaven of the Sun (*Par.* 10.93–99), whose contribution to Latin astrology was chiefly a bibliography of astrological works that Christians might legitimately consult. Three further astrological authorities can be identified among the philosophers in the Noble Castle (*Inf.* 4.131, 132, 142): Aristotle, whose physiognomic works were an integral part of the medieval astrological corpus;[23] Plato, whose astrological doctrines in the *Timaeus* were given qualified approval by Beatrice (*Par.* 4.49–57); and Ptolemy, author of the *Centiloquium* and *Quadripartitum* (or *Tetrabiblos*), which were both university texts in astrology.[24] But Dante's regard for the works of professional astrologers has been cast in doubt by the presence of two of them, Michael Scot and Guido Bonatti, among the diviners in *Inferno* 20.115–118. This circumstance has suggested to many that Dante disapproved of astrologers, and of these two in particular, and I believe that this assumption, more than anything else, has discouraged Dantists from studying astrology with the same care that they accord to the other branches of medieval culture.

A close reading of *Inferno* 20, however, can put these apprehensions to rest. Elsewhere I have argued that the diviners who precede Michael Scot in the procession through this *bolgia* were each endowed with a special gift of prophecy that enabled him, or her in the case of Manto, to foresee what divine judgments lay in the future. This foresight was not in itself sinful; the fault lay rather in failing to accept the divine judgment as the unchangeable will of God.[25] Astrologers, of course, possess no special gift of prophecy, but by studying the heavens they too can discover the will of God, and either accept it or attempt to circumvent it. Scot was certainly guilty of the latter, for he tried to prevent his own death as foretold to him by the stars;[26] but that did not discredit his study of astrology. Dante in fact indicates his approval of Scot's major astrological work, the *Liber introductorius*, by using its most popular part, a treatise on physiognomy, to characterize the author himself. For Dante's description of Scot as one "who is so spare in the flanks" (*Inf.* 20.115) indicates, according to Scot's own system of physiognomy, one "who is sagacious, bad, and just with respect to what is good."[27] Thus Dante could approve Scot's learning and at the same time could condemn the man for presuming to defraud God by attempting to forestall what God had willed. Hence the way now stands open to consult Scot's works, and also presumably those of Bonatti, as possible sources of Dante's astrology.

The present book is a preliminary reconnaissance into this virtually unexplored territory. My primary goal throughout has been to determine whether Dante made substantial use of astrological materials in the *Commedia*. Rabuse had shown that an approach by way of Hell was possible, but the lukewarm reception of his study did not encourage a second attempt via this route. Perhaps, I reasoned, he had taken up the stick by the wrong end. After all, nothing is clear or conclusive in Dante's Hell; the process of clarification only begins in Purgatory and reaches its culmination in Paradise. Of the two, Paradise seemed the better place to look because the seven planets themselves provide the *mise en scène* for the first two-thirds of the cantica. If astrology plays some part in the poem, it would be like Dante to make that role most evident when the Pilgrim visits the sources of astral influence. Therefore I decided to concentrate my search on the seven planetary heavens in *Paradiso*.

The other half of my problem was what to look for. Even the simplest manuals of astrology bristle with technicalities that can be applied to literature, as J. D. North has done for Chaucer and J. M. Richardson for Spenser.[28] But I hesitated to emulate them, both because I lacked their technical expertise in astrology and because I suspected that few Dantists would be convinced by arguments based on the technicalities of an esoteric and unfamiliar discipline. To carry conviction, my study would be better conducted in terms with which both I and my readers were more familiar. Fortunately, such a nontechnical approach to astrology was a regular feature of elementary handbooks on the subject, for the astrologers compiled long lists of the "properties of planets." Such a list begins with the characteristics that are proper to the planet itself, such as the elements for which it has an affinity, its strength by night and by day, and its sexual nature. The greater part of the list, however, is a catalogue of things on earth that the planet signifies, or indicates. The best example is provided by al-Biruni, who methodically listed forty categories for each planet, four of which defined the planet's own nature, while the remaining thirty-six classified its terrestrial influences.[29] A few sample rubrics will illustrate the broad scope of the classification: a planet can indicate smell, taste, and color; countries, climates, and kinds of terrain; metals and gems; trees, crops, and fruits; animals, classified as quadrupeds and birds; human passions, temperaments, and powers of growth; parts of the human body; kin relationships; personal disposition, aptitude, manners, and morals; social classes, trades, and professions; and kinds of religious life.

Such planetary properties were ideal for my purpose because their presence in the *Commedia* could be readily ascertained without astrological expertise. The requisite methods were already well known to philologists as those of *Quellenkunde*: the close comparison of texts for verbal, or at least conceptual, echoes. Thus my study would be accessible to the judgment of most of my intended audience. The diversity of the lists was also an advantage, because the wide range of subjects treated promised many points of comparison with Dante's text.

Scot and Bonatti, the two astrologers named in *Inferno* 20, both included exceptionally long lists of these planetary properties, but I thought it wise to cast my net more widely. Could I find other lists that Dante was likely to have consulted? I began, as I thought Dante might have done, with the bibliographical guide to astrology compiled by Albertus Magnus, who was one of the poet's favorite scholastic authorities, especially on scientific matters.[30] His *Speculum astronomiae* in fact recommends eight books on the principles of judicial astrology, which include the study of properties.[31] Identifying and locating these texts was facilitated by Carmody's repertory of Latin astrological texts.[32] Two of Albertus's references were eventually discarded,[33] but the other six usefully supplemented Scot and Bonatti. Another treatise, by Abraham Ibn Ezra, was included in the survey although it was not mentioned by either Dante or Albertus. Thus I had nine lists of planetary properties to look for in the *Paradiso*. Here are the full citations, listed in chronological order:

Ptolemy, *Quadripartitum* 2.8 (with Firmicus Maternus, *Astronomicon*, 3rd ed., Basel: Hervagius, 1551), pp. 29–32.

Albumasar, *Introductorium in astrologia* 7.5 (Venice: Sessa, 1506), fols. g5r–g7r.

Alcabitius, *Opus ad scrutanda stellarum magisteria isagogicum* 2.1–7 (Venice: Liechtenstein, 1521), fols. 9r–12v.

Haly Abenragel, *De iudiciis astrorum* 1.4 (Venice: Sessa, 1503), fols. 3r–4v.

John of Seville, *Isagoge* 13–19 (Nuremberg: Montanus and Neuber, 1548), fols. D1–D2.

Abraham Ibn Ezra, *In re iudiciali opera* 1.4 (Venice: Liechtenstein, 1507), fols. E2v–F2r.

Anonymous, *Liber novem iudicum* 13.3 (Oxford, Bodleian Library, MS Digby 149), fols. 210rb–212va.

Michael Scot, *Liber introductorius* 3 (Munich, Staatsbibliotek, MS Clm. 10268), fols. 100ra–104vb.

Guido Bonatti, *De astronomia* 1.3.1–7 (Basel: n. p., 1550), cols. 97–119.

Since most of these lists fill only a few pages and proceed planet by planet, it seems superfluous to repeat the full reference each time the author is cited. Instead, I cite only the author on the understanding that the reader is referred to the list above for the full citation.[34] Biographical and bibliographical notes on these sources will be found in Appendix 1.

Once I had these astrological texts in hand, I proceeded to compare them with what Dante had written about the seven planetary heavens. Since both Dante and the astrologers used the planets as their organizing principle, I followed the same course and studied one planet at a time. First I made an index card for each mention of a property, including even those I had no expectation of finding in the *Comedy*. With these gleanings in mind, I then read and re-read Dante's text, again noting on cards every passage that might possibly refer to a planetary property. I next combined the two sets of cards and organized them by categories, such as "professions" and "parts of the body." In the final stage, I scrutinized each category for correspondences between the astrologers and Dante, and in the process discarded about two-thirds of the cards.[35]

The cards that remained were my results. I could have presented them in the order they appear in the *Commedia*, as Edward Moore did in his study of Scripture and classical authors in Dante,[36] but that seemed inappropriate because Dante often made multiple use of the same property, which could be brought out more effectively by discussing each property in turn. Although this information, too, could be presented in an itemized list that was organized systematically by categories, a less austere and more readable approach seemed preferable, especially because the results often required, or at least invited, interpretation, which could better be done in essay form.

Although the mechanics of my method have been simple, progress has been neither easy nor routine, because Dante's use of his astrological sources becomes increasingly complex as he moves closer to God. In the lower heavens, the poet appropriates the indications of the astrologers in a straightforward, though selective, way; in the higher heavens, above the Sun, however, astrology is tempered by theology, becoming most clearly what I call Dante's Christian astrology. This development is, I think, another instance of Dante's conviction that human reason must be guided by divine revelation. The details of this thesis will be presented in due course, but the general tendency of my argument should be made plain at the outset, lest anyone imagine that I am attempting to substitute astrology for the better known sources of the poem. To be sure, because my subject is astrology, I usually consider it in isolation; only by exception do I consider Dante's other sources, when astrology alone provides an insufficient explanation.

The correspondences between Latin astrology and the *Commedia* are the core of this book. I have included all the parallels that seemed plausible, as well as a very few that are tentative. If the text sometimes seems overburdened by the accumulation of detail, it should be remembered that my primary purpose is to demonstrate that Dante used astrological materials in the poem. While a few points of contact, however apt, might be dismissed as coincidence, the probability of a causal connection approaches certainty as the number of cases grows. My demonstration that Dante used astrology rests, in large part, on the sheer weight of the evidence.

Once the presence of astrology in the poem is established, this fact raises new questions. Do these allusions to astrology enhance our understanding of the poem? Do they resolve disputes over obscure passages? Do they reinforce the already impressive coherence of the poem? And, perhaps most tantalizing of all, are they omnipresent in the poem, or just concentrated in the planetary heavens? I will offer some provisional answers to all but the last of these questions, but by no means do I pretend to have treated Dante's use of astrology exhaustively, even in the first two-thirds of the *Paradiso*. At best I hope to show that interpreters of the poem must take astrology into account no less than the other disciplines that Dante drew on.

1. The Moon

In a moral poem such as the *Commedia*, the most important influence of astrology will be exercised on human character. Indeed, as we have seen, the poet has assured us through the veracious medium of two blessed souls that they bear the imprint of the planets in which the Pilgrim encounters them.[1] Therefore, the search for astrological allusions in the heaven of the Moon can best begin where it is most assured of success. If we can find clear indications of Lunar influence at work in the life and character of the souls that appear in the first heaven, then we can proceed with some assurance to seek other uses of astrology in the same heaven.

The only souls to be identified in the heaven of the Moon are Piccarda and Costanza. Both are women, and this is an encouraging start, since astrologers agreed that the Moon, like Venus, is a feminine planet.[2] Unlike Venusian women, however, the women of the Moon exhibit "little lust";[3] instead, they are honorable, respectable women ("mulieres honestas")[4] whose lives were untouched by the sort of scandal that made Cunizza notorious. In fact each woman is first presented to the reader in terms of her family relationship, and in each case it is a relationship that is governed astrologically by the Moon. Piccarda is first mentioned in *Purgatorio* 24, where her brother Forese identifies her as "la mia sorella" (13), and her sisterhood is appropriate to the Moon, which signifies sisters, especially when adults.[5] "La gran Costanza" is similarly identified with reference to her family position, as mother of the Emperor Frederick II (*Par.* 3.118–120), just as the Moon also signifies mothers.[6] As the paternal aunt of the last Norman king of the Regno, her marriage to the future Emperor Henry VI brought the crown of Sicily to the Hohenstaufen dynasty, and this pivotal relationship to her brother's son is one that again is proper to the Moon.[7]

Thus Lunar astrology has provided the poet with some basic categories that seem to have guided his choice of characters who appear in the first heaven. In their sex, social standing, and genealogical position, both Piccarda and Costanza are appropriate to the Moon. But the Moon's influence on them goes beyond these general categories to pervade their entire character and career.[8]

Reluctant Secularization

The two women may be treated together because in the most significant particulars they are in fact two parallel examples of the same set of Lunar influences. Comparison of the two cases is immediately invited because both are presented in a single speech (*Par.* 3.97–120) and, moreover, their similarity is emphasized by the express statement that what is said of one is to be understood of the other (112). Let us accordingly review the two cases as Piccarda presented them, collect the features that are common to both, and then see to what extent these generalizations are founded in Lunar astrology.

Piccarda's speech is a clarification for the Pilgrim, who, although he knew her well enough to inquire after her by name when he met her brother (*Purg.* 24.10), still is apparently puzzled to find her among those whom Beatrice has told him were "assigned here for failure in their vows" (*Par.* 3.30). Piccarda had elaborated this only in general terms, explaining that "this lot, which appears so lowly, is given to us because our vows were neglected and void in some particular" (*Par.* 3.55–57). After she had assured him that she is content with her place in Paradise, he next wants to know what the vow was that she had failed to fulfill (*Par.* 3.94–96). In response, Piccarda begins by specifying for the first time the kind of vow in question:

> "Perfetta vita e alto merto inciela
>   donna più sù," mi disse, "a la cui norma
>   nel vostro mondo giù si veste e vela,
> perché fino al morir si vegghi e dorma
>   con quello sposo ch'ogne voto accetta
>   che caritate a suo piacer conforma."   (*Par.* 3.97–102)

"Perfect life and high merit enheaven a lady more aloft," she said to me, "according to whose rule, in your world below, are those who take the robe and veil themselves that they, even till death, may wake and sleep with that Spouse who accepts every vow which love conforms unto His pleasure."

This vow is a religious one, which is described with legal precision in terms of a formal constitution or rule ("norma," 98). The particular religious order is not expressly identified, although the Poor Clares would seem to be implied because it was the only one that had received its rule from a woman.[9] This reticence is significant, not only as a practical exercise of humility, but also because it directs the reader's attention away from the features peculiar to Saint Clare's rule and stresses instead those elements that were common to all orders of nuns. Thus what is said of Piccarda's vows can also apply to Costanza's, which were taken before the foundation of the Poor Clares. The point, then, is that the vows in question are the solemn vows taken by a nun. Again with legal precision, Dante leaves no doubt about the character of these vows. They include, but are not limited to, the profession of virginity, symbolized by the veil; in addition, they involve the assumption of a religious habit ("veste," 99), which distinguishes the wearer as a member of a particular community. As the bridal veil suggests, the vows are for life ("fino al morir," 100), the nun having taken Christ as her bridegroom ("sposo," 101), who is the object of her contemplative life in an enclosed community.

Having established this context, Piccarda swiftly sketches first her own history and then that of Costanza:

> Dal mondo, per seguirla, giovinetta
>   fuggi'mi, e nel suo abito mi chiusi
>   e promisi la via de la sua setta.
> Uomini poi, a mal più ch'a bene usi,
>   fuor mi rapiron de la dolce chiostra:
>   Iddio si sa qual poi mia vita fusi.
> . . . .
> ciò ch'io dico di me, di sé intende;
>   sorella fu, e così le fu tolta
>   di capo l'ombra de le sacre bende.
> Ma poi che pur al mondo fu rivolta
>   contra suo grado e contra buona usanza,
>   non fu dal vel del cor già mai disciolta.   (*Par.* 3.103–108, 110–117)

From the world, to follow her [Clare], I fled while yet a girl, and in her habit I clothed me and promised myself to the way of her order.

Then men, more used to evil than to good, snatched me from the
sweet cloister: and God knows what then my life became. . . .
[Costanza] understands of herself that which I say of me. She was a
sister, and from her head in like manner was taken the shadow of the
sacred veil. Yet, turned back as she was into the world, against her
will and against right custom, from her heart's veil she was never
loosed.

Clearly the two biographies are parallel, and indeed so similar that they
appear to be two instances of the same phenomenon. I would suggest that
the poet does this at the beginning of *Paradiso* in order to teach us how to
read this third part of the poem. On finding two cases of the same sort,
the reader's attention is naturally drawn by comparison to the general features they have in common. At the same time, Piccarda's vagueness about
particulars, which we have already noted at the beginning of this speech,
discourages any counter-tendency to dwell on the contrasting features that
individualize each case. In short, we learn from this presentation to take
the characters in Paradise as particular illustrations of general categories.

The generalized picture that emerges from such a comparison is easily
drawn. The composite is a well-born woman who has taken solemn religious vows to live as a nun in a religious community, and most particularly she has assumed the veil as a token of perpetual chastity. However,
she is forced to break this vow by leaving the convent and contracting a
marriage to which she would really rather not be a party. The identity of
those men who bring about this change does not seem to be important;
what is stressed is that theirs was an act of violence, as the verbs imply
("mi rapiron," "fu tolta," and "fu rivolta," *Par.* 3.107, 113, 115), and that they
should have known better because their offense was not only a technical
violation of canon law but also a breach of the customary good behavior
of their own society (105, 116). The purpose for which she was taken from
the cloister is wholly irrelevant and consequently is indicated only by implication: it must have been marriage because at the conclusion of the
speech Costanza is identified with reference to her husband and son
(118–120). The main point is that for the rest of their days both women
preferred their former life: this is explicitly stated about Costanza (117) and
is implicit in Piccarda's genteel expression of distaste for her postclaustral
life—a distaste that we may gather was lifelong because she is still main-
taining it in the afterlife. Sources outside the poem in fact justify the infer-

ence that Piccarda, too, was married off, to a member of her brother's political party, Rossellino della Tosa.[10]

The Moon and Religion

Since an attachment to virginity is the constant factor in both careers, anyone conversant with ancient mythology could detect some evidence of Lunar influence, inasmuch as Diana, goddess of the Moon, was the patroness of virgins. Strange to tell, hardly any trace of this classical connection between the Moon and virginity remains in medieval astrology.[11] Instead, the astrologers provide even more specific reasons for the presence of these nuns in the heaven of the Moon. According to Albumasar, the Moon gives one "the intention to contemplate high things,"[12] and although this may simply mean that the Moon enkindles "the soul's affection for rational knowledge,"[13] a substantial body of astrological opinion understood the contemplative life fostered by the Moon to be that of religion. Alcabitius, in the most popular medieval handbook of astrology, flatly stated that "in matters of faith, the Moon signifies religion."[14]

These terse, somewhat ambiguous indications provided by the Arabic astrologers are expanded by their Latin successors in a way that unmistakably applies to Piccarda and Costanza. One is the Christian priest Michael Scot, whom Dante's reader has already met in *Inferno* 20.115–117; his *Liber introductorius* states:

> Among the various sects of the faith, the Moon signifies a life that is holy and hard, for example a hermit, or a religious life that is more for women than for men.[15]

Scot's method, here and throughout his works, is to take the sparse, not to say gnomic, utterances of his predecessors and to flesh them out by paraphrase, elaboration, and example. Here he begins with the Arabs' slender indications that the Moon is associated with the contemplative and religious life and converts them into a more specific and elaborate formulation. Thus there can be no doubt that with Scot the Moon governs certain specific forms of religious life. On the one hand it signifies a hard and holy way; on the other, presumably because of the Moon's female influence, it also signifies any religious order that is intended primarily for women. The latter sense was undoubtedly the primary one for Dante because the Basilian Greek rule followed by Costanza[16] was hardly as rigorous as that of the Poor Clares, with whom "the austerity of the rule went far beyond any that women had previously undertaken."[17] Thus Dante follows Scot to the extent that the only nuns in his poem appear in the heaven of the Moon, but he differs from the astrologer in limiting these to nuns who have failed in their vows (*Par.* 3.30).

To clarify Dante's treatment of nuns, it may be useful to determine whether nuns who persevered in their vows have a place allotted to them in the plan of the *Paradiso*. Although strictly speaking no nuns *appear* in the poem after the first heaven, still the text makes it clear that one nun at least belongs to a higher heaven, for Piccarda says of Saint Clare that "perfect life and high merit enheaven a lady more aloft" (*Par.* 3.97–98). Presumably her heaven is that of Saturn,[18] where the founders of religious orders appear together with those of their followers who kept their vows, as Saint Benedict suggests by identifying several other founders of orders—Macarius and Romuald—who are with him in the heaven of Saturn, and then by adding that in the same heaven "are my brethren who stayed their feet within the cloisters and kept a steadfast heart."

> Qui è Maccario, qui è Romoaldo,
>   qui son li frati miei che dentro ai chiostri
> fermar li piedi e tennero il cor saldo.   (*Par.* 22.49–51)

By "my brethren," Benedict is referring, not to monks in general, but specifically to Benedictines who follow his *Rule* as it was understood in Dante's time, for the two criteria he specifies are precisely equivalent to *stabilitas loci* and *stabilitas cordis*, which were often considered to be the characteristic features of Benedictine life.[19] Generalizing from this analysis, it appears that Saturn is the proper heaven not only for the founders of religious orders but also for those of their followers who accept such a rule of life and persevere in their profession.

Surely this is true for male members of religious orders, but is it true of females as well? Dante tells us that Clare belongs to a higher heaven than the Moon, and not because she was a foundress but because of her "perfetta vita e alto merto" (*Par.* 3.97). Her "perfect life and high merit," I would argue, are the same qualities that qualify Benedict's blessed monk for the heaven of Saturn. Outwardly, his life is perfect because he lives it out within the community he joined, and thus conforms to the rule or way of life he had professed; inwardly, he is deserving of "high merit" because his heart remains firm, that is, he perseveres in his original intention. In this dichotomy, merit must be associated with internal rather than external acts in accordance with the Dantesque principle, revealed by Beatrice, that merit is produced by a combination of grace and free will: "mercede, / che grazia partorisce e buona voglia" (*Par.* 23.112–113). Thus it appears that Clare owed her position to the same virtues that served to beatify Benedict's brethren, and consequently one can infer that not only Clare but other virtuous nuns are rewarded in the same heaven as similarly qualified males.[20]

If this analysis is correct, one would expect the same categories could apply to nuns who fell short of their vows, and this is in fact the case with Piccarda and Costanza. In their external adhesion to the rule, both nuns failed to maintain *stabilitas loci* because they left the convent; however, because they both preferred to remain in "la dolce chiostra" (*Par.* 3.107) and wished to observe their vow of chastity, their absolute will persevered in *stabilitas cordis*, while their conditioned will was swayed by circumstances and hence merited the lesser reward.[21] Presumably the same criteria would apply to men as well as to women, so the heaven of the Moon would be equally appropriate for a monk who was forced to break his vows. Thus the first and last of Dante's planetary heavens are devoted to members of religious orders, both male and female. What distinguishes one from the other is simply success or failure in observing their vows.

Broken Vows and Lunar Instability

Obviously, Dante's treatment of nuns owes little to Michael Scot. At most, the astrologer may have suggested to the poet that it would be appropriate to people the first heaven with nuns, but if so, other sources suggested modifications so extensive that Scot's influence in this respect must be accounted minimal. A far more likely astrological source for Dante's twofold treatment of monasticism is the other Latin astrologer that the poet placed in Hell—Guido Bonatti (*Inf.* 20.118), who like Scot advised Frederick II and who was a more popular author than Scot because he was compendious but not unduly verbose. He, too, links the Moon with monasticism, but with a variation that most closely approximates Dante's conception:

> In matters of belief, [the Moon] signifies the religious life, since many Lunar personalities enter religious orders, especially when they are young; however

sometimes they do not keep their promises to God well, and rarely do they persevere well in religious orders, and hence they become the butt of common gossip.[22]

In their views about the Moon's influence on human religious life, Bonatti and Dante are similar in several remarkable respects. First, both men and women are influenced indifferently to take monastic vows, for Bonatti, unlike Scot, does not use the Moon's gender to modify its impulses toward the religious life. Less striking is the observation that the Lunar type is especially prone to conversion while young. Although this doubtless was true of most medieval monastic vocations, still it is notable that Piccarda expressly states that she fled from the world when she was still a young girl ("giovinetta," *Par.* 1.103). Furthermore, since the secularization of both Costanza and Piccarda gave rise to legends that are independent of the *Comedy*,[23] we can be sure that each case was the subject of common gossip ("fabule"), just as Bonatti's *obiter dictum* leads us to expect. Much the same expectation is implicit in Piccarda's repeated assertion that contemporaries did not regard secularization as a good practice (*Par.* 3.106, 116), and consequently they would consider it scandalous and inevitably gossip about it.

The most important similarity, however, is obviously that Bonatti, like Dante, associates the Moon with the breaking of religious vows. Furthermore, unlike Scot, he does not see the Moon as the only planet that encourages monasticism; instead, again like Dante, Bonatti assigns religious orders, and especially Benedictines, to Saturn:

> And [Saturn] has to signify black clothing and those who use black garments because it is their nature to do so, both religious or cloistered persons and others.[24]

Thus Bonatti provides the astrological basis for Dante's dichotomy between the persevering religious of Saturn and the inconstant ones of the Moon.

Bonatti is by no means unique in stressing the instability of the Lunar personality; rather, his contribution is that he took a general principle that was commonly recognized by his predecessors and applied it to the religious life in particular. The earliest astrologers had associated the Moon with change because of its rapid monthly revolution through the zodiac and its attendant and readily observed changes of phase. Ptolemy, the earliest astrologer known to Dante, had already attributed physical change to the Moon, most especially noting its degenerative power.[25] Albumasar extended the Moon's scope to include psychological changes as well, and for him the Lunar type was "one who is suitable to all changes and who is nonetheless agreeable."[26] Such affable flexibility was seen in another light by Haly, who declared that the Lunar personality "is not firm in anything": he has "neither perfect love nor perfect friendship."[27] Finally, Abraham Ibn Ezra gave this line of thought its most encompassing formulation: "and as a general rule, [the Moon] tends to change every kind of nature."[28]

Strange to say, Michael Scot makes more of the Moon's influence over change than does any other astrologer Dante might have known. He begins by asserting that the Moon "signifies a thing that, when it happens, does not last long. The reason is that [the Moon] remains for only a short time in a [zodiacal] sign, and when the sign changes, the influence is changed."[29] The Moon itself is fickle, he writes, "and hence the future things it signifies are inconstant and of short duration (*cum brevitate perseverantie*)."[30] Again, the Moon "is a planet of the feminine kind . . . often deceitful, apt to be turned quickly in either direction, and that which it promises by signification it quickly performs, and this lasts for a short while."[31] Yet again: "This planet always promises to someone anything with doubt, and such a thing will last but a little while. . . . Hence the Moon always signifies a simple person who is unstable and quickly turned either way."[32] Scot not only often repeats the principles laid down by his predecessors, he also elucidates them by similes:

> In its stages, the Moon is like a shapely girl whose promise is uncertain. It is like the hope of a man concerning a girl whom he cherishes and very much desires for the effect she has on him, because his hope sometimes waxes, sometimes wanes. And when one believes that the Moon may bring about good, time brings about the opposite or something contrary. And according to its times and stages, the Moon behaves likewise in other respects. It is a feminine planet, and for that reason it is said to be weak, timid, lacking fortitude, having brief power, and with good reason it is called the goddess of fortune.[33]

Furthermore, the Moon's general ability to promote change is a principle that Scot readily applies to particular cases of its influence. For instance, what is characteristic of Monday, the Moon's day, is "motion, instability, and ease of conversion from one thing into another, as from good into evil or vice versa."[34] When Scot tabulates each planet's indications concerning fame, he lists the Moon's significance as fame that is "easily altered."[35] Similarly, the Moon can signify "things which cannot be expected to last for a long time, for example dew, rain, cold, the traveler's complaints to the sailor, and so forth."[36] Thus Scot was abundantly aware of the Moon's influence over change, and yet, as we have seen, he made no use of this in his discussion of religious professions.

Varieties of Lunar Ambiguity

Nevertheless, Scot's portrait of the changeable Lunar personality fits Piccarda in so many ways that it would seem that Dante, having taken his skeletal concept of an unfaithful nun from Bonatti, then went to Scot to flesh out the character with qualities appropriate to the Moon.

This is best seen in Beatrice's exposition of the distinction between the absolute and the conditioned will, because Piccarda, having drunk the water of Lethe, has no memory of her sin, and consequently gives the reader no insight into her reasons for leaving the convent. This omission is supplied by Beatrice, who explains how a nun could break her vows and still be faithful to them (*Par.* 4.100–114). The answer is that, being placed under compulsion to marry, the nun who consented would act out of fear, but the choice was nonetheless up to her, so she was blameworthy even though she would rather have acted otherwise. This doctrine, as is generally recognized, comes directly from Aristotle's *Nicomachean Ethics* (3.1, 1109b30–1110a34), and the poet makes his source unmistakable by borrowing from it the example of Alcmeon.[37] It is from Aristotle rather than from Beatrice that one learns explicitly that such a choice is motivated by fear ("propter timorem maiorum malorum"),[38] although this is implicit in her statement that the choice is made "in order to escape from danger (*per fuggir periglio*)" (*Par.* 4.101). The difference, then, between a steadfast nun and one who allows herself to be secularized under compulsion is that the latter is motivated by fear, or to be more precise, by fear of man rather than of God.

Fear. According to the astrologers, this quality of fearfulness is imparted by the Moon. Rabbi Ibn Ezra, for example, described the Lunar person as "the most timorous" and "the least magnanimous" of all the planetary types.[39] Scot, however, develops this theme more than most astrologers. He says that in general the Moon "signifies weak things and those that are done with fear (*cum timore*) and with little virtue,"[40] and with particular reference to human personality, this means that a Lunar character tends to be

> easily fearful (*pavidus*), peaceful, and generally obedient and serviceable enough to another, but highly unreliable inasmuch as a thing willed is often unwilled.[41]

Scot does not explain in so many words why *Lunares* are inclined to fear, though their constitutional weakness probably provides a sufficient explanation. In his summary table of planetary qualities, Scot describes Lunar persons as "weak" in power and "prone to fatigue" in their senses.[42] Similar but more pointed is the explanation supplied by Albumasar, who declared that the Moon type was especially "concerned about the health of the body."[43]

Pacificity. Other, less physical, causes of fear are suggested by Scot. In the passage given above, he characterizes Moon children as "peaceful," and elsewhere he says that "their lifestyle is . . . peacemaking about everything."[44] Thus fear of conflict could also be a motive, so that a timid person such as Piccarda might accede to her relatives' demands just to keep peace in the family. What she should have done instead was to conform her will to God's, for, as she herself explains, this brings the true peace which is the goal of all creatures (*Par.* 3.85–87). Although we cannot be sure whether this Moon-given pacific tendency contributed to her tragedy on earth, she certainly displays it in heaven.

Piety. The Lunar inclination towards peace, then, is morally ambiguous: it can lead man to God or away from him. Similar to this is another Lunar trait—piety. Scot says that the Lunar personality makes itself pleasing to another by being "pious, sympathetic, and serving."[45] Piety, of course, can be devotion to any one of several duties—to God, to country, or to family—but as a way of being gracious to someone else, affectionate behavior towards relatives is most probably what Scot had in mind. Such a Lunar disposition might well have been a factor influencing Piccarda or Costanza in her decision: on the one hand, she would be inclined to do her duty to God, which would be to fulfill her vows; on the other, family piety would urge her to do her duty to her relatives. Again, as in the cases of a timorous or pacific nature, the Moon poses a moral dilemma by imparting a virtue which can be directed towards either God or some lesser object.

Servitialis. This bipolar pattern appears in still other ways. According to Scot, the Moon makes one "generally obedient and serviceable enough to another"—in a word, *servitialis*, or "serving" (above, at nn. 41 and 45). Such a propensity would conduce towards the monastic life, which is based on submission of one's will to a rule, so that obedience "is the primary characteristic of the cenobite";[46] but the same servility would make one apt to obey some rival authority, such as the family.

Female roles. In the poem, this ambiguous position is reflected by the term "sister (*sorella*)," which is applied to both Costanza and Piccarda in a monastic sense (*Par.* 3.45, 113), in contrast with the normal genealogical one, which in Piccarda's case had been established previously (*Purg.* 24.13). As we have already seen, adult sister is one of the female roles governed by the Moon (above, at n. 5), and it is this twofold sistership, in both a spiritual and a physical family, that placed both nuns in their moral predicament.[47]

In addition to sisterhood, the Moon also governs woman's role in the home after marriage. The whole range of marital attributes is exhibited by Albumasar, who associated marriage with the Moon, together with pregnant women, mothers, nurses, and matrons;[48] whereas John of Seville sums it up in one word—"wife."[49] Not all women would be astrologically suited to such a life, for the Venerian type, Cunizza for example, shuns such responsibility in preference to a life of pleasure, which has little appeal to the *Lunaris*.[50] Thus a Lunar woman such as either of Dante's nuns would be naturally disposed on the one hand to a religious life of chastity in the domestic role of Christ's bride ("quello sposo ch'ogne voto accetta," *Par.* 3.101), but on the other hand she would be equally attracted to a more mundane form of domesticity. Nature, operating through the stars, establishes the parameters of her psychological nature, within which limits she can function comfortably and efficiently, but she is not predestined to any particular form of Lunar life.

Having viewed the Lunar character of Piccarda and Costanza in its various facets, we are now in a position to see what Beatrice meant when she said that to some extent the praise or blame for human acts properly belongs to the planets that influence those acts (*Par.* 4.58–60). The Moon can be praised for disposing both women to the religious life, and for endowing them with the qualities that make a good nun: piety, obedience, chastity, and a love of peace. But the Moon can also be blamed for their failure to keep their vows, first because it made an alternative domestic way of life as wife and mother equally attractive to them by nature, and moreover because it disposed them to exchange one way of life for another for a variety of reasons. Being *Lunares*, they were naturally prone to alter their decisions, and this propensity was reinforced by other aspects of their disposition. When family pressure was brought on them to change their minds, they were easily coerced because their Lunar nature made them afraid of physical violence and also inclined them to be peaceloving, unassertive, obedient, and subservient to the needs of others, especially out of an innate sense of duty to family. In short, the Moon disposed these nuns to change as they did, and hence this is a case in which the Moon deserves some blame for human actions. Still, Costanza and Piccarda, though astrologically inclined to be weak, were not altogether deprived of moral choice. What they could do, they did: each in her heart remained true to her vows, and this absolute act of will alone qualified her for beatitude. But nowhere in Paradise will the power of the stars be more apparent than in the case of these two nuns whose lives were largely conditioned for better and for worse by the planet that most dominated them. Our conclusion, then, must be that their moral predicament was imposed by nature as it was perceived and described by the astrologers, and especially by Bonatti and Scot, who now emerge as a major source for the moral structure of the poem.[51]

Collateral Uses of Astrology

The principal function of astrology in the *Paradiso* is to define the character that is appropriate to the blessed souls in each heaven, but Dante makes use of astrological materials in many other ways.

Physical appearances. For example, the women whom the Pilgrim meets in the Moon are the only blessed souls whose features are discernible to the human eye, and their earthly beauty there appears marvelously enhanced (*Par.* 3.48, 58, 110), all of which fits nicely with the astrologers' notion that the Moon confers "a beautiful appearance."[52] Again, Piccarda's face appears so indistinctly to the Pilgrim that the narrator compares it to a reflection "so faint that a pearl on a white brow (*perla in bianca fronte*) comes not less boldly to our eyes" (*Par.* 3.14–15). Although, strange to say, the Latin astrologers do not associate the Moon with pearls,[53] Michael Scot does connect it with white or fair skin, and he goes on to state that "the Moon naturally causes the human face to be as it were without color."[54] Admittedly, neither correspondence is close enough to establish an astrological origin beyond a doubt, but these parallels and many like them deserve brief mention because, given Dante's reliance on the astrologers, such an origin is plausible. Although individual cases may remain doubtful, still as the number of undoubted borrowings grows, so does the likelihood that an astrological reference was intended in the borderline cases as well.

Veracity. On occasion Dante chose to ignore the properties of the Moon, and indeed was at pains to assure the reader that the Moon did not affect his characters as astrology would lead one to expect. Just as the Pilgrim is about to address Piccarda, Beatrice assures him that he can believe what he hears without reservation (*Par.* 3.31–33), because, as she later puts it, "a soul in bliss cannot lie," and this is "for certain (*per certo*)" (*Par.* 4.94–96). Such an assurance was particularly necessary in the heaven of the Moon because that planet was often associated with falsehood. According to Scot, the Moon's indications are themselves extremely deceptive,[55] while the Moon's children are not only credulous but are also unreliable witnesses who often tell falsehoods.[56] Therefore it would seem likely that the poet selected the heaven of the Moon as the appropriate place in which to establish the veracity of blessed souls precisely because his astrologically sophisticated reader would be expecting the opposite.

Moderation. Sometimes an astrological generalization can lead us to remark things in the poem that otherwise might have passed unobserved. For instance, Michael Scot summarized the Lunar character in a single phrase: "its manner is to be moderate in praise and blaming."[57] Does this fit Piccarda, the only Lunar character that Dante presented in detail? She does praise Saint Clare, ascribing to her "perfect life and high merit" (*Par.* 3.97), which is moderate indeed when compared with the rhetoric lavished later by Thomas on Saint Francis and by Bonaventure on Saint Dominic (*Par.* 11.28–121, 12.37–105). Similarly, against those who forced her and Costanza to leave their convents, Piccarda can only say that they were "men more used to evil than to good," who acted "against right custom" (*Par.* 3.105, 116). Certainly these phrases do imply blame, but as vituperation they pale before the pyrotechnic fulminations of Folco, Peter Damian, Benedict, and Simon Peter (*Par.* 9.122–142, 21.130–135, 22.73–96, 27.40–63). Thus Piccarda in her unassuming, low-keyed judgments exhibits not only humility but also an authentic Lunar characteristic— moderation in blaming and praising.

Forgetfulness. In one particular, at least, the Moon seems to have affected the Pilgrim himself while he was in its sphere. When he first sees Piccarda, he does not recognize her but is told that he will recall who she is "if your mind be searched well" (*Par.* 3.47), and he responds by admitting that "I was not quick in remembering, but now that which you tell me helps me so that I more clearly recall your features" (61–63). This lapse of memory is proper to the Moon, which Albumasar, Ibn Ezra, and Scot agreed was responsible for human forgetfulness.[58]

Revelations. The most prominent feature of the Pilgrim's visit to the Moon is the lengthy and learned discourses delivered to him by Beatrice. Following hard on her exposition of cosmic order in the first canto (*Par.* 1.103–142) comes the explanation of the spots on the Moon (2.49–148); then she lays the theoretical bases for Dante's position on astrology in response to two questions, first admitting that the stars do influence human behavior and then qualifying this by asserting that the absolute will is not bound by circumstances, including those produced by astral influence (4.16–142); and finally she goes on to expound the conditions under which vows to God may be broken (5.1–84). The cumulative mass of these lectures is imposing: not counting the 39 preliminary verses, the Lunar discourses proper run to some 309 lines. All this comes to the Pilgrim as—literally—a revelation, that is, a revealing of truths that are hidden from human reason under ordinary, earthly conditions. That these secrets are revealed at this time in the heaven of the Moon is astrologically appropriate because, according to Guido Bonatti, the Moon promotes the concealment of secrets when Luna herself is concealed by the Sun, whereas the reverse is true when, passing from conjunction to opposition, she is fully revealed to sight.[59] The latter, of course, was the case during the Pilgrim's journey,[60] so revelation of secrets is particularly to be expected at this propitious time and place. Presumably the same influence promotes the revelations that the Pilgrim receives in subsequent heavens, but they are more profuse in the Moon, where the impulse originated, than in any other planet.

The Moon is the only planet where revelations are made by Beatrice herself. Elsewhere the Pilgrim's informant is a native of the planet: Justinian in Mercury, Carlo Martello in Venus, Aquinas in the Sun, Cacciaguida in Mars, the souls composing the Eagle in Jupiter, and Peter Damian in Saturn. Evidently Piccarda is an exception, and astrology explains why it would be inappropriate for her or any other Moon child to deliver magisterial discourses. Scot is particularly insistent that "the Moon always signifies a simple person," one who is "more simple than truly wise."[61] Thus astrology would seem to have indicated to the poet not only that the full Moon was the proper time and place for revelations, but also who was best fitted to make them. What astrology did not control was the subject matter of these discourses, which seems to have been selected with little reference to astrology except indirectly, inasmuch as the discussion of will and vows was occasioned by the nuns' weakness, which in turn was imparted by the Moon.

Astrological Imagery

Thus far we have been concerned with the poet's use of astrological materials in his treatment of the *dramatis personae* and the themes developed through them. Since astrology was chiefly concerned with human actions, it was particularly suited to suggest such character-related concepts, but it was also a rich potential source for poetic imagery.

Water. Scot, elaborating as usual on traditional astrology, lays down the general principle that "the Moon effects coldness and wetness, and by its nature it signifies the dominance of all cold and wet things, of which it is the significator, e.g., of women, of the sea, and of phlegm."[62] In consequence, Scot can flatly assert that "among the substances, [the Moon] signifies . . . water,"[63] and hence also various forms of water, such as dew, rain, and the sea,[64] as well as water-related occupations, such as seafaring and fishing.[65]

Given the Moon's lordship over water in all of its forms, one is not surprised to find a profusion of water imagery in Dante's Lunar heaven. The planet itself receives the travelers "as water (*acqua*) receives a ray of light" (*Par.* 2.35); the narrator compares the indistinct appearance of Piccarda to a reflection seen "through clear and tranquil waters (*acque*)" (3.11); and he says that she finally disappears "as some heavy thing through deep water (*acqua*)" (3.123). The narrative also implies water in images based on thirst (2.19, 3.70–72), on voyages by sea (2.1–9, 13–18), and on melting snow (2.106–108). These aquatic variations find their climax as the narrator praises one of Beatrice's explanations by calling it "the rippling of the holy stream which issues forth from the fountain from which every truth flows."

> Cotal fu l'ondeggiar del santo rio
>   ch'uscì del fonte ond'ogne ver deriva   (*Par.* 4.115–116)

An image as complex as this can only be the product of self-conscious artifice, and hence it is the poet's way of assuring the reader that these water images are no accident: he has contrived them by design. The implication clearly is that the occult influences at work in his heaven are understood, not only by the poet, who might pretend to be ignorant of them, but also by the narrator. Whether consciously or not, the travelers too make use of such images. The figure just quoted is immediately followed by the Pilgrim's own reaction to Beatrice's 99-line speech: he says it "inundates me (*m'inonda*)" (*Par.* 4.119),[66] which admittedly need not refer to a wave of water, though that is certainly strongly suggested by the multiple aquatic images that directly precede it. Finally, Beatrice herself employs an explicit water image when she warns Christians not to think "that every water (*acqua*) may cleanse you" (5.75).

Nutrition. In addition to this lavish application of water imagery, Dante also makes use of the Moon's less obvious connection with nutrition. The core of this concept would seem to be the Lunar influence over child rearing, which as we have already seen includes not only mothers but nurses (*nutrices*);[67] by generalizing the nurse's function, the Moon had also come to be associated with nutrition (*nutritura*). Albumasar, the earliest of our Arabic astrologers, links the two terms ("nutritura et nutrices") and goes on to associate the Moon with any "means of subsistence by nourishing foods."[68] Similarly, Alcabitius assigns to the Moon "the feeding of the young . . . and the preparing of foods."[69] Haly, following a different line of reasoning, links the Moon specifically with food production. Since whatever is brought to fruition by water can be predicted through the Moon, that planet by its influence on rainfall is one of the indicators "of the abundance or of the high cost of bread (*panis*)."[70]

In the *Paradiso*, however, the stress is on the consumption of food rather than on its production, and what nourishes is the spiritual food of heaven. As Beatrice and the Pilgrim are about to enter the first sphere, the reader is encouraged to press on only if he is hungry for "the bread of angels (*pan de li angeli*), on which men here [on earth] subsist, but never become sated of it" (*Par.* 2.10–12). What the reader finds waiting for him in the heaven of the Moon is in fact an intellectual feast, which its purveyor, Beatrice, expressly compares to a meal: "it behooves you to sit a while longer at table," she tell the Pilgrim as she is explaining how vows can be commuted, "for the tough food (*cibo*) which you have taken still requires some aid for your digestion" (*Par.* 5.34–39). Astrology evidently makes this nutrition metaphor appropriate to the Moon. Indeed, the biblical description of manna as the "bread of angels" (Ps. 77.25; Sap. 16.20), which had already suggested the title metaphor for Dante's *Convivio*

(1.1.7), is doubly appropriate to the heaven of the Moon because, as Beatrice reveals much later in the poem, that heaven is also the heaven of the angels (*Par.* 28.126).

Sheep. Twice in the Lunar cantos Dante made prominent use of images based on sheep. The keynote of canto 4, which explains how free will triumphs over the apparent necessity imposed by nature, is sounded by three variations of the dilemma that was later to become famous as the problem of Buridan's ass:[71] A man, a lamb, and a dog are successively presented as placed between two objects that are equally desirable or, in the case of the lamb, the reverse:

> sì si starebbe un agno intra due brame
>   di fieri lupi, igualmente temendo   (*Par.* 4.4–5)

All three are images of the Pilgrim's own dilemma as he could not decide which of two questions to put first to Beatrice. She resolves the deadlock by answering first one and then the other in a long discourse that runs on into the next canto, and in concluding it she returns to the ovile imagery previously employed by the narrator. "Christians," she warns, "should not be foolish sheep (*percore matte*)" but instead should be guided by "the shepherd (*pastor*) of the Church" (*Par.* 5.80, 77), and she concludes with this admonition:

> Non fate com' agnel che lascia il latte
>   de la sua madre, e semplice e lascivo
>   seco medesmo a suo piacer combatte!   (*Par.* 5.82–84)

> Be not like the lamb that leaves its mother's milk and, silly and wanton, fights with itself at its own pleasure.

This interconnected series of references is appropriate to the heaven of the Moon, which astrologers identified with sheep. John of Seville uses the general term *pecudes*, which refers especially to sheep, just as does Beatrice's use of the closely connected form *pecore*.[72] Other astrologers make the association obliquely: Abraham Ibn Ezra lists a sheep fold (*ovile*) among the animals (*sic*) that are subject to the Moon,[73] and in assigning to it all birds and snakes that are white, he also suggests the principle that makes sheep proper to that planet by similarity.[74] Michael Scot, on the

other hand, includes the job of shepherd ("pastor gregis") among the occupations in which Lunar man is inclined to engage,[75] which again is
echoed by Beatrice. Finally, her images of the lamb and of the sheep who
are silly ("matte" and "semplice," *Par.* 5.80, 83) accord well with the
Moon's dominion over "all simpletons (*omnes simplices*)," to which Scot
repeatedly refers.[76]

White and silver. Before concluding, a few slight correspondences deserve passing mention. According to most astrologers, the Moon signifies
the color white,[77] although Michael Scot has a significant variation: for
him, "her color is pure silver."[78] To be sure, astrologers commonly associated the Moon with silver, but usually not as a color but rather as a metal
or a substance.[79] Dante, however, faintly reflects Scot's variation by using
white to signify silver when he has Beatrice refer to Peter's silver and gold
keys as "la chiave bianca e de la gialla" (*Par.* 5.57). The color white is also
alluded to by Beatrice in a simile based on snow, which when warmed by
the Sun "is left stripped both of the color and the coldness which it had"
(*Par.* 2.108). The allusion is equally appropriate to the Moon's capacity to
replace its natural, but not necessary, coldness with a warming effect, similarly when under the influence of the Sun's warming rays.[80]

Archangels. Another minor correspondence is offered in one of Beatrice's examples that illustrates how the intellect can be introduced to immaterial objects by representing them to the senses as material ones: "Holy
church represents to you with human aspect Gabriel and Michael and the
other who made Tobit whole again" (*Par.* 4.46–48). This fits because
angels, of course, are messengers, as their name indicates (ἄγγελος), and
as such they are engaged in an activity governed by the Moon. "Among
the kinds of work," wrote Alcabitius of the Moon, "it has missions and
commissions."[81] Albumasar also mentions commissions (*mandata*) but instead of missions (*legationes*) he specifies messengers (*nuncii*),[82] whereas
Michael Scot includes the equivalent of all three terms.[83] Admittedly, insofar as Gabriel, Michael, and Raphael are all archangels, they would be
more fittingly mentioned in the heaven of Mercury, since "Arcangeli" come
next to last in Beatrice's descending angelic hierarchy (*Par.* 28.125); but
evidently the poet has chosen here to stress their function as divine agents
in individual cases, specifying only Raphael's mission to Tobit (Tob.
11.1–15), although he could also count on every reader to recall Gabriel's
role as angel of the Annunciation. Thus, though archangels in rank, they
appear here doing what is common to all ranks of angels, namely serving
as divine messengers.[84] Furthermore, the archangel Gabriel is expressly

assigned to the Moon by Michael Scot, who names one angel as the *rector* of each heaven.[85] To be sure, Dante himself did not limit the angelic movers to one per sphere[86] and consequently would not have agreed with Scot, but the astrologer's assertion may well have suggested to the poet that Gabriel be named here, and perhaps he added Michael and Raphael to dissociate himself from Scot's position.

The Lunar eye. Our ultimate image is a more striking one. Although, as noted above, Beatrice's long dissertation on the cause of the spots on the Moon draws none of its substance from astrology, still that discipline may have suggested the remarkable simile with which Beatrice concludes her discourse. She compares the maculated Moon to a great eye turned earthward:

> Per la natura lieta onde derive,
>   la virtù mista per lo corpo luce
>   come letizia per pupilla viva.   (*Par.* 2.142–144)

> Because of the glad nature when it flows,
>   the mingled virtue shines through the body,
>   as gladness does through a living pupil.

Some astrologers said that the Moon signifies a single eye—the right one in women and the left one in men.[87] Moreover, according to Bonatti, *one* eye of the Lunar person would eventually suffer damage. Perhaps it would undergo some major internal change, perhaps a blow would damage it from outside. Whatever the mode might be, Bonatti felt unusually confident about the result: "And, that I may foretell the truth to you briefly, one of the eyes shall by no means be free from defect."[88] According to Aristotle, however, one defect hardly ever found in the Lunar eye was absence of coloration.[89] Thus the Moon suggested a colored eye, and Messehalla went so far as to specify that such eyes were "not completely black," which I take to mean that they were, like the Moon itself, black in blotches. Although this describes the appearance of the Lunar person, the description is in some part based on that person's resemblance to the physical features of the Moon itself, since Messehalla not only says that the *Lunaris* has a "round face" but also assures us that this is the sign by which this type can be readily identified.[90] Thus Beatrice's simile could have been compounded from two astrological indications: on the one hand, the Moon signified a single eye; on the other, eyes spotted black. Combined, these two elements suggest that the Moon itself should be compared to a single eye flecked with black. Another element in the image—that the Moon, like the eye in the extramission theories of vision in the Platonic tradition[91] itself emits rays—has no astrological basis, but in a lyric mood an Arabic astrologer did exclaim that the Moon, "borrowing light from the Sun, spreads joy."[92]

2. Mercury

Dante pairs Mercury with the Moon. Just as his heaven of the Moon represents a defect in the life of contemplation, exemplified by passive women, so his heaven of Mercury signifies a defect in the life of action, exemplified by active men. Dante's guiding principle for Mercury is clearly set forth by Justinian: "This little star is adorned with good spirits who have been active in order that honor and fame might come to them."

> Questa picciola stella si correda
>   d'i buoni spiriti che son stati attivi
>   perché onore e fama li succeda.   (*Par.* 6. 112–114)

This weakness for honor and fame is an integral part of the Mercurial character as depicted by the astrologers. According to Albumasar, Mercury signified "fame, rumors, ambition motivated by a desire for greater glory."[1] Michael Scot also took this view and elaborated both the theme of fame and that of honor. The native of Mercury, he says, "takes much care to have a good reputation (*famam*) throughout the world";[2] he desires to know everything that will be useful and make him famous.[3] This thirst for fame is so great that the *Mercurialis* finds notoriety and ill fame just as attractive as a good reputation,[4] but he is inclined towards good by a correlative desire for honor. "Mercury," wrote Alcabitius, "also signifies honor (*honorem*)."[5] Michael Scot as usual rings many changes on this theme; the Mercurial man, he states, "always longs to achieve great and useful things that will bring honor (*honoris*) and riches."[6] Instead of the word *honor*, Scot often substitutes some other word derived from it; thus Mercury's native by his nature prefers work that is "honorable (*honorabili*),"[7] he "loves respectability (*honestatem*),"[8] and his lifestyle is consequently peaceful and respectable (*honesta*).[9]

Accordingly, Mercury motivates one "to perform ingenious and subtle things that please other people and are praised by being accorded signal marks of honor (*incignamento*)."[10] Indeed, this hunger for recognition often leads to vainglory, which is to say empty, as opposed to true, glory: the Mercurial man "is vainglorious of his knowledge or of another's property that has been loaned to him."[11] But for the most part, the desire for honor imparts to those under Mercury's influence a drive to work. Thus Alcabitius says that Mercury "also signifies work (*opus*),"[12] while Scot twice states that the planet is an indicator of "labor."[13] This propensity for work is reflected in Dante's description of the souls in Mercury as *attivi* (*Par.* 6.113): they too are active in their pursuit of honor and fame. Hence we may conclude that when Dante characterized his Mercurians as "spirits who have been active in order that honor and fame might come to them" (*Par.* 6.113–114), all the essentials of this description—activity, honor, and fame—were already recognized as Mercurial traits by the astrologers, and especially by Michael Scot.

To personify these principles, Dante chose two men, in contrast to the two women who represented the Moon. It would have been difficult to do otherwise, since few women had distinguished themselves in the pursuits governed by Mercury, but the choice of men as types of Mercurian influence was also suggested by astrology. Although the god Mercury was, of course, male, the earliest astrologers considered the planet Mercury to be of common gender because it produced both the qualities of moisture and dryness, which were considered to be feminine and masculine respectively.[14] By Dante's time, however, this distinction was of little importance in astrology, and the masculine character of the planet tended to be stressed. Thus Scot twice stated that Mercury is "more masculine than feminine,"[15] while a generation later Robertus Anglicus (fl. 1271) simplified this to the flat assertion that "Mercury is masculine."[16]

Although the two pairs of souls differ in gender, the way in which they are presented in the poem is significantly similar. In each case, the Pilgrim interviews only one member of the pair, who tells him about the other member. In the heaven of the Moon we found that this arrangement was used to direct the reader's attention to the characteristics that Piccarda and Costanza shared in common, which proved to be the qualities conferred on them by the Moon. Now when the reader finds the same arrangement is repeated in the heaven of Mercury, he is justified in supposing that this symmetry is the poet's way of inviting a similar comparison of the characteristics of Justinian and Romeo. To begin, let us extract the biographical portions of Justinian's speech, which takes up the whole of canto 6:

> I was Caesar, and am Justinian, who, by will of the Primal Love which I feel, removed from among the laws what was superfluous and vain. And before I

had put my mind to this work, one nature and no more I held to be in Christ, and with that faith I was content; but the blessed Agapetus, who was the supreme pastor, directed me to the true faith by his words. I believed him, and what he held by faith I now see as clearly as you see that every contradiction is both false and true. So soon as with the Church I moved my feet, it pleased God, of His grace, to inspire me with this high task, and I gave myself entirely to it, committing arms to my Belisarius, with whom Heaven's right hand was so joined that it was a sign for me to rest from them.

. . . .

And within the present pearl shines the light of Romeo, whose noble and beautiful work was ill rewarded; but the Provençals who wrought against him have not the laugh, and indeed he takes an ill path who makes harm for himself of another's good work. Raymond Berenger had four daughters, each of them a queen, and Romeo, a man of lowly birth and a pilgrim, did this for him. And then crooked words moved him to demand a reckoning of this just man, who had rendered him seven and five for ten. Thereon he departed, poor and old, and if the world but knew the heart he had while begging his bread morsel by morsel, much as it praises him it would praise him more. (*Par.* 6.10–27, 127–142)

Superficially, Justinian and Romeo resemble one another far less than did the two nuns, yet the parallel structure of the two accounts urges us to look deeper. Since astrology explained the resemblances in the previous heaven, we are justified in the expectation that astrology will again indicate points of resemblance between the two characters. We can begin with what we already know: that Mercurians lead active lives in pursuit of honor and fame. The activity of both men is obvious. In Romeo's case, it assumed an altered form when he left his position at court, for he became a wanderer, begging his bread, whereas, if he were governed by Saturn or the Moon, he would have retired from the world as well to lead a secluded life of contemplation. The concern with fame and honor is also evident in both cases, but most vividly in that of Justinian, who reveals this Mercurial aspect of his character in his speech. Throughout the passage given above (10–27), he is concerned first of all to make known his role in the compilation of the *Corpus Iustinianum*, which is his chief claim to honor and fame. He is, in fact, vainglorious, because he claims in his speech to have done the work himself, although anyone conversant with his *Corpus* would certainly also know that the actual work was done by a team of jurists whom he had appointed, for the emperor himself left a detailed account of the process in his rescripts that initiated and promulgated various stages of the project.[17] To be sure, Dante's Justinian gives God due credit for his part in the codification, but at the same time he does not give his human associates their due. In heaven, then, Justinian is still greedy for all the fame and honor he can get, even vain, or false, glory that is not properly his due. And we should not be surprised that this fault persists in Paradise, because without it he would not belong in the heaven of Mercury.

Romeo's preoccupation with honor is perhaps less evident, but it is nonetheless a major component of his character. The crisis of his life came when his honor was questioned, first by Provençals who defamed him out of envy, then by the count of Provence, whom they persuaded to demand an audit of Romeo's accounts. Even though the charge of graft proved to be unjustified, still Romeo was dishonored by the accusation and still more by his master's lack of confidence in his honesty. For Romeo it was not enough that an audit could verify his honesty, for the injury to his reputation (*fama*) would linger on. As a Mercurian who worked above all to acquire fame and honor, Romeo was frustrated by this stain on his good name, and accordingly he resigned and became a wandering beggar rather than continue in a career that he now considered to be pointless.

Thus with the help of astrology our first comparison of Justinian and Romeo has shown how both exemplify the Mercurian obsession with honor and fame. This interpretation is, as it were, a preliminary reconnaissance that has pursued the poet's explicit indications. Now that the astrological basis of his Mercurian principle has been established, we can systematically explore the astrology of Mercury in detail in order to fill in the portraits that have been lightly sketched in this first comparison. My plan is first to continue the search for astrological traits that both characters have in common; this inquiry will provide a general description of the Mercurial character. Once this is achieved, we will turn next to consider those aspects of Mercury's personality that are exemplified mainly in one character—for example, legal aptitude in Justinian. Finally we shall see how geography and theology each combine with astrology to unify the Mercurian cantos.

The Planet of Ingenuity

When Dante had Justinian explain that Mercurians were souls that had been active in pursuit of fame and honor, he meant to indicate the fatal defect that placed them in a lower state of bliss. Although this criterion forms an integral part of the Mercurian's character, it is by no means an adequate definition of that character, because the true natives would not gain distinction in fields that require, for example, physical strength or spiritual humility. Instead, Mercury's natives excel in their chosen activity by exercise of great wit.

Subtle ingenuity. No doubt the fabled cleverness of the god Mercury established the planet's character at the beginning of Greek astrology. Ptolemy characterized Mercurians as men who are "subtle in their ingenuity."[18] Arab astrologers continued to stress the sharp intelligence and understanding imparted by this planet, and hence Alcabitius assigned to it those endeavors that require intellectual effort—in a word, *cogitatio*.[19] As a result, the opinions of a Mercurian were characteristically "acute and wise,"[20] and most astrologers offered a variety of other synonyms and qualities, which one extended example from Michael Scot will serve to illustrate.

> When anyone is more Mercurial, to that extent he is subtle of spirit, most ingenious (*ingeniosus*) in matters that require careful consideration, in making subtle distinctions, in working well or perfectly, and in persevering enough in his work. It is also found that this is a planet . . . the property of which is voice, knowledge, ingenuity, eloquence, labor, thought, and making one able to know and perform all things that exist and are done by the ingenuity of a subtle mind and by admirable art. . . . Hence Mercury is called the planet of genius (*ingenii*) and the god of the sciences, who is eloquent, wise, ingenious, clever, and especially concerned with, and expert in, those things that require subtlety and ingenuity of mind.[21]

The Mercurian, then, excels in a large and bewildering variety of activities, but in essence they all involve some form of *intellectual* activity. Accordingly John of Seville assigned to Mercury all the works of man's rational soul, which he then proceeded to list.[22] This broad generalization can evidently accommodate both Justinian's laws and Romeo's negotiations and accounts, but we do not have to rely on inference, because the astrologers themselves indicate in detail those categories of human activity that are especially governed by Mercury. They include the liberal arts, business, and administration, each of which we shall now consider in turn.

Liberal arts. Varro's canon of seven liberal arts was peculiar to Latin culture, but the arts themselves were well known to the Arabs, and given Ptolemy's attribution to Mercury of all skills requiring intellectual acuity, it was only natural that Arabic astrologers would include grammar, logic, rhetoric, arithmetic, geometry, music, and astronomy in the lists they compiled of Mercurian pursuits.[23]

More to the point than these rambling lists was the classification of

Mercurian talents into two broad categories, one concerned with verbal skills and the other with mathematical ones, which of course correspond to the Latin distinction of the seven arts into the *trivium* and the *quadrivium*. Since Mercury governed the rational soul, it was natural that it would also influence the power of speech, and accordingly Haly took the planet to be the significator of both speech and reason in the interpretation of natal horoscopes.[24] Similarly but more specifically, John of Seville ascribed the tongue to him.[25] "Combat of words without physical violence" was Ibn Ezra's apt characterization of Mercury's strongly verbal character.[26] The Arabs were even more impressed with Mercury's power over mathematics. For Haly, it was "the planet of computations";[27] for Alcabitius it especially conferred an aptitude for working with numbers.[28] Thus, in ruling both the *trivium* and the *quadrivium*, Mercury presided over the liberal arts in substance if not in name, although one translator of Arabic astrology even recast al-Kindi's thought into the traditional Latin terminology, so that Mercury is said to possess the "artes liberales," and later the *trivium* and *quadrivium* are specified as well.[29] Michael Scot, a source certainly close to Dante, likewise linked Mercury to the liberal arts: "for he signifies . . . the study of letters" and "an abundance of subtle liberal knowledge."[30]

Dante, on the other hand, had his own private system of correspondences between the seven arts and planets. In the *Convivio* (2.13.9–50), he equated the Moon with grammar, Mercury with logic, and so on through Saturn and astronomy. To be sure, he had often altered his views by the time he wrote the *Paradiso*—the cause of spots on the Moon is a case in point—but no shift in this position has been detected up to now because we have not known where to look. Astrology now suggests that, as an alternative to the system of the *Convivio*, Dante may have assigned all of the liberal arts to Mercury, just as the astrologers did.

Once one looks with this principle in mind, the answer is readily found: Justinian in his canto-long speech somewhat ostentatiously displays his familiarity with all seven of the *artes*. With a grammarian's pedantry, he glosses the cognomen of Lucius Quinctius, otherwise known as "Curly" (*Cincinnatus*): "named from his neglected locks" (*Par.* 6.46–47).[31] His familiarity with logic is demonstrated with reference to the fundamental law of noncontradiction: "that every contradiction is both false and true" (21). Mastery of rhetoric is in evidence throughout the speech, but most memorable in the figure of the Roman Eagle, which is literally the "sign" or "standard" of the Roman state ("segno," 32; "pub-

blico segno," 100) Twice Justinian draws on the art of arithmetic to em-
bellish his speech, once at the beginning to define the Eagle's residence in
Constantinople for "a hundred and a hundred years and more" (4), and
again at the end, making as it were a frame, when Romeo is said to have
"rendered seven and five for ten" (138). Similarly Justinian draws on the
science of music to say that "diverse voices make sweet music" (124) and
on astronomy to describe the Eagle's return to the East as being "counter
to the course of the heavens" (2).

Among the seven liberal arts, only geometry is not obviously included, but its apparent absence is perhaps only one of those enigmas
with which Dante liked to tease his reader's understanding. At any rate,
there was a widespread medieval definition of geometry that went far beyond the principles of the subject as they were expounded in Euclid's
Elements. When Geometria appears in Martianus Capella's popular introduction to the liberal arts, she "reminds her audience of the literal meaning
('Earth-measuring') of her name. The bulk of the lengthy discourse that
follows . . . is devoted not to definitions, axioms, and propositions but to
a conspectus of the known world."[32] Just so Justinian, who alludes to all
the major parts of the Roman world in his sketch of the Eagle's progress
through France, Spain, Italy, Africa, Greece, Asia Minor, and Egypt.

Thus Dante depicts his typical Mercurian as not only conversant with
the seven arts but also as vainglorious enough to flaunt his learning. As if
to assure us that this is characteristic of the place and not peculiar to the
person, the narrator also makes similar allusions proper to Mercury, evok-
ing the art of music in his anticipation of Justinian's canto ("as the next
canto sings," *Par.* 5.139) and grammar in his play on the syllables of Beatrice's name ("only by *Be* and by *ice*," 7.14).

Business. In the ancient world, the liberal arts were an occupation
reserved for those who could pursue theoretical studies without regard to
any practical application. Mercury, however, did not share this elitist attitude; he had also been the ancient god of commerce, in which the same
verbal and mathematical skills could produce a profit, and the astrologers
never forgot it. Alcabitius assigned to Mercury all work that involved ne-
gotiation and the making of estimates,[33] Albumasar more specifically indicated that these were the negotiations of merchants,[34] and Ibn Ezra
noted that such Mercurians tended to be outstanding in their fields.[35] Of
Dante's astrologers, Guido Bonatti had the most to say about the influence
of Mercury on negotiations: "Mercury signifies the knowledge of business

(*negotiationis*); he knows how to conduct many kinds of business, he involves himself in many of them, and he knows how to carry them to a successful conclusion."[36] Moreover, Bonatti had his own explanation of why Mercury is associated with *negotiatores*: the planet instills two qualities that businessmen ought to possess—they are exceedingly careful to provide for future contingencies and they thrive by diversifying their interests.[37]

Although neither Justinian nor Romeo were strictly speaking merchants, these Mercurian traits affected them both. The influence is most evident in the case of Romeo, whose greatest success was as a negotiator of marriages for his master's four daughters, who all became queens through his skillful diplomacy (*Par.* 6.133–135). Something of the mercantile quality of his character is, indeed, suggested by the commercial terminology that the poet applies to the count's demand for an audit ("dimandar ragione," 137) and to Romeo's services, which like an account are said to have been "rendered (*assengò*)" (138).[38] In the case of Justinian, the qualities that Bonatti said make a good merchant are also present, but they are directed towards greater goals. Thus, although the emperor did not share the businessman's managerial concern to avoid future difficulties by wording contracts with care and by accounting for his assets and liabilities, still Justinian as a legislator was deeply concerned with the rules by which all negotiations are concluded, and his law books attempted in their abstract way to provide for every contingency, just as the merchant on a lesser scale does his best to plan ahead. Early in his reign Justinian also seems to have been naturally inclined to diversify his interests, as Bonatti says Mercurian merchants do, but the emperor's inclination to distinguish himself as a theologian was overcome by his faith in Pope Agapetus, while a sign from heaven indicated to him that he was to leave warfare to his general Belisarius and concentrate his own energies instead on legislation (*Par.* 6.13–27). Thus the versatility that was his Mercurian birthright was eventually modified by his own free will in response to revelation.

Stewardship. Another mythological function of Mercury was service, notably as messenger of the gods, and this too became part of astrology. For Alcabitius, Mercury signified "servants,"[39] for Albumasar, "service,"[40] and for Ibn Ezra, "ministers."[41] Moreover, the Mercurial man is the ideal servant who above all else is intent on obeying his master.[42] Michael Scot especially elaborates on the character of the Mercurian servant: he serves to the best of his ability; though subject to human error, he is highly conscientious; he tries to serve loyally and with a good will; like the god Mercury, he is both dutiful and ready to serve—in a word, he is *officiosum*.[43] Furthermore, Scot particularly sees him as being motivated by affection, for the Mercurian is useful to his friends, whom he will faithfully serve as soon as he begins to like them, and they can then trust him to carry out commissions solely for the sake of friendship.[44] Finally, this Mercurian capacity for service can be exercised at the highest levels of government or even of religion. Ptolemy had already associated Mercury with "divine service (*officium divinum*),"[45] and Haly claimed that Mercury "had great and trustworthy significance concerning the officeholders of a lord or of a kingdom."[46]

In Dante's heaven of Mercury, this higher kind of service appears as a theme that unifies the apparently diverse careers of Romeo and Justinian. Romeo clearly fits the pattern. Of humble origin ("persona umìle," *Par.* 6.135), he rose to eminence wholly on his merits as a servant to Count Raymond Berenger, whom he served with such devotion that it can be said that he gave more than he received (138). Although Dante does not indicate what position Romeo held in the county of Provence, he leaves no doubt that it was important, describing the work first as "l'ovra grande e bella" (129) and then as "ben fare" (132), and giving the royal marriages of the count's daughters as the outstanding example (133–135). The historical Romeo of Villanova did in fact rule in the count's name, being described in contemporary documents as his "vicar" or "bailiff," and eventually rising to be "bailiff of his entire land (*bailum totius terrae suae*)."[47] The precise terminology is important because it is the title of *baiulus* that equates him to the emperor Justinian. In its Italian form, the term occurs in the *Comedy* only once, at *Paradiso* 6.73, where Caesar's successor, the Emperor Augustus, is not named but instead is identified by reference to his office as the "succeeding bailiff (*baiulo*)." Similarly, Dante elsewhere called Rome's first seven kings "the bailiffs and tutors as it were of her childhood" (*Conv.* 4.5.11) and described the Emperor Henry VII as "the bailiff of the Roman state" (*Ep.* 6.25). Thus throughout Rome's history, he understood her rulers to be agents of some higher power, just as in medieval society a bailiff was an agent who acted for his lord.[48] Since the imperial succession passed from Augustus through Justinian to Henry VII, it follows that Justinian, like the other emperors, must have been a "bailiff of the Roman state." Consequently both Romeo and the ruler of Rome now appear as two instances of the same stewardship to which both were adapted by the influence of Mercury.[49]

MERCURY CONJUNCT

The planet Mercury, as we have seen, is associated with raw intelligence that can be readily adapted to many uses. Thus the astrologers stress its ambiguous character: depending on circumstances, it can be masculine or feminine, diurnal or nocturnal, fortunate or unfortunate.[50] To be more precise, Mercury's character is determined by the planets that happen to be in his vicinity. He is "convertible," Haly remarks, "being masculine with the masculine planets, and feminine with the feminine ones, fortunate with the fortunate, and unfortunate with the unfortunate."[51] In short, as Ptolemy explained, Mercury is "generally speaking in nature like whatever of the other planets may be associated with him."[52] Later astrologers broadened this generalization to make Mercury susceptible to almost every influence from another planet, the most extreme formulation being that of Scot: "In its effect, this planet is extremely weak, useless, and diverse, for when Mercury is near another planet, he influences almost everything just as the other planet does."[53] Both Scot and Bonatti particularly stress the moral aspect of such influences, which can be for good or evil depending on Mercury's relation to other planets.[54] Consequently, the character of the Mercurians whom Dante encountered in the sphere of Mercury depends in large part on the planets under whose influence it stood at the time. For example, we have seen that Mercurians make good servants, but the kind of service depends on how Mercury is aspected. Thus, if Mercury were joined to the Moon—which was not the case at the time of the poem—the result, according to Bonatti, would be a Mercurian "who will know how to serve in the courts of kings, magnates, nobles, and others, for example, to place a tray before diners and to cut bread and meat in their presence, and such like."[55] Other aspects that favor more exalted service were operative on 14 April 1300. The position of the planets on that day was a most unusual one that was especially notable for the conjunction of Mercury with both the Sun and Jupiter (see below, Appendix 2). The astrologers provide us with ready-made interpretations for both cases.

    Sun. "The status of Mercury vis-à-vis the Sun," Haly declared, "is the status of a secretary: he is active, obedient, and wise in reasoning and writing about affairs of state."[56] Alcabitius took Mercury to signify some use of numbers, such as accounting or the scansion of verse, and accordingly "if the Sun is joined to Mercury, it signifies that through the use of numbers one is to be the chief person of a king or to control the property of houses."[57] Michael Scot offered slight variations on the same theme: "If

Mercury is joined to the Sun, it signifies the use of number in relation to a king, to houses, especially a monastery, and to authority over men."[58]

Evidently conjunction with the Sun brings out those qualities of Mercury that we have already noted in Romeo and Justinian. It is in this situation that Mercury produces bailiffs, stewards, and secretaries rather than merchants, scholars, or inventors. The Sun particularly disposes Mercurians to apply their talents to political administration (*regnum*) as rulers exercising authority over those committed to their care. Such a conjunction, it should be noted, is a fairly common event, which for example occurred four times in the year 1300,[59] so Mercurians with these Solar qualities are not great rarity.

Jupiter. Conjunctions of Mercury with Jupiter, on the other hand, are only of annual occurrence, and consequently the Jovial qualities of Mercury are considerably less common. According to Alcabitius, Mercury conjunct Jupiter signifies number in connection with either chanting or divine books.[60] Scot interprets this to mean the scansion of verses written in books, and he adds that the same combination could also signify arithmetical calculations done aloud with a sing-song intonation.[61] Bonatti enlarges the musical applications to include not only the scansion of melodies but also writing them for ecclesiastical use, and he adds that the Jovial Mercurian is adept at song and dance in general.[62] This musical proclivity is present in Dante's heaven of Mercury, but hardly more than the other liberal arts (above, pp. 43–44).

The special influence of Jupiter was, however, susceptible of a broader interpretation that seems more characteristic of Romeo and Justinian. Haly singles out the relationship between Mercury and Jupiter for certain features that they have in common; Mercury, he states, "participates with Jupiter in his wisdom, instruction (*documento*), knowledge, and intellect."[63] Thus Mercury's distinct but weak potentiality in all of these areas would be greatly enhanced by a conjunction with Jupiter, and when the Sun was added to the configuration, the result would be men who not only ruled as another's agent but did so with great knowledge and wisdom. This most desirable combination of knowledge with authority—the secular equivalent of the powers of gold and silver keys (*Purg.* 9.121–126)—would produce just such superior administrators as Romeo and Justinian.

Taken together, then, Dante's two natives of Mercury exemplify a single facet of the planet's diverse influence. In the broadest sense, Mercury governs the intellect, and consequently its natives excel in any matter that requires *ingenium*—innate intellectual talent or genius. Although the unlearned can exhibit Mercurian cleverness as nimble opportunists in trade or in crime, such a nature finds its perfection in occupations that require the practice of the seven liberal arts, for which it has the greatest aptitude. Mercurians make better businessmen, for instance, when they are able to read, write, and calculate; by the same token, they can be excellent administrators at any level. These proclivities are strengthened and channeled when Mercury is well aspected, as it was on 14 April 1300, so that Dante's Mercurians, exemplify the highest practical application of the Mercurian temperament. Both Romeo and Justinian exercise their talents in government, not as rulers in their own right but as agents of a higher power whom they serve, as Mercurians will do, in hope of attaining honor and glory. Mercury's conjunction with the Sun qualifies them both for government administration at the highest level, while its conjunction with Jupiter insures that wisdom and understanding will be added to their mastery of technique. Thus astrology suggested to Dante that his Mercurians should both present types of political stewardship. But at the same time it also suggested to him ways in which they should differ, and consequently we must pass now from the general to the particular and consider how which each character manifests certain Mercurian traits that are not prominent in the other.

Romeo

Descriptions of Mercurian stewardship often fit Romeo better than Justinian. For example, the collection of taxes from the lower classes[64] is more properly the work of a fiscal officer than of an emperor. Alcabitius's description of the significance of Mercury conjunct the Sun fits both men because it was highly generalized (above, n. 59), but when Bonatti repeats it, he adds details that apply so specifically to Romeo that it would seem to be the text that suggested him as a companion figure to Justinian:

> If Mercury is joined to the Sun, it signifies one who, through the use of numbers, is to be the chief person of kings or who is to be in charge of the property of lords, magnates, nobles, or rich men, for he knows how to put their affairs in order, how to rule their households (*familias*) and how to make their domestic affairs (*familiaria facta*) prosper.[65]

Since Romeo was employed by the count of Provence, Bonatti's express inclusion of rulers of lesser magnitude would suggest Romeo's case more readily than the generalized formulation of Alcabitius. Still more suggestive of Romeo's career are the two references to the employer's *familia*, an ambiguous term that Bonatti doubtless used in the common medieval sense of "household," but which also possessed the more restricted sense of "family." Romeo had of course made his master's affairs prosper in both senses, but because by Dante's time the feat of making the count's four daughters queens was already legendary, Romeo's career made the point better than that of some other effective but colorless administrator.

Counsel. The Mercurian servant was especially noteworthy for his excellent advice. Albumasar lists "prudent counsel" among the Mercurian virtues,[66] and Scot elaborated this into a sketch of the ideal counselor: in character the Mercurian is a man

> of upright counsel, with great foresight in practical matters, answering another's questions by telling the truth, and acting with wisdom and with suitable secrecy.[67]

This characteristic would hardly suit an emperor, who by virtue of his position took counsel rather than gave it, but it fits the Romeo of legend perfectly, for Villani's account of how Romeo made the four daughters queens represents Romeo as the count's counselor in the matter. He advises Raymond Berenger to spare no expense to marry off his first daughter so well that the other sisters will be sought in marriage for the sake of their illustrious brother-in-law. And again, Romeo advises the count to marry his last daughter to a capable man who can succeed him as count.[68]

The same Mercurian virtue of counsel is echoed twice by Beatrice in the heaven of Mercury: she begins her long speech in canto 7 by assuring the Pilgrim that her opinions are always correct: "Secondo mio infallibile avviso" (*Par.* 7.19). And again she identifies her opinions with God's: "Fix your eyes now within the abyss of the Eternal Counsel (*l'etterno consiglio*), as closely fastened on my words as you are able" (*Par.* 7.94–96). In both cases she represents herself as the perfect counselor whose opinions are always true; as such she contrasts with the fallibility of even the best human counselor whose advice, though ingenious and prudent, cannot always be correct. Needless to add, these references to counsel are suitably made in the sphere of Mercury.

Romeo's temptation. In Paradise, the stress is on Mercury's power to promote good, but its potentiality for evil must not be overlooked. Mercurians are easily inclined to move from one extreme to another, so that a good Mercurian represents a triumph of free will over temptations presented by the darker side of his nature. Thus his energetic activity can be replaced by listless inanition, his natural benevolence by equally natural malevolence, and hence the loyal Mercurian with a capacity for friendship can turn into a traitor who nurses enmities; likewise, his native ingenuity makes him adept at fraud, deception, and underhanded theft,[69] while his aptitude for the literate arts enables him to be an accomplished forger of written documents.[70] All these sinister tendencies were special temptations to Romeo because he was a native of Mercury, and consequently we should be all the more impressed at his virtue when we learn that he was "active" (*Par.* 6.113), that his works were "noble and beautiful" (129) and "good" (132), and that he himself was not only "just" but even generous in giving his master more than was strictly due him (137–138). Clearly his salvation was not determined by the stars; they enabled him to do evil as well as good, and it was by the exercise of his own free will that he resisted his innate temptations and instead developed his equally inborn capacity for good.

Romeo's departure. The essence of Romeo's story is that in temporal goods he was always poor. When he arrived at the count's court, he was a poor pilgrim; he did not profit unduly from his successful service while he was there; and he departed "poor (*povero*) and old . . . begging his bread morsel by morsel" (*Par.* 6.139–141). All this was in accordance with astrology, for the Mercurian often was a pauper.[71] Scot particularly stresses this facet of Mercury's influence: "He signifies scarcity of riches that are of great consolation to the body," so the Mercurian should expect, "not temporal wealth for his enjoyment," but rather "poverty in temporal goods such as money."[72] Indeed, as a Mercurian Romeo should not have expected to profit from his good service to the count, because according to Scot:

> those whom he has preferred to serve often fail to give him what he deserves, because, like the scorpion who first blandishes his prey before attacking it, fortune favors the master, and therefore the result is good for him but not for his servant.[73]

The circumstances surrounding Romeo's departure were also typically Mercurian. The talented *homo mercurialis* tends to excite the envy of his less fortunate associates, as Scot observed:

> The Mercurian's neighbors are a source of misfortune to him, and accordingly he keeps away from them, and thereby greatly reduces their injuries to him, which for the most part he receives from no fault of his own, since he would willingly benefit another and is careful not to do much harm.[74]

When the envious Provençals prompted the count to have his steward's accounts audited, Romeo's reaction was to drop everything and leave, even though the suspicions were not justified. His motive was injured honor (above, p. 41), which he did not bear patiently as a Lunar personality would have done; instead he reacted like the Mercurian he was, with "strong feelings of anger and abiding resentment due to injured pride."[75] Had he retained his position, as Villani says the count urged him to do, such powerful emotions would have tempted him to revenge himself on his detractors. Instead, since the Mercurian takes pains *not* to injure others, whom he would rather benefit, Romeo behaved as Scot says Mercurians do and simply absented himself from those who had injured his honor. Thus the climax of Romeo's career was wholly typical of the Mercurial temperament: its brilliance attracts undeserved injuries from the envious, which wound his sensitive honor and arouse his anger and disdain, but rather than repay their evil in kind, he prefers to break off all relations with his enemies and live instead in congenial poverty.[76]

Justinian

Although Romeo is a secondary figure whom Justinian mentions as an afterthought, I have examined his Mercurial connections first because he is, as it were, a textbook case of Mercurialism, whereas Justinian's affinities with the second planet are less evident. It is in Romeo that the medieval reader might be expected to recognize the Mercurian temperament at the very end of the episode, and such recognition would naturally turn him back to look for traces of the same character in Justinian as well. They are there to be found, but probably only a professional astrologer would be able to detect them, for Justinian's Mercurialism is of a more subtle sort than Romeo's. Thus it has been easier to discover in Romeo evidence of the Mercurian talent for official service, but only a careful reading of the text revealed Dante's conception of Justinian as God's steward (above, after n. 39). Now we must examine the emperor's character for further Mercurian traits of which he is the poem's best representative; generally speaking, they fall into two areas—religion and law.

Piety. Ibn Ezra simply lists "piety" as one of Mercury's gifts,[77] but other astrologers were less certain of this. Scot, again extrapolating from Mercury's tendency to swing from one extreme to another, presents a qualified view of Mercurian piety: the native pleases others by being "moderately pious and impious."[78] How this works out in practice is best explained by Guido Bonatti in a passage that in fact provides the astrological key to Dante's Justinian:

> In relation to religious sects, Mercury signifies the cultivation of true unity, of reasonable laws, and of similar things; and it signifies doing so with hypocrisy and simulation, pretending that one is better than one is, but without falling into heresy.[79]

In religious matters, the Mercurian's desire for honor and fame inclines him to be a hypocrite, so his piety is most likely to be superficial. Both in public and in private the Mercurian serves God as he serves earthly masters, to the best of his ability, but this is limited by his Mercurian character, which diverts his love from God to lesser objects (*Par.* 6.115–117).[80] His impiety, then, does not extend to such positive expressions as heresy but is rather the hypocrite's weakness for doing "the right thing for the wrong reason." Accordingly we may well wonder about Romeo's motives as a pilgrim, which in his latter days at least seem to have been pique rather than piety, but at any rate the theme is better exemplified in Justinian.

The former emperor tells us that he indeed had been a heretic in his early days, but a sincere one who was content to believe that Christ's nature was wholly divine and in no way human (*Par.* 6.13–15). He was saved from this, as he says, by Pope Agapetus, who "directed me to the true faith by his words" and "I believed him" (*Par.* 6.16–19). Justinian stresses that both before and after his conversion it was for him a matter of faith: first he believed one doctrine and then another, but only in heaven is the truth of the matter apparent to him (19–20). In this readiness to believe, Justinian was purely Mercurian, for the planet signifies both "credulity" and the "credulous."[81] Even more to the point, Justinian was especially disposed to believe in the exclusive divinity of Christ because, according to Albumasar, Mercurians are naturally inclined to have "faith in divinity."[82] Moreover, the Mercurian is apt to be converted by preaching (as Justinian was) because he speedily believes what he hears:[83] "when begged or counselled by others, he quickly changes his mind."[84] This proclivity to change views is tempered, however, by the Mercurian's innate aversion to evil, so he is "more readily inclined to good than to evil."[85] As a result, the

Mercurian is usually a true believer whose character Bonatti delineates in detail: "He will have credulity and will devoutly frequent churches' sanctuaries and places of prayer, and he will be a man of good faith and catholic opinion."[86]

Agapetus. The story of Justinian's conversion provides Dante with an opportunity to introduce yet another type of Mercurian into the poem, for the clerical hierarchy has a special affinity for Mercury. Even the pagan Ptolemy seemed to associate the planet with "houses of prayer,"[87] and Rabbi Ibn Ezra said it was the Mercurian's nature "to know prayers,"[88] but it took a Christian like Michael Scot to develop these indications in the context of Catholic Europe: "Mercury signifies ecclesiastical offices such as the mass etc., prayers, fasts, clerics, and prelates, prophets and prophecies, gospels, epistles, and any kind of religious order."[89] From this broad ecclesial spectrum, Dante singled out a single element, the prelates, whom he exemplified in the person of a pope, the chief prelate. All that Agapetus does is preach to Justinian, and in doing so his behavior is characteristically Mercurian, for both Alcabitius and Scot list "preaching" among the works typical of Mercury,[90] and Bonatti enlarges on the theme, asserting that "if the Mercurian shall be a cleric, he will be a good and pleasing preacher."[91]

Agapetus is more than just an ordinary preacher and Justinian is no mere parishioner; they are respectively pope and emperor, and their interaction is Dante's paradigm for the proper relationship between *sacerdotium* and *regnum*, between church and state. The pope does not compel the emperor but teaches him the truth, while the emperor for his part humbly listens to the gospel and believes. As Dante explains at the end of the *Monarchia*, mankind is guided by two leaders: "there is the Supreme Pontiff who is to lead mankind to eternal life in accordance with revelation; and there is the Emperor who, in accordance with philosophical teaching, is to lead mankind to temporal happiness."[92] The point of the *Monarchia*, of course, is that the emperor does not derive his authority from the pope but directly from God. Nonetheless Dante insists that the pope does command a certain respect from the emperor, and accordingly his concluding sentence provides a precise description of Justinian's relation to Agapetus: "Caesar, therefore, is obliged to observe that reverence towards Peter which a first-born son owes to his father; so that when he is enlightened by the light of paternal grace he may the more powerfully enlighten the world, at the head of which he has been placed by the One who alone is ruler of all things spiritual and temporal."[93] Thus in the heaven of Mercury we learn by example how the chief persons of Christendom are related, and this too is astrologically appropriate because, according to Scot, it is Mercury that governs "the order of persons."[94]

Law. For the Mercurian, the practice of religion is closely connected with the subject of law. Thus Guido Bonatti saw a tendency in Mercury that opposed religious divisions by "the cultivation of true unity and of reasonable laws" (above, n. 79). More than any other, this key passage explains why the emperor who codified Roman law was for Dante the Mercurian par excellence. Although no other astrologer describes Justinian's work with such precision, Mercury's association with law was a well-established tradition in medieval astrology. Ptolemy himself had linked the planet with "changes of customs and laws,"[95] and Albumasar represented the Mercurian as one concerned with "the observance of law, who presents both sides of a case truthfully,"[96] while Haly noted that he also had a tendency to be litigious.[97] Thus Michael Scot included law as one of the studies to which the keen Mercurian mind was apt to devote itself with a zeal that he considered to be religious:

> Among the kinds of faith, Mercury signifies the student's single-minded cultivation day and night of the art of writing or of such learned subjects as grammar, logic, *laws*, physical science, astronomy, experiments, and the exercise of any art that requires a keen mind.[98]

Furthermore he asserts that it is the property of the Mercurian to take pleasure in such studies, among which he again expressly includes "the laws."[99]

In Justinian, this concern with the law was combined with the Mercurian's special regard for books. According to Scot, Mercury signifies those things that are done through the study of books,[100] and Haly placed books first among the things that a young Mercurian prized,[101] while one astrologer went so far as to claim that the mature Mercurian "was a wise man who would rather read than do anything else."[102] Most astrologers, however, stress the Mercurian's active role as a producer of books, for typically he is a scribe by profession,[103] following the influence of his planet, which governs writing and documents.[104] The Mercurian's concern for books goes beyond mere transcription, however, for he also writes commentaries[105] and compiles books himself.[106] Dante's Justinian is of course chiefly concerned with only the last of these bookish activities—"the compilation of books (*compilatio librorum*)"—which in fact is made explicit by one of the poet's favorite astrologers, Michael Scot.

None of the astrologers expressly connect the Mercurian's legal interests with his literary activities, although Bonatti approaches it when he lists "proverbs and writing" as characteristic activities of the Mercurian, immediately adding by way of a gloss that "he will be good and moral."[107] Presumably the Mercurian moralist who is in a position to be a legislator will prescribe conduct, not in proverbs, but in the more authoritative form of written law. There is even a hint in Michael Scot that rhetoric and Roman law, the studies for which Bologna was most famous, were especially under the guidance of Mercury: "for the god of sciences is supreme among the Romans, and especially the Lombards, and all who are learned by nature and by art in noble and great sciences."[108]

A closer connection is provided by Dante himself, who in the *Convivio* (4.9.8) translated *ius*, the broadest Latin term for "law," as "ragione scritta" or "written reason." Mercury governs both components of "written reason," for by virtue of the planet's identification with the rational soul, it controls "genius, reason (*ratio*), eloquence, and the observance of their precepts."[109] Moreover, Dante goes on to link his Mercurian *ragione scritta* with the Roman emperor: "For writing down, declaring, and enforcing this Law [*ragione scritta*], that officer of whom we are speaking, viz. the Emperor, has been appointed. . . ."[110] Thus it is not surprising that Dante exemplified the planet of reasoning and writing by the most famous single source of Written Reason—Justinian himself.

The *Corpus Iustinianum*

As befits a Mercurian who was activated by a desire for fame and honor, Dante's Justinian identifies himself by reference to his greatest achievement, the *Corpus iuris civilis*: "I was Caesar, and am Justinian, who, by will of the Primal Love which I feel, removed from among the laws what was superfluous and vain (*il troppo e 'l vano*)" (*Par.* 6.10–12). Thus Dante's reader is referred to a work outside the poem, and in fact the intertextual reference is even more precise, because the description of his work echoes a recurrent theme in the seven imperial constitutions or decrees that Justinian published to initiate and promulgate various parts of the project.[111]

A few examples will suffice to establish the correspondence. Throughout his codification, Justinian was insistent that the editors should omit whatever was superfluous (*il troppo*): in the *Institutes* and *Digest*, he claims, "We divested all the ancient law of superfluous prolixity," and similarly in the *Code* he "removed all that is superfluous in resemblance and all iniquitous discord."[112] Dantists have no difficulty in finding the *troppo* echoed in Justinian's prefaces, but the *vano* has been a matter of controversy, some taking it to be a loose equivalent of the contradictory matter that Justinian ordered to be excised, others taking it to be a redundant equivalent of *troppo*, and yet others taking it *strictu sensu* to mean what is void and hence useless.[113] The third approach, based on a careful consideration of Dante's usage, is doubtless the most convincing, and there is more textual support for it in Justinian's prefatory constitutions than has been noticed before. The *Institutes*, for example, are promulgated so that student may learn "nothing useless (*inutile*),"[114] and a revised version of the *Code* was issued in which both the *troppo* and the *vano* appear side by side, when Justinian relates how his editors had been instructed to remove passages "where any of the constitutions were superfluous, or had been annulled (*vacuatas*) by any of Our subsequent decrees."[115] Another possible echo, which has passed unobserved, may be found in the reference Dante's Justinian makes to the law of noncontradiction, on which the historical Justinian relied when he repeatedly banned contradictory matter from his *Corpus*.[116] These parallels, then, leave no doubt that as Dante was writing *Paradiso* 6 he had in mind Justinian's prefatory decrees to the *Corpus iuris civilis*; consequently by intertextual reference they become as it were an extension of the poem, and hence a likely place to seek further exemplification of Justinian's mercurial character.

Justinian's contribution. The historical Justinian makes it clear in his prefaces that he had little to do with the actual work of preparing the *Corpus*, which was delegated to Tribonian and other legal experts; his own contribution was to initiate and to organize the work, and both functions are typically Mercurian. According to Scot, the Mercurian "all by himself will discover many new things that are of great utility."[117] Just so, Justinian stresses the novelty of his enterprise, "which no one before Our reign ever hoped for, or even thought to be hardly possible for human effort to accomplish."[118] Similarly, organization is one of the Mercurian's strong points; Alcabitius says he excels in work that involves putting things in order ("dispositionem rei"),[119] and Ibn Ezra simply says that he likes "to organize."[120] Justinian in his prefaces exhibits this Mercurian trait: in the *Code* he brought together in one authoritative source "enactments which are scattered through various constitutions,"[121] and thus they were "reduced to one consistent system."[122]

The emperor's organizational genius is in fact repeatedly manifested in the decrees themselves. The constitutions *Haec* and *Deo auctore* announce the projects of compiling the *Code* and the *Digest* respectively, and each presents a rationale for the enterprise, appoints a commission to implement it, and lays down definite guidelines for the commissioners to follow. Again, when the *Digest* was completed, it was promulgated by the decree *Tanta*, a large part of which describes the organization of the *Digest*, proceeding systematically through all fifty of its books.[123] At the same time, since the *Digest* was intended for use in the law schools, Justinian took its appearance as the occasion to reorganize legal instruction by imperial decree, and he outlined the new five-year curriculum in the constitution *Omnem*. These instances of Justinian's talent as it appears in his decrees show that above all he had a genius for organization such as one would expect in a Mercurian administrator.

Perfectionism is another Mercurian trait that is much in evidence in Justinian's prefaces. Scot describes this quality in much the same way that his Arab predecessors had: "the spirit of perfection in any given art."[124] This certainly was the spirit in which Justinian had his own *Code* revised and issued in a second edition "so that nothing which has been begun by us may be left imperfect."[125] Elsewhere he attributed any errors in the *Digest* "to the innate weakness of human nature," though this was to be expected because "only divine things are perfect."[126]

Closely allied to perfectionism is the Mercurian "cultivation of true unity and reasonable laws" that Bonatti saw as the Mercurian's characteristic approach to religious differences (above, at n. 79). This is evident in Justinian's *Code*, the first title of which reads: "Concerning the Most High Trinity and the Catholic Faith, and that no one should dare to dispute about them in public."[127] Such Mercurian fondness for unity was not necessarily limited to religious matters, however, for Bonatti notes that when Mercury approaches conjunction with the Sun, as was the case at the time of the poem, "it signifies . . . concord and the search for it."[128] This accords well with Justinian's insistence that contradictory matter be eliminated from his compilations, as when he claimed that his *Code* "brought into perfect harmony (*consonantiam*) the Imperial Constitutiones hitherto involved in confusion."[129] Unification in a political sense agreeable to the author of the *Monarchia* was also a theme to which Justinian frequently returned. Several of his prefaces record the progress of his reconquest of the Roman world, culminating in his boast that "all peoples in fact, are now governed by laws either promulgated or compiled by Us."[130]

Justinian, then, appears in his prefaces as the initiator and organizer of the *Corpus* that he meant to be the well-nigh perfect means of uniting mankind into one harmonious Christian-Roman society. The work itself, as he is careful to record, was carried out by experts at his command. In

the case of the *Digest*, the most ambitious of the compilations, he names
not only the seven members of the commission but also eleven other lawyers who assisted them.[131] It is hard for the historian to determine to what
extent Justinian himself participated in their labors. His most definite
statement is that he approved the short treatise of the *Institutes* "after having read and examined them."[132] A similar but less precise claim in the case
of the immense collection of the *Digest* suggests that, although he may in
fact not have read the entire work, still he did at least make a number of
important editorial decisions himself: "and our majesty also relying upon
the heavenly divinity and constantly examining and scrutinizing the matter
compiled by these men, have corrected whatever has been found to be
ambiguous or doubtful and reduced it into proper order."[133] An astrologer
would recognize that Justinian played a part particularly congenial to Mercurians, who according to Albumasar are led by their ambition for glory
to investigate questions[134] and are attracted by subjects that are "doubtful
and involved."[135] Scot suggests that the Mercurian may indeed be over-
ambitious because he "wants to be acquainted with great questions, but
without any study, and to know as it were all the answers."[136] Justinian
certainly conformed to Albumasar's description and perhaps to Scot's as
well; at any rate, his confidence in his own intellectual abilities was truly
Mercurian.

Glory to God. Intermixed with these matter-of-fact descriptions of
how the *Corpus* was compiled are statements of quite another order, which
acknowledge God's help in the work. The compilation of the *Digest*, for
example, would otherwise have been "nearly impossible";[137] but Justinian
"wished God to become the author and head of the whole work" and
accordingly placed it under divine protection;[138] thus he could eventually
claim that the project was "accomplished by the grace of God and the favor
of the Supreme Trinity," or alternatively that is was "completed by the aid
of Our Lord God Jesus Christ, who has rendered the task possible for Us
as well as for Our ministers,"[139] and accordingly the *Digest* is finally offered
to God with thanks[140] and is held to be "a proof of the wisdom of Almighty God."[141] A similar sentiment is voiced by Dante's Justinian, who
in heaven recognizes that the work was done "by will of the Primal Love
which I feel" (*Par.* 6.11), although the reader gathers that, due to his love
of fame and honor, he felt it rather less while on earth (*Par.* 6.112–117).
We have already learned from the astrologers that Mercurians are prone to
make displays of their piety and that these can be expected to be relatively
shallow and often hypocritical as well (above, n. 79), and consequently we

need not take the piety of Justinian's prefaces at face value but can appreciate it for its Mercurian character.

Fame and honor. The insincerity of these pious ornaments is betrayed by Justinian's own ego, for in true Mercurian fashion the emperor never misses an opportunity to enhance his personal honor and fame, whether deserved or not. With justification he can claim credit as the project's initiator and patron, and he does so in the most laudatory terms: "this compilation is to be ascribed to the extraordinary liberality of our imperial will."[142] But he is just as ready to take credit for the work that others have done. Although the *Digest* is an anthology of jurisprudence, Justinian wanted it understood "that it shall all be entirely ours" because he had approved it.[143] The compilers are informed that Justinian will give their work the force of law,

> so that all those most learned men whose opinions are included in this book may have the same authority as if their studies had been based upon the imperial constitutions promulgated by our own divine power; for we very properly consider all those things to be ours which have obtained their sanction from us; for he who corrects what has not been skillfully done is more praiseworthy than he who is the original author of the same.[144]

Moreover, law students are assured that they should consider themselves honored and happy because the books that they study "issue from the mouth of your sovereign."[145] Thus even first-year law students, by studying Justinian's *Institutes*, will "be able to learn the first principles of the law . . . from the imperial splendor,"[146] and accordingly he decreed that hence forward their nickname should be "the New Justinians."[147] Similarly, he planned from the start to have the new code issued "under our auspicious name,"[148] and subsequently so designated it himself—"the Justinian Code."[149] These and many similar passages in Justinian's prefaces fully justified Dante in his opinion that the emperor was one of those ambitious Mercurians who were "active in order that honor and fame might come to them" (*Par.* 6.113–114).

JUSTINIAN'S ORATION

Insofar as Dante had any detailed knowledge of the character of the historical Justinian, it must have been derived from the emperor's prefaces to his legislation, and so it has seemed useful to examine their Mercurial character in detail. From them Dante doubtless derived one other feature of his treatment of Justinian, for just as in life the emperor framed his decrees as eloquent orations delivered to an audience, so Dante's Justinian is endowed with this same proclivity for formal discourse adorned with all the flowers of rhetoric, and he fills the whole sixth canto of the *Paradiso* with it. This disposition, too, is characteristically Mercurian because the astrologers single out rhetoric as a liberal art in which the *Mercurialis* particularly excels. Thus Alcabitius said that the planet signified "oratio" and produced works of "rhetoric." [150] This identification was based on the fabled eloquence of the god Mercury, whose planet accordingly confers skill in speech,[151] making its native "soothing and suave in speech, arranging the words of his speech well." [152]

The Roman Eagle. Justinian's oration is Mercurian not only in its general conception but also in many of its most prominent features. Chief of these is the Roman Eagle, to whose progress over half of the canto is devoted (*Par.* 6.1–9, 28–96). Although no astrologer specifically names the eagle in connection with Mercury, Ibn Ezra says that among birds the planet governs "the starling, bees, and every one that flies with agility." [153] Quickness, of course, is a quality of Mercury,[154] which brings other quick things under the influence of his planet *per similitudinem*. Since the swiftness of eagles is proverbial, occurring for example three times in the Bible [155] (not to mention Justinian's oration, 62–72), it follows that the eagle is one of the birds appropriate to Mercury. To be sure, elsewhere Ibn Ezra lists the eagle by name as one of Jupiter's birds, but this is hardly a difficulty, since Dante, too, gives the bird a prominent place in both heavens. Indeed, it would be especially appropriate to emphasize a property common to two planets when they are conjunct, as Mercury and Jupiter are in the *Comedy*'s horoscope (above, after n. 49). Finally, it is noteworthy that the canto opens with a reference to the course of the Eagle from west to east when "Constantine turned back the Eagle counter to the course of the heavens" (*Par.* 6.1–2), which in astronomical terms is a retrograde movement, appropriate because at the time of the poem the planet Mercury was itself moving retrograde towards the Sun (see below, Appendix 2).

War. After introducing himself, Justinian turns to his main theme, which is to censure the modern use of the Roman Eagle as the Ghibelline standard (*Par.* 6.28–111). His basic premise is the thesis that Dante proved in the second book of the *Monarchia*, "that the Roman people acquired the Empire of the world by right," [156] but Justinian develops the argument more simply by contrasting the great deeds that were formerly done under the standard of the Roman Eagle to its present partisan use. Accordingly the greater part of this section describes the victories by which the Romans enlarged their empire, and this stress is also an appropriate one for the heaven of Mercury, since Alcabitius and Bonatti agree that "it signifies earthly things and the augmentation of things by growing in size."[157] The Eagle also defeats Hannibal in Italy and emerges triumphant from various civil wars, just as the same authorities state that Mercury "signifies fear, and invasion and war, and enmity, sedition, and opposition."[158] Hence both the wars of the Roman Eagle and of the Guelfs and the Ghibellines are properly a Mercurian theme.

Up to now, this warlike aspect of Mercury has not concerned us for the simple reason that Justinian, as he tells us, refrained from leading his armies when he accepted the victories of Belisarius "as a sign for me to rest from them" (*Par.* 6.25–27). In other words, Justinian was by his astral nature fitted to be a general, but he was prevented from developing this talent by a special judgment of God, for according to Dante, God's will can be revealed indirectly through a trial between forces opposed in combat.[159] Nonetheless, astrologers did associate Mercury with warfare, notably Haly, for whom it was "the planet of wrongdoing and violence,"[160] so that in four signs of the Zodiac it signified different kinds of warfare, including the origins of strife in Aries.[161] Scot and Bonatti, on the other hand, were inclined to stress Mercury's warlike aspects chiefly in conjunction with Mars.[162] Thus, although Justinian suppressed the violent side of his Mercurian nature in later life, still it is completely in accordance with his astral character that he should devote much of his speech to the congenial subject of wars foreign and domestic.

Lilies. Justinian's complaint is that the Roman Eagle has come to be nothing but the symbol of the Ghibelline political party, like the French fleur-de-lis, which was adopted by the opposing Guelf party as its arms. Mentioned twice by him, these "yellow lilies" (*Par.* 6.100, 111) are also an image borrowed from Mercurian astrology. Alcabitius and Bonatti both declare that Mercury "signifies alezeminium, which is a certain color like the color of the lily of the field."[163] Thus astrology justifies not only the underlying theme of Justinian's oration but also both of its principal images.

Geography

Although by now it is abundantly clear that both Romeo and Justinian are astrologically appropriate to the heaven of Mercury, we have not quite exhausted Dante's reasons for placing them there. Perhaps the oddest of them all, at least to the modern mind, is provided by geography, which accordingly I give last place, as a kind of postscript.

Geographers in Dante's time divided the habitable world into seven zones or climates (*climata*),[164] to which Dante himself referred on six occasions.[165] Since the climates, like the planets, numbered seven, some astrologers systematically paired them off. Thus Rabbi Ibn Ezra has Mercury governing the sixth climate.[166]

Unfortunately, there was no general agreement on the precise location of the *climata*, so at least two systems were available to Dante. One was that of Alfraganus, from whom Dante drew other technical details of astronomy. In this system, the sixth climate was a band about 210 Arabic miles wide (257.5 English statute miles = 414.3 km), extending from 43 2/5° to 47 1/4° north latitude.[167] The other system was found in the astronomical tables of Alcoarismi (al-Khwârizmî), which were translated into Latin by Adelard of Bath in 1126.[168] According to this reckoning, the sixth climate lay approximately two degrees farther south, extending from 41 1/3° to 45 1/3° north latitude. Alcoarismi's system was fully described by Albertus Magnus in his *De natura locorum*[169] in a chapter (1.9) that Dante himself cited, though not with any indication that he preferred this climatic system.[170] Happily, we do not have to determine which system Dante considered correct, because my point can be made equally well in terms of either location of the sixth climate.

The point is that both Justinian and Romeo did in fact flourish in the sixth climate. Assuming that climate to be the smaller band common to both systems and extending only from 43 1/2° to 45 1/3° north latitude, we find that according to medieval astronomers that zone includes both Provence and Byzantium. The actual latitude of Istanbul-Constantinople-Byzantium is 41° 4' north, but the astronomical tables available to Dante both agreed that it lay some 4° more to the north, at 45°.[171] Moreover, Alfragnaus explicitly includes Constantinople in his description of the principal cities lying within the sixth climate.[172] Marseilles, the principal city of the county of Provence, is not so well documented, but in a supplementary entry to a copy of the *Toledo Tables*, its position is given as 44° north, whereas its actual latitude is 43° 17' north,[173] so Ptolemy in his *Almagest* (2.6.14) was more nearly correct in placing it at 43° 4'.[174] Thus, whatever medieval climatic authority Dante might have consulted, he would have arrived at the same conclusion: both Byzantium and Marseilles were included within the sixth climate.[175]

Accordingly, the poet has Justinian, in his canto-long Mercurian declamation, allude appropriately to both places. The canto opens with an allusion to the transfer of imperial administration from Rome to Constantinople (*Par.* 6.1–9), and long before the Provençals are expressly named in connection with Romeo (130), their region has been evoked as the scene of some of the Eagle's victories. The Var river near Nice is undeniably a reference to Provence (58), and although narrowly speaking Provence as a political entity was the county, which is in effect the valley of the Durance river, still the linguistic influence of Provençal flowed up "the Isere . . . and every valley whence Rhone is filled" (59–60). Certainly Hannibal, too, followed one of those valleys to reach the watershed of the Po, though neither Dante nor we know which one (50). To be sure, these are minor touches compared with the prominent connections between Justinian and Constantinople and between Romeo and Provence, but nonetheless they perform a useful function in the poem. To the reader who suspects that Dante selected Justinian and Romeo as his typical Mercurians not only because of their temperament but also because they flourished in the sixth, Mercurial climate, these geographical allusions serve as a reassurance that he is on the right track, because they clearly indicate that the poet considered these places significant and therefore multiplied his references to them in *Paradiso* 6.

Jesus

Almost half of Dante's sojourn in Mercury is devoted to yet another person, for the theme of canto 7 is the redemption of mankind by God's incarnation as Jesus of Nazareth. Beatrice explains in detail why it was most appropriate that mankind, which had lost free will through Adam's fall, should be redeemed by one who was both God and man. This theme had already been foreshadowed in the previous canto, when Justinian related how he had been converted to the orthodox theological doctrine that Jesus had two natures, one human and the other divine (*Par.* 6.13–21).

The theme is especially appropriate to Mercury because that planet signifies both natures. On the one hand, "it signifies deity," according to Alcabitius,[176] and this facet of the Mercurian character is hinted at by the poet when he has Beatrice tell the Pilgrim to address the Mercurians "and trust even as to gods" (*Par.* 5.123). On the other hand, as we have repeatedly remarked (above, pp. 42, 48, 56), Mercury also signifies the rational soul, which is the specifically human part of *homo sapiens*. Moreover, the planet is also suited to signify the combination of these two natures into one person, because of Mercury's ambiguous nature that includes opposing tendencies.[177] Indeed, Haly actually stated that "Mercury is the planet . . . of a composite person (*composite persone*),"[178] by which he probably meant what we might call a "composed person" in whom conflicting components were resolved into a peaceful and harmonious union, although to a Latin Christian reader the phrase could readily suggest the composite person of Christ. Thus the subject of Christ's geminal nature is fittingly considered in the heaven of Mercury.

What is more, by invoking a familiar medieval variation on the theme of Christ's *gemina persona*, Dante is able to integrate the doctrine Beatrice expounds in Mercury with the souls encountered there. "I was Caesar, and am Justinian" says the leading character (*Par.* 6.10), thereby making use of a distinction now familiar to scholars as "the king's two bodies."[179] Every autonomous medieval official was conceived to be a figure of Christ because he combined in his person both his natural, physical person and an office that was conferred by divine grace. Justinian expressly makes this distinction, and furthermore it is implicit in the related Mercurian theme of stewardship, in accordance with which both Romeo and Justinian are represented as officers doing their duty. Since Dante believed that the office of emperor was conferred directly by God (*Mon.* 3.15.13), his representation of Justinian as God's *baiulo* epitomizes the human who rules by divine grace.

The role was especially appropriate for Justinian not only because of the part he played in the Monophysite heresy over the twofold nature of Christ but also for its prominence in his decree *Tanta*, which begins: "So great is the providence of divine humanity (*divinae humanitatis*) concerning us. . . ."[180] Repeatedly in the same decree, he contrasts the imperfection of human nature with the perfection of divinity.[181] This contrast is implicit in Dante's treatment of the Mercurian character, which strives to gain recognition of its natural genius, but which can be nonetheless redeemed by grace when its energies, guided by faith, are directed towards goals that are in themselves good.

This twofold nature of Mercury and the Mercurian explains why "double light is twinned" (*Par.* 7.6) in the natives when the Pilgrim provides them with a new means of showing their love, so that their joy, and hence their brightness, is increased (*Par.* 5. 105–108, 124–126, 131–132).[182]

3. Venus

Dante loved to test his reader's understanding by posing problems, often in the form of ambiguous statements that were equally apt to lead or mislead. He begins the cantos of Venus with just such a conundrum, which directs the reader's attention to an erroneous belief about Venus, but it is not immediately clear what the poet is condemning.

> Solea creder lo mondo in suo periclo
> che la bella Ciprigna il folle amore
> raggiasse, volta nel terzo epiciclo;
> per che non pur a lei faceano onore
> di sacrificio e di votivo grido
> le genti antiche ne l'antico errore. . . . (*Par.* 8.1–6)

The world was wont to believe, to its peril, that the fair Cyprian, wheeling in the third epicycle, rayed down mad love; wherefore the ancient people in their ancient error not only did honor to her with sacrifice and votive cry. . . .

But, he goes on to say, they also honored her mother Dione and her son Cupid, the latter being Desire personified, and especially sexual desire; consequently they named the third planet after the goddess Venus (7–11).

At the least we may be sure that Dante, as a Christian, considered it an error to deify the planets, a practice which indeed has already been explicitly described and condemned by Beatrice (*Par.* 4.61–63). She conceded at the same time that the stars do influence human affairs (58–60), so that cannot be part of "l'antico errore" of Venus's devotees, but it is unclear whether they were correct in their belief that the planet "rayed down mad love (*folle amore*)."

The ambiguity of the opening sentence of canto 8 is only a minor problem until the reader discovers that in this heaven he is not explicitly given any principle that explains how this planet has conditioned the souls that appear there. In the Moon, both Beatrice and Piccarda explained that failure to observe vows was the reason (*Par.* 3.31–32, 53–57); in Mercury, Justinian identified the cause as the pursuit of fame and honor (6.112–114); but in Venus neither Beatrice nor the three souls who speak to Dante define the effect of Venus in so many words. Instead, the reader is introduced to four characters who provide him with clues from which he can, perhaps, infer why they are there. If, like most medieval and modern readers, he assumes that "mad love" is the principal effect of Venus, he will quickly discover that Dante had a broader concept of Venusian astrology. To make this apparent, let us briefly consider each case in turn.

(1) Canto 8 is almost wholly devoted to Carlo Martello, titular king of Hungary and heir apparent to the kingdom of the Two Sicilies and to the county of Provence. Although we incidentally learn that he was married and had offspring before he died prematurely at the age of twenty-four, there is nothing about him either in the poem or in history or legend to suggest that he was under the influence of "mad love." Instead, the stress in the poem is on his friendship with Dante, which presumably flourished during the prince's three-week visit to Florence in March 1294. Thus, in the course of the canto, the concept of love is enlarged by Carlo's example to include friendship (*amicitia*) as well as the *folle amore* mentioned in the opening lines.

(2) The next canto, however, presents three cases in which erotic love plays a greater part. In the case of Cunizza da Romano, the eroticism is implied rather than expressed. The only biographical details that Cunizza provides in the poem are that she was born near Treviso and was the sister of its infamous lord, Ezzelino da Romano. True, she acknowledges the influence of Venus, but in terms so general as to tell nothing about her life: "I am refulgent here because the light of this star overcame me (*mi vinse*); but I gladly pardon in myself the reason of my lot" (*Par.* 9.32–35). Dante leaves the reader to gather from the writings of chroniclers and troubadours that Cunizza led a varied erotic life that included at least two marriages and perhaps as many as four, as well as two famous affairs, one with the troubadour Sordello and the other with Enrico da Bonio, a knight of Treviso, who accompanied her for over ten years as they wandered together in a peripatetic life of luxury.[1] Given the notoriety of her love affairs, there can be little doubt that Dante meant her career to be understood as an example of the influence of "il folle amore." Furthermore, it should be noted that her amorous disposition is expressly

attributed to the influence of Venus, so the ambiguity of the narrator's introduction is now resolved: the ancients were *not* in error when they believed that Venus had this effect on humanity.

(3) What Cunizza leaves the reader to discover from sources outside the poem is made explicit by the third and final speaker, Folco of Marseilles, a troubadour who, according to his biographer, conducted a courtly and carnal affair with his lord's wife until her death, after which he became a Cistercian monk and had his wife and children also take religious vows. Folco's conversion opened a second career to him, for he soon rose to be abbot and then was elected bishop of Toulouse (1205–1231), where he played a leading role in the Albigensian crusades.[2] In the poem he acknowledges the erotic influence of Venus, saying that he was imprinted by the planet as were such classical lovers as Dido, Phyllis, and Hercules, "who burned not more than I, as long as it befitted my locks" (*Par.* 9.97, 99). What is more, by explaining that middle age had cooled his venereal passions, he establishes that the influence of Venus is natural and physical, and a few lines later he attributes it to "the Power that ordained and foresaw" (105), thus making his case an instance of God's orderly and providential distribution of talents, which Carlo Martello had previously described in a generalized way.

(4) Taken together, Cunizza and Folco are Dante's examples of "mad love," but his typology of love is not yet complete: the final stage is reached when Folco introduces the silent soul of Rahab, the prostitute of Jericho who entertained Joshua's spies and helped them to escape from their pursuers (Jos. 2.1–24; 6.15–25). As a professional lover for whom sexual relations were a matter of business rather than of passion, she can hardly be taken as an example of "mad love." Yet we are told by Folco that she represents the highest type of Venusian: "our order is sealed by her in the highest degree" (*Par.* 9.116–117). Since Rahab was not emotionally involved with Joshua's spies, her love is clearly not the friendship displayed by Carlo Martello, so it follows that Rahab must represent a third type of Venusian love, higher than the others. What that may be is not stated, so the cantos of Venus end as they began with a puzzle for the reader.

By scrutinizing the effects of Venus on each of the four characters, we have discovered that these effects are apparently not as simple as those of the Moon and Mercury. They at least include "mad love," friendship, and the unknown quality of Rahab. In fact, there are a great many more effects that the poet includes by allusion, but the three kinds of influence already made apparent in the Venusian souls themselves are enough to make the reader aware that Venus has diverse effects. His problem, then, is to ascertain the full range of the planet's influence, and for this one would naturally turn to the astrologers. In this chapter, therefore, we shall not concentrate on the qualities of the characters, as we have done before, but instead let us systematically pass in review all those qualities of Venus that are reflected in the poem. This will enable us to see what Venus meant to Dante, and from this vantage point we can then return at the end of the chapter to the four characters and not only see how they embody these qualities but also solve the riddle of Rahab.

Venusian Appetites

The search may well start with some astrological properties of Venus on which Dante laid particular stress. Let us begin where he did, with the ancient misconceptions about the influence of Venus, and see how they can be rectified by astrology. By seeing how Dante uses astrology to correct the errors of the ancients, we will be able to expand the common, sexual concept of Venusian love to include a broader range of human activity.

Idolatry. Dante began the Venusian cantos by stating that "the ancient people in their ancient error . . . to her did honor with sacrifice and votive cry" *because* they believed that the goddess rayed down mad love from her planet (*Par.* 8.1–6). Ironically, their idolatry itself was an effect of Venus of which they were apparently ignorant. The kind of religious sect that Venus signifies is "the worship of idols" according to Alcabitius,[3] "the cult of idols" according to Scot,[4] and simply "idolatry" according to Bonatti.[5] Moreover, like Dante, Scot specifically mentions "sacrifices," while the others speak of ritual eating and drinking. Since idolatry is itself a form of love, the stress the poet lays on it serves as an early warning that Venusian love is not limited to sex.

Desire. Another ancient error mentioned in Dante's *principium* is the honor paid to desire personified as Cupid, so that Dido's sexual desire could be represented by having him sit on her lap. The error, as in the case of Venus, is that desire is an effect of the planet, not a person, much less a god. Dante himself would agree that love produces desire, for this is the doctrine that Virgil teaches in *Purgatorio* 18.19–39, but there both qualities are used to describe every kind of human appetite and not just the sexual ones with which "mad love" and Cupid are concerned. In the course of the Venusian cantos, Dante suggests as much by referring to nonsexual, and indeed nonphysical, kinds of desire. After once hearing the souls cry "hosanna," the narrator says "that never since have I been without the desire (*disiro*) to hear it again" (*Par.* 8.29–30); when Folco is slow to speak, the Pilgrim asks him "Why then does your voice . . . not satisfy my longings (*disii*)" (*Par.* 9.76, 79); and Folco tells him about Rahab "in order that you may bear away with you all your desires (*voglie*) fulfilled which have been born in this sphere" (109–111).

This broader conception of desire is also found in astrology, where Venus is associated with the appetitive soul by Ibn Ezra.[6] Indeed, the astrologers have no need for either personification or deification; for them it is a straightforward fact that the planet Venus controls the erogenous parts of the body, including not only the loins (*lumbi*)—the anatomical equivalent of Dido's lap ("grembo," *Par.* 8.9)—but also the reproductive organs, as well as the liver (*epar*), which as the organ that produced the *spiritus naturalis*, was considered to be the ultimate source of the passions. Because sexual desire originates in the liver, Michael Scot moralizes that this organ may also be regarded as the source of one's humanity (*humanitas*) because "by it one is moved to the love not of himself but of someone else."[7] Thus Alcabitius and Bonatti declare that Venus governs longing or desire (*desiderium*).[8]

Peace and quiet. Not all desire is Venusian: the natives, for example, do not desire the intellectual activity of Mercury or the physical activity of Mars; instead, Venus inclines one to a life of leisure—*otium*.[9] Accordingly, Michael Scot describes the *homo Venereus* as one who is "peaceful and quiet in his relations with others" and "peaceful in his actions"; similarly, in the larger sphere of politics, the planet itself signifies "truce, concord, peace."[10] Scot finds this peaceful quality of soul reflected in the native's appearance, for his face is "placid as that of an angel," and also in his conduct, which is likewise *placidus*, for no matter what he is doing he moves along with deliberate speed.[11] All of these qualities are consistent with the phlegmatic temperament that Scot also attributes to Venusians.[12]

In view of these peaceful and placid qualities, it is appropriate that Rahab, the paragon of Venusian souls, should be characterized as being tranquil ("tranquilla," *Par.* 9.115). The same quality is perhaps also echoed in the disposition of the souls to cease their wheeling on the planet's epicycle: "we are so full of love that, in order to please you, a little quiet (*quïete*) will not be less sweet to us" (*Par.* 8.38–39).

Joy and gladness. The pacific tendencies of Venus are remarked only by

Michael Scot, but almost every astrologer associates the planet with joy (*gaudium*).[13] Dante too stresses this quality in the heaven of Venus, by using both the equivalent Italian verb *gioiri* ("ti gioi," *Par.* 8.33) and noun ("gioia," 9.37), the latter in the sense of "jewel," and hence doubly appropriate to Venus (see below, n. 80). Moreover, he uses *allegrezza* to convey the same sense of joy: "allegrezza nova che s'accrebbe . . . .a l'allegrezze sue" (8.47–48). Even more he stresses the closely related quality of gladness (*letitia*), which Scot says people seek through the social amusements, which Venus signifies.[14] In heaven, to be sure, gladness proceeds from less trivial causes, but it is nonetheless much in evidence, *lieto* and related forms being used six times (8.52, 85, 91; 9.34, 67, 70), not counting the same sense conveyed by *trastulla* (9.76).

Joy and gladness are of course to be found throughout the *Paradiso*, but one kind is peculiar to Venus. Carlo tells the Pilgrim "I rejoice in you" ("di te mi giova," 8.137), and the narrator says that Cunizza spoke "as one rejoicing (*giova*) to do a kindness" (9.24). The Latin equivalent is the verb *iuvare*, which like its Italian offspring means either "to help" or "to delight," and the astrologers apply it to Venus in both senses: the planet is "adiuvatrix et iuvatilis" according to Scot and "stella iocunditatis" according to John of Seville.[15]

The Varieties of Love

Love, as our initial analysis has already established, was central to Dante's conception of Venus. In this he was certainly following the lead of the astrologers, for whom love (*amor*) was the essential Venusian quality.[16] In contrast, those qualities we have just considered are but the accompaniments of love: peace and quiet provide the proper ambience for loving, which in turn produces joy and gladness in the lover. Accordingly, Dante relegated them to the background, as it were, but nonetheless suggested their presence in the heaven of Venus by an occasional verbal echo. The poet's treatment of love itself is more straightforward: he stressed those aspects that serve to expand and qualify the oversimplified view that Venusian love is nothing more than an erotic mania. This distinctive emphasis can best be seen by surveying the varieties of love that the astrologers attribute to Venus and by seeing to what extent Dante took care to include allusions to each variety.

Sexual love. Strictly speaking, there is no astrological equivalent of

Dante's "mad love." The astrologers of course mention love in connection with Venus, but they neither adjectivally qualify the term nor otherwise suggest that it is an irrational passion.[17] Instead, they join other related terms to *amor* that indicate their understanding of the limits of that term. Many, but not all, of these synonyms associate Venus with erotic love. Some, like *luxuria* and *lascivia*, are ambiguous, indicating respectively luxury and playfulness on the one hand and on the other lust and wanton indulgence in sensuality.[18] Ambiguity was the exception rather than the rule in their descriptions of erotic love. Michael Scot's term for it is *libido*,[19] whereas Albumasar preferred to call it *fornicatio*, which he defines broadly but specifically as

> every kind of fornication, both natural practices and those contrary to nature, performed with either sex, and both legitimate acts and illicit ones.[20]

Many astrologers were even more explicit about the various acts involved, and almost all specified at least copulation, which Alcabitius, Scot, and Bonatti simply call "coition,"[21] although euphemisms, such as "lying with women," are also used.[22] With his usual verbal exuberance, Scot also repeatedly lists kisses, hugs, and blandishments, all of which Bonatti at one point dismisses with a curt "et similia,"[23] although elsewhere he remarks that the fornicator "shall practice the whole cult of love with pleasure."

In Dante's heaven of Venus there is no overt reference to copulation, although it is tacitly understood that all four of his Venusian characters indulged in it on occasion: Carlo Martello because he had offspring (*Par.* 9.1–3) and the others because of what is known of their lives from other sources. Carlo's allusion to the Sicilian Vespers (*Par.* 8.73–75) may also be a covert sexual reference, since Villani relates how the uprising was provoked when "a Frenchman in his insolence laid hold of a woman of Palermo to do her villainy."[24] In fact, the only overt reference to sex is figurative, when, in the last word of the Venusian cantos, Folco indignantly brands the preoccupation of the pope and his cardinals with canon law rather than with the teachings of the Gospels and the Fathers as "adultery (*avoltero*)."[25] The term itself is not used by the Latin astrologers, although its sense is conveyed by *fornicatio*, and especially the illicit kind specified by Albumasar.[26]

The astrologers recognized that the sexual appetites inspired by Venus were not necessarily heterosexual. Alcabitius said that the planet also signified "unions of males,"[27] and as usual Bonatti provided a more explicit gloss: "the union of males with one another in a way that is not only shameful and forbidden but also abominable and abhorrent."[28] Albumasar included homosexuality in his definition of fornication (above, at n. 20), and Ibn Ezra remarked that Venus caused men "to desire sexual intercourse, whether it shall be natural or otherwise," and also "to love boys."[29]

Once it was established that Venusian sex can be homo- as well as heterosexual, one is led to wonder whether this may not be exemplified in the relationship between Carlo Martello and Dante. Carlo's description of their mutual love is at least open to a physical interpretation, for it is cast in the most general terms: "Much did you love me, and had good cause; for had I remained below, I would have shown you of my love more than the leaves."

> Assai m'amasti, e avesti ben onde;
>   che s'io fossi giù stato, io ti mostrava
>   di mio amor più oltre che le frondi.   (*Par.* 8.55–57)

If, for the sake of argument, we take this to refer to something more physical than friendship, then it would seem that it remained only a possibility that bore neither flowers nor fruit. But as far as I know there is no hint outside the poem that Carlo was so inclined, and until some evidence is forthcoming that he was bisexual, this possibility must be regarded as one that is extremely remote.

Nonerotic love. Far more likely is the traditional view of their relationship, which was adopted in our preliminary analysis of the characters (above, pp. 67–68) as being one of nonerotic friendship. This, too, is an astral effect emanating from Venus, which governs friendship (*amicitia*) according to Haly, John of Seville, Michael Scot, and Guido Bonatti,[30] so that Scot describes the planet itself as "friendly (*amicus*)."[31]

Closely associated with friendship is the broader concept of society. Thus Haly says that Venus is "the significatrix . . . of friendship and society,"[32] and Michael Scot explains that the planet's influence is most evident in those activities that man does in consequence of being a social animal.

> When a conjunction of Venus occurs, it is a sign of . . . things that are ordinary and worth little, as when among people (*inter gentes*) there is rejoicing, consoling, negotiation of marriages, conviviality, quarreling, embracing, dance, truce, concord, peace, etc.[33]

It will be noted that all the activities on Scot's diversified list are interpersonal, and hence social, acts that require two or more participants. Note, moreover, that Scot's examples are drawn from many different levels of social interaction: they run from "embracing," which people almost always do in pairs, through interfamily negotiations and a variety of other group activities that are characteristic of family social life, finally to culminate in relations that are clearly political, such as "truces," since they imply the existence of a social unit that is larger than the family, namely some form of the political state. Thus at every level of society the influence of Venus finds expression in acts that are based on mutual good will. The astrologers commonly attribute this quality to Venus, which they describe as the planet "of good will," being both "benevolent" and "benign."

Dante of course recognized the social value of this kind of nonerotic love, for the second half of his *Inferno* is dedicated to the various frauds that break "the bond of love that nature makes" (*Inf.* 11.56). This sociopolitical form of love accordingly has its place in the cantos of Venus. Carlo Martello explains that divine providence works through the stars to supply mankind with whatever is necessary for its well-being, and since man is better off when he lives in society, the stars provide whatever is needed for him to live as a member of a community (*Par.* 8.97–117). Carlo then goes on to stress the need for specialization and exchange, which is provided for by endowing men with diverse talents (118–135), but the need for mutual good will is equally necessary, as Aristotle suggested shortly after the passage to which Carlo plainly refers (120).[35] In a society that lived in accordance with nature, each person would be motivated by love of his fellow citizens to do for them what he was best fitted by nature to do, and conversely those who are not so benevolent will ignore their natural duties and disrupt society. These implications of Carlo's doctrine are later taken up by Cunizza, who prophesies disaster for the march of Treviso because "her people are stubborn against duty" (*Par.* 9.46–48), namely their duty to the emperor.[36] Still later Folco offers another variation on the theme in his prophecy that Rome will soon be rid of those popes and cardinals who do not do their duty by preaching and practicing the Christian Gospel (*Par.* 9.131–142). Thus the nonerotic love that nature diffuses through the planet Venus makes that heaven the appropriate place for Dante to treat the theme of duty to fellow men.

In Paradise there is of course a kind of love that is higher than earthly nonerotic loves because it is based on greater understanding (*Par.* 28.109–114); this presumably is the love that fills the souls on Venus, which are said to be "pien d'amor" (8.38). But the planet infuses the Pilgrim with another kind of love, which is not based on knowledge because he declares that he feels it for the first soul he meets *before* learning his identity: "'Say who you are' was my utterance, stamped with great affection (*afetto*)" (8.44–45). Consequently this must be regarded as the planet's *natural* effect on the Pilgrim; it is the same quality that promotes human friendship and good will to all men. Among the astrologers, only Albumasar gives it a name: "charitas."[37]

Mothers and children. Like the Moon, the planet Venus is feminine in gender, and both stars govern women,[38] but the astrologers hasten to add that Venus is particularly concerned with woman in her role as wife and mother: in the words of Alcabitius, Venus "is the significatrix of women and wives and mothers."[39] Dante accordingly alludes to both roles in the heaven of Venus. The Venusian cantos begin and end with references to motherhood: in his opening, the narrator mentions Dione, whom the ancients honored as mother of the goddess Venus ("per madre sua," *Par.* 8.8), and in the closing lines Folco complains of the pope and cardinals that "their thoughts go not to Nazareth whither Gabriel spread his wings" (9.137–138), thus recalling the maternity of the Virgin Mary. As for wives, the multiple marriages of Cunizza make her the poet's prime example (see above at n. 1) but another may be concealed in the ambiguous address to Carlo's "bella Clemenza" (9.1), which can refer either to his wife, Clemence of Habsburg, or his daughter, Clemence of Anjou.[40]

A reference to Carlo's daughter would, astrologically speaking, be equally apt, for Venus not only signifies mothers but also their offspring. Ptolemy had already identified Venus with "many children,"[41] and Bonatti explains at some length why the planet signifies offspring.[42] Indeed, a reference to King Carlo's daughter would be especially appropriate because at the time of the Pilgrim's visit, the planet Venus was in the sign of Taurus (see below, Appendix 2), which Haly says is an indication of great or famous events "concerning kings *and their children*."[43] Moreover, she would be doubly appropriate to Venus because she was the youngest of Carlo's three children, and having been born in 1293, she was only seven at the ideal state of the poem. This circumstance again relates her to Venus because the astrologers assigned younger or minor sisters ("sorores minores") to Venus, just as older or adult ones were given to the Moon (above, pp. 17, 28).[44] We do not have to solve the question of Clemence's identity to discover a younger sister in the heaven of Venus, however, since Cunizza was also her parents' youngest child,[45] and in the poem she draws particular attention to the fact that she was the *sister* of Ezzelino da Romano: "I and he sprang from the same root" (*Par.* 9.31).

As offspring, sons are signified by Venus as well as daughters, and Dante did not fail to include them too. He refers to the ancient belief that Cupid-Desire was Venus's son ("figlio," *Par.* 8.8), and in the same passage he alludes to the episode in the *Aeneid* in which Cupid appears disguised as Ascanius, the son of Aeneas (8.9, *Aen.* 1.657–660). Again, when speaking of Daedalus, the poet slips in otherwise irrelevant references to Icarus, his son ("figlio," 8.126). To these explicit references to sons can be added several implicit ones and many more that concern the birth of famous persons. Sonship is implicit in Cunizza's declaration that she and Ezzelino sprang from the same stock (9.29–31), and the narrator obliquely alludes to the way in which another son, Carobert, Carlo Martello's heir, was excluded from the kingdom that was rightfully his (9.2–3).

This stress on children reaches its climax in Carlo Martello's explanation of the reason why good fathers often produce bad sons (*Par.* 8.94–148). The question is suggested by the case of his brother, Robert, "mean descendant from a generous forebear" (8.82–83), and in the course of answering it Carlo refers to half-a-dozen famous men as examples of the diverse talents with which men are endowed at birth (124–132). Although all these cases are appropriate to Venus because they concern the generation of these men, one in particular is unmistakably linked to another, related property of the planet. Romulus, we are told, was an illegitimate son: "Quirinus comes from so base a father that he is ascribed to Mars" (8.131–132). Combining Venus's proclivity for fornication with her patronage of offspring, the astrologers deduced that she consequently signified "the children of fornication" or, more precisely, "all illegal offspring."[46] Thus the illegitimacy of Romulus is a theme especially appropriate to Venus, and all the more so because of her fornication with Mars in classical myth, which Haly used to explain how two planets so dissimilar in nature could interact.[47]

Astral aptitude. The question that prompted this cluster of references to inborn aptitude is itself related to Venus, for the Pilgrim had asked "how from sweet seed (*seme*) may come forth bitter" (*Par.* 8.93). Because Venus presides over reproduction, one of the parts of the human body that the astrologers assigned to her was semen, seed, or sperm (*sperma*).[48] Elsewhere in the Venusian cantos the poet used *seme* and its equivalents in other senses that are no less appropriate to the theme of reproduction: Esau differed from Jacob "per seme" (8.131), that is, "at birth";[49] Carlo's descendants are "his seed (*semenza*)" (9.3); and nonhuman principles of growth are "every other kind of seed (*semente*)" (8.140).

These variations, indicating as they do the poet's concern with natural generation, accent the major doctrinal content of these cantos, which is conveyed in Carlo's solution of the difficulty raised by the Pilgrim. Divine providence, he explains, works through the stars to provide not only the nature of each thing but also the well-being of each creature, and these provisions must necessarily be effective because God and the angelic intelligences by means of which he imparts his power to the heavens both are perfect. Since man is a social animal whose well-being requires him to live in organized communities, mankind needs a diversity of skills that will enable society to function through specialization and exchange. Hence it is necessary for God to endow individual men with the various talents and aptitudes that are required for their collective well-being. These aptitudes are distributed through the influence of the stars, which when operative overrides the weaker influence of parental heredity, and this explains why children are often different from their parents (*Par.* 8.94–135). Carlo concludes by adding a "corollary" to his explanation: every person should develop his own natural aptitudes, for if one born to be a warrior is put into a monastery, for example, nature will be frustrated and nothing good will result (8.136–148).

> Sempre natura, se fortuna trova
>   discorde a sé, com' ogne altra semente
>   fuor di sua regïon, fa mala prova.
> E se 'l mondo là giù ponesse mente
>   al fondamento che natura pone,
>   seguendo lui, avria buona la gente.
> Ma voi torcete a la religïone
>   tal che fia nato a cignersi la spada,
>   e fate re di tal ch'è da sermone;
> onde la traccia vostra è fuor di strada.   (*Par.* 8.139–148)

Ever does Nature, if she find fortune discordant with herself, like any kind of seed out of its proper region, come to ill result. And if the world there below would give heed to the foundation which Nature lays, and followed it, it would have its people good. But you wrest to religion one born to gird on the sword, and you make a king of one that is fit for sermons; so that your track is off the road.

The whole discussion of the causes of inborn aptitudes is obviously pertinent to the heaven of Venus, which controls human reproduction, but Carlo's corollary is also remarkable for another reason: it unmistakably echoes an excursus that Guido Bonatti makes for no discernible reason in the course of his chapter on the planetary properties of Venus. In the midst of telling us that the Venusian native excels in making musical instruments and playing board games, in the crafting of jewelry and clothing, and in other leisure-related pursuits, including fornication, Bonatti interjects these general observations that could apply to the influence of any planet:

> These are the functions (*officia*) of one for whom Venus is the significatrix. They are the activities that are closer to his nature and which he will know how to do better if he chooses to devote himself to them, and if he devotes himself to other kinds of activity, he will neither learn nor know them as well as these. . . . And he shall know how to work . . . if he sticks to these skills. And this is because it [nature] sometimes does not permit people to achieve perfection in their professions or occupations (*magisteriorum seu officiorum*) because they make use of skills and tasks (*artibus et officiis*) which those people do not possess by nature. Such things they never learn perfectly; whatever they do grasp of such matters, they learn with effort, but they learn easily and well those things that pertain to them by nature.[50]

By now it is no surprise to find Dante borrowing from Bonatti, but this parallel is particularly valuable because it gives us a glimpse of the poet's mind at work. While perusing Bonatti's description of the effects of Venus, Dante evidently encountered this *obiter dictum* that could have been made in connection with any planet, but the poet assimilated it to his plan nonetheless. Perhaps it gave him the idea of treating the whole question of astral aptitude in this heaven; perhaps he already had Carlo's main argument in mind and Bonatti suggested to him that a relevant appendix could be added to it—we can never tell which.

The Life of Leisure

The astrologers associated the planet Venus with a specific lifestyle that was conducive to love and friendship. Like the youth culture of today, this was a way of life for which the young and well-to-do were best suited, though it might nonetheless attract those who lacked those qualifications. The astrologers are in effect describing what we in retrospect call the cult of courtly love, but they avoid such labels and are content to list the kinds of people that are most influenced by Venus and the kinds of activity they enjoy.

Youth. Since Venus governs reproduction and growth, together with the carnal appetites that promote these functions, the influence of the planet is strongest during the period of human life in which they are more prevalent. Somewhat vaguely Alcabitius identifies that period as "youth or adolescence (*iuventutem vel adolescentiam*),"[51] and later astrologers continue to waver between the two terms. At one point Scot says that Venus "with respect to age is like adolescence, signifying the beginning of youth," but later he declares that the planet controls "all women, youths, and boys, but not an old person."[52] Bonatti likewise tries to include both stages: "And concerning human age, Venus has to signify adolescence, and especially when youth is unmixed, which is from the fourteenth to the twenty-second year."[53]

In the *Convivio*, Dante used the same terminology, but he distinguished sharply between adolescence and youth, precisely assigning the first twenty-five years of life to adolescence and the next twenty, through age forty-five, to youth (4.24.1–3). From the classification in the *Convivio*, however, one cannot be sure how he would accommodate the astrologers' system to his own, for he explains there that adolescence (*adolescenzia*) means "the increase of life" and that *gioventute* is "the age that can be helpful (*giovare*)," whereas according to the astrologers both growth and helpfulness are characteristic of Venus (above, at n. 15). In the heaven of Venus it is possible that he introduced examples of both, for adolescence can be represented by Cupid-Ascanius (*Par.* 8.7–8), Icarus (9.126), and perhaps Clemenza (9.1), but undoubtedly the greater stress is on *gioventute* as defined in the *Convivio*, for the influence of Venus on at least two of the major characters was greatest during this period of their lives. Folco, speaking with the veracity of the blessed, says that Dido burned with love no more than he did "as long as it befitted my locks" (9.99). This change must have occurred at about age forty-five, which Dante set as the limit between youth and middle age ("sennetute"), and in consequence it follows that Dante had assimilated the *iuventus* of the astrologers to his own concept of *gioventute*, preferring his own chronological limits to those indicated by Bonatti. Thus Folco emerges as Dante's prime example of the close connection between Venus and youth. Once we have determined what the poet's definition of youth was, it is also evidence that Cunizza's amorous adventures took place during this period of her life, for she was first married in late adolescence at about the age of twenty-two, but in early youth she began her relations with Sordello, leaving her husband in 1226 when she was perhaps twenty-eight and finally settling down at her brother's court after 1239 when she was in her early forties.[54]

Royalty and nobility. Carlo Martello (1271–1295), however, is definitely not an example of youth, for he died in his twenty-fourth year before entering the age of *gioventute*. He represents not youth but the other qualification for the Venusian life of leisure—a noble lifestyle. As early as Ptolemy the luxurious way of life fostered by Venus was seen to apply especially to kings.[55] Later astrologers occasionally associated Venus specifically with royalty,[56] but the idea of including a great prince like Carlo in the third heaven was probably suggested to Dante, not by astrology, but by theology, for Venus is the heaven ruled by the angelic order which Paul called "the Principate" or guiding principle ("Principatus," Eph. 1.21 and Col. 1.16). Toward the end of the *Paradiso*, Dante identifies these angels by their medieval name, "Principati" or "Principalities" (28.125), but in their own heaven he calls them simply "princes" ("principi," 8.34). Thus it was fitting in the heaven of Princes to have the most prominent soul be himself a prince, who in turn has much to say about other princes. Since *princeps* could signify any leader or chief, Cunizza's remarks about her brother Ezzelino and his march of Treviso may be a continuation of this theme, as Folco's mention of the princes of the Church certainly is ("cardinali," 9.136).

The Venusian character of Carlo lies not only in his rank itself but also in the life of leisure and luxury that accompanied it. In Villani's *Chronicle* he is remembered for nothing but the magnificence and courtesy of his court, which visited Florence in the spring of 1294. He arrived

> with his company of 200 knights with golden spurs, French and Provençal and from the Kingdom, all young men, invested by the king with habits of scarlet and dark green, and all with saddles of one device, with their palfreys adorned with silver and gold, with arms quarterly, bearing golden lilies and surrounded by a bordure of red and silver, which are the arms of Hungary. And they appeared the noblest and richest company a young king ever had with him. And in Florence he abode more than twenty days, . . . and the Florentines did him great honour, and he showed great love to them all.[57]

Such courtly life is one of the few things that Carlo had in common with the other Venusian souls who speak to the Pilgrim. Cunizza's milieu was evidently courtly, too, for she met the troubadour Sordello at her first husband's court in Verona, and afterwards he was her brother's courtier at Romano. Folco too was a courtier, especially at the court of Barral de Baux, viscount of Marseilles, but he also enjoyed the patronage of Alfonso VIII of Castile and Richard the Lionhearted.[58] No doubt a case could be made that all three characters speak in a courtly manner, but it is enough to note that an allusion to the life of courts is worked into each of their speeches. Cunizza demonstrates her courtly values by ironically referring to the bishop who violated the laws of hospitality as "this courteous priest" ("questo prete *cortese*," *Par.* 9.58). Carlo similarly displays his sympathy with a truly chivalric concept of courtliness by disparaging his brother's courtiers, evidently a *noblesse de la robe* and not *de l'épée*: to regain his subjects' good will, the king "would need a knighthood (*milizia*) that gave not its care to the filling of coffers" (8.83–84).[59] Folco likewise complains of the avarice displayed by another court, the Roman curia, verbally linking his complaint to Carlo's earlier one by repeating the term "milizia" (9.141), this time with reference to "the soldiery that followed Peter" to martyrdom as the pope's ideal courtiers. The true knights are, of course, appropriate to Mars, while efficient civil servants belong to Mercury; but the idle courtier is the child of Venus: Bonatti and Scot leave no doubt about that. According to the former,

> A man whom Venus signifies shall live in luxury. And he knows how to lead his life better, to live more luxuriously, and to be more courtly (*curialius*) than someone else to whom he is otherwise inferior.[60]

Bonatti limits himself to essentials, but Scot goes on to show in detail how these traits are exemplified by the courtier.

> [The native of Venus] delights in living luxuriously if he can do so, especially if he does not have to work for it. An example is someone who, being unwilling to work, stays with some lord or lady as a companion the better to eat and drink, to hug and kiss, to copulate often, to gossip and dance, to delight in acquaintanceships and to repress sadness, and to have fun playing like boys and girls, or simply to be at leisure.[61]

Sweet words and music. The astrologer offered a variety of specific activities connected with courtly life, such as dancing and games, that Dante chose not to incorporate into his Venusian cantos.[62] Instead, he represented his Venusians as engaged in two courtly activities at which they excel—speaking sweetly and singing.

"Venus," said Alcabitius, "signifies the mastery of all sounds, such as music and so forth."[63] Michael Scot elaborated on this theme more than any other astrologer. While recognizing that instrumental music fell within the province of Venus,[64] this for him was secondary to song, which he stressed again and again. *Cantus* is a property of the planet, a Venusian quality of mind, and one of the arts of Venus;[65] therefore the native delights in "making songs, eagerly learning and singing them, . . . [and] listening . . . to songs being sung."[66]

In the heaven of Venus it is not at first clear to the reader that the souls are singing: he is told that "within those that appeared most in front *Hosanna* sounded (*sonava*) in such wise that never since have I been without the desire to hear it again" (*Par.* 8.28–30). Evidently he heard a delightful sound, but at this point it is not altogether clear that it was music in the strictest sense. Later, however, when Cunizza, one of these foremost souls, finally speaks, the narrator reveals that previously she had in fact been singing—"ella pria cantava" (9.23)—the song, of course, being "Hosanna."[67] Still later, the Pilgrim assumes that Folco (and presumably the other Venusians as well, since he has as yet no notion whom he is addressing) sing forever with the Seraphim in heaven (9.76–79). This little chain of progressive revelation is accompanied by two other clues that also suggest the musical character of Venus. One is the musical image with which the narrator describes the spectacle of luminous souls moving within the larger light of the planet: "as a voice within a voice is distinguished when one holds the note and another comes and goes" (8.17–18). The other is the reference to Dante's own *canzone*, which Carlo Martello cites by its incipit: "Voi che 'ntendendo il terzo ciel movete" (8.37).

Although Dante's *canzone* is a song in name, and hence appropriate to the musical theme set by Venus, it is primarily a poem, as Carlo indicates by specifying that rather than being sung it was *said* by the poet ("dicesti," *Par.* 8.36). To be sure, the content of this particular *canzone*, which is addressed to the intelligences, or angels, that move the planet Venus, makes it appropriate *per se* to this heaven, but the astrologers supply another, more general reason that could apply to any of Dante's lyric poems. According to Haly, Venus, as opposed to Mars, is distinguished by "good words"; they are "gentle (*mansueta*)" and "tasteful (*saporosa*)."[68] With Bonatti, however, the stress is on their sweetness: "The Venusian man pours forth words that are soft and sweet (*dulcia*); in every respect he has ways of speaking that are sweet flowing (*dulciflua*)."[69] Therefore the heaven of Venus provides the exact astrological context for Dante's "sweet new style" ("dolce stil novo," *Purg.* 24.57).

Apparently Venus is capable of inspiring other styles as well, for each of the souls displays a fondness for rhetorical ornament. Carlo Martello, for example, takes nine lines of geographical periphrasis to identify the kingdoms of Hungary and the Two Sicilies (*Par.* 8.61–69); Cunizza requires only six to similarly establish her connection with Romano and

Ezzelino (9.25–30), while Folco, being a professional poet, is able to fill thirteen lines saying Marseilles in other words (9.81–93). In part this kind of elaboration proceeds from the Venusian taste for ornament, of which more later, but the important point here is that the ornamentation is rhetorical. In the *Convivio*, when Dante assigned one of the seven liberal arts to each of the planets, he identified Venus with rhetoric (2.13.13–14), but we have several reasons to believe that he discarded this system in the *Comedy*. Certainly he no longer maintained the fiction that the movers of this heaven were authors who instilled in him the love of philosophy (2.15.1), as he makes clear by transferring one of them—Boethius—to the heaven of the Sun (*Par.* 10.125–129). Moreover, we have seen that in the *Comedy* the seven liberal arts are present in Mercury for astrological reasons (above, pp. 42–44). How, then, does one account for the Venusians' obvious affinity for rhetoric? The answer would seem to lie in a distinction between Latin and vernacular culture. Mercury governs the formal learning of the seven Latin liberal arts that were studied as curriculum subjects; it is in the spirit of the well-schooled *literatus* that Justinian vaunts his mastery of them. But in the heaven of Venus, the stress is placed instead on the vernacular literature produced in noble courts. Carlo admires Dante's Italian poem; Folco recollects his career as a Provençal troubadour; and Cunizza was celebrated in Sordello's Provençal lyrics, not to mention the comments that other troubadours made about their affair.[70] Just as vernacular poets could and did learn from Latin rhetoric how to sweeten their speech without ever becoming curriculum authors, so Dante's Venusians adorn their speech with rhetorical devices but not in order to be admired for their learning; their purpose, rather, is to delight others. The contrast, then, would be between the Latin *literatus* who is motivated by the ambitious but exclusive Mercurial desire for fame and honor on the one hand, and on the other the vernacular author whom love of others impels to create and share beauty with his fellow men and women. Rhetoric can serve them both, but intention makes the difference.

Convivio. This distinction recalls the first tractate of the *Convivio*, which justifies Dante's use of the vernacular rather than Latin in that commentary on his *canzoni*. Since the one cited by Carlo forms the first course in Dante's banquet, the *Convivio* is implicitly cited by him as well. And astrologically speaking, a work of that title, based on an extended analogy to a feast in which each of the component treatises is to form one course (*Conv.* 1.1, esp. § 14), is completely appropriate to the heaven of Venus, the star that, according to Scot, presides over entertainment and feasting—his precise word is "convivium."[71] Most other astrologers associate Venus with "eating and drinking,"[72] which Bonatti says Venusians are especially eager to do "in company,"[73] but only Scot fuses these into the exact Latin equivalent of Dante's "convivio." As if to assure us that he was aware of the gastronomic connotations of Venus, the poet has Carlo use an appropriate metaphor: "with one thirst (*sete*) we revolve with the celestial Princes" (*Par.* 8. 35–36).

Venusian Arts and Crafts

"Every kind of luxury" belongs to Venus,[74] including not only the pleasures of the flesh and the entertainment that accompanies them, but also "the enjoyment of wealth" in the most material sense.[75] As the goddess of beauty, Venus governs "decoration" in general, and in particular "the adornment of the body" by cosmetics, clothing, and jewelry.[76] Proceeding as usual by the association of ideas, the astrologers consequently assign to Venus the production of these luxurious adornments by such craftsmen as jewelers, goldsmiths, weavers, embroiderers, and cosmeticians.[77]

Dante's Venusians display an analogous concern, for in their heaven, Folco says, "we contemplate the art which so much love adorns (*addorna*)" (*Par.* 9.106–107), while Carlo, prompted it would seem by his innate affinity for the arts that create beauty, twice speaks of astral influence in terms of art: "Circling nature . . . performs its art well" and its effects are themselves *arti* (8.128, 108). Earthly arts are not always transposed to a heavenly context, for they haunt the Venusians' thoughts. Although the personal beauty of these souls is now outwardly expressed by the light that reflects their inner feelings, their minds still bear the stamp of Venus, as the poet is able to show by having them make specific reference to those beautifying arts that once were so important to them. Because these references are so specific in character, they serve perhaps better than any others to establish Dante's use of astrological sources for this heaven.

Mirrors. Among the arts that attract the Venusian native, Michael Scot lists that of "constructing mirrors."[78] Accordingly in the heaven of Venus this artifact so characteristic of Venus is mentioned by Cunizza, though she uses the term to describe the Thrones in the heaven of Saturn: "Aloft are mirrors (*specchi*)—you name them Thrones" (*Par.* 9.61).

Jewels. Since both gems and other kinds of jewelry are precious ornaments, the astrologers assign them all to Venus.[79] Hence it is appropriate that Cunizza should describe Folco as "this resplendent and precious jewel (*cara gioia*)" (*Par.* 9.37).[80] The accuracy of her description only becomes apparent when, as the Pilgrim turns his attention to Folco, the narrator refers back to Cunizza's words and reports how Folco made them appear apt: "The other joy, which was already known to me as precious (*cara*), became to my sight like a fine ruby (*balasso*) on which the sun is striking" (9.67–69).

Since Cunizza is the Venusian soul who displays a special affinity for jewelry, a similar allusion may be intended in her remark that the blood to be shed by the treacherous bishop of Feltre will be so great in quantity that it would "weary him that should weigh it ounce by ounce" (*Par.* 9.57). Porena's suggestion that she was referring to the medical practice of letting blood by the ounce seemed macabre and inappropriate to Mattalia,[81] but it would be entirely fitting if the reference was instead to the transactions of jewelers and like dealers in precious objects that are weighed out in the most minute quantities. The suggestion then would be that blood is extremely precious, and, moreover, the allusion would be both thematically proper to Venus and in character for Cunizza.

Crowns and garlands. When Alcabitius lists "the construction of crowns and their use" as one of the areas of Venusian expertise,[82] one naturally supposes that he is referring to a product of the goldsmith's art, and in that sense we find Carlo speaking of the royal crown of Hungary ("corona," *Par.* 8.64). But Bonatti uses *corona* in its more basic sense of a wreath or garland woven of flowers: the native, he says, "will know how to construct *coronas et serta.*"[83] The relevant sense of "coronas" is indicated by its being joined with "serta," which unambiguously means "wreaths" or "garlands of flowers." Scot had already said that the Venusian "may know how to use and make . . . *serta* of flowers," the use of which includes wearing, selling, and giving them.[84]

The poet seems to have had this second sense of *corona* in mind when he had Carlo tell the Pilgrim that "I will have a corollary (*corollario*) cloak you round so that you may know that I delight in you" (*Par.* 8.137–138). In Latin, a *corollarium* is basically "a garland, often given as a reward," and hence by transference "an additional or unsolicited payment, a gratuity, extra, bounty, douceur."[85] Thus in the first sense a *corollarium* is one of the artifacts of Venus and in the second sense it is Carlo's *corollario* or bonus. The play on words is itself appropriate, for we learn from Scot and Bonatti that Venusians are prone to joke and play.[86] Further, as if to resolve any doubt whether the poet had garlands in mind while writing the Venusian cantos, he later uses the term as a verb: "inghirlanda" (9.84)

Tailors and textiles. Clothing is another of the luxury products with

which Venusians are especially concerned: they make "every kind of artifact that is done by sewing and dyeing."[87] It is consonant with this theme
that Carlo Martello says that he wants to give the Pilgrim a corollary as a
cloak or mantle ("t'ammanti," *Par.* 8.138). The implication, as commentators have often noted, is that the Pilgrim has been progressively dressed
by Carlo's discourse, and now the corollary will supply the outermost garment.[88] Although the Venusian concern with clothing would have been
enough to suggest this metaphor to the poet, his immediate source may
well have been Bonatti, who does specifically name "mantles" among the
kinds of Venusian handwork.[89] Venusians not only sew cloth, they weave
it as well, just as we have seen that they weave garlands and wreaths, and
what is more, this weaving brings even cobwebs and nets within the scope
of Venus's influence.[90] Thus it is astrologically appropriate for Cunizza to
base a metaphor on webs when she prophesies the downfall of the lord of
Treviso "for catching whom the web (*ragna*) is already being made"
(*Par.* 9.51). Similarly, Carlo Martello compares himself to a silkworm:
"My joy, which rays around me, holds me concealed from you and hides
me like a creature swathed in its own silk—*quasi animal di sua seta fasciato*"
(8.52–54). The reference is specific because silk is one of the luxury fabrics
that astrologers assign by name to Venus.[91]

Natural Substances and Qualities

From artifacts and *objects d'art* we may pass on to consider briefly several
natural substances and qualities that the astrologers mention without connecting them to any craft or art.

   White and clear. Among astrologers there was widespread agreement
that the color proper to Venus was white, or at least whiteness.[92] In the
Venusian cantos this quality manifests itself only in Carlo's use of the verb
imbianciare, "to whiten": "Do you wish this truth to be made still clearer
to you (*ti s'imbianchi*)?" (*Par.* 8.112).

   The planet Venus was noted for its limpid quality, and consequently
clearness was one of its astrological affinities.[93] This being so, we may
perhaps discern a more or less faint reflection of this quality twice in the
heaven of Venus. Limpid water, used in a comparison by Folco, provides
an instance of clearness in the literal sense: Rahab, he says, "sparkles here
beside me as a sunbeam on clear water (*acqua mera*)" (*Par.* 9.113–114),

while figurative clarity is found in the narrator's statement that Carlo "had enlightened me—*m'ebbe chiarito*" (9.2).

Sulfur and emerald. Two substances deserve separate treatment because they suggest, however faintly, that Dante included references to another medieval occult science, namely alchemy. Carlo parenthetically remarks that the dark clouds issuing from Mount Etna are due to "sulfur in formation (*nascente solfo*)" (*Par.* 8.70). Although the astrologers do not mention sulfur by name, Ibn Ezra does attribute to Venus "every [metal and mineral] issuing forth from the bowels of the earth."[94] Moreover, Dante's reference to "nascent sulfur" has a *prima facie* relevance to the generative powers of Venus, so it widens their scope to include metals, rocks, and minerals. Sulfur has a further generative significance in alchemy, where, according to the widespread Arabic "sulfur-mercury theory," sulfur is "the father of metals," which it produces through a union, often represented by sexual imagery, with the element mercury.[95]

Another curious alchemical echo occurs in Folco's speech: "Here we contemplate the art which so much love adorns, and we discern the good by reason of which the world below again becomes the world above."

> Qui si rimira ne l'arte ch'addorna
> cotanto affetto, e discernesi 'l bene
> per che 'l mondo di sù quel di giù torna. (*Par.* 9.106–108)

This echoes several of the precepts of the famous *Tabula Smaragdina* or *Emerald Tablet* of Hermes, probably the oldest monument of occidental alchemy, and a text highly esteemed in the Latin Middle Ages. The outstanding parallels are these:

> 2. What is below is like that which is above, and what is above is like that which is below, to accomplish the miracles of one thing.
> 8. Ascend with the greatest sagacity from the earth to heaven, and then again descend to the earth, and unite together the powers of things superior and things inferior.[96]

Alchemical texts, as is well known, can be understood in a spiritual as well as a physical sense, so the passages quoted above can have the same sense as Folco's analogue. To be sure, Folco's image might be drawn from other sources, but a reference to the *Emerald Tablet* seems the most likely inasmuch as the astrologers attributed jewels in general to Venus.[97]

Geography and Meteorology

Ibn Ezra, who identifies the seven planets with the seven climates, equates Venus with the fifth of the climatic zones, adding that Spain is typical of that region.[98] As before (above, pp. 62–64), we must take into account two different systems of dividing the climates: according to al-Farghani the fifth climate extends from 43 1/3° to 39° north latitude, while Alcoarismi places it somewhat more to the south, between 41° and 36°.[99] This time, however, we are able to determine which system Dante was following, because in the heaven of Venus he refers to "Malta" (*Par.* 9.54), which by medieval reckoning lay precisely on the thirty-sixth parallel that serves as Alcoarismi's southern boundary for the fifth clime, while according to al-Farghani it lies in the next climate.[100] Thus we can take Alcoarismi to have been Dante's authority for the location of the climates, and in that case the poet's fifth climate begins just south of Rome and extends southward to the parallel of Malta, and consequently contains the entire kingdom of the Two Sicilies.[101]

These data apply unmistakably to Dante's heaven of Venus, where the principal speaker is Carlo Martello, heir to the two Sicilies, to each of which he devotes a tercet—the mainland at *Par.* 8.61–63 and the island at lines 67–69. If this were not enough, the affairs of the Regno are also discussed in the same heaven: Carlo comments on the succession, the Sicilian Vespers, and his brother's misrule (71–81), alludes to one of its kings (147–148), and prophesies its future (9.1–3). Furthermore, his reference to Catalonia (8.77) is also appropriate to the fifth climate if one takes it to include all of Spain, as Ibn Ezra stated.

The climatic system was not the only way in which astrologers assigned lands and peoples to Venus. Ibn Ezra says that "the peoples belonging to Venus are the Arabs and everyone professing the faith of the Saracens."[102] Alcabitius, however, presents it somewhat differently, attributing to Venus the *lands* of the Arabs, rather than the people themselves.[103] Bonatti repeats this, adding his own obscure but intriguing explanation, namely that the influence of Venus is more apparent in Arab lands than elsewhere.[104] Dante accordingly put three references to Arab or Saracen lands into Folco's speech: Marseilles lies on almost the same meridian as Bougie in North Africa ("Buggea," *Par.* 9.92); Rahab "favored Joshua's first glory in the Holy Land" ("la Terra Santa," 125); and the pope and cardinals give no thought to Nazareth ("Nazarette," 137). Although the last two refer to Christian sacred places, by 1300 both were wholly in the hands of the Moslems and hence qualify as "lands of the Arabs." A fourth instance of this theme, also associated with Folco, occurs when the narrator compares his appearance to "a fine ruby (*balasso*) on which the sun is striking" (69). The *balasso*, according to Singleton, was "a kind of ruby that took its name from the region in Asia from which it was imported, Arabic *balaksh*, the modern Persian province of Badakhshân."[105]

Clouds, rains, and rivers. Yet another opportunity for geographical allusion was provided by the aquatic associations of Venus, which were in fact some of her oldest astrological attributes. In Ptolemy's system these occupied a prominent place; he says that Venus supplies "moist and very nourishing winds" that bring "generous showers of fertilizing waters," which in turn cause "the full rising of rivers."[106] Haly explains that this humidifying effect of Venus results from the planet's conjunction with the Sun (as at the ideal date of the *Commedia*), which is like a woman lying with a man and makes her "the significatrix of rains, clouds, and showers."[107]

Dante made lavish use of the planet's connection with clouds and rivers: early in the Venusian cantos he introduces a comparison involving rain clouds (*Par.* 8.22–24), and he goes on to inundate us with some fifteen references to rivers—the Rhône and the Sorgue (56), the Tronto and the Verde (63), and the Danube (65); the Brenta and the Piave (9.27), the Tagliamento and the Adige (44), the Bacchiglione (46–47), the Sile and the Cagnano (49), the Ebro and the Magra (89); even the Mediterranean is described as being like a river that lies "in the greatest valley in which the water spreads from the sea that encircles the world" (82–84).

Blood. Michael Scot offered the poet yet another opportunity for astrogeographical allusion:

> Venus governs the provinces of Tuscany, Friuli, and others that are similar to them in nature by being hot and humid. Such places naturally delight in the singing of songs, coition, and all their accompaniments, such as elegance, ornament, etc.[108]

Since neither Tuscany nor Friuli is given much prominence in the Venusian cantos, it would at first seem that Dante ignored this tempting invitation, but closer inspection suggests that he did indeed make use of it in a less obvious way. According to Scot, a province comes under the influence of Venus if it is "hot and humid," which are the elemental qualities that he repeatedly ascribes to Venus.[109] The reason for this influence is not far to seek: the combination of these two qualities produces people of sanguine temperament by creating an excess of blood. Scot allowed that other provinces than Tuscany and Friuli might be similarly affected, and Cunizza plainly designates her native march of Treviso as one of them.[110] She concludes her catalog of its faults (*Par.* 9.41–60) by saying that the blood ("sangue," 56) shed by the bishop of Feltre will be, as it were, a gift to the Guelfs, and significantly she adds that "such gifts will suit the country's way of life" (59–60). Beneath the surface sense, that the inhabitants of the province are prone to shed blood, is a deeper meaning, that they are sanguine by temperament, which explains why the march of Treviso is given prominence in the heaven of Venus, with the luxurious Cunizza as its sanguine representative. Similarly, Folco describes his own place of origin, which Dante seems to have thought was Marseilles,[111] as "the city whence I came, which with its own blood (*sangue*) once made its harbor warm" (9.92–93).

Thus the geographic origins of all the principal characters are astrally determined: Carlo Martello by the fifth climate, Cunizza and Folco by the sanguine temperament of their respective birthplaces, and Rahab, of course, by her association with the Holy Land, which the Arabs control.

The Dark Side of Venus

Although Venus is on the whole an amiable and pleasant planet, some of its effects can be otherwise, as we have just been reminded by the bloody results of a sanguine temperament. Scot and Bonatti agree, for example, that Venus gives rise to disputes and quarrels (*rixae*),[112] and Haly adds killing, evil doing, and property seized and held by violence to the list when Venus is unfavorably aspected.[113] Such qualities seem to fit Cunizza's description of her brother, the "firebrand that made a great assault on the country round" (*Par.* 9.29–30), as well as the other battles, murders, and bloodshed with which she taxes her native region (44–60). Likewise these *rixae* may be reflected in the contentiousness of lawyers, which Folco implies is the attitude of the pope and cardinals who study only canon law (133–136).

Gullibility is another Venusian trait noted by both Scot and Bonatti. The former says that the native "readily believes what he hears said," and in consequence he is "easily turned in either direction";[114] the latter adds that such persons are subject to fraud: "they confide in others and are often deceived by them."[115] Passing reference is accordingly made to these qualities in the heaven of Venus: Carlo reveals what frauds ("li 'nganni") his descendants will suffer (*Par.* 9.2); the narrator directs an apostrophe against "souls deceived (*anime ingannate*)" who turn from the Good to vanity (10); and the poet takes the gullibility of Venus's ancient devotees as his opening theme: "Solea creder lo mondo . . ." (8.1).

Finally, the behavior of Alessandro Novello, the Trevisan bishop of Feltre, is Venusian in several aspects. He had made himself infamous by receiving thirty fugitives from Ferrara, giving them his protection and hospitality, but then treacherously returning them to Ferrara, where they were all executed.[116] Since the bishop came from Treviso, we must understand that he bore the stamp of Venus, and Albumasar provides some particularly relevant traits: the Venusian tends to receive others of his own free will; he is also inclined to use "deceit, often a lie and indeed perjury," and cruelty comes easily to him.[117]

Four Venusian Characters

Above all, the stars shape human character, and consequently in each heaven we must expect that its influence will be most evident in the character of the souls encountered there. So far in this chapter, the character of the *dramatis personae* has been a secondary consideration, although while ascertaining the uses Dante made of the astrological properties of Venus, we have observed in passing many particulars that are indicative of character. Now to conclude our study of astrology in the Venusian cantos, let us return to the characters whom we examined cursorily at the beginning of this chapter and apply what we have learned to construct a full-length portrait of each as a Venusian.

Carlo Martello. We now understand how Carlo came to be included in the heaven of Venus. First Dante wanted a prince, to match the Principalities that govern Venus; that he should be a prince from the Regno was suggested by Venus's connection with the fifth clime, and Carlo was selected as the most Venusian of such princes. His friendship with Dante qualified him to exemplify one nonerotic variety of Venusian love, but more important is the nature of the bond between them: it seems to have been Carlo's appreciation of poetry that brought them together. Above all, Carlo represents the courtly patron, who lives in luxury but not lust, so that references to silks, garlands, and mantles come easily to his lips. His speech also reveals him to be a lover of art, for he adorns his discourse with the flowers of rhetoric, not out of pedantry but from a love of elegance, in emulation of the beauty of the vernacular poetry that he prized as one of the chief ornaments of his court. Carlo's love of art begins with superficial, material things, but passing to the abstract, immaterial beauty of the word, it finds there its highest creativity, as we learn when he uses an analogy to art to explain the part played by God and nature in the generative process (e.g., *Par.* 8.108). All in all, he represents the Venusian role of princely connoisseur, one who consumes the arts and crafts that suit courtly leisure.

As such, he is closely identified with a Venusian trait appropriate to noble patrons, namely generosity. Indeed, Dante has constructed Carlo's canto so that this quality forms the pivotal point of the action. Carlo's first speech ends with the complaint that his brother is avaricious and lacks his father's magnanimous generosity ("larga," *Par.* 8.82); this observation prompts the Pilgrim's question in response to which Carlo explains how astral influences can override heredity. This generosity is a Venusian characteristic, for Alcabitius, Scot, and Bonatti all specifically attribute *largitas* to Venus,[118] though before them Ptolemy had already associated the effects of such lavish generosity with Venus, which he said brought improvement of status, increase of property, and honor in general.[119] Some such munificence, it would seem, was to have been the flower and fruit of Carlo's love for Dante (8.55–57), to whom Carlo may well have offered a position in his chancery as *dictator pulcherrimus*.[120] Significantly, Haly says that the ability "to write beautifully (*pulchre scribere*)" is conferred by a combination of Mercury and Venus.[121]

Cunizza. Like Carlo Martello, Cunizza too typifies many aspects of courtly society over which Venus presides. Like Carlo and Folco, but on a more modest scale, she affects the ornate language of vernacular courtly rhetoric, and moreover the language of luxury comes easily to her, especially thoughts of jewelry. Significantly, in heaven she is found next to a troubadour, just as on earth she was famous for her association with Sordello. In life it was her lot to be the sister of a powerful man who married her off to effect political alliances; in these circumstances no less than in love she was influenced by Venus, because the star indicates noble relatives and marriage alliances.[122] This unfortunate combination made Cunizza a *malmariée*, but her Venusian nature impelled her to seek a more satisfying, erotic relationship; once she was free to remarry, she did so, perhaps repeatedly,[123] not out of erotic motives, for she was by then middle aged, but because marriage comes naturally to the natives of Venus.[124] Thus, paradoxically, both in adultery and in marriage she can be said not only to have followed her star (cf. *Inf.* 15.55), but to have been conquered by it, as she says: "perché mi vinse il lume d'esta stella" (*Par.* 8.33). In her case it would seem that astral influence dominated her life until its force waned with advancing age, whereupon she was able to separate herself from sin and gain a place in Paradise. Hers thus is a textbook case of "mad love."

Folco. The troubadour of Marseilles belongs to the same courtly milieu as Carlo and Cunizza; indeed, the three of them provide a paradigm of the essential social roles involved in the troubadour's creative process: Folco is the poet himself, Cunizza the lady who inspires him to write, and Carlo the princely patron whose court brings them both together. The astrological reasons for recalling Dante's *canzone* in this heaven also make a troubadour appropriate;[125] in fact Dante cites Folco's work in the *De vulgari eloquentia* (2.6.5–6) as an example of the style that is appropriate to the *canzone*, which is the same style affected by all of the Venusian characters, and most extensively by Folco himself. Cunizza assures us that Folco's poetry will make him famous for five centuries (*Par.* 9.37–39), and this too is appropriately Venusian, for "glory" is another astrological property of the planet.[126]

Cunizza, however, implies that fame has little value because, no matter how prolonged, it is still temporary compared with external beatitude: "See if man should make himself excel, so that the first life may leave another after it!" (*Par.* 9.41–42). When Folco eventually identifies himself, he does so with modesty, for he suggests that his name was known only in the past and then not to everyone: "Folco people called me to whom my name was known" (94–95).[127] As a matter of fact, he hesitated to speak at all and had to be coaxed by the Pilgrim (73–81). Both his hesitancy and his modesty are typical of a Venusian native, who according to Scot "speaks sweetly and begins his words with fear" because "with strangers [he is] tremendously timid and shy."[128] Folco has not, however, lost his equally Venusian impulse to excel, since his whole speech strives for the rhetorical effects that Dante had admired in his poetry. Moreover, like Carlo Martello, he perceives the work of God and nature in terms of art; what is more, he assures us that all the Venusian souls do so as well: "Here we contemplate the art which so much love adorns" (*Par.* 9.106).

In heaven, as in life, he is more than just a troubadour, however; his final rebuke of the Roman Curia's avarice shows him in his other earthly role, as the zealous Cistercian abbot and bishop of Toulouse. This, too, is the product of Venus: according to Alcabitius, the planet signifies "houses of prayer,"[129] and Ibn Ezra says that it is the nature of the native "to associate himself in every case with righteousness and the cult of God."[130] Folco admits that until his erotic passions were cooled by advancing age, he had been obsessed by "il folle amore" that Venus inspires (*Par.* 9.95–102), but he stresses that he, like all the Venusians, now sees that their astral nature, however much it may have led them into sin, was ultimately good, for in accordance with God's plan it eventually brought them to heaven (103–108).

Astrology suggests that this generalization applies to Folco's case in ways he does not specify, for Venus not only made him an adulterer and a troubadour, but also gave him an innate sense of piety that eventually transformed both his life and his poetry. Although other astrologers connected Venus with piety, Michael Scot makes the most use of this connection; he mentions it no less than seven times, for example listing "pietatem" as one of the qualities of mind bestowed by Venus.[131] Moreover, the astrologers recognized that in certain circumstances the Venusian talent for music could be channeled into the service of God. Thus Bonatti writes:

> If Venus is joined with Jupiter, it signifies that the native will excel at voicing ecclesiastical lections and chants, and at making all kinds of music relating to clerics and religious and to using both altars and praise of the lord Jesus Christ and houses of prayer.[132]

In *Paradiso* Venus was so aspected (see Appendix 2), making it appropriate to have a singer of divine songs among the souls who greeted the Pilgrim. After Folco's conversion he certainly qualified for such a role, being successively a monk, an abbot, and a bishop. But doubtless Dante meant us to remember that Folco had turned his talents as a troubadour from profane to sacred themes; the inference, I think, is inescapable, because Folco had celebrated his conversion with an *alba* or dawn song that was addressed to the day star—his star, the planet Venus:

Vers Dieus, el vostre nom et de sancta Maria
m'esvelharai hueimais, pus l'estela del dia
ven daus Jerusalem, que m'ensenha qu'ieu dia:
    estatz sus e levatz,
    senhor que Dieu amatz!
Que·l jorns es aprosmatz

e la nuech ten sa via;
e sia·n Dieus lauzatz
per nos et adoratz
e·l preguem que·ns don patz
a tota nostra via.
La neuch vai e·l jorns ve
ab clar cel e sere
e l'alba no·s rete,
ans ven be' e complia.

True God, in your name and Saint Mary's
I shall be wakeful from this day forth,
for the morning star rises toward Jerusalem and teaches me to say:
  Arise, stand,
  you lords who love God,
  day has come,
  night passes on:
  now let us praise
  God and adore him;
  and pray Him give us peace
  all our days.
Night passes, day comes,
the heaven is calm and bright,
the dawn does not hold back,
it rises fair and full.[133]

The literal sense of this subtext is that the poet is inspired by the coming of dawn, heralded by the rising of *lucifer*, the day star, as Venus was commonly called when it preceded the Sun.[134] But in a Christian context such as this, the underlying meaning is supplied by a verse of Scripture containing the only biblical use of the word *lucifer*:

Et habemus firmiorem propheticum sermonem: cui benefacitis attendentes, quasi lucernae lucenti in caliginoso loco, donec dies elucescat, et lucifer oriatur in cordibus vestris. (2 Peter 1.19)

And we have the more firm prophetical word: whereunto you do well to attend, as to a light that shineth in a dark place, until the day dawn, and the day star arise in your hearts.

This is assuredly the experience that Folco is commemorating in his poem: the rising of the day star in his heart, which in the medieval exegetical tradition was understood to mean coming to love Christ.[135] Here, then, is that "praise of the lord Jesus Christ" that Bonatti taught us to expect from a singer gifted by a conjunction of Jupiter and Venus. Folco could well smile in contemplating the providential influence of Venus by which he was no less a poet of sacred than profane love.

Rahab. There remains the riddle of Rahab: what form of love does she represent that would justify Folco's assertion that "our order is sealed by her in the highest degree." Her biblical story is well known from Joshua 2, but the principal facts bear repeating. She was a prostitute (*meretrix*) in Jericho, who entertained Joshua's spies, unwittingly it would seem, and when their mission was made known to her by the police who came to arrest them, she hid the spies, sent the officials off to follow a false trail, and managed the escape of the spies in return for their promise that she, her family, and its property would be spared when Joshua conquered Jericho. Rahab's speech in the biblical account clearly indicates that she was motivated by a firm conviction that Joshua was certain to win because he was being helped by the one true God: "for the Lord your God he is God in heaven above, and in the earth beneath" (Jos. 2.11). Accordingly when faith is defined and exemplified in the epistle to the Hebrews, Rahab is one of his examples: "By faith (*fide*) Rahab the harlot perished not with the unbelievers, receiving the spies with peace" (Heb. 11.31). After Joshua's victory, she married Salmon and, giving birth to Boaz, became of one the ancestors of Jesus (Matt. 1.5), so she must be one of the unnamed Hebrew women in the Mystic Rose whose seats, like a Tree of Jesse, form the wall between the souls of the old dispensation and the new, who believed respectively in Christ yet to come and Christ already come (*Par.* 32.16–27). Thus, like all the blessed who were born before Christ's coming, she had faith in that future event. But Folco informs us that when Christ harrowed Hell "she was taken up by this heaven before any other souls of Christ's triumphs" (8.118–120). The reason Folco gives for so honoring her is that, because "she favored Joshua's first glory in the Holy Land," she prefigured the redemption of sinners by Joshua's homonym Jesus (8.121–125).[136]

Rahab, then, is for Dante a *figura* of faith, just as she exemplified the same virtue for Paul. In this, no less than in her harlotry, she was a true daughter of Venus, for the astrologers ascribe that virtue to the planet's natives. Scot says that the Venusian "is faithful (*fidelis*) enough to all,"[137] and Bonatti claims that the native frequents churches in order to retain his faith,[138] though this is a cynical paraphrase of Alcabitius's flat assertion that "he maintains faith."[139] Thus it is that Folco can say that Rahab was taken up from Hell "by this heaven (*da questo cielo*)" (*Par.* 9.118), for Venus had disposed her towards the saving virtue of faith.

Rahab has another astrological association that is made apparent by the standard medieval scholastic commentary on the Bible, the *Glossa ordinaria*, which offers this interlinear gloss to the description of Rahab as a prostitute:

> *Harlot* (Jos. 2.1): the church, namely the congregation of the gentiles, which in the desires of the flesh was previously fornicating with idols; whence it is said "the harlots shall go into the kingdom of heaven before you" (Matt. 21.31).[140]

This brings us back full circle to the image of idolatry with which Dante began the Venusian cantos and which we have seen is astrologically appropriate to Venus (above, pp. 66, 69). It also establishes a contrast between the states of Rahab before and after her profession of faith: before, she was literally a whore and figuratively fornicated with idols; after her conversion she worshipped the true God, married a respectable Jew, and gave birth to Christ's ancestor. Like Folco, she moved from a lower form of Venusian life to a higher one. To emphasize this resemblance, Dante describes them both in similar terms: Folco is like a *balasso* ruby—the kind distinguished by its clearness—and Rahab "sparkles as a sunbeam on clear water" (*Par.* 9.69, 114). The clarity that they have in common is an effect of Venus, which itself shines with a clear light (above, at n. 93), but not all Venusians display it. Just as in the physical world the earth's conical shadow extends to the heaven of Venus but no farther (9.118), so the shadow of worldliness touched the lives of all the natives we have met in Venus and the lower planets as well; but unlike Carlo and Cunizza, both Folco and Rahab were able to realize the higher part of their astral nature. Certainly Rahab enjoys the honor of being the first redeemed Venusian, but otherwise Folco's case does not seem greatly different from hers. As one subject to innate modesty, Folco probably was speaking in character when he indicated that "our order is sealed by her in the highest degree" without noting that the same could be said of himself. The answer to the riddle of Rahab, then, is that through faith she, like Folco, turned to the higher love of God while still living.

4. The Sun

In Dante's universe, the Sun is the most important star. Astronomers calculated that it was the largest heavenly body,[1] and everyone knew it was the brightest. Above all, the Sun was the primary source both of heat and of light, and not only for earth but also for the stars.[2] Today we consider light and heat to be natural phenomena, and consequently we are not apt to associate them with astrology, which in the modern view is concerned only with occult, supernatural occurrences. But in the Middle Ages, they were the concern, not of astronomy, but of astrology, for the former was limited to the mathematical description of the motions of heavenly bodies, while the latter was, to adopt Ptolemy's definition, the study of "the *changes* which they bring about in that which they surround."[3] To be sure, other sciences—such as meteorology, physics, and medicine—took into account particular aspects of astral influence, but insofar as they did so, they were considered to be "subordinate" to astrology, that is, dependent on it for the general principles that they applied to specific cases. Therefore the Sun's effects on the earth, which we assign to natural science, fell primarily into the province of astrology as it was defined in the Middle Ages. What is more, because no one can deny that the Sun's heat and light have an effect on earth, they justified the whole science of astrology by providing manifest examples of astral influence. Thus Ptolemy, when constructing a rationale for astrology in his *Quadripartitum*, offered as his prime example an impressive catalogue of the changes on earth effected by the Sun:

> For the sun . . . is always in some way affecting everything on earth, not only by the changes that accompany the seasons of the year to bring about the generation of animals, the productiveness of plants, the flowing of waters, and the changes of bodies, but also by its daily revolutions furnishing heat, moisture, dryness, and cold in regular order and in correspondence with its positions relative to the zenith.[4]

Since Dante in his art tried to follow nature, it is not surprising that most of these physical Solar phenomena find a place in his heaven of the Sun.

Of course these are influences that anyone could associate with the Sun without recourse to astrology, but in Dante's case we can reasonably take them to be instances of astrological allusion because by now it should be clear to the reader that in his treatment of the planets he took astrology as his guide. Accordingly, the first sections of the present chapter shall be devoted to "natural" effects of the Sun's heat and light, which Dante, together with most medieval philosophers, would have considered proper to astrology. These "natural" Solar influences will be considered first because they are the premises from which the astrologers deduced the "supernatural" influences that form the conceptual core of these cantos. But since such conclusions do not come readily to the modern mind, it will be well to make the connection plain at the outset, lest this crucial relationship be lost in a multitude of details.

The physical heat and light with which the Sun fills the macrocosm has its spiritual analogue in man the microcosm. According to the astrologers, the Sun ruled two parts of the human body in particular—the head and the heart. Although the astrologers do not explain why these human members are essentially Solar, the reason is not far to seek. The head contains the two human organs that are especially associated with light: the eyes, by means of which we perceive physical light, and the brain, by which we apprehend spiritual, or intellectual, light. Similarly, the heart provides the body with both physical and spiritual heat, for according to medieval medical theory, the body's natural spirit, after being produced in the liver, flows to the heart, where it is heated and so becomes the vital spirit that conveys warmth to the other members of the body. In addition to this physical heat, the heart is also the seat of a spiritual heat—"the intense heat (*ardor*) of desire" (*Par.* 33.48)—for the heart is the source of human passions, desires, and feelings, or affects.[5] Thus the human head and heart function in the microcosm as the Sun does in the macrocosm: both are the source of light and heat.

Heat and light accordingly furnish Dante with the organizing principles in his heaven of the Sun. The twenty-four souls encountered there are divided into two groups of twelve each, which form concentric circles around Beatrice and the Pilgrim. The Dominican Thomas Aquinas speaks for the inner circle and the Franciscan Bonaventure for the outer circle; each praises the founder of the other's order, and their eulogies typify not only the characteristic virtues of Dominic and Francis and of the orders they founded, but also those of the two circles of souls in which their followers appear. The key lies in Thomas's lapidary characterization of the two founders: "The one [Francis] was all seraphic in ardor (*ardore*), the other [Dominic], for wisdom (*sapïenza*) was on earth a splendor of cherubic light."

> L'un fu tutto serafico in ardore;
>   l'altro per sapïenza in terra fue
>   di cherubica luce uno splendore. (*Par.* 11.37–39)

Ardor, or intense heat, therefore, is characteristic of Francis, and light (*luce*) of Dominic, and hence presumably of their respective mendicant orders as well, and also of the two Solar circles which are differentiated by the presence of Dominicans in one and Franciscans in the other. To be sure, neither order has an exclusive claim to its characteristic virtue, which is shared by the other to some extent, but Dante elucidates this complex interrelationship by indicating that it is the same one that obtains between the Cherubim and Seraphim, the two highest orders of angels. One has but to consult Thomas Aquinas to discover that, although all angels possess all the spiritual perfections, some possess them more abundantly than others. Both the Cherubim and the Seraphim take their names, Aquinas says, from the spiritual perfection of which they have an excessive amount. The name "Cherubim" means "fullness of knowledge (*plenitudo scientiae*)" and is fitting because, among other things, these angels receive the divine light fully and shed it on others. The name "Seraphim" means "ardors (*ardori*)" or "fires (*incendii*)" and refers to their "excess of charity," which makes them comparable to fire that continually moves upward and at the same time has the power both to the excite fervor in others and to purge them.[6] Consequently there is no fundamental difficulty in the correspondences I am proposing. The souls of the inner circle, including the Dominicans Thomas Aquinas and Albertus Magnus, are cherubic like their prototype Dominic, because like him they fill the earth with the divine light they perceive; on earth their wisdom reflected their full vision of the divine light. The souls of the outer circle, including Bonaventure and two other Franciscans, are seraphic in their ardor because, like Francis, they were remarkable for their superabundance of charity. Thus the two circles represent the highest activities of the human head and heart, which correspond respectively to the light and heat of the Sun. Accordingly in this chapter we shall pass from the Sun's effects in the macrocosm to its corresponding influence in the microcosm of man, considering first the human organs that the Sun dominates and then the characteristic activities of the Solar man.

Light and Heat

Most astrologers do not bother to expound the physical properties of the Sun as Ptolemy did; instead, they take them for granted or mention them only in passing. Haly, for example, begins by declaring that "the Sun is the light and candle of the heaven,"[7] and Michael Scot explains its placement midway between the other planets in terms of the Sun's function as their source of light: "It is the prince of all the planets, and for that reason it is located in fourth place, illuminating the upper ones as much as the lower ones."[8] Moreover, its function as the source of physical light also makes the Sun a symbol and astrological significator of "light (*lumen*)."[9]

Dante, as we have already seen, used the light and heat of the Sun to give structure to his Solar cantos, but he also makes explicit reference to physical and spiritual light in connection with the Sun. Physical sunlight is the brightest light that our eyes know (*Par.* 10.48); nonphysical light is the subject of two of the principal doctrinal passages in these cantos. Aquinas accounts for human wisdom, and indeed all perfection in the universe, in terms of light (13.37–87): everything that Nature generates is a reflection of the "living light" (55) of divine wisdom that streams downward in rays from its eternal source to be embodied in individuals created by universal Nature, who accordingly possess some portion of this light (43–45). Again, the soul of Solomon explains another light-related problem in *Paradise* 14.37–60: whether blessed souls after the Resurrection will retain the brilliant light in which they are now clothed and, since that is the case, how their eyes will be able to stand such intense light. These two extended examples will suffice to attest to the prominence Dante gave to light in the Solar cantos.

To be sure, much more could be said of Dante's use of light in these cantos, but his refinements owe little to astrology. One point of contact does, however, deserve passing mention. The Latin astrologers quite naturally tend to describe the Sun's light as a *splendor*, i.e., as a brightness or brilliance that shines or radiates. Thus Scot states that the Sun "causes heat, dryness, and *splendor*,"[10] and for him it signifies light that is shining ("lumen spendidum"),[11] while Alcabitius takes it to signify simply *splendor*.[12] Dante, too, especially associates splendor with the Sun, and for him it is essentially brightness that is borne by a ray of light, as he makes clear by distinguishing between incident and reflected light: "a first splendor [surpasses] that which it throws back" (*Par.* 12.9). Thus all contingent beings are splendors of the divine idea that gives them form (13.53); Dominic is a splendor of cherubic light (11.39); the Pilgrim is distracted by the splendor of Beatrice's smiling eyes (10.62); and Thomas says that he is a brilliant reflection ("resplendo") of the ray of eternal light into which he gazes (11.19).

Another small point is worth noting in connection with light. The narrator expressly excludes color from his description of the Solar souls; they manifest themselves "not by color but by light" (*Par.* 10.42). This exclusion of color may well have been prompted by the fact that the astrologers were of many opinions as to the color proper to the Sun, for John of Seville said it was white, Ibn Ezra yellow or moderately red, and Scot gold, while Alcabitius and Bonatti thought its color was variable.[13]

Finally, we must note the few references to heat. As we have seen, Dante connects ardor with the Seraphim, whose name indicated that they are ardent, flaming, or fiery (*Par.* 11.37), and we have argued that he connects this quality primarily with the outer ring of souls that has Francis as its archetype and Bonaventure as its spokesman. Nonetheless, as is evident from the *Summa theologiae*, the same quality is a less prominent property of all the angels, and also of all the blessed, since by divine grace they are made equal to the angels.[14] In the heaven of the Sun, this truth is exemplified by the souls of the inner ring, whose physical appearance causes the narrator to describe them as "blazing suns (*ardenti soli*)" (10.76), and later we learn from Solomon that after the Resurrection the ardor of the blessed will be increased (14.37–51). Otherwise, heat plays no part in Dante's Solar cantos, except as an implicit condition of thirst (10.89, 123, 11.100) and in Thomas's extended metaphor of the seal and the wax (13.67–75). The astrologers, however, generally follow Ptolemy in attributing the qualities of hotness and dryness to the Sun, usually in a moderate degree,[15] although Albumasar puts it another way, saying that the Sun's nature is that of "moderate fire."[16]

Water and Other Inanimate Substances

Planetary influence on earth is effected, in large part, by affinities between the planets and the elements, and since there are seven planets and only four elements, the astrologers assigned the same element to several planets. Thus we should not be surprised to find water once again appearing as a planetary property. The Sun's astrological association with water is specific rather than general, for according to Haly "the descent (*decursus*) of waters is caused by the Sun."[17] Dante twice incorporates this Solar effect into elaborate comparisons. The first is put into the mouth of Aquinas, who expresses his willingness to answer the Pilgrim's questions by saying that he could hardly do otherwise because one who refused "would no more be at liberty than water that flows not down to the sea" (*Par.* 10.90). Haly's *decursus* here is taken in the classical sense of "the action of running downhill,"[18] and the implication is that the Sun inclines those who have received cherubic light from above to pass it on downward just as the Sun inclines waters to flow downwards.[19] The same idea is later developed by Bonaventure in his description of Dominic's mission, which is the poet's exemplar of the cherubic mode of Solar influence.

> si mosse
> quasi torrente ch'alta vena preme;
> e ne li sterpi eretici percosse
> l'impeto suo, più vivamente quivi
> dove le resistenze eran più grosse.
> Di lui si fecer poi diversi rivi
> onde l'orto catolico si riga,
> sì che i suoi arbuscelli stan più vivi.   (*Par.* 12.99–105)

He went forth like a torrent which a lofty vein presses out, and on the heretical stocks this force struck with most vigor where the resistances were most obstinate. From him there sprang then various streamlets whereby the catholic garden is watered, so that its bushes are more living.

Dominic himself is the original rush of energy that flows hard and fast as the torrent first drops from its upland source and strikes with most force where it encounters resistance, while in his followers this force is dissipated as the primary stream branches off into many lesser ones that bring life-giving water to the lower, more fertile regions, but with diminished vigor. In addition to these metaphoric rivers, the poet names several actual ones in the course of these cantos. Four—the Topino, the Tiber, the Arno, and the Ganges (*Par.* 11.43, 51, 106)—are mentioned without reference to their downward flow, but this feature is stressed in the case of two others. The sluggish river Chiana serves to exemplify the slowest moving things in the universe (13.23), and Assisi is located by reference to the Chiascio, "the stream that drops (*L'acqua che discende*) from the hill chosen by the blessed Ubaldo" (11.43–44). Finally, since *decursus aquarum* does not always imply the downward motion of water but can simply mean that water runs or flows,[20] we may apply Haly's words to the movement of water described in the opening lines of *Paradise* 14: "From the center to the rim, and so from the rim to the center, the water in a round vessel moves, according as it is struck from without or within."

Haly also mentions other ways in which the Sun promotes the down-pouring of waters: "Through it clouds are produced and rains come."[21] The poet works both of these Solar functions into his text: the formation of clouds is implied in the simile that identifies the nymph Echo as she "whom love consumed as the sun does vapors" (*Par.* 12.15); the rain, however, appears as a metaphor for the outpouring of divine grace on the blessed: "lo refrigerio de l'etterna ploia" (14.27).[22]

Substances. According to Alcabitius and Bonatti, the Sun "signifies every kind of substance."[23] Given this carte blanche, it is noteworthy that Dante in the cantos of the Sun repeatedly directs our attention away from material substances to spiritual ones. The term *substantia* itself appears in its Italian form, "sustanza," and is used to describe the human soul (*Par.* 14.14), as is the related term "sussistenze" (*subsistentia*, subsistence), which is applied not only to souls in beatitude but also to angels (13.59, 14.73). A small thing in itself, this shift becomes significant when taken in conjunction with Dante's treatment of specific material substances that are also associated with the Sun.

"Among the substances," Scot informs us, "the Sun signifies a thing of great value, such as gold, cloth of gold, tapestries, gems, perfumes, etc."[24] In the Solar cantos, Dante alludes to three kinds of precious objects listed by Scot—gold, jewels, and cloth—but in each case the material object assumes a spiritual, or at least an immaterial, value. Above all, the astrologers would lead us to expect frequent references to gold, for they agree almost unanimously that this is *par excellence* the metal of the Sun.[25] But, contrary to expectation, gold appears only twice in the Solar cantos, both times in proper names associated with the saints: first in "Ciel-dauro"—literally, "heaven of gold"—the name of the place where the earthly remains of Boethius rest (*Par.* 10.128), and second in "Crisos-tomo," or "golden-mouthed," the cognomen of Saint John Chrysostom (12.137). This immaterial use of gold might seem to be a coincidence were not gems given similar treatment. They are not as characteristic of the Sun as gold, but Scot listed them among the valuables that the Sun can signify, and Ibn Ezra's list of Solar metals includes "precious stones, such as dia-monds."[26] In the *Comedy*, these Solar gems appear only in metaphor: the narrator tells us that the song of the *spiriti sapienti* was one of the "many gems (*gioie*) so precious and beautiful that they may not be taken out of the kingdom" (10.71–72). Finally, Scot also mentioned valuable textiles; elsewhere he assures us that the Solar man delights in "clothing that is beautiful in color" and in "cloth goods that are noble by reason of their wool and color."[27] For these splendid material garments Dante substitutes the splendid light of eternal glory: "As long as the feast of Paradise shall be, so long shall our love radiate around us such a garment (*vesta*)" (14.37–39). This is the clothing in which the souls of the Solar heaven truly find delight; on earth, the Mendicants who typify the Solar souls are dis-tinguished instead by the simplicity of their dress, as Dante reminds his reader by an allusion to their familiar habit: "they are so few that little cloth (*panno*) suffices for their cowls" (11.131–132).

In dealing with specific substances of great value, then, Dante accepts the Solar associations ascribed to them by the astrologers, but by a sort of poetic alchemy he transmutes them from material to spiritual objects. This same process can be seen in a more generalized way in his treatment of wealth. Scot repeatedly asserts that copious riches ("copia divitiarum") are the heritage of the Sun's native.[28] Dante's Solar souls do indeed have wealth, but it is not the sort that Scot had in mind. When Aquinas tells how Francis's pursuit of poverty so impressed Bernardo da Quintavalle that he gave up his position of wealth and importance in Assisi to be-come the first Franciscan, Dante has Thomas exclaim, "Oh wealth un-known, oh fertile good! (*Oh ignota ricchezza! oh ben ferace!*)" (*Par.* 11.82). Paradoxically, then, poverty is the true wealth of the seraphic soul; in the cherubic mode, however, it would seem that wealth is the light of divine wisdom. Thus Dante compares Peter Lombard, the founder of scholastic theology, to the widow who offered her mite (Luc. 21.2), because in his *Liber sententiarum* he, too, "offered his treasure (*tesoro*) to Holy Church" (10.107–108). The true nature of the Lombard's treasure is revealed in his preface, to which Dante's allusion refers us: Peter Lombard writes "desiring to contribute somewhat of our poverty and our little store [of knowledge] to the treasury of the Lord, as did the poor widow [her two mites]." [29]

Plants and Animals

"Life," Scot said, "is the property of the Sun." [30] John of Seville agreed but added "soul (*anima*)" as an equivalent, [31] while other astrologers combined the two into a single concept, associating the Sun with the "vital soul" or the "animal spirit." [32] Ibn Ezra's attempt to express the underlying thought through paraphrase is, if anything, more obscure: "The Sun impresses the amount of vigor each thing has by its nature." [33] Haly's way of putting it is somewhat clearer: the Sun's "nature and action are apparent in all things, both in animate beings in general [including heavenly bodies] and in all those that exist on earth." [34] Still better is his matter-of-fact statement of what every farmer knows: "through it every thing that has birth is born, every growing thing is increased, every leaf grows, and every fruit is matured." [35]

In the cantos of the Sun, its connection with life and the soul provides the poet with a structuring theme that is no less important than light and heat. Aquinas's first discourse on Saint Francis is offered to clarify his obscure metaphor based on the growth of animals: "the path where there is good fattening if they do not stray" (*Par.* 10.94–96, elucidated in 11.22–139). This is followed by Bonaventure's encomium on Saint Dominic, in which he represents him as Christ's agriculturist ("agricola," 12.71) with a variety of figures based on the life of plants and animals (12.37–126). Then Aquinas returns to explain why the gift of prudence that Solomon received as a king is not comparable to the perfection of Adam and Christ because it was not conferred by nature, and at the core of this explanation stands the *Comedy*'s most general statement on the process by which souls and life are generated (13.37–45). Finally, the life of the soul in glory is clarified by Solomon (14.13–60). Diverse as these subjects seem to be, they all concern life—the life of plants, of animals, of man, and of the blessed. Therefore another underlying structural element of the Solar cantos becomes apparent: because in nature the Sun animates every living soul, the poet gave life in all its variety a leading role in his heaven of the Sun.

Since these effects of the Sun, like light and heat, are common knowledge, one cannot infer from their presence in the poem that the poet borrowed them directly from the astrologers. But the immediate source of inspiration is relatively unimportant; what is important is that the poet realized that these commonplace examples of the Sun's influence were also recognized by the astrologers. In a few cases, of which the "fattening" theme is a good example, the reference is so specific that an astrological source is certainly indicated. This does not mean that all the others were suggested by the same sources, but it does permit us to infer that Dante knew that they were *in accord* with astrology. The distinction may seem a fine one, but it makes a great deal of difference to our appreciation of the poem. If we take the modern point of view—that the Sun is of course responsible for the growth of vegetation, so it is appropriate for the poet to scatter references to plants throughout his heaven of the Sun—such allusions appear highly artificial and arbitrary, because the poet places them in the mouths of intellectuals like Bonaventure and Aquinas for whom it would not be characteristic to employ vegetational imagery. But if, on the other hand, we adopt the medieval viewpoint and see that these images are astrologically appropriate, then it appears only natural that Solar souls should express themselves in terms that are an outward manifestation of their innate astrological characters. Thus, just as Mercurians are pedantic and Venusians luxurious, so Solarians, even scholastic theologians with no "grass roots," can display an inborn affinity for plants and animals. Hence, in what follows, we will not be belaboring the obvious in pointing out the various forms of plant and animal life that appear both in the astrologers and in the cantos of the Sun. Whenever such correspondences can be established, the astrological context of the poem is enriched by the realization that the allusion is appropriate.

Since we already know from Haly that the Sun is responsible for the growth of plants, let us begin by seeing how that is reflected in the poem. The term "plant" (*pianta*) occurs three times in these cantos, and each time it is used metaphorically, standing in one instance for the Dominican order (*Par.* 11.137) and in two others for human souls (10.91; 12.96). Thus Aquinas, who is the speaker in all three cases, displays a Solar inclination for vegetative imagery. Similarly, when he wishes to commend a good idea because it is spreading, he calls it "fertile (*ferace*)" (11.82). The maturation of fruit, another of Haly's Solar functions, is also never far from the mind of the poet. Thus he has Francis return to "the harvest (*frutto*) of the Italian field" (11.105). Likewise, his Thomas says that one should not "count the ears in the field before they are ripe" (13.132), just as we would say that chickens should not be counted before they hatch; Aquinas even describes his own professional activity—rational investigation—in terms of threshing grain (13.34–36). Bonaventure exhibits the same Solar affinity for agrarian images: Dominic is both "the marvelous fruit" and God's *agricola*, while his followers work in "the catholic garden," which yields tares when badly cultivated (12.65, 71, 104, 118–120). Moreover, as in previous heavens, Beatrice is speaking under the influence of her environment when she announces the Pilgrim's need "to go to the root (*radice*) of another truth" (14.12).

Roses. In addition to these generalized references to vegetation, Dante also alludes to certain phases of plant life, particularly to flowers, fruits, and seeds, all of which also appear in the astrologers. According to Ibn Ezra, for example, the rose is one of the flowers that belongs to the Sun,[36] and so Dante twice works this flower into the fabric of his Solar cantos, most notably when Aquinas uses it as an example of how deceptive appearances can be: "for I have seen first, all winter through, the thorn display itself hard and stiff, and then upon its summit bear the rose (*rosa*)" (*Par*. 13.133–135). Roses, like plants in general, are also used as a figure for the souls in this heaven, whom the narrator describes as "two garlands of those sempiternal roses" (12.19). Earlier, Thomas had compared his circle of souls to a garland or wreath of flowers that he promised to identify: "You wish to know what plants these are that enflower (*s'infiora*) this garland" (10.91–92, 102). At the literal level he had proceeded to introduce each soul, but a figurative, botanical answer was also possible, and this is what the narrator later supplies when he takes up the metaphor (12.19). The theme is further developed in the last canto of the series by Beatrice, who specifies that the flower in the figure is in fact "the light wherewith your substance blooms (*s'infiora*)" (14.13). Needless to add, this catena of images prepares the reader for the culmination of this theme in the Empyrean, where the Mystic Rose composed of all the blessed souls "breathes forth odor of praise unto the Sun which makes perpetual spring" (30.125–126). The fitness of this final image was previously established in the Solar heaven and was based on the astrological connection between roses and the Sun.

Fruit. Ibn Ezra assigns to the Sun a variety of trees bearing fruits, including dates, grapes, olives, apples, cherries, and figs.[37] Aquinas could be referring to any of these when he says "that one same tree (*legno*), in respect to species, fruits (*frutta*) better or worse" (*Par*. 13.70–71). Again, his allusion to the forbidden fruit eaten by Eve (13.37–39) is not inappropriate in this connection. But the only Solar fruit to which specific reference is made in these cantos is the grape. Viticulture provides an analogue to the teaching mission of Saint Dominic, who "set himself to go round the vineyard (*vigna*), which soon whitens (*imbianca*) if the vine-dresser is negligent" (12.86–87). Wine, the produce therefrom, also appears twice, first explicitly as a metaphor for the wisdom dispensed in this heaven (10.88), and later implicitly in a reference to Bacchus (13.25).

Lions and sheep. The Sun is also associated astrologically with several animals that appear in the Solar cantos. "Among living creatures," Ibn Ezra names only "man, horses, lions, and rams, especially from overseas."[38] Of these, Dante makes use of the lion and the ram, both of which were doubtless suggested to Ibn Ezra because the Sun bears a special astrological relations to the zodiacal signs of Leo and Aries, for he rules the former sign both by night and day, while in the latter he is exalted.[39] Dante's use of the lion is minor but obvious: Dominic was born in Old Castile "under the protection of the mighty shield whereon the lion is subject and sovereign" (*Par.* 12.53–54). The ram plays a greater role in the heaven of the Sun, but he is less readily recognized because he has been stripped of his aggressive, sex-related qualities and appears as a simple sheep in the pastoral metaphor that Dante employs to characterize the Dominican order. The theme is introduced by Thomas Aquinas, who uses it to identify himself and at the same time to deplore the present state of his order: "I was of the lambs of the holy flock which Dominic leads on the path where there is good fattening if they do not stray."

> Io fui de li agni de la santa greggia
>   che Domenico mena per cammino
>   u' ben s'impingua se non si vaneggia.   (*Par.* 10.94–96)

Almost the whole of canto 11 is a commentary on this passage; in it Thomas recalls the mission of Francis and Dominic, and after using the former to exemplify the positive side of the mendicant movement (11.22–120), he finally explicates his earlier remark by expanding the original pastoral metaphor (11.124–131). Dominic here is a shepherd ("pastor," 131), the Dominicans are the sheep ("pecore," 127) of his flock ("peculio," 124). Although some of the sheep still stay close to the shepherd who leads the flock to pastures where there is "good fattening," most of them now leave him because they are "greedy of new fare" (124–125) and go far afield into less nourishing pastures, and the farther they stray, "the more empty of milk do they return to the fold" (129). To be sure, the image of the good shepherd and his sheep is drawn ultimately from biblical sources, but astrology makes it appropriate to the Solar cantos.[40] The novel, nonbiblical feature of this pastoral metaphor is the phrase that Thomas took as his text: "where there is good fattening (*s'impingua*) if they do not stray" (*Par.* 10.96 and 11.139). This element is clearly astrological in origin, for Scot repeatedly stresses the Sun's influence over fat. According to Scot, the face of the Sun itself appears to be "shapely and fat (*pinguis*)"; hence in general the Sun "controls things that are fat (*pingues*)," and in particular "the Sun naturally makes a man large and fat (*pinguem*) in the trunk of his body," so the Solar man's appearance is "handsome and fat (*pinguis*)."[41] It would seem that the poet started with two Solar properties—rams and fatness—and combined them into a single metaphor, which he then developed in biblical terms; but far from trying to pass off the result as a traditional commonplace, he drew the reader's attention to the novelty of his combination. "Good fattening" puzzles the Pilgrim precisely because it is *not* a familiar Christian topic. The meaning must be explained to him, and the elaborate explanation makes the reader at least conscious that there is something out of the ordinary about fatness in this context, and it might perhaps prompt him to seek out its origins in astrology.

Closely related materials are introduced elsewhere in the heaven of the Sun. Scot, probably working deductively from the observed fatness of the Sun and its children, also declares that the Solar man "eats and drinks well."[42] Eating well, as the case of Dominic's flock suggests, requires proper guidance. At the beginning of the Solar cantos, the reader himself receives such direction from the narrator, who introduces him to the astronomical setting and then urges him to make the most of the clues he has been given. This exhortation takes the form of a nutritional metaphor: after giving the reader a foretaste ("preliba"), the narrator tells him, "I have set before you; now feed yourself" (*Par.* 10.25). The good host, like the good shepherd, has shown where there is good fattening; both are concerned that their charges, like Scot's Solar man, should eat well. In both allegories, food represents knowledge, true doctrine, or *scientia*; it is, I think, to be identified with "the true manna" for the love of which Dominic became a teacher, as we are told elsewhere in these cantos (12.84–85). Thus the Sun's influence over growth provides the occasion for a series of nutritional metaphors that are interconnected in much the same way as the vegetational ones.

Heart and Head

Of all the creatures on earth that the Sun generates and nourishes, mankind seemed the most noble, and therefore the astrologers thought it only
proper that the Sun should be associated with its higher, no less than its
lower, powers. Thus, when Ibn Ezra names the living things that especially
belong to the Sun, *homo* stands at the head of his list.[43] Man and the Sun
are also closely connected in the *Commedia*, for the Sun's part in the making of man is one of the most important doctrines revealed in the Sun's
heaven (*Par.* 13.37–87). Although the perfection of Adam and Christ provides the pretext for the discourse, the poet makes it clear that they are to
be understood as the highest manifestations of "human nature" by using
the term twice in the course of the exposition ("natura umana," 43;
"umana natura," 86). And human nature is again treated in the next canto,
where Solomon explains how its limitations will be transcended after the
Resurrection (14.37–60). These two discourses are specifically concerned
with the Sun's action on the two parts of the human body that it affects
most directly, the heart and the head, for "whatever of light it is allowed
human nature to have" is infused in the "breast (*petto*)" (13.37, 43–44),
while it is the eyes, the organs of vision, that will be strengthened to bear
the light of glory (14.59–60). Although these are the principal instances
of heart and head in the cantos of the Sun, they are not the only ones, and
the lesser allusions serve both to emphasize the major ones and to establish
closer links to the Sun of the astrologers.

"In the person, the Sun by nature rules the heart," writes Scot, and
the same correspondence is attested by Alcabitius, John of Seville, Ibn
Ezra, and Guido Bonatti.[44] Just as we have seen Dante spiritualizing the
material substances controlled by the Sun, so it is not the human heart's
material function of heating the vital spirits that he stresses, but rather its
immaterial, psychological roles. Although there are only two references to
the human heart, they represent the opposite extremes of human feeling.
At the lower end is "baseness of heart (*viltà di cuor*)," which was conspicu-
ously absent in Saint Francis (*Par.* 11.88), while at the upper extreme is the
Pilgrim's heart, of which we hear when Beatrice exhorts him to give
thanks for being raised to the heaven of the Sun: "Never was heart of
mortal (*cor di mortal*) so disposed unto devotion and so ready, with all its
gratitude, to give itself to God, as I became at those words" (10.55–58).

Most astrologers name the head as another human organ ruled by the

Sun; indeed, according to Guido Bonatti, "its virtue and power is most especially in the head."[45] They also, however, associate the Sun with specific parts of the head—notably with the face, the mouth, the eyes, and the brain—and for some obscure reason Dante chose to allude to each of these parts rather than to the head as a whole. Each of these parts must therefore be considered separately.

Face. To begin with the face, Alcabitius and Bonatti agree "that the Sun signifies the image of man's countenance."[46] Of course only the face of Beatrice is actually seen in the heaven of the Sun, but another, more remarkable one does occur in a curious metaphor. As examples of theologians who fell into error through lack of caution and skill, Aquinas mentions Sabellius, Arius, and "those fools who were to the Scriptures like swords, in rendering straight countenances (*volti*) distorted" (*Par.* 13.127– 129). Here the true sense of the Bible is compared to the features of a human face, which appear distorted when seen reflected in the curved surface of a sword.[47] Thus the metaphor substitutes one way of seeing the image of God for another, for the Eternal Word can be seen in the Scriptures by the mind, whereas the image and likeness of God can be seen in man's face by the eyes, even as the Pilgrim literally sees it at the end of the poem (33.131). Although this resemblance between God and man is a revealed truth (Genesis 1.26–27), its physical basis is natural rather than supernatural, since according to the astrologers man owes his facial features to the Sun.

Mouth. None of Dante's astrologers says directly that the mouth is one of the parts of the human body that belongs to the Sun, though several of them take that for granted, given the Sun's control of the head, and assign to the Sun every infirmity connected with the mouth.[48] Dante follows them in this, comparing himself to a mute inasmuch as certain things he has experienced in heaven cannot be described to those who have not been there: they "await tidings thence from the dumb (*muto*)" (*Par.* 10.75). Dante also mentions one organ of the mouth, Eve's "palate (*palato*)" (13.39), and similarly in the proem to this series of cantos he twice speaks of the sense of taste. He who contemplates the order of the macrocosm and microcosm "cannot but taste (*gustar*) of Him" (10.6), and afterwards the narrator leaves the reader to reflect on "this of which you have a foretaste (*preliba*)" (10.23). Elsewhere, both voices and charity are said to be "sweet" (10.66, 13.36), but the astrological fitness of this is doubtful, since only John of Seville assigns "sweetness of taste" to the Sun, in contrast to others who indicate instead a sharp, pungent, or acrid taste, while Scot offers a compromise flavor somewhere between those two extremes.[49] It is also possible that the Sun's hot and dry nature, on which all astrologers agree,[50] may account for Dante's repeated references to thirst in these cantos ("sete," 10.89, 123, 11.100).

Eyes. Since the eye is part of the head, astrologers agree in associating it also with the Sun, but always with a variety of qualifications. Some say the Sun rules only the right eye,[51] others that it rules the right eye by day and the left one by night,[52] and yet others that it signifies the right eye in men, though they differ as to whether the Sun or the Moon controls the left eye in women.[53] Faced with an array of conflicting opinions, Dante retained only the general association of the Sun with the eye,[54] but he made liberal use of it in the Solar cantos, perhaps because this generality made it possible for him to fill the Solar cantos with an abundance of ocular allusions.

Although Dante does use eyesight as an analogue for nonphysical perception, he also makes literal reference to the eye more often than to any other physical organ or object, probably because he regarded vision as the least material of the human senses. Here, as throughout the cantica, the eyes of Beatrice and of the Pilgrim interact with the environment. In the Solar heaven, the eyes of Beatrice are, like the Sun itself, remarkable for their "splendor" or brilliantly reflected light (*Par.* 10.62). The eyes of the Pilgrim, on the other hand, cannot stand the splendor of the third ring of souls (14.78), and thus they serve to illustrate the limitations of normal human vision, which a few lines earlier have been the subject of Solomon's discourse (14.37–60). This concluding theme of the Solar cantos had been foreshadowed at the beginning of the series by the narrator's assertion that the human eye is unable to perceive anything brighter than the Sun: "ché sopra 'l sol non fu occhio ch'andasse" (10.48). Not all the allusions to eyes are negative, however, for the coordinated movement of the two circles of Solar souls is compared with that of the eyes, "which, at the pleasure that moves them, must needs be closed and lifted in accord" (12.26–27).[55]

Physical eyesight, of course, is often used as an image of understanding by the light of human reason. When Aquinas wants the Pilgrim to exercise his intellect, on one occasion he urges him to direct his "discerning eyes (*li occhi chiari*)" to the key word of the problem (*Par.* 13.106); on another he tells him, "Now open your eyes to that which I answer you" (13.49); and on a third, he assumes that the Pilgrim is not only letting his eyes pass around the ring from soul to soul as they are being introduced but also is following with "the eye of the mind (*l'occhio de la mente*)"

(10.121). Similarly, the reader is urged by the narrator to visualize the location of the Sun: "Lift then your sight with me, reader" (10.7–8). Finally, the problem of Solomon's prudence is posed in visual terms: his knowledge ("saver") was so great that "there never rose a second of such full vision (*veder*)" (10.113–114; cf. 13.104–105), which is particularly fitting for the virtue that Dante elsewhere personified as a lady with an extra eye to symbolize her foresight (*Purg.* 29.132).

The mind's eye of man, however, is ultimately an image of the Eye of God, for Dante twice describes the Father's knowledge of the Son in visual terms. Indeed, the *oculus Dei* image provides the key note for the Solar cantos, which begin by recalling the inner relations between the persons of the Trinity: "Looking upon (*guardando*) His Son with the love which the One and the Other eternally breathe forth, the primal and ineffable Power made everything that revolves through the mind or through space" (*Par.* 10.1–4). Later, Aquinas uses the same image to describe God's direct creation of the human soul: "Yet complete perfection is there acquired if the fervent Love, the clear vision, and the primal Power disposes and imprints" (13.79–80).[56] Thus both in God and man the eyes for Dante are the organs associated with the highest intellectual powers. It is noteworthy that in this he departs from the astrologers, who also assign the brain to the Sun as one of the organs of the human head.[57] For Dante, the brain, like the mind it contains, is hidden from our view; physically it is most manifest through the eyes, the windows of the soul, and its contents are known to us, not immediately, but through their effects.

The Human Mind

Since the astrologers associate the Sun with the brain, they naturally also give it influence over the human mind. Alcabitius says that the Sun signifies a mind that is broad or ample.[58] In Dante's heaven of the Sun, this quality is best exemplified by the array of experts in many fields of human learning, but the principle itself is stated at the outset as the narrator reminds the reader that God "made everything that revolves through the mind (*mente*)" (*Par.* 10.4–5). The astrologers are more precise about what fills the mind, for they assign to the Sun both knowledge (*scientia*)[59] and wisdom (*sapientia*).[60] We have already seen that Dante equates these qualities with the light of the mind, exemplified by Saint Dominic, who "for wisdom (*sapïenza*) was on earth a splendor of cherubic light" (11.38–39).

Thus it is proper that one of the Solar cantos be devoted to Aquinas's exposition of the natural and supernatural origins of human wisdom in explanation of Solomon's peculiar kind of wisdom ("senno," 13.95).

Truth. The Solar man attains wisdom because, according to Scot, "he delights much in being told the truth and he detests lies,"[61] and indeed the astrologer considers the cultivation of truth to be a religious act.[62] Dante's Aquinas repeatedly displays just such concern, claiming that Solomon's wisdom was unique "if the truth is true" (*Par.* 10.113), announcing that he will reconcile his views with the Pilgrim's "in the truth" (13.51), and finally urging caution in the pursuit of truth (13.112–142). The truth is often knowledge of the causes or reasons of things, and hence Albumasar lists *ratio* as one of the qualities of the Sun, and Dante similarly uses *cagion* twice in this context (11.78, 13.92).

Becoming wise. Several other parallels concerning the acquisition of wisdom are more striking because more particular. For example, Scot says that the *homo Solaris* "appears attentive in listening (*in audiendo attentus*),"[63] so Dante has Aquinas tell the Pilgrim that his point will be clear "if your listening has been intent—*se la tua audïenza è stata attenta*" (*Par.* 11.134). Again, Scot describes the religious life of the Solar man by listing its characteristic activities, including "the study of agreeable doctrine,"[64] and elsewhere he indicates that the native also delights in learning honorable and praiseworthy doctrine (*doctrina*) such as laws and natural or physical science.[65] Dominic, Dante's paragon of wisdom, professes doctrine as Francis does poverty: "he became a mighty teacher (*dottor*)" who opposed ignorance and heresy "con dottrina" (12.85, 97), while a less militant form of teaching is exemplified by Donatus (12.137–138). Finally, Scot and Bonatti agree that when the Sun is joined with Mercury, as it is in the *Comedy*, the making of books is indicated, doubtless because they are the repositories of wisdom.[66] Dante developed the Solar indication of book-making into an elaborate metaphor for the order of Friars Minor, which he has Bonaventure compare to a volume that is being continually written by its members, some of whom reproduce their exemplar faithfully while others depart from it or abridge it (12.121–126).

Prudence. Because the natives of the Sun are wise, they make good counselors. Albumasar says that the Sun itself signifies "judgment" and also "opinion" (by which he means correct opinion, because elsewhere he explains that the Solar man makes "a good evaluation by habit"), and furthermore he has the Sun govern the formal occasions on which counsel is given—"councils and meetings of men."[67] Alcabitius, however, sums it all up in a single word: *prudentia*, or prudence.[68] These qualities do in fact appear in Dante's heaven of the Sun, but with important qualifications. That "regal prudenza" which is Solomon's peerless virtue (*Par.* 13.104) was conferred on him, not by nature, but by a special act of divine grace, so it is not an instance of the influence of the Sun. Moreover, Dante has his Aquinas warn us that a precipitate opinion ("l'oppinïon corrente," 119) is often wrong, and that at any rate man's moral judgments may not be God's, so we should "not be too secure in judgment (*troppo sicure / a giudicar*)" (130–131).[69] Paradoxically, Thomas is urging us to be prudent by recognizing the limitations of human prudence. Three times in these cantos Dante reinforces this theme by attributing counsel (*consiglio*) only to God: poverty was Christ's first counsel (12.75) and no human can fathom the divine counsel (11.29, 13.141). By treating prudence in the heaven of the Sun, Dante accepts the astrological view that human prudence is conferred by the Sun *naturaliter*, but he himself stresses its ultimate origin in God, whose omniscience men can only approximate imperfectly.

Speech. Because the tongue is one of the organs of the head, which the Sun rules, that planet also governs eloquence.[70] Thus both Thomas and Bonaventure display their Solar gift of eloquence. Although both are called "barons" (*Par.* 16.123), they do not speak as Michael Scot would lead us to expect, for he says that the Solar man "in speaking plays the lord (*baronizat*)," "boasting about himself and being magnanimous to his followers."[71] Quite to the contrary, each mendicant spokesman praises the other's order and criticizes his own harshly. In having them do this, however, Dante may simply be ignoring Scot and instead following Albumasar, who takes the speech of the Solar native to be like the heat of the Sun itself, which is more harmful to those closer to it, so the Solarian tends to degrade his intimates with oppressive speech while praising those who are not.[72]

Nonrational mentalities. In addition to rational thought, the mind also has activities that are nonrational, and the Sun governs these as well. Chief of these is faith, which the Sun signifies according to Alcabitius, Scot, and Bonatti.[73] And in the *Comedy*, it is faith to which Dominic devotes himself: just as Francis was the lover of Poverty, so Dominic is "the ardent lover of the Christian faith" (*Par.* 12.55–56), and his baptism is described as a marriage between him and Faith, where each endowed the other (61–63). Another nonrational Solar activity, according to Albumasar, is "contemplation of the highest divinity,"[74] and this is exemplified by Richard of Saint Victor, "who in contemplation was more than man" (10.132).

Finally, the Sun can signify the divination of future events,[75] and accordingly *Paradise* 12 has four distinct references to prophecy: Dominic's mother is a "profeta" (60), and a dream foretold Dominic's future to his godmother (64–66); Nathan, too, is identified as a "profeta" (136), and Joachim is said to have been "endowed with prophetic spirit (*spirito profetico*)" (140).

Fathers and Rulers

The Solar qualities of mind, which we have just surveyed, are often manifested in certain concrete roles and occupations. Prudence, for instance, is characteristic of leadership, whether by the father within the family or by the ruler within the state. These positions are typically male roles, since the Sun itself is, astrologically speaking, a masculine planet,[76] and accordingly all of the two dozen souls introduced in Dante's Solar heaven are males. They also exemplify the diversity of ways in which Solar qualities of mind can be rightly utilized in human society. Roughly speaking these functions can be divided into two categories: on the one hand, positions of authority, of which fatherhood with its attendant power is the type, and on the other, positions of service, typified by brotherhood in peer relations. In this section and the next we shall see how the Sun fits its children for these two kinds of tasks.

Fathers. Just as astrologers generally assimilated mothers to the Moon, so they associated fathers with the Sun.[77] And conversely, as Haly put it, the Sun "is like fathers in his forms and actions."[78] Dante clearly makes the same connection, because he begins the Solar set of cantos with a reference to God the Father (*Par.* 10.1–3), who a little later is said to be the "alto Padre" of the family of Solar souls, as of all others in Paradise (10.50), and still later is referred to as "our Sire" (13.54). But physical fatherhood is also commemorated in these cantos, for the narrator thinks that all the souls in the Sun seem to be hoping for eventual reunion with their earthly fathers (14.16), and Adam, the common ancestor of mankind, is called the "primo padre" (13.111). Thus in the eulogies of Francis and Dominic, the fathers of both saints are given prominence (11.59, 63; 12.79), but in each case we are told that the saint himself became a father in a third, spiritual sense, which is neither divine nor physical: Dominic is "nostro patrïarca" (11.121) and Francis "quel padre e quel maestro" (11.85). This third form of fatherhood, of course, is the most pervasive of all in these cantos, for many of the souls in this heaven are Fathers of the Church.

Rulers. The Sun is the "governor of the world," Haly says, and "a planet of great lordship."[79] It controls the planets by providing their light, and hence is their ruler; it is located in their midst, with three planets below the Sun and three above, in order to maximize the distribution of sunlight. Thus, Haly explains, the Sun is "like a wise king (*rex sapiens*) who maintains his rule by keeping himself well informed and who in order to do so places his capital in the center of his kingdom."[80] Consequently, the Sun signifies "rule and headship (*regimen et principatum*)."[81] This, indeed, is the primary astrological meaning of the Sun when combined with the other planets or with the zodiacal signs. For example, when the Sun is joined with Venus, the combination signifies the *rule* of women or courtiers; again, with Mercury, the advisers of the ruler.[82] The astrologers go on to specify the different kinds of rulers, such as emperors and kings, that the Sun signifies, and we shall examine each of them in turn, but before turning to these specific types, we may note that in several ways Dante also made reference to rulership *in genere.* Just as the Sun is the chief planet ("princeps omnium planetarum," says Scot),[83] so Francis and Dominic are said to be two "chiefs (*principi*)" (*Par.* 11.35). Another and more striking reference to monarchy in general is Dante's use of the crown, the generic sign of rulership, which he adopts as his visual symbol of the Sun. The souls in its heaven appear to the Pilgrim in the form of a ring, which is described as a *corona* (10.65), and we can be sure that this refers to a jeweled diadem because it is compared to the crown of Ariadne (13.14), which was so described by Ovid (*Metamorphoses* 8.177–182).

Ranking highest among rulers in Dante's estimation was, of course, the emperor, and Scot assures us that this office is signified by the Sun.[84] Dante does not make this an occasion to display his devotion to the Holy Roman Empire, however; the only emperor so called in the heaven of the Sun is God himself: "lo 'mperador che sempre regna" (*Par.* 12.40). Earthly empire appears nonetheless, but disguised, as it were, in a reference to Julius Caesar as he appeared incognito to hire a dingy from the poor fisherman Amyclas (11.67–69). Since elsewhere Dante indicates that he considered Caesar to be the first emperor,[85] this, too, must be accounted a reference to emperorship, but by making it obscure Dante once again places his stress on the spiritual rather than the material sense of his Solar allusions.

Kings. The commonplace example of Solar rulership, both for Dante

and his astrological sources, was not the emperor but rather kings (*reges*).
For John of Seville, the Sun is the "star of kings"; similarly, Albumasar,
Ibn Ezra, Scot, Bonatti, and the *Liber novem iudicum* all list kings among
the great officers governed by the Sun.[86] Dante distributes his references
to kingship much as he did those to fatherhood: they range from literal
kings on earth through kings in a spiritual sense to culminate in the kingdom of heaven. At the bottom of the scale are those who "reign through
force" (*Par.* 11.6), and the assertion that although there are many kings,
the good ones are rare (13.108). The kingdom of Castile is mentioned as
the place of Dominic's birth, being identified by its arms on which "the
lion is subject and sovereign" (12.54). Dante is also careful to bring out the
royal connotations inherent in the Latin name of Saint Bonaventure's
birthplace, *Balneum Regis*, "King's Bath," by using the Latinate form
"Bagnoregio" (12.128) rather than the then current form, "Bagnorea."
Saint Francis is the type of a higher, spiritual kingship, for though of
ignoble birth, when he approaches Pope Innocent III to secure approval
for his new order, he does so "royally (*regalmente*)" (11.91). His kingdom, however, is not of this world, for when Francis dies he goes "al suo
regno" (11.116). There, of course, it is God who "reigns" (14.30), with the
blessed as his "court" and Paradise as his "kingdom" (10.70, 72). These
passing references to kingship are dwarfed, however, by the figure of King
Solomon, the "most beautiful" of the souls in the Sun (10.109); his virtue
of "regal prudence" is the subject of Aquinas's second discourse (esp.
13.94–108). As if this were not enough, Dante further exalts the kingship
of Solomon in his continuing series of astro-climatic allusions.

Geography and kingship. In the two preceding heavens we have seen
that Dante made extensive use of the correlations between planets and
climates. Ibn Ezra, apparently his authority for these correspondences, assigns the Sun the next climate to the south: "Among the climates, his is
the fourth, for example the land of Babylon . . . and Israel."[87] Albumasar,
who up to now has not connected the planets with climatic zones, makes
an exception in the case of the Sun, to which he assigns "the middle habitable zone."[88] Since Ptolemy's seven *climata* were by definition longitu-
dinal belts or zones that were habitable, of which the midmost would be
the fourth, Albumasar is following the same system that Ibn Ezra uses.
Perhaps there are faint reflections of the same system in Scot and Bonatti
as well, for both mention the "sultan of Babylon" in connection with the
Sun. Scot says that the Sun signifies "fathers and magnates, such as the
pope, the emperor, kings, and other barons, such as the sultan of Babylon,

etc.,"⁸⁹ but the climate plays no part in this association, since Scot also says that the Sun controls "Saracens, all Indians and Ethiopians," the last named of which belong, not to the fourth, but to the first and southernmost of the climates.⁹⁰ Bonatti, too, assigns countries to the Sun without reference to climata, and in another connection he asserts without explanation that "the king of Babylon" is signified by the Sun *naturaliter*.⁹¹

A sultan does indeed appear in the cantos of the Sun, but the Babylon over which he rules is the one in Egypt, where Saint Francis preached the Gospel "in the proud presence of the Sultan (*Soldan*)" (*Par.* 11.101). To verify the accuracy of the reference in terms of climata, we must again turn to Alcoarismi (al-Khwârismî), who gives the boundaries of the fourth climate as 36° and 30° 22′ north latitude,⁹² and to the positions appended to the *Marseilles Tables*, which include one city in Lower Egypt, the scene of Francis's mission, namely Alexandria at 31° north latitude, well within the fourth climate.⁹³ To this minor reference we can add another, more important one, for Ibn Ezra quite correctly placed Israel in the fourth climate, the latitude given for Jerusalem in the *Marseilles Tables* being 32°.⁹⁴ Hence it is fitting that two of the souls in the heaven of the Sun are associated with Jerusalem and Israel: the prophet Nathan in the outer circle (12.136) and in the inner one, King Solomon, a major figure to whom some 108 lines are devoted, including his own speech (10.109–114, 11.34–111, 14.37–60). If this were an isolated instance, the correspondence might well be ascribed to coincidence, but the author shows it is part of his plan by making such climatic allusions according to a fixed pattern that now emerges. Romeo, Justinian, Carlo Martello, and the Sultan have all proved to be climatically appropriate; they are a diverse group, but one thing they all have in common—all have been *rulers* of the areas in question. Since it is the kingship of Solomon that Dante stresses—his "regal prudence" (13.104)—Solomon, too, fits into this pattern, and indeed he must be said to constitute its culmination, both because he is Dante's type of the good king and because his kingdom stands not only in the midmost climate but also at the geographical center of Dante's world.

Solar warfare. "The Sun is the most powerful planet of all for signifying and influencing both good and bad, both peace and war."⁹⁵ Thus Michael Scot brings out a perhaps unexpected association between the Sun and war, which Dante nonetheless maintains in the heaven of the Sun. As we have learned to expect by now, this appears in a spiritualized form. Francis and Dominic "warred (*militaro*) for one same end" (*Par.* 12.35); they fight in the service of God, the generalissimo (*imperator*) of "Christ's army," which they are sent to rally as its champions (37–45); they are the two wheels "of the chariot in which Holy Church defended herself and on the battlefield overcame her civil strife" (106–108). To sum up all these military metaphors, Bonaventure alludes to Dominic as "cotanto paladino" (142), which suggests that he was a count palatine of God's empire, a knight-errant or champion, and a hero of the caliber of Roland and his peers at Charlemagne's court in medieval romance—we need not decide which meaning Dante had in mind, for in any case the image is a military one.

All this might seem astrologically more appropriate to Mars than to the Sun unless we read our astrologers with some care. Each planet plays its part in warfare, and the respective roles are best grasped from their significance in conjunction. "If Mars is joined to the Sun," Alcabitius writes, "it signifies leadership of an army (*ducatum exercitus*) and investigation into wars."[96] Thus it appears that in a military context, the Sun stands for those who exercise command, just as it signifies rulership or leadership in general.[97] This, in fact, is the precise function that Dante assigns to Francis and "l'altro duca" (*Par.* 12.32), namely Dominic. The Sun gives one intellectual mastery of warfare, either as a practical strategist or as a theoretical student of military science ("investigationem bellorum").[98] It is concerned with warfare as an object of knowledge, and it is in this cognitive sense that Scot is speaking when he assures us that the Sun "makes war known (*notificat guerram*)."[99]

The Sun also supplies war-related images, for astrologers assign to it a variety of projectile weapons, including arrows, darts, javelins, lances, and spears, all reminiscent of the powerful rays that the Sun projects.[100] Accordingly, Dante introduces two such weapons into the Solar cantos: at the Crucifixion, Christ's side was "pierced by the lance (*lancia*)" (*Par.* 13.40), as Dante has Aquinas note gratuitously, and later Thomas compares his own intention to an arrow or dart ("stral," 105).

Spiritual rulers. We have seen that Dante presented a scale in Solar rulership, ranging from the divine through spiritual self-mastery down to the actual exercise of material power by earthly emperors and kings. But alongside the civil hierarchy of rulers he also recognized an ecclesiastical one that we would expect would also be reflected in this heaven because elsewhere in the *Comedy* he compared its head, the pope, to the Sun itself: "Rome, which made the world good, was wont to have two Suns, which made visible both the one road and the other, that of the world and that of God" (*Purg.* 16.106–108). Few of Dante's astrological sources, however, justified the inclusion of ecclesiastical prelates among the rulers signified by the Sun. His Moslem authorities did not of course mention the Christian hierarchy, and they did not provide a corresponding list of Moslem religious leaders because in Islam the caliph united both temporal and spiritual authority in a single office. Since the Arabic tradition was ambiguous on this point, Christian astrologers were left to decide whether the leaders of their religion fell under the Sun's influence or not. Bonatti decided to exclude them, limiting Solar rulership to "lay dignities,"[101] while Scot expressly named the pope along with the emperor as instances of the "fathers and magnates" signified by the Sun.[102] This was especially true when, as was the case at this point in the *Comedy*, the influence of the Sun was joined with that of Jupiter, which signified "headship of the faith, such as a great prelacy or an election, e.g., of a cardinal to be pope."[103]

In Scot, Dante found the astrological authority he needed to bring the hierarchy of the Church under the influence of the Sun, and thus authorized he made this heaven reflect a wide spectrum of spiritual fathers. At the summit of the hierarchy, the papacy is represented by references both to the office and to individuals who filled it, most probably by design, since Dante reminds the reader that the papal office must be distinguished from its incumbents: the attitude of Peter's see ("sedia," *Par.* 12.88) has changed "not in itself, but in him who sits on it and deviates" (89–90). The pope authorizes Dominic's "officio apostolico" (98), and the parallel passage in the life of Francis has him likewise secure approval of his order, first from Pope Innocent III and later from Honorius III (11.92, 98). A third pope, John XXI, appears in his private capacity as Peter of Spain (12.134), and three other persons appear in these cantos who are named after Saint Peter, the first pope: Peter Lombard (10.107), Peter Bernadone (11.89), and Peter Mangiadore, or Comestor (12.134). Another papal name is borne by the Franciscan Silvester (11.83), whose pursuit of poverty contrasts with Pope Silvester, "il primo ricco patre" of *Inferno* 19.117.

Next after the pope in the ecclesiastical hierarchy are the cardinals of the Roman Church, at least three of whom are included in these cantos: one explicitly, since Henry of Susa, cardinal-bishop of Ostia, is referred to by his curial title ("Ostïense," *Par.* 12.83), and two others only implicitly, namely Bonaventure (127) and Matthew of Acquasparta (124).[104] Below the cardinals we have archbishops represented in the "metropolitano Crisostomo" (11.137–138) and Isidore of Seville (10.131) and bishops in Albertus Magnus (10.98) and Peter Lombard (10.106–108), as well as another bishop implicitly presiding over the "spiritual court" where Francis was united with Poverty (11.61–63), while the lowest level of the hierarchy is reached with an allusion to "priesthood" in general ("sacerdozio," 11.5), exemplified by the smallest light of Orosius (10.118–120). Two other ecclesiastical titles are applied metaphorically to Saint Francis, who is said to be his order's "patriarch" (11.121) and "archimandrita," or "chief shepherd," a Greek title that in Latin is most often used as a synonym of *abbas*, "abbot." Both might equally well be applied to Joachim, "il calavrese abate" (12.140), who founded the order of Fiore. Spiritual fatherhood is especially indicated here at the summit of the hierarchy, since *abbas* originally meant "father."[105]

Brothers and Servants

The heraldic lion that Dante characterizes as being both "subject and sovereign" ("soggiace il leone e soggioga," *Par.* 12.54) may be taken as an emblem of the Solar occupations, for the lion signifies the Sun in astrology,[106] and that planet itself exercises influence not only over those in positions of authority, as we have just seen, but also over those who are subordinate to authority and serve as its subjects.

Brotherhood. Just as fathers are the prototype of the former, so brothers are of the latter.[107] According to Bonatti, the Solar man will love his father and brothers above all else until his familial role is altered and he himself becomes the father of sons.[108] It is not blood brotherhood, however, that Dante celebrates in the cantos of the Sun but rather religious brotherhood, and particularly mendicant *fratres*, or friars, whose founders and leading theologians are, with Solomon, the most prominent persons in this heaven. Brotherhood was, of course, a major theme for both the Franciscan and Dominican orders, whose members were styled "brothers" (*fra*, or friar, from *frater*) and who so addressed all men save those placed in authority: "fra Tommaso," spoken by Bonaventure (12.144), illustrates both usages. For the most part Dante seems to take this mendicant fraternalism for granted, though as if to place the point beyond doubt, he applies the term *fratre* to at least one member of each order: Albertus is Aquinas's "brother" (10.97) and Francis commends Poverty to all of his "brothers" (11.112).

The spirit of brotherhood that the Mendicants exemplify is not, for Dante, limited to their orders alone; instead, a broader extent is defined by the twenty-four souls in this heaven, who display a variety of monastic affiliations: three Benedictines (Bede, Anselm, and Rabanus: 10.131, 12.137, 139), three canons regular, all from Saint-Victor (Richard, Hugh, and Peter Comestor: 10.131, 12.133–134); a Camaldolese (Gratian: 10.104), and a Cistercian who also founded his own order of Fiore (Joachim: 12.140–141). This is not an exhaustive list of medieval monastic orders, of course, but the assortment is sufficiently various to suggest that any kind of religious brotherhood, and not merely the Mendicants, comes under Solar influence. The astrologers confirm this impression, for Ibn Ezra says that the human impulse to join together into communities ("communitatis coniunctio") comes from the Sun,[109] and Scot defines that impulse as the tendency "to bear sweet love towards neighbors and friends."[110] It is in accordance with this Solar inclination to form associations with those who are near and dear that Bonaventure terms the souls in his circle a "company (*compagnia*)" (12.145). By the same token we can gather that in heaven the old earthly associations have been transcended, for these Solar souls have formed themselves into new orders that include elements of the old—the Franciscans being in one *compagnia* and the Dominicans in the other—but also other souls of similar temperament.

Service. The good will that leads the Solarian to associate with his fellow men also impels him to serve them. Scot, claiming that the *Solaris* "is more useful to others than they to him," especially elaborates on this tendency:

> When he can serve another, he does so with a good will, even if when invited to serve he realizes that he will be ill rewarded if he serves, so it is said that he wastes many services that he performs to the advantage of another and in good faith.[111]

Such willingness to help others is abundantly evidenced by the books written by all but three of the Solar *sapienti* (the exceptions are the prophet Nathan and the early Franciscans Illuminato and Augustine). The element of service is most strongly stressed in the case of Donatus, who wrote an elementary Latin grammar rather than the more learned works that he might have written instead (*Par.* 12.136–137),[112] but Gratian's contribution to canon law is also represented as a service rendered: he "served (*aiutò*) the one forum and the other so well that it pleases in Paradise" (10.104–105). Authorship, however, is not the only means of placing one's talents at the disposal of others. Nathan did it through prophesying, Bonaventure by putting spiritual concerns before material ones in his administrative duties ("grandi offici," 12.128) as minister-general of the Franciscans and as cardinal, and Dominic by undertaking the "apostolic duty (*officio apostolico*)" (12.98) of preaching the Gospel. Indeed, each of the Solar souls devoted himself to God's service in one way or another, and in so doing was in a lesser way imitating the example of the Sun, which Dante, doubt-less echoing the astrological tradition, called "the greatest minister (*ministro*) of nature" (10.28).

Bona cultura. Such service is in accord with the Solar character, which in a religious context expresses itself through activities that promote good.[113] How well this broad category fits the diverse ministries of Dante's Solar souls appears from the illustrations supplied by Michael Scot:

> In matters of religious faith, the Sun signifies attention to good activity, such as legality, truth, the study of uncontroversial doctrine, praiseworthy mod-esty, magnanimity, and by being humble he enables himself to correct sub-jects easily.[114]

All of Dante's Solarians pursued truth, most of them in the form of Chris-tian doctrine, and a few with a marked attachment to law as well, such as Solomon, Isidore, Gratian, Donatus, and perhaps even Orosius, "quello avvocato de' tempi cristiani" (*Par.* 10.119). Probably some trace of modesty, magnanimity, or humility could be discovered in the life of each of the twenty-four, but these qualities are already sufficiently evident in the speeches of the major characters. The Mendicants, who on earth were prone to praise their own order at the expense of its competitor, now appear magnanimous in praising the other's founder and humble in ad-mitting their own order's latter-day faults. All these Solar souls were fa-mous in their way and deserving of praise, as the astrologers say they ought to be, for the Sun does signify fame and praise.[115] This indeed is what they receive in this heaven, for when Aquinas is presenting his circle to the Pilgrim, he describes his introductions as "my praises (*le mie lode*)" (10.122). But the greater part of the praise in this heaven is reserved for God himself, whose praises are twice said to have been sung by the assem-bled souls (13.25–27 and 14.23–33) and who may have been the unstated subject of their earlier songs as well (10.64–81, 139–148; 12.6). By referring their glory to God, who made possible their achievements, these Solarians are of course displaying true humility. And a model for this virtue is pro-vided by Saint Francis, whose principal merit consisted "in making himself humble (*pusillo*)" (11.111). This, the poet makes plain, was not a matter of the saint's humble birth, for neither that nor being despised troubled him; instead, Francis chose to be humble by pursuing Poverty, and his choice is symbolized by the sign of his order, "the humble (*umile*) cord" (11.87). The exception might seem to be Solomon, famous on earth for his glory and in heaven the most beautiful light of his circle (10.109; 14.34–35); but any suspicion of pride is allayed by Thomas's elaborate reminder that Solomon owed his wisdom on earth to his humility (91–96, with an implicit reference to 3 Reg. 3.11), which virtue he still possesses in heaven, where he speaks with "a modest voice (*una voce modesta*)" (14.35).

Medicine and law. The souls in the Solar heaven, then, show the many ways in which the love of God can combine with the love of wisdom in a career of service or ministry. In contrast to their examples of right conduct, the poet twice offers us counter examples of the improper use of knowledge. The first is a long list of human goals that do not lead to heaven, at the head of which stands the study of law and medicine: "One was following after the law (*iura*), another after the *Aphorisms* [of Hippocrates]" (*Par.* 11.4–5). The second example singles out only law and medicine to typify studies that are pursued, not for love of true wisdom, but for love of the world: men labor to master the canonistic commentaries of Hostiensis and the medical ones of Taddeo d'Alderotto (13.82–85). Dante insists on these two studies because the astrologers associate both of them with the Sun. We have already seen that Scot considered *legalitas* to be a typical concern of the religious Solar man, but other astrologers assign laws (*leges*) in general to the Sun.[116] Thus broadly defined, *lex* would include all the general principles that are the object of knowledge, such as the laws of nature that are the basis of *physica*, the science on which the physician bases his art; but, lest there be any doubt, among things signified by the Sun one astrologer listed both medical men and law.[117]

Dante, by his references to the *Aphorisms* of Hippocrates and to the medical commentaries of Taddeo d'Alderotto, obviously also considered physicians to be appropriate to the Sun. This raises a problem because, although he gives examples of both good and bad lawyers, he does not seem to include a good physician among the *spiriti sapienti*. The answer is simply that Dante's good doctor of medicine has not been recognized for what he is. He can be found in the greater circle of souls, which contains "Peter of Spain, who down below shines in twelve books."

> Pietro Spano,
> lo qual giù luce in dodici libelli.   (*Par.* 12.134–135)

Without doubt the twelve books are those of his treatise on logic, the *Tractatus* or *Summulae logicales*.[118] But Thomas, here our infallible informant, states that these books add luster to their author's name back on earth, leaving us to wonder what is the cause of his glory in heaven. The most plausible answer would seem to be another work, for which he was equally famous, namely a compilation of medical cures entitled the *Thesaurus pauperum*.[119] This book he complied, as the title indicates, for the benefit of the poor, though at the time he wrote (1272–76), he himself was far removed from them, being personal physician to Pope Gregory X and, since 1273, a cardinal as well.[120] Thus, at the pinnacle of his profession he performed an act of charity that stands in sharp contrast to the avid pursuit of gain that Dante complained was all too often characteristic of physicians.[121] Moreover, the spirit in which the work was composed is attested in a brief preface, which has no counterpart in his *Summulae logicales*:

> In the name of the holy and indivisible Trinity, who created all things, who endowed them all with their proper virtues, by whom all wisdom is given to the wise and knowledge to those who know, I am undertaking a work that is beyond my abilities because I trust that He will aid me who performs all our good works through us as through an instrument. Therefore I dedicate this work, which is named the *Treasure of the Poor*, to Him who is called "the father of the poor" [Job 29.16]. If this work be read attentively, in it will be found a means of healing almost every illness that will be effective and easy if the physician works in cooperation with Him who created medicine from earth [John 9.6].[122]

Here Peter of Spain displays all the virtues Michael Scot attributed to the Solar man in the good activities that are the characteristic form of his religious self-expression. The very conception of the work is magnanimous, since without thought of personal gain it gives the treasures of the medical art to those who need it. Furthermore, Peter is modest about his own abilities and even the efficacy of his prescriptions; above all, he is humble, ascribing all wisdom and knowledge to God, to whom he dedicates his work and commends those who would use it rightly. Truly this must be the work for which he shines in the heaven of the Sun, for it epitomizes the Solar virtues that Dante borrowed from the astrologers and made the criteria for his *spiriti sapienti*.

The Masters of Salvation

Each planet confers mastery (*magisterium*) in certain arts and sciences—Venus, for example, in the making of jewelry, or Mars in armaments—and the one proper to the Sun, according to Scot, is the salvation of the soul (*salus animae*).[123] Naturally the souls whom the Pilgrim met on other planets knew how to attain salvation for themselves, but the ones on the Sun also knew how to teach that art to others. Most of them are authorities in some branch of knowledge that contributes to human salvation, and generally it is as authors of authoritative works that they convey their knowledge to others. Not necessarily so, however, for a Solar *magisterium* can also be the personal relationship of teacher to student, as in the case of Albertus Magnus, who Thomas says "was my brother and my master (*maestro*)" (*Par.* 10.98). Or, transcending the world of learning, it can be a spiritual *magisterium* such as Saint Francis, "quel padre e quel maestro" (11.85), exercised over his disciples. Both academic and spiritual mastery are comprehended in the general formulation of Albumasar, who declared that the office of *magister* was proper to the Sun.[124]

Alta ac magnifica. Although Scot is the only astrologer who mentions the art of salvation in so many words, others associate the Sun with equivalent conditions, such as perfection, honor and reward, joy and happiness, all of which are also reflected in Dante's heaven of the Sun. The fundamental idea is that the Sun brings success or victory,[125] which as often as not the astrologers interpret in worldly terms. Thus Scot writes:

> This planet always allows everyone to have high and magnificent things (*alta ac magnifica*), such as wealth, merit, and honor. Hence it causes anyone to be happy (*beatum*) in his life unless its influence be disturbed by that of other planets, e.g., Saturn or Mars.[126]

Elsewhere, as we have already noted, Scot offers a higher view of beatitude as the "health of the soul," so he exemplifies the astrologers' ambivalence about happiness, which they sometimes take to be in this life, sometimes in the next. Dante himself certainly shared this view that man has a twofold beatitude: it forms the conclusion of his *Monarchia* (3.15.3–8) and is one of the most original features of his philosophy.[127] In the heaven of the Sun, however, it is the otherworldly beatitude that he stresses, just as he regularly emphasized the spiritual aspect of the other Solarian influences. Let us now see what use he made of those astrological indications that are related to salvation.

Alcabitius and Bonatti agree that the Sun signifies perfection.[128] Likewise Dante twice makes human perfection a major issue in the heaven of the Sun: first, when he contrasts the natural "perfezion" of Christ and Adam (*Par.* 13.81, 83) with the infused wisdom of Solomon; and again, when it is explained that the blessed will eventually be reunited with their bodies in order to make them more perfect (14.41–45).[129]

Honor and glory are two other analogues of beatitude that astrologers attributed to the Sun's influence. Albumasar, for example, associated moral rectitude (*honestas*) with the Sun; Alcabitius added that the Solar man would also have those qualities of soul that *honestas* entails, namely munificence and glory,[130] while the *Liber novem iudicum* states that the Sun signifies *gloria* for kings.[131] Honor enters into Dante's heaven of the Sun only as a passing allusion to Pope Honorius (11.98), doubtless because the poet wished to stress human humility instead, chiefly reserving honor, like praise, for God (see above, after n. 115). Glory, however, he attributes to his Solar souls, both now and after the Resurrection. The circle of souls is "la gloriosa rota" (10.145); one of them is "the glorious life of Thomas" (14.6); and after the Resurrection their flesh will be "gloriosa et santa" (14.43).

Finally, joy (*gaudium*) and gladness (*laetitia*) are astral properties of the Sun,[132] as well as of certain other planets, notably Venus. Dante's Solarians manifest this through their harmonious dancing and singing, for we are told that "the holy circles showed new joy (*gioia*) in their revolving and in their marvelous melody" (*Par.* 14.23–24, cf. 13.30), which is compared to the "letizia" of singing circle dancers (14.19).[133]

The Trinity and the Sun

Dante devoted more space to the heaven of the Sun than to any of the other planetary heavens, and so it is not surprising to find it is correspondingly richer in astrological allusions, but the number and diversity of these Solar influences may easily obscure the conceptual unity that underlies them. Dante associates the Sun with such a wide range of creatures because for him the Sun is an image of God himself, or to be more precise, of the Trinity.

The terms of this correspondence are abundantly displayed in the cantos of the Sun, where the Trinity is described three times, each time stressing the function of another of its persons. The cantos open with the narrator's affirmation of God's ordaining power, in which all three persons of the Trinity participate, although, according to Aquinas, it is most properly referred to the Father.[134]

Guardando nel suo Figlio con l'Amore
  che l'uno e l'altro etternalmente spira,
  lo primo e ineffabile Valore
quanto per mente e per loco si gira
  con tant' ordine fé. . . .   (*Par.* 10.1–5)

Looking upon His Son with the love which the One and the Other
eternally breathe forth, the primal and ineffable Power made
everything that revolves through the mind or through space. . . .

In this first Trinitarian passage, the three persons are readily identified
(*Valore, Figlio, Amore*), and the stress is put on the first by making it the
grammatical subject; in the second passage, spoken by the soul of Aquinas,
the role of the Son is emphasized, and moreover his relations to the Father
are represented in terms of light imagery.

Ciò che non more e ciò che può morire
  non è se non splendor di quella idea
  che partorisce, amando, il nostro Sire;
ché quella viva luce che sì mea
  dal suo lucente, che non si disuna
  da lui né da l'amore ch'a lor s'intrea,
per sua bontate il suo raggiare aduna. . . .   (*Par.* 13.52–58)

That which dies not and that which can die are naught but the
splendor of that Idea which in His love our Sire begets; for that
living light which so streams from its Lucent Source that It is not
disunited from It, nor from the Love which is intrined with
them. . . .

In the first tercet, the three persons are easily recognized: "il nostro Sire"
as the Father, who begets his son, the Logos ("quella idea"), in the Holy
Spirit of love ("amando"). All creatures, we are told, are the "splendor" of
the Son, who is accordingly the person on whom the stress here falls. The
second tercet explains how the other members of the Trinity contribute to
the creative process: the Father is the source ("lucente") of "that living
light (*quella viva luce*)" that is the Son, while both are joined by the Holy

Spirit ("l'amor ch'a lor s'intrea"). Although the subsequent account of creation is no doubt based on the speculative metaphysics of light that was the most prominent Neoplatonic element in thirteenth-century Scholastic thought,[135] the luminal roles ascribed to the Trinity are firmly based in traditional Christian doctrine, for the Nicene Creed describes the Son as the "light from light" ("lumen de lumine"). This in turn serves to clarify the third, much disputed, Trinitarian passage, which occurs later in the same speech.

> Però se 'l caldo amor <e> [136] la chiara vista
>   de la prima virtù dispone e segna,
>   tutta la perfezion quivi s'acquista.   (*Par.* 13.79–81)

> Yet, if the fervent Love <and> the clear Vision from the primal
> Power disposes and imprints, complete perfection is there acquired.

Now the role of the Holy Spirit ("'l caldo amor") is the one emphasized, by listing it in first place, while the Son, who had previously been described as "Idea" and "living Light," appears here as "the clear Vision," which in accordance with the Nicene formula is said to be derived from ("de") the Father, "la prima virtù" (cf. "lo primo . . . Valore," 10.3).

Thus in three passages the Trinity is described in four different ways, and what is more, the three persons are presented in each case as participants in the creative process. Thus the *Valore* that is the Father "made everything that revolves through the mind or through space with such order" (*Par.* 10.4–5); all creatures can be called the "splendor" of the Idea that is the Son because they are produced by the angelic intelligences on which the ray ("il suo raggiare") of the Son's "viva luce" is concentrated by reflection, as it were, since it remains itself eternally united with the other two persons (13.58–60). Finally, in the direct creation of Adam and Christ, the "fervent love" of the Holy Spirit, acting together with the other two persons, produced "perfezion" (13.81). Consequently these Trinitarian tercets present the creative process in three successive aspects, showing how each person contributes to the process in relation to the other two. What is important for our present purpose are the various terms that Dante applies to the several persons and the result of their interaction. These terms may be conveniently summarized in tabular form. These same terms recur in the last canto of the Solar set, but there they serve to explain

Paradiso	Father	Son	Spirit	Result
10.1–3	primo . . . Valore	Figlio	Amore	quanto . . . fè
13.52–54	nostro Sire	Idea	amando	splendor
13.55–58	il suo lucente	viva luce	Amor	il suo raggiare
13.79–81	prima virtù	chiara vista	caldo amor	perfezion

how the light of glory is produced by blessed souls rather than how God produces his effects. In this passage, Solomon first explains the general rule, which is true both before and after souls are united with their bodies:

> Quanto fia lunga la festa
> di paradiso, tanto il nostro amore
> si raggerà dintorno cotal vesta.
> La sua chiarezza séguita l'ardore;
> l'ardor la vïsione, e quella è tanta,
> quant' ha di grazia sovra suo valore.   (*Par.* 14.37–42)

As long as the feast of Paradise shall be, so long shall our love radiate around us such a garment. Its brightness follows our ardor, the ardor our vision, and that is in the measure which each has of grace beyond his merit.

Here the order recedes from effect to cause, from "the light wherewith your substance blooms" (14.13–14), the garment whose brightness is radiated by their ardent love, which in turn is produced by their vision, the extent of which is finally determined by the amount of grace each soul receives beyond its own merit ("valore"). Having explained how the light of glory is produced in general, Solomon proceeds to explain how it will be increased when the souls are reunited with their flesh. Because they will then be complete, they will be more pleasing ("più grata," 45):

per che s'accrescerà ciò che ne dona
   di gratüito lume il sommo bene,
   lume ch'a lui veder ne condiziona;
onde la visïon crescer convene,
   crescer l'ardor che di quella s'accende,
   crescer lo raggio che da esso vene.   (*Par.* 14.46–51)

wherefore whatever of gratuitous light the Supreme Good gives us
will be increased, light which fits us to see Him; so that our vision
needs must increase, our ardor increase which by that is kindled, our
radiance increase which comes from this.

In this second statement, the soul's "grace beyond its merit" appears as a
"gift of gratuitous light," which enhances its "vision," and this intensifies
love's heat ("ardor"), which in consequence emits a ray ("lo raggio") that
is more brilliant than before. How closely this process parallels the earlier
descriptions of creative emanation from the Trinity can best be shown by
adding two more entries to the table given above. Clearly man, when in
the state of beatitude, is truly an image of God. Just as the Father is the
source of light ("lucente") that makes possible the Son's "clear vision," so
beatified man receives illuminating grace that increases his vision; similarly, his ardor corresponds to the love of the Holy Spirit, and finally the
result is externalized as a radiance or splendor.

Paradiso	*Father*	*Son*	*Spirit*	*Result*
14.37–42	grazia sovra suo valore	visïone	ardor(e)	chiarezza
14.46–51	dona di gratüito lume	visïon	ardor	lo raggio che da esso vene

How does this all relate to the heaven of the Sun? Dante's reader who
has observed these correspondences in the text may well wonder why they
are given such prominence in this particular heaven. Here astrology can
provide the connection. The Trinity and its reflection in man are most
appropriately displayed in the heaven of the Sun because that planet, ac-

cording to Michael Scot, "makes deity known (*notificat deitatem*)."[137] Scot
does not explain how the Sun does this, but Dante's threefold analysis of
the Trinity places all the essential points of comparison at the reader's
disposal, so the analogies are readily apparent. The Sun is like God the
Father, the source from which not only the "living light" of the Son proceeds (cf. "lucente," 13.56), but also the "hot Love" ("caldo Amore," 13.79)
of the Holy Spirit, inasmuch as the Sun has the power to produce both
light and heat. This power, which corresponds to the Father's *virtù* or
valore (10.3, 14.80), is its essence or nature, while the light and heat produced by this Solar power are analogous respectively to the Son and the
Holy Spirit. Moreover, these three aspects of the Sun form a unity, for
considered in itself the Sun has both light and heat and the power to
produce them both. Finally, the Sun's power to heat and to illuminate
emanates from it as a splendor or ray, just as the power, light, and love of
God are concentrated in a single ray that is reflected in the nine heavens
(13.58–60). Thus the Sun so closely resembles God that it in itself can be
rightly said to "make known deity."

The Sun makes deity known not only in itself but also in humanity,
for it is the astrological influence of the Sun that normally determines how
much a person will resemble the Trinity. In the afterlife, as we have seen,
beatified souls have their natural powers enhanced by gratuitous light that
is conferred on them directly by God, and this increases their vision, their
ardor, and ultimately their visible glory. This supernatural process is paralleled, however, by the natural one that precedes it, in which the Sun
plays a crucial role. In the natural process of embryological development,
a human being comes into existence "as soon as the articulation of the
brain in the fetus is perfect" (*Purg.* 25.68–69); then the brain receives the
ability to think from God directly ("sanza mezzo," *Par.* 7.142). It is this
gift of intelligence that turns the fetus into an animal that is rational, and
thus into a human being, since by Aristotelian definition man *is* a rational
animal. Of course, people are not all equal in intelligence, but this is not
the fault of God, who confers the same potentialities on every human soul.
Souls differ in intelligence because they differed in their capacity to receive
and develop God's gift, and this capacity was in turn determined by three
factors: the disposition of the father, the complexion of his seed, and the

> When the human seed falls into its receptacle, the womb, it brings with it a
> threefold power: that of the generating soul, that of the heavens, and that of
> the elements of which the seed is comprised, that is, of its own constitution.

> It matures and disposes the matter to receive the formative power, which is given by the soul of the male parent. The formative power prepares the organs to receive the power of the heavens, which brings the soul into life from the potency latent in the seed. As soon as this is brought into being, it receives the potential intellect from the power of the Mover of the Heavens. . . . Since the constitution of the seed can be better or less good, and the disposition of the man who generates the seed can be better or less good, and the disposition of the heavens to bring this effect into being can be good, better or best (depending on the constellations, which are in a constant state of change), it comes about that the soul which is brought into being from this seed and from these powers is of greater or less purity. Correspondingly, it is in proportion to the soul's purity that the power called the potential intellect spoken of above descends into the soul, in the manner stated above. (*Conv.* 4.21.4–5, 7)[138]

configuration of the planets at the moment of conception (*Conv.* 4.21.7). In other words, these three factors determine how much of deity ("dei-tade") will descend into the soul. Although some think that under optimal circumstances the result would be "almost another God incarnate" (*Conv.* 4.21.10), Dante has Thomas assure us that nature will never be quite perfect (*Par.* 13.76–78). Only when God himself performs the function of these natural factors, directly disposing the matter as well as infusing the form, as was the case with both Adam and Christ, will the result be a person that is the perfect image of God (13.79–84). (Of course, a soul that is imperfect by reason of nature can be perfected subsequently by grace, as was the case with Solomon.) Nonetheless, insofar as anyone is intelligent, he is an image of God; to that extent it can be said that "deity" has descended into his soul.

Furthermore, man is an image of the Trinity, since the way in which he acquires and uses the light of natural reason is analogous to the Trinitarian light-vision-ardor sequence by which the light of glory is produced in man's beatified state (*Par.* 14.37–51).[139] Just as the beatified soul receives gratuitous light that is analogous to the *virtù* of God the Father, so the fetal brain receives "the possible intellectual virtue" (*Conv.* 4.21.7), which, when realized, results in the inner vision that is understanding or *intellectus*; this, in turn, gives rise to love, as when the mind assents to an attractive object (*Purg.* 18.25–27), so that all three persons of the Trinity are reflected in the human psychology of love.[140]

Therefore, the extent to which a given man resembles God depends in large part on the influence of the planets. And because the Sun is the planet that most resembles God, inasmuch as it has the power to produce both light and heat, it is reasonable to infer that the influence of the Sun, more than that of any other planet, disposes the fetal brain to receive the light of natural reason by making the matter of this transaction *similar* to the form it will receive. Thus the Sun is the factor that especially causes men to differ in their powers of heart and head. Because of the Sun, some men have greater prudence, and thus make better rulers, whether of families or of kingdoms, while other men have superior understanding in various different ways; yet other Solar men are distinguished for their ardor, being affected to serve their fellows with exceptional zeal. Whichever way, the Solar qualities of the Godhead are more evident in such men than in others, and hence they can, like the Sun, be said to "make deity known."

5. Mars

Astrologically speaking, the Martian cantos confront the reader with a paradox. On the one hand, the poet's use of astrology is more evident here than in the previous heavens, because the qualities popularly attributed to Mars are readily apparent. The medieval reader knew that the planet Mars governed warfare, and accordingly his expectations were fulfilled when he found that the souls displayed there are all famous warriors: Joshua and Judas Maccabaeus, Charlemagne and Roland, the legendary William of Orange and his sidekick Renouard, the crusader Godfrey of Bouillon, and Robert Guiscard, famous for his part in reconquering southern Italy from the Moslems (*Par.* 18.37–48). Cacciaguida, the principal character of the Martian cantos, clearly deserved his place among these warriors, for he was made a knight by Emperor Conrad III and died fighting against the Moslems on the Second Crusade (15.139–148). This military stress is reinforced by Cacciaguida's long list that celebrates the feudal nobility of Florence in his youth, circa 1100, contrasting it unfavorably with the non-military families that dominated Florentine society two centuries later (16.46–147).[1] Moreover, the reader should recognize that this emphasis on Florence is astrologically appropriate because, following the doctrine of signatures, which assigns each place on earth to the influence of a particular planet, Florence is ruled by Mars, its original patron (*Inf.* 13.143–150, *Par.* 16.47, 145–147). This Martian character not only disposed the Florentines to extend their boundaries by conquest but also made them prone to civil strife—both tendencies that Cacciaguida repeatedly deplores. Finally, to these military tendencies associated with Mars one can add its more general reputation among astrologers as "the lesser malefic," the bringer of misfortune, which makes this heaven the appropriate place for Dante to learn of his impending exile.

On the other hand, there is more to the heaven of Mars than strife, warfare, and misfortune. The warriors named in the heaven of Mars are not famous for fighting all comers; instead, what they have in common is warfare that was directed against the enemies of God. Cacciaguida, our extended example of a Martian soul, indeed seems little inclined to dwell on his military career, which he summarizes in a few vague phrases (*Par.* 15.141, 145–146) that omit the gory details that were the stock in trade of feudal epics and chivalric romances. Judged by his discourse, Cacciaguida is no stereotypical knight; indeed, his character as it is revealed in the three cantos in which he is the principal speaker appears to be more that of a man of peace than one of war. His interests, to judge from their relative prominence in his speeches, lie first with the family, then with the community, and last and least with the larger world of the Christian Empire. Family affection is uppermost in his exchange with the Pilgrim, for that is what brings them together. It is family life in general that he praises in his vignette of the Florence of his youth (15.97–129), and it is in terms of families rather than of individuals that he describes the more prominent Florentines of his day. Like Aristotle, he conceives the community to be a cluster of families, so that civic character is altered by the immigration of new families (16.46–72). His ideal Florence, then, is a community of families living together in peace and harmony. In this picture there is no place for partisan politics; instead, there is unswerving loyalty to the emperor, who nonetheless is a remote figure impinging on the Florentine scene only when the good of the Christian commonwealth is concerned. Knighthood for Cacciaguida came almost by accident; his lifelong role was that of paterfamilias, and it is in that capacity that he speaks to us in the *Commedia*.

The essentially nonaggressive character of Cacciaguida could be analyzed at yet greater length, but enough has been said to establish the paradox with which we began. This paradox is also evident in the Martian hymn with which the Pilgrim is greeted. Although he is impressed by the harmony and concord of the music (*Par.* 14.118–120), which are the very qualities that characterize Cacciaguida's Florence, still the only words of the song that he can understand are precisely those militant terms he would be expecting—"Arise" and "Conquer" (14.125). Thus the reader is warned that the true nature of Mars surpasses, but does not exclude, common preconceptions about the planet's influence.

How is this paradox to be explained? One possibility is that the nature of Mars was somehow muted on 14 April 1300. Normally it is the planet's nature to be immoderately hot and dry, which accounts for its violent effects; but Michael Scot assures us that these can become praiseworthy when this characteristic complexion is moderated.[2] There are various ways in which this moderating effect might be achieved. Haly, for example, says that Mars varies its effects according to the season, being like the Sun hottest and driest when it stands highest in the heaven during the summer.[3] But this explanation is of no help, because Haly goes on to explain that the difference is caused by the earth's wet and misty atmosphere, which cools and dampens Mars's rays more in the winter when the planet is low in the heaven,[4] so the effects of the planet differ on earth while its nature remains constant in heaven, where the Pilgrim observed it. The planet's nature might also be affected by the zodiacal sign through which it was passing, which could temper the extremely hot and dry complexion of Mars, but this explanation also is of no help in the present case, because in April 1300 Mars was in Aries, a fire sign that would reinforce, rather than temper, its nature and which was accordingly reckoned to be its natural place (*domus*), where it exercises lordship.[5] Yet another possibility is that the nature of Mars might be moderated by Venus if the two planets stood in a favorable relationship, or "benefic aspect" in astrological jargon.[6] But in fact, at the time of Dante's visit they stood in adjacent signs (see Appendix 2) and consequently were "dissociated," which is to say their relationship had no astrological significance. Even if this were not the case, the occasional tempering of Mars's nature by another planet is irrelevant to the present inquiry because it only explains how Mars can be beneficent *sometimes*, whereas we are trying to see how Mars might *always* be better than the planets beneath it.

Far more likely than these explanations, however, is the possibility that the nature of Mars was at least normal when the Pilgrim visited it, if not actually enhanced by its placement in Aries. Certainly the planet was freed from earthly influences, for the Pilgrim's first impression of Mars was that, when viewed from its own heaven, it "seemed to me ruddier (*più roggio*) than it usually is" (*Par.* 14.87). When viewed from the earth, Mars assumes such heightened redness only under exceptional meteorological circumstances, "as when, suffused by dawn, Mars glows ruddy (*rosseggia*) through the thick vapors low in the west over the ocean floor" (*Purg.* 2.13–14).[7] Nonetheless the redness of Mars is an intrinsic quality of the planet itself, as is evident from Ptolemy's description:

> The nature of Mars is chiefly to dry and to burn, in conformity with his fiery colour and by reason of his nearness to the sun, for the sun's sphere lies just below him.[8]

Dante's use of this passage in the *Convivio* (2.13.21) leaves no doubt that he regarded the color of Mars to be an inherent quality of the planet:

> <As Ptolemy says in the *Quadripartitum*>, this same Mars by its own power dries up and burns everything because its heat is like that of fire; this heat is the reason why he appears suffused with the colour of fire, sometimes more, sometimes less, according to the density or rarity of the vapours which attend him. . . .[9]

In this view Mars is assimilated to fire by reason of their having two properties in common: first, intense heat, and secondly, a reddish color that is caused by the heat. Variations in this color are attributed to sublunar causes, namely the hot vapors or exhalations in the upper air. We can be sure that Dante by no means imagined these vapors to be in the vicinity of the planet Mars, because in the *Convivio* the influence of Mars on its vapors is compared to the influence of music on the vapors, or spirits, of the human heart: both are cases of action at a distance. Hence, if the vapors that alter the planet's appearance are not present in the heavens above the Moon, it follows that the color of Mars must be constant when viewed in its own heaven. And since for Dante Mars's color was an effect of its heat, it would further seem that the planet's heat is also invariable in its own heaven, which is to say that the planet's nature is itself constant. Consequently, what the Pilgrim reports of the heaven of Mars must be taken as typical of that planet's nature and can by no means be construed as an anomaly arising from some weakening of its power.

It would seem, then, that for Dante Mars is a more benign planet than the astrologers supposed it to be. And indeed in Dante's universe one could hardly expect it to be otherwise, placed as it is closer to God than the beneficent Sun. For in the Dantesque cosmos there is a scale of goodness descending from the absolute Good that is God, who is located beyond the outermost sphere of the world, down to the center, which is the most evil place because it is the most remote from God. Since the nine heavens are the principal means by which this goodness is conveyed to earth, one might suppose that they too differ in goodness in proportion to their distance from God, but this principle is not made explicit in either one of the poet's extended descriptions of the emanation process (*Par.* 2.112–138; 13.52–78). Nonetheless, the poet's belief in the moral gradation of the planets is made plain in other ways. Physically it is indicated by the earth's shadow, a cone that terminates in the heaven of Venus ("in cui l'ombra s'appunta / che 'l vostro mondo face," *Par.* 9.118–119). Commentators generally take this as a sign that the three lowest heavens contain souls "who were too much influenced by mundane considerations."[10] We have seen that in each case the influence was astral in origin: Piccarda's timidity comes from the Moon, Justinian's ambition from Mercury, and Carlo Martello's luxury from Venus. Thus we can be sure that the lower planets as a group confer a lesser grade of goodness than the upper ones. This establishes that the heavens are not uniform in their goodness, but we may still wonder whether each heaven represents a different grade of goodness in a scale ascending up to God. The answer becomes apparent from the effects of each heaven on the Pilgrim, who experiences progressively greater happiness as he ascends. As the narrator explains, holy pleasure "becomes the purer as one mounts—*sì fa, montando, più sincero*," *Par.* 14.139). This augmentation of happiness, of course, is expressed in the eyes of Beatrice, which appear more beautiful to the Pilgrim in each successive heaven, and the progression is expressly remarked in the heaven of Mars, where "her aspect surpassed all it had been at other times, even the last" (18.56–57). In Dante's cosmos, then, Mars represents a higher degree of goodness even than the Sun, not to mention the lower planets.

A Christian Astrology

Evidently the malignant character of Mars, which was stressed by the pagan and Arabic astrologers, did not fit into Dante's Christian view of the cosmos. What he needed was a Christian astrology that equated the planets with the orders of angels, but no such system was available, since his Christian authorities on astrology—John of Seville, Michael Scot, and Guido Bonatti—had been content to transmit and elaborate the work of their non-Christian predecessors. Consequently, Dante had to create a new system of astrology that was in accord with his theology. In other words, to account for the differences between Dante's Mars and that of the pagan astrologers, we must ask how his Christian view of the cosmos differed from that of the philosophers. The answer is well known: following the lead of scholastic theologians, the intelligences that Aristotelian philosophers posited as separated substances responsible for celestial motion were identified by Dante with the angels whose existence was revealed in Sacred Scripture.[11]

In the *Commedia*, Beatrice reveals to the Pilgrim that the nine types or orders of angels named by Saint Paul correspond with the nine heavens in the order that they are given in Ephesians 1.20–21, which had been preferred by Dionysius the Areopagite, rather than the order found in Colossians 1.16, which Gregory the Great had favored (*Par.* 28.98–126).

She divides the nine orders of angels into three triads and names the angels in each, proceeding from the highest to the lowest. Thus the middle triad contains "first Dominions, then Virtues (*Virtudi*) and the third are Powers" (122–123), which correspond with the planets Jupiter, Mars, and the Sun. In Dante's cosmos, then, we can be sure that the planet Mars is moved by the angelic intelligences known as Virtues (*Virtutes*).

Paul had simply named each of the nine kinds of angels, and from these revealed names theologians, beginning with Dionysius, attempted to deduce the character and function of each angelic order. We have already found Dante using Aquinas's interpretation of the Cherubim and Seraphim (above, chapter 4, n. 6), and so it is reasonable to suppose that he turned to the same authority to characterize the Virtues as well. The correctness of this assumption is confirmed by striking correspondences between Aquinas's treatment of the Virtues and Dante's Martian astrology, but let us defer the comparisons until we have assembled the relevant texts from the *Summa theologiae*.

AQUINAS ON FORTITUDE

In the *Summa theologiae* Aquinas argued that the angelic orders had been properly named by Paul (I q.108 a.5), and to sustain his argument he had to explain how one order could be called Virtues when each order undeniably had its own virtue. He did so by making a distinction:

> Virtue can be taken in two ways. First, commonly, considered as the medium between the essence and the operation; and in that sense all the heavenly spirits are called heavenly virtues. . . . Secondly, as meaning a certain excellence of strength (*fortitudinis*), and thus it is the proper name of an angelic order. Hence Dionysius says that the name "virtues" *signifies a certain virile and immovable strength* (*fortitudinem*) first, in regard to those divine operations which befit them; secondly, in regard to receiving divine gifts. Thus it signifies that they undertake fearlessly the divine behests appointed to them; and this seems to imply strength of mind (*fortitudinem animi*).[12]

For Aquinas, then, the name "Virtues" indicates that these angels possess the virtue of fortitude. Several articles later he makes the same point more succinctly: "this name [*Virtutes*] expresses a certain strength (*fortitudo*), giving efficacy to the inferior spirits in the execution of the divine ministrations."[13]

Dante, who frequently was guided by the principle that "names are the consequences of things,"[14] apparently reasoned that if Mars was moved by the angelic order of Virtues, and if the name *Virtutes* signified a kind of fortitude, then *fortitudo* must be the specific astrological property of the planet Mars. Revelation, by supplying the name of the angels associated with Mars, served to indicate the human virtue that the planet governed. Once that virtue was identified, Dante's concern was with the fortitude of men rather than of angels, and once again he turned to Aquinas for an authoritative discussion of *fortitudo*.

In the system of the *Summa theologiae*, fortitude, along with justice, prudence, and temperance, is one of the four cardinal, or principal, moral virtues (I-II q.61 a.2) to which all other moral virtues can be reduced: for example, "every virtue that makes the soul firm against any of the passions can be called fortitude" (a.3). The *Summa* in its definition of fortitude per se closely follows Aristotle's discussion of the virtue in his *Nicomachean Ethics*, on which Thomas had, of course, written a commentary.[15] The Greek term that Aristotle analyzed was *andreia*, "manliness," the spirit especially appropriate to the adult male,[16] which Aristotle defines as a mean between feelings of fear and recklessness (*Nic. Eth.* 2.7, 1107a35–34). For Aristotle the purest expression of this manly spirit—"courage" or "bravery," as we would call it—is fearlessness "in the face of a noble death, and of all emergencies that involve death; and the emergencies of war are in the highest degree of this kind."[17] For Aquinas, too, these are the chief characteristics of fortitude: it is a mean between timidity and audacity, and it most properly concerns perils of death, especially in a just war, but also in other emergencies.[18]

Therefore Aquinas, like Aristotle, viewed fortitude primarily as a military virtue, but from this central concept he developed a broader definition of the virtue, thereby adapting it to play a key role in his Christian system of morality. Thomas finds that fortitude is a virtue in the widest sense because it enables the will to overcome difficulties that impede it from following the dictates of reason.[19] In this extended sense fortitude amounts to a kind of "firmness of mind (*firmitas animi* or *mentis*)" that is required in the exercise of any virtue; but Thomistic fortitude also has its own province, which is somewhat larger than that assigned to it by Aristotle, for *fortitudo* "implies firmness of mind in bearing and resisting those things in which it is especially difficult to be firm, namely certain grave dangers."[20] The difficulty arises from the nature of such perils, which are *terribilia*, things that inspire fear or dread of bodily harm, the greatest of which is death.[21] Some deaths are more virtuous than others, however, so the purest, or proper, form of fortitude occurs when risking one's life in a good cause. Like Aristotle, Aquinas regards death in battle as the supreme occasion for fortitude, but for Thomas it must be in a just war fought for the common good. Moreover, Aquinas stretches the concept of war to include any form of assault (*impugnatio*), so that the brave person can be a Christian martyr who dies for God, the highest good, or he can be a civilian who risks his life for justice, e.g., a judge who makes a just judgment despite threats against his life. Indeed any deadly peril qualifies, provided only that it is undergone in a good cause. Thus the *fortis* can risk death by attending a friend who has a deadly and infectious disease, or he can travel on some pious errand despite risk of shipwreck.[22]

All the forms of fortitude we have mentioned so far are virtues that are natural and proper to man, but Thomas recognizes another kind of fortitude that is a gift of the Holy Spirit, which enables a man to do by grace what he could not do otherwise. Specifically, the Spirit can infuse confidence (*fiducia*) into the mind that will enable one either to achieve an unfinished work or to escape from imminent danger or evil.[23]

Aquinas not only expanded Aristotle's definition of fortitude but also enlarged its connotations by connecting other virtues with this cardinal one. He divides fortitude into four constituent parts and establishes the interrelations between the various virtues by making a complex series of distinctions that I shall for the most part pass over, because for our purpose it is enough to know which were the virtues that he associated with fortitude.[24] Following Cicero (*De inventione* 2.54), Aquinas divides fortitude into four principal parts: *fiducia* or confidence; *magnificentia*, which he defines etymologically as the virtue of "doing great things"; patience; and perseverance.[25] Confidence, however, Thomas presently identifies with magnanimity, to which the greater part of his discussion is devoted.[26] The magnanimous man seeks honor, which is the greatest exterior good for man;[27] other exterior goods, such a money, power, and friends, are not as important to the magnanimous man as his honor. Possession of such good things is conducive of magnanimity because they provide the magnanimous man with opportunities to exercise his virtue, but whenever pursuit of these lesser goods would diminish his honor, he scorns them.[28]

In Aristotelian fashion, Thomas further defines magnanimity as a moderate pursuit of honor, that is, as a mean between striving for honor too much or too little. Thus the virtue of magnanimity is associated with certain vices arising from an immoderate concern with honor. One who fails to make the greatest possible use of his potential is said to be pusillanimous or "small-souled," in contrast to the great-souled or magnanimous man, who does the best that is within his power.[29] At the other extreme stand those who are excessively desirous of honor; their sins are of three main kinds: presumption, ambition, and vainglory. The presumptuous man overstrives for honor by attempting what is beyond his powers; the ambitious man has an inordinate appetite for honor; and the vainglorious man goes to extremes in making his own excellence known to others.[30] Vainglory in turn begets several other sins—called its "daughters"—when they are committed for honor's sake. Three aim directly to give others a good opinion of the vainglorious man by boasting, or by pretending to great deeds (hypocrisy), or by attempting to do wonderful, unheardof things that are in fact beyond his powers (*novitatum praesumptio*). The others serve vainglory indirectly by seeking to show that the sinner is not less in some respect than another person. Thus one can obstinately refuse to accept better opinions than one's own (*pertinacia*), or willfully disagree with others (*discordia*), or be quick to take issue with others (*contentio*), or simply disobey the order of a superior (*inobedientia*).[31]

The parts of fortitude include one other virtue that is fittingly mentioned last because it is the ultimate goal of fortitude, namely safety or security (*securitas*). Fortitude, it will be recalled, is exercised in overcoming fears, and the most perfect form of this is a sense of security. On earth the brave man strives to overcome his fears, but in heaven he will enjoy "full security from exertion and evil."[32]

THOMISTIC FORTITUDE IN THE MARTIAN CANTOS

From the foregoing sketch of Aquinas's treatment of *fortitudo* and its associated virtues and vices, it is at once clear that the *Summa theologiae* offered Dante the possibility of attributing a complex of related properties to Mars. It remains to be seen whether these properties do in fact figure prominently in his Martian cantos. The obvious place to begin is the one passage in the poem that plainly states the astrological properties that Dante associated with Mars, namely Cacciaguida's prophecy concerning Can Grande:

> With him you shall see one who, at his birth, was so stamped by this strong star (*stella forte*), that notable shall be his deeds. . . . [Before 1312] some sparks of his virtue shall appear, in his caring naught for money or for toils (*affani*). His magnificence (*magnificenze*) shall

hereafter be so known, that his very foes will not be able to keep
silent tongues about him.

> Con lui vedrai colui che 'mpresso fue,
>   nascendo, sì da questa stella forte,
>   che notabili fier l'opere sue.
> . . . .
>   parran faville de la sua virtute
>   in non curar d'argento né d'affanni.
> Le sue magnificenze conosciute
>   saranno ancora, sì che 'suoi nemici
>   non ne potran tener le lingue mute.   (*Par.* 17.76–78, 83–87)

At the outset Mars is identified with fortitude, for it is the "strong star
(*stella forte*)" that imparts the abstract quality of "strongness (*fortitudo*)."
This, of course, could be said of Mars without recourse to Aquinas, but
the virtues that Can Grande will display in consequence of this natal influence are not all Martian properties in traditional astrology. His willingness
to trouble himself with difficult affairs ("affani")—probably military ones
in this context—is typical of the *fortis* and not particularly Thomistic,[33]
but his Martian character is also manifested by two virtues that Aquinas
associates with fortitude, although the connection is neither commonplace
nor self-evident: first, "his caring naught for money" (84), which is one of
the marks of the magnanimous man, who places honor above all other
exterior goods; second, his "magnificenze," which will be so famous that
even his enemies must speak of the magnificent things he has done.[34] According to Dante, then, the star of fortitude disposes one to magnanimity
and magnificence, which in the Thomistic system are parts of the cardinal
virtue of fortitude. This is our most explicit indication that the *Summa
theologiae* provided Dante with the materials for his Christian astrology.

Once the connection has been established between Dante's Mars and
Thomistic fortitude, other points of correspondence can also be discerned.
An obvious example is Cacciaguida's Christian martyrdom, an act of fortitude unknown to the pagans but recognized as such by Aquinas.[35] On a
far larger scale, one could analyze Cacciaguida's characterization of the
Florentine nobility in 1100 and 1300 in terms of Thomistic fortitude and
its related virtues and vices, for the ideal feudal nobleman is readily iden-
tifiable with Thomas's magnanimous man who seeks honor principally in

the dangers of battle, though also in performing acts of justice;[36] but a less extended example will suffice to show the extent to which Thomas's treatment pervades these cantos. The Pilgrim, too, displays the Thomistic type of fortitude: he is told to make his wishes known in a voice that is "confident, bold, and glad (*sicura, balda e lieta*)" (*Par.* 15.67), and somewhat later he acknowledges that Cacciaguida has given him "full boldness (*baldezza*) to speak" (16.17), more so than had been his wont. This boldness imparted by Mars is most fully displayed in his subsequent request to learn precisely what calamity awaits him in the future "because an arrow foreseen comes slower" (17.27). Dante's analogy echoes the opinion of Gregory the Great from which Aquinas argues that fortitude is not exclusively concerned with emergencies: "shafts that are foreseen strike less forcibly."[37] Although none of the principal parts of *fortitudo* are expressly named in Cacciaguida's prophecy, it is easy to see that the Pilgrim will need them all: he will require patience and perseverance to endure the hardships of his exile, and confidence and magnificence to undertake the writing of the *Commedia*, not to mention fortitude as a gift of the Holy Spirit in order to complete his *magnum opus*. What *is* made explicit is that he will need courage to write truthfully about the sins of his contemporaries, for peril of death is involved, not only for his soul but also for his *fama*, if his writing is deficient in fortitude, which is to say timid: "if I am a timid (*timido*) friend to the truth, I fear to lose life among those who shall call this time ancient" (*Par.* 17.117–120). This, of course, is completely in character for the magnanimous man, who aims above all else at honor, and this goal is approved by Cacciaguida—speaking with the invariable veracity of the blessed—when he assures Dante that to tell the truth without respect of persons, as he should do in the *Commedia*, "is no small proof of the honor of the writer" (17.135).[38]

With this example we must cut short our excursus on Dante's Christian astrology, because enough has already been said to establish the essential point for the present inquiry. We are now in a position to see, if only dimly, why traditional astrology alone cannot explain the qualities displayed by Dante's heaven of Mars. More properly it might be called "the heaven of fortitude," for that virtue and its allies, as expounded by Thomas Aquinas, constitute a great part of the planet's positive influence on human affairs. At its best, then, Mars produces noblemen like Cacciaguida, who are brave soldiers but also good Christians. They direct their aggression against the enemies of Christian society; at home they live in concord with one another, each doing what is truly honorable without either vainglory or ambition. Unlike the latter-day Florentines, they neither conquer their neighbors nor squander their resources in ostentation and self-indulgence; instead, they make the most of their material and spiritual potentialities by doing as much good as they can, especially for the good of the whole community. Thus a gentleman like Cacciaguida will strive to be a good citizen and paterfamilias, a prince like Can Grande will aim to rule well, and an artist of Dante's genius will undertake the *Commedia* for the benefit of mankind. Each in his Martian way does such true works of magnificence as are within his power. The structure of the *Comedy* contrasts Cacciaguida, the exemplary Florentine noble, with the three corrupt Florentine nobles of *Inferno* 16, who dissipated their energies in endless intramural rivalries, competing and fighting with one another, as appears most clearly in their symbolic circling that the poet compares to wrestlers each seeking the advantage in a match, which is really a mismatch because it is three-sided (*Inf.* 16.19–27).[39]

The Martian cantos, then, are unified by the theological concept of fortitude rather than by any doctrine of traditional astrology. We have gone to great lengths to establish this point before considering Dante's use of astrology in these cantos because it teaches us not to expect too much from the astrological references taken alone. They exist in profusion, but they do not in themselves form a conceptual complex around which the cantos were built, as was the case in the lower heavens. Instead, the traditional astrological references in Mars will seem to bear little relation to one another unless they are recognized to be part of a larger pattern supplied by theology. In that paradigm, as we have seen, warfare plays the leading part, so the military aspect of Mars that figures so prominently in the astrological tradition fits in readily, but Dante took other, nonmilitary properties from pagan astrology because they agreed with the Martian principles he had derived from theology, and these are apt to be dismissed as astrological applique employed for decorative effect unless the underlying principles that governed their selection are recognized. This subordination of astrology to theology suggests that we cannot hope to fully appreciate the appropriateness of his choices until the theological principles have been fully explicated. To do so lies beyond the scope of the present work, and the most we can hope to accomplish here is to identify Dante's uses of astrology and to indicate in a general way how these fit into the larger pattern provided by the theological paradigm of fortitude. Consequently the astrological materials can most conveniently be presented systematically in four chief categories: (1) the planet's astrological principles; (2) its most familiar, military associations; (3) other Martian virtues and vices; and finally (4) miscellaneous properties. After we have completed this survey, we will be in a position to consider whether the traditional view of Mars as the malevolent planet is compatible with Dante's Christian astrology.

The Nature of Mars

Although we have already touched on the nature of Mars somewhat in passing, now we must survey the essential qualities of the planet systematically. From Ptolemy onwards, all the astrologers agreed that by nature Mars was hot and dry.[40] As we have seen, the Sun also possesses the same qualities of hotness and dryness, but with a difference, because whereas the Sun has them in a moderate degree, Mars is hot and dry without moderation.[41] The point is made most forcefully by Michael Scot: "The nature of Mars is without temperateness because it is extremely hot and dry, and in this respect it is extremely different (*discors*) from the others."[42] Mars is most closely allied to the Sun by their common qualities, as Haly makes clear:

> [Mars] is inclined to the Sun by the love he has for him and is defended by his aid, inasmuch as the Sun is exalted in the domicile of Mars [sc. Aries] and the Sun controls him by giving him heat and dryness.[43]

This seems to be what Cacciaguida had in mind when he said that the fire of Mars is rekindled ("rinfiammarsi") when it returns "to its Lion" (*Par.* 16.37–39), the fire sign Leo, which belongs to Mars inasmuch as they both partake of the same hot and dry nature, but which is ruled by the Sun, whose house (*domus*) is Leo both by day and night.[44] This close relationship between Mars and the Sun also explains why Dante twice in these cantos compared God's gifts to the Martian souls with the action of the Sun. The Pilgrim, marveling at their light and color, returned the glory of their adornment to God, whom he appropriately addressed as "Helios" (*Par.* 14.96). Likewise reminiscent of God is the Pilgrim's declaration that "the Sun that illumined and warmed you [Cacciaguida] is of such equality with its heat and light that all comparisons are inadequate" (15.76–78).

Although the nature of Mars is derived from the Sun, it is influenced by other stars as well. According to Haly, the zodiacal signs that possess the quality of heat, namely the fire and air signs, "strengthen and fortify the nature of Mars, which is weakened by the wet signs that oppose its natural dryness.[45]

Dryness and thirst. While the qualities of heat and dryness figure prominently in the Martian cantos when combined as fire, there are few allusions to either one independent of the other. Thirst, however, is an exception. It is induced by Mars, whose property is, Scot said, "to influence dryness."[46] Ptolemy had attributed to Mars drought, "the failure of the water of rivers, the drying up of springs, and the tainting of potable waters,"[47] and Ibn Ezra extended this to the human body, which Mars could also dry out,[48] with the result that the Martian man, as characterized by Scot, is one "often suffering thirst."[49] Thus it is appropriate that Dante used metaphors based on thirst twice in these cantos.[50] Cacciaguida says that the holy love of which he is always conscious "makes me thirst (*asseta*) with sweet longing" (*Par.* 15.65–66), and Beatrice urges the Pilgrim to speak "in order that you may learn to tell your thirst (*sete*), so that one may pour out drink for you" (17.11–12).

FIRE

In Aristotelian physics, the qualities of hotness and dryness combine to form the element of fire. Since Mars possesses these qualities to a greater degree than the Sun, fire belongs to Mars. According to Haly, the planet itself appears to be "glowing hot (*fervens*)" and is by its nature "fiery (*igneus*)."[51] Because elemental fire lacks moderation, Scot says that Mars produces not only heat but also blazing fire ("arsura") in the sublunary world, especially when the planet is itself in a fire sign, such as Aries, which reinforces this power to induce combustion.[52] Consequently, in astrological interpretations the planet signifies all kinds of burning up (*combustio*),[53] including such medical conditions as fevers and inflammations—Bonatti specifically mentions impetigo.[54]

Accordingly, in the poem the planet Mars itself appears "fiery (*affocato*)" (*Par.* 14.86), and the narrator makes frequent use of fire images in his metaphors, especially when describing Cacciaguida and the other Martians. Thus when Cacciaguida first appears he is compared to a meteor, which in accordance with Aristotelian meteorology is described as a "fire (*foco*)" that is "kindled (*s'accende*)" in the sky (*Par.* 14.13–18). Again, as he moved he "seemed like fire (*foco*) behind alabaster" (24). Similarly, he is called "the holy lamp (*la santa lampa*)" (17.5), though in this case fire is only implied. Like all the souls above the Moon, his surrogate body is so radiant that inner love cannot be discerned from his invisible features but instead is expressed by an increase in the intensity of his light. In Cacciaguida's case, this intensification causes his light "to be brilliant (*risplendere*)" in a way that reminds the narrator of a coal that "quickens into flame (*fiamma*) at the breathing of the winds" (16.28–30). On another occasion, he resembles lightning when his affection is manifested "in the blazing (*fiammeggiar*) of the holy bolt of lightning (*folgór*)" (18.25). The other Martian souls likewise appear to the Pilgrim as flashes across the planet's cross, which Cacciaguida compares to lightning, for they flash "as in a cloud its swift fire (*foco*) does" (18.36). As usual, Beatrice assumes something of the character of the heaven; here there is fire in her eyes, within which "a smile was burning (*ardeva*)" (15.34).

Although fire is most frequently used to describe characters, there are other ways in which the same theme has been worked in. The narrator opens canto 17 by comparing the Pilgrim with Phaëthon in respect to his burning curiosity, which Beatrice refers to as "the flame (*vampa*) of your desire" (*Par.* 17.1–8). Phaëthon's legend occasions other fire-related allusions as well, for his inept driving, as described by Ovid, has the effects that astrologers attribute to Mars: rivers dry up, vegetation burns, and the very mountains of earth are set ablaze, while Phaëthon himself is said to resemble a meteor (*Metamorphoses* 2.210–226, 318–322). The Pilgrim, too, burns as he thanks God with a "burnt offering (*olocausto*)" made figuratively by "the burning (*ardor*) of the sacrifice in my breast" (14.88–92). Several times Cacciaguida's words also recall the fiery associations of his planet: once he predicts that the "sparks (*faville*)" of Martian virtue shall appear in Can Grande (17.83), and on another occasion he recalls Mars's control over inflammations of the skin as he advises Dante to let those whom his poetry justly offends "scratch where the itch is" (17.129).

The God of War: The Most Obvious Qualities

That Mars is the god of war is one of the familiar commonplaces of classical mythology. All the astrologers accepted this identification and constructed their interpretation of the planet around it. Thus, according to Ptolemy, Mars "brings about wars";[55] for Ibn Ezra and Scot the planet signifies *bella* and makes those under its influence *bellicosi*.[56] Battle in the open field is only one aspect of Mars's influence on warfare; Scot lists— among other martial effects of Mars—looting, shattering, destroying, revolting, and bloodshed.[57] Albumasar, however, subsumed war under a broader generalization: Mars governs "every bloody means of causing death."[58]

Given this consensus that Mars signifies war, one might expect Dante to make warfare as prominent in his Martian cantos as love was in the Venusian ones. But the poet surprises us, for war is never mentioned directly in these cantos. To be sure, the Pilgrim shared the readers' expectation, for he was attuned to hear only the few militant words—"rise up again" and "conquer"—in the Martians' opening hymn (*Par.* 14.125). This hymn is a sort of emblem of Mars's true significance, for most of the words, like Cacciaguida's first speech, transcend the Pilgrim's understanding (15.38–45). The astrologers perceived only that part of Mars's influence that they were capable of understanding and consequently placed undue stress on the martial nature of Mars. The poet rectifies this false perspective by relegating warfare to the background,[59] so that the reader, like the Pilgrim, learns by example to view the military tendencies of Mars in the true perspective of Christian astrology. We are, as it were, viewing the bright upper side of a coin of which warfare is the dark, unseen reverse. Thus Cacciaguida's idyllic picture of twelfth-century Florence depicts the city "in her last period of peace" (16.147), which implies that the murder of Buondelmonte on Easter 1216 marked the beginning of a correlative period of war, when Florence ceased to be "in such repose that she had no cause for wailing" (16.149–150).

Warfare, therefore, is constantly implicit in these cantos but rarely surfaces, and then it is referred to only indirectly. The nobles of Cacciaguida's Florence, for instance, whom he catalogues in such detail, all belonged to the class of feudal warriors, although their primary, military function is never made explicit. At best it is hinted at in the rank of knighthood ("milizia") to which the Great Baron, Hugh of Brandenburg, raised six Florentine families in the eleventh century (*Par.* 16.127–132), just as Cacciaguida himself was knighted on the Second Crusade (15.140).[60] Even the sanctified warfare of the crusade is described rather than named (16.139–144) and repeatedly is implied by references to the Cross, the badge that identified those who had dedicated themselves to a Holy War (14.100–108, 18.34, 37, 48).[61] If there is any doubt that war lurks behind the peaceful picture of Cacciaguida's Florence, it is dispelled by his use of the military census to calculate the size of the city: he reckons in terms of "all those able to bear arms (*da poter arme*)" (16.47). This is distinctive of Mars, which Scot calls "the arms-bearing star (*stella armigera*)" (M, 101va).

Thus the Pilgrim uses a metaphor appropriate to the planet when he declares that "it is good that I arm myself (*m'armi*)" (17.109).

Dante's reluctance to follow the astrologers in simply equating Mars with warfare reaches its climax at the end of the episode, when Cacciaguida names eight souls who are with him in this heaven. Modern commentators generally label the group "warriors for the faith,"[62] but this is a generalization inductively derived from the legendary character of these eight souls. In fact, Dante, speaking through Cacciaguida, says nothing at all that suggests they were fighters, for the Faith or anything else; instead, he categorizes them as "blessed spirits which below, before they came to heaven, were of such great renown (*di gran voce*) that every Muse would be rich with them" (18.31–33). To say that these warriors were "living legends" may seem trite, but actually it is the clue that leads to Dante's point: they were all men worthy of honor, which, as we have learned from Aquinas (above, at n. 25) is the mark of the magnanimous man, who, for the sake of honor, exercises the Martian virtue of fortitude by "doing great things" with moderation. Thus Dante's Christian astrology is superimposed on the traditional notion that Mars simply produces warriors. The less accurate formulation is not discarded, for the eight heroes were undoubtedly warriors, but neither is it stressed; instead, Dante preferred to give prominence here to the highest virtues instilled by Mars.[63]

Although Dante avoided direct references to war in his Martian cantos, still he found a variety of ways to refer to the subject indirectly. The astrologers provided him with many war-related subjects that were appropriate to the planet: arms, fortifications, victory, capture and bondage, destruction, and violent death. To complete our survey of the martial attributes of Mars as they appear in the *Paradiso*, we must consider each of these categories in turn.

Arms. Mars, according to Alcabitius, governs every craft "that is done by means of iron and fire, as is the forging of swords with hammers."[64] Scot is more explicit, assigning to Mars "the preparation of arms, e.g., long and short swords, breastplates, lances, arrows, etc."[65] Accordingly Dante sprinkled his Martian cantos with allusions to swords, arrows, and spurs. A sword is implied when Cacciaguida says that Emperor Conrad "girt me with [the swordbelt of] his knighthood—*mi cinse de la sua milizia*" (*Par.* 15.140); again it is implied by reference to "the hilt and pommel gilded" that was a status symbol of the Florentine knight (16.102),[66] but it is mentioned directly and most memorably in Cacciaguida's condemnation of overpopulation: "oftentimes one sword cuts better and more than five *spade*" (16.71–72). If anything, the weapons of archery figure more prominently than the sword in these cantos. The Pilgrim wants to know his future "because an arrow (*saetta*) foreseen comes more slowly" (17.27), and Cacciaguida obliges by foretelling that he will have to leave all that he loves best, and this "is the arrow (*strale*) which the bow of exile shoots (*saetta*) first" (17.56–57). The narrator, too, employs the imagery of archery in an elaborate metaphor to convey how Cacciaguida's first speech missed its mark by being too lofty for mortal mind to comprehend (15.42–45). Finally, the spur, which like the sword was one of the insignia of knighthood, appears in another figure of speech: the Pilgrim sees "how time spurs (*sprona*) toward me" (17.106).[67]

Fortifications. Albumasar ascribes "the castles of kings" to Mars, while Ibn Ezra generalizes this to any kind of castle or tower, and adds as well that Mars "signifies . . . digging through walls [and] breaking doors."[68] In rapid succession Cacciaguida lists five cases of rural noble families that moved to Florence when their castles—Aguglione, Simifonti, Montemurlo, Montecroce, and Montebuono—were either destroyed or sold (*Par.* 16.56, 61–66).[69] Actual walls and gates are likewise referred to repeatedly. Florence's twelfth-century walls are "la cerchia antica" (15.97), and this "little circuit was entered by a gate (*porta*) named after the Della Pera" (16.125–126). The palace of the Conti Guidi is metanomically indicated by its "porta" (16.94–95), and heaven itself has its door ("ianua," 15.30). The latter was, of course, neither military nor manmade, and hence was not produced by the arts Mars rules; but Dante does manage to enlarge the scope of authentic Martian artifacts, "which men with skill and art contrive for their defense (*difesa*)" (14.116–117), to include the construction of sunshades, thus once again mitigating the military image of Mars.

Captivity and flight. From Ptolemy onwards, the astrologers associated Mars with captivity and imprisonment.[70] This association is only faintly reflected in the *Paradiso* by repeated allusions to various forms of bondage. The narrator recalls that his love of Beatrice grew so great in Mars "that till then nothing had bound me (*mi legasse*) with such sweet bonds (*vinci*)" 14.128–129). The cords of various stringed instruments ("corde," 14.119) hardly qualify, but two allusions to the entrapment of birds—by birdlime and by nets (17.32, 95)—do pertain to the theme of captivity.

In the astrological tradition, flight seems to have been an offshoot of this theme, for Albumasar ascribed to Mars "difficulty of fleeing (*fugiendi difficultas*)," which the *Liber novem iudicum* extended to make Mars signify "fugitives."[71] Dante echoes this in his reproach to Buondelmonte: "how misfortunate that you fled (*fuggisti*)" from a marriage alliance with the Amidei (*Par.* 16.140). Although the astrological tradition for Mars's governance of fugitives is admittedly slight, it is worth noting because it may explain why the bulk of *Paradiso* 17 is devoted to Dante's exile (lines 13–99), in which he was a fugitive from Florentine justice. This somewhat tenuous connection is strengthened by other Martian elements in the sentence of condemnation passed on Dante and his associates in 1302, which provided that "all the goods of whoever does not pay [the fine] are to become public property, to be laid waste and destroyed, and let the title to whatever is laid waste and destroyed pass to the commune."[72] Both provisions pertain to Mars, for Ibn Ezra took Mars to signify sequestration of property,[73] while, as we shall see next, the planet's destructive influence was generally recognized.

DESTRUCTION

Mars is "the destroyer planet"; its "destructive quality" is responsible for "breaking," for "dispersing,"[74] and, according to Ibn Ezra, for "a man's losses (*perditiones*), whether by nature or habit."[75] The destruction of Dante's goods, implied by the prophecy of *Paradiso* 17, is paralleled by the destruction of castles alluded to in the previous canto (above, at n. 69), which also mentions two families whose houses were destroyed by the commune in 1293 in the first application of the Ordinances of Justice.[76] Destruction is indeed one of Cacciaguida's major themes:

> Se tu riguardi Luni e Orbisaglia
>   come sono ite, e come se ne vanno
>   di retro ad esse Chiusi e Sinigaglia,
> udir come le schiatte si disfanno
>   non ti parrà nova cosa né forte,
>   poscia che le cittadi termine hanno.
> Le vostre cose tutte hanno lor morte. . . .   (*Par.* 16.71–79)

If you regard Luni and Urbisaglia, how they have perished, and how Chiusi and Senigallia are following after them, it will not appear to you a strange thing or a hard, to hear how families are undone, since cities have their term. Your affairs all have their death. . . .

With this introduction, Cacciaguida goes on to catalogue almost twenty families that had declined or disappeared by 1300.[77]

Violent death. As the bringer of war, Mars, according to Ptolemy, also "brings about . . . sudden deaths arising from such causes."[78] Ptolemy himself extended this influence to include "murder,"[79] and later astrologers generalized it to embrace every form of "killing (*occisio*)."[80] Such effects are not altogether excluded from the *Paradiso*, but one must look closely to find them, for again Dante has at once minimized and elevated this dire influence of Mars. Thus Cacciaguida says, "Your [human] affairs all have their death (*morte*) even as you have" (*Par.* 16.79–80). Here the stress is on natural death, but later in the same speech he alludes to death by violence, though only in a metaphorical sense. Addressing the city of Florence, he says that the Amidei family, by murdering Buondelmonte and thus initiating a period of civil strife, "has slain you (*v'ha morti*) and put an end to your glad living" (16.137–138). Moreover, Dante included two cases of death by violence, each of which had their redeeming feature. The first is the martyrdom ("martiro") of Cacciaguida himself, which brought him swiftly to heaven (15.148). Such a death, we have learned from Aquinas (above, at n. 22), results from the purest kind of fortitude—the virtue appropriate to Mars—and hence it is the occasion for good rather than evil. The same, of course, is true of Christ's crucifixion, when "the Lamb of God who takes away sins was slain (*fosse anciso*)" (17.32). Once again the astrological tradition has been accommodated to Christian principles.

CONTRADICTION AND DISSENT

The astrologers added to Mars's warlike qualities others that gave rise not only to war but also to similar dissensions in the civil sphere, such as arguments, lawsuits, and lawlessness. Underlying all these manifestations is Mars's affinity for "contradiction."[81] From this root spring "contention," "controversy," "dissension,"[82] and all kinds of quarrelling.[83] Within a state these tendencies produce violent political discord (*seditio*) of various sorts—for instance, between factions or between the establishment and its critics, which conduce respectively to civil war and to rebellion, either singly or collectively, against the government.[84]

Dante acknowledged that Mars could promote such dissident behavior, for he has Cacciaguida deplore it, but he emphasizes that this is not a positive use of Martian energy. For Dante, only ill-disposed Martians are disruptive; well-disposed ones are not. Thus the exemplary souls in Mars act together in harmony rather than with discord: they not only sing in unison but "become silent with one consent (*concorde*)" (*Par.* 15.9), because, as the narrator explains, their will was disposed to do good rather than evil ("Benigna volontade . . . iniqua," 15.1–3). Although the main thrust of this argument is borne by the poet's military and political examples, there are also a number of lesser instances of Martian contradiction woven into these cantos, and to these we shall now turn.

Falsehood and truth. The Martian proclivity for contradiction is so strong that it often takes the form of denying the truth. Michael Scot summarizes the common opinion of the astrologers in this regard: the native of Mars "often lies to another and deceives him,"[85] even to the point of committing perjury.[86] In Dante's heaven of Mars, the narrator reflects something of the devious quality of the Martian, but he deploys it in the service of truth rather than falsehood as he accuses himself in order to excuse himself so the reader "may see that I speak truth (*dir vero*)" (*Par.* 14.137). Cacciaguida, however, recommends a more forthright approach; when the poet recounts his pilgrimage, he should make all of his vision manifest, having "set every falsehood aside (*rimossa ogne menzogna*)" (17.127).[87] Consequently it would seem that for Dante Mars's influence, if joined with a "benigna volontade" (15.1), could induce a special concern for the truth; otherwise, he recognizes the baleful effects of the planet in two particular forms of falsehood. (1) Because the Martian tends to be a liar, he is often involved in transactions that are fraudulent, such as falsifying documents, counterfeiting money, and making false accusations,[88] so that "he is extremely suspect of dealing in bad faith."[89] This tendency is represented in these cantos by an allusion to the fraud practiced by a member of the Chiaramontesi family, who, while administering the Florentine municipal salt monopoly, enriched himself by measuring out salt for sale in a bucket that contained less than the legal measure.[90] An earlier allusion to the same scandal assures us that the poet knew that "those who blush for the bushel" (16.105) did so because it had been altered fraudulently by removing one of the staves (*Purg.* 12.105). (2) The Martian penchant for falsification also qualifies the natives as "perfidious (*perfidii*)," as several astrologers remark,[91] and the poet twice works this quality into his heaven of Mars. Thus Dante will have to leave Florence as Hippolytus left Athens "by reason of his pitiless and perfidious (*perfida*) stepmother" (*Par.* 17.47), but he will live to see his neighbors punished for their "perfidies (*perfidie*)" (17.99).

Accusations and litigation. The Martian's capacity for dissent makes him apt to make accusations,[92] and accordingly the poem's narrator exhibits a harmless form of this proclivity when he accuses himself ("io m'accuso," *Par.* 14.136). More often the result is a dispute, and especially a legal one, so that traditional astrology gives Mars rule over lawsuits (*litigia*).[93] In Paradise this association is reflected in Cacciaguida's disparaging reference to two lawyers, one of whom was distinguished for his fraudulent transactions: Florence must "endure the stench of the churl of Aguglione, and of him of Signa, who already has his eye sharp for jobbery (*barattare*)" (16.55–57).[94] Somewhat more pointedly Martian is the reference to a corrupt judge, Lapo Salterello, who was notorious for taking bribes (15.128),[95] which makes him an appropriate example of the "perverse judges" that, according to Albumasar, are the spawn of Mars.[96] Finally, Cacciaguida occasionally employs juridical turns of speech that are perhaps prompted by his Martian nature. Thus, "vengeance shall bear witness (*fia testimonio*) to the truth which dispenses it," and "their own conduct shall afford the proof (*farà la prova*) of their brutish folly" (17.53–54, 67–68).

Lawlessness. The dissident influence can take yet another form: the Martian "undertakes things that are prohibited in law,"[97] dissenting against the law rather than against truth or his neighbor, as in the previous cases. Thus he is an outlaw, one bound by no law—in a word, "exlex" (Albumasar). Other astrologers express the same idea with a variety of terms: Mars is the felon planet that promotes brigandage, theft, robbery, plundering, pillaging, piracy, and general lawlessness.[98] Dante accordingly seasons Cacciaguida's discourses with several appropriate allusions. The gate of the Conti Guidi's palace "is at present laden with new felony (*fellonia*)," namely that of the Cerchi, who had occupied it since 1280 (*Par.* 16.94–95).[99] Indeed, Cacciaguida represents himself as a kind of outlaw, for he describes his crusade as an action "against the iniquity of that law (*legge*) whose people . . . usurp your right (*giustizia*)" (15.142–144). In other words, it is permissible, and even laudable, to oppose a *lex* that lacks *ius*; an unjust law is deserving of dissent and thus sanctifies an otherwise undesirable influence of Mars. The narrator, too, insinuates an allusion to robbery, saying that the sinner "robs himself (*si spoglia*) of that [eternal] love" (15.12).

BLOOD AND NOBILITY

As the hot, red planet, Mars was naturally associated with blood. So fundamental is this association that, astrologically speaking, it probably justifies the identification of the red planet with the war god of classical mythology. Be that as it may, the astrologers were agreed that Mars "signifies blood" and "everything bloody."[100] Consequently, it governs those parts of the human body that are especially related to the production and distribution of blood, such as the liver, kidneys, veins, and heart.[101] Moreover, the astrologers commonly combined these sanguinary associations with Mars's reputation for violence to make the planet signify "bloodshed" and hence "wounds."[102]

Dante accepted the astrologers' view that blood was one of the planet's most basic associations. As soon as the Pilgrim realized he was in the heaven of Mars, he made a burnt offering "with all my heart (*core*)" (*Par.* 14.88). The wholeheartedness of his thank offering is itself appropriate, for the Martian "puts his whole heart into the things he does."[103] Although blood itself is mentioned infrequently, both occurrences are, like the one just noted, emphasized by primacy of place. Thus the first words of Cacciaguida are "*O sanguis meus*—O my blood" (15.28), and the use of Latin serves to heighten their impact. The same theme is developed at the opening of canto 16: "*O poca nostra nobiltá di sangue*—O our petty nobility of blood!" (16.1). There Dante justifies pride in his lineage, and incidentally explains why Mars is the appropriate heaven for the exemplification of Dante's theories on the nature of inherited nobility, which he had previously expounded in *Convivio* 4. True nobility, he had argued there, is not inherited but comes from God; this gift leads its possessor to virtue because it inclines him to love the mind, his noblest part, more than the body, and hence to cultivate it and use it in the exercise of the moral and intellectual virtues (*Conv.* 4.22). The crux of this process is the individual's love of mind: "it loves the mind (*ama l'animo*) more than the body or anything else."[104] This kind of nobility, no less than nobility of blood, was appropriate to Mars, for several astrologers took that planet to signify "love of mind (*animi amorem*) in all things."[105]

Cacciaguida blames the latter-day problems of Florence on the enlargement of her *contado* to include new, non-Florentine territories from which whole families emigrated to the city. Formerly, he says, "the citizenship, which is now mixed with Campi, with Certaldo, and with Figline, saw itself pure down to the humblest artisan" (*Par.* 16.49–51). This intermingling of populations—"le confusion de le persone" (16.67)—was the ruin of the city, not for the racist reasons adduced by Brunetto Latini, but because the population exceeded the natural limits of a functional community.[106] Cacciaguida's complaint does have an astrological basis, however, since Mars, Florence's patron planet, promoted contamination as well as the tendency to favor outsiders over one's neighbors.[107]

Nonmilitary Aspects of the Martian Character

Any reader with a moderate acquaintance with classical mythology could discern the basic, warlike qualities of Mars without recourse to the astrologers, but the planet promoted other character traits, many of which were not derived from the mythographic tradition and would only be recognizable to one versed in astrology. These traits include various manifestations of hot passions, such as anger, courage, and impiety; moreover, the deadly sins of pride, envy, and gluttony fall into Mars's province. The impetuous Martian is also prone to folly and fickleness, and finally he expresses himself in characteristic kinds of speech. To round out our portrait of the astrologer's Martian and his mirror image in the *Paradiso*, each of these areas must be considered in turn.

HOT PASSIONS

Mars controls "the hot passions of the body."[108] This phrase of Albumasar's encapsulates a complex of physiologic theories that determine the Martian character. In humoristic psychology, the fiery nature of Mars (*Par.* 14.86) corresponds to the choleric temperament, since both fire and choler are compounded of the qualities hotness and dryness. Thus the astrologers ascribed to Mars both choler, or bile, and the gall bladder that produces that substance;[109] they further agreed that the person in whom choler was the predominant humor was inclined to wrath (*ira*), which was consequently one of the principal psychologic effects of the planet Mars.[110] Carried to the extreme, wrath afflicted the Martian with such distinctly morbid states of uncontrolled passion as frenzy (*rabies*) and fury (*furor*).[111] Only once does Dante expressly refer to such a state in the Martian cantos, but then he unmistakably echoes Michael Scot, who wrote that Mars "signifies impious and furious persons (*impie et furiose*) without any measure of discretion."[112] Their counterparts in the *Commedia* are Dante's fellow exiles, who, Cacciaguida tells him, "will become all ungrateful, all mad and impious (*tutta matta ed empia*) against you" (*Par.* 17.64–65).

Beyond this clear allusion to anger and its allies, these cantos yield several doubtful, inferential references,[113] but these do not exhaust the instances of anger, for the choleric character imparted by Mars is exemplified by Cacciaguida. Whenever the good and simple knight touches on evil in his discourses, he shows his displeasure more or less strongly. The contrasts between his Florence and Dante's in canto 15 are relatively restrained, although an undercurrent of anger is implied by his thesis that the latter-day Florentines are no longer peaceful, sober, and chaste (*Par.* 15.97–129, esp. 99). In that canto his venom is largely vented through sarcasm, such as the comparison of noble Romans with unworthy Florentines (127–129), but an unmistakably angry note emerges at the end, when quite gratuitously he blames the papacy for the Christians' failure to recover the Holy Land (144). In the next canto, however, when asked to identify the worthy Florentines of his day, his reply (16.49–154) repeatedly manifests his anger against their opposites: for instance, the Adimari are tagged "the insolent breed (*L'oltracotata schiatta*)" (115), and he wishes that the Buondelmonte might have been jailed as soon as they had arrived in Florence (142–144). Indeed, his anger becomes increasingly evident in the course of the interview, so that in canto 17 he goes out of his way to condemn the Roman curia as "the place where every day Christ is bought and sold" (51), while he ascribes to Dante's enemies such qualities as "perfidies" and "brutishness (*bestialitate*)" (99, 67). In daily conversation we readily recognize repressed anger when it surfaces in disparaging remarks, and similarly the reader can detect Cacciaguida's passionate feelings from these and many other lapses from his superficial attitude of lofty serenity. The cause, of course, is his choleric, Martian character, which in heaven still can be vented in righteous anger.

The varieties of courage. The Martian, like his planet, is "strong and powerful—*fortis, potens*,"[114] as Dante acknowledged by terming Mars the "stella forte" (*Par.* 17.77). One might imagine that the astrologers would unhesitatingly proceed to transform the physical sense of this virtue into a moral one, but in fact only Ibn Ezra lists "fortitudo" among the properties of Mars. Consequently, in the introduction to this chapter, I have stressed Dante's dependence on Aristotle and Aquinas in shaping his view of Mars as the star of fortitude (above, after n. 32). Nonetheless, the astrologers did recognize certain component parts of the Thomistic virtue of *fortitudo*. For example, the quality of constancy or persistent endurance, which the Pilgrim is exhorted to practice in his exile, is a Martian trait noted by Alcabitius, among others.[115] Instead of *fortitudo*, the astrologers preferred to characterize courage in terms of audacity or "boldness (*audacia*)."[116] Dante does work this quality into these cantos, but it appears stripped of its heroic and military connotations. At one point, the narrator fears that the reader may find an assertion "too daring (*troppo osa*)" (*Par.* 14.130); much later, the Pilgrim screws up his courage to ask Cacciaguida a question by claiming that "you give me full boldness (*baldezza*) to speak" (16.17). Several astrologers also associate Mars with the opposite of boldness, namely "fear and trembling,"[117] which the poem echoes, likewise in a nonmilitary sense. The birth of a daughter instills the dowry-conscious father with "fear (*paura*)" (15.103), and the Pilgrim says that he fears ("temo") that the fame of his poem will not endure long "if I am a timid (*timido*) friend to the truth" (17.118–119).

Elation. The Martian soul is "full of spirit (*animosus*),"[118] and consequently experiences "great elation."[119] Thus Cacciaguida in his first outpouring of affection surpasses the Pilgrim's comprehension (*Par.* 15.37–45), and eventually he has the same effect on Dante, who tells him that "you so uplift me (*mi levate*) that I am more than I" (16.18).[120]

DEADLY SINS

Christians might well regard Mars as the most evil planet, for it promotes cupidity, which according to Aquinas is well said to be the root of all evils inasmuch as *cupiditas* is "a certain inclination of corrupt nature to desire corruptible goods inordinately."[121] That Mars promotes cupidity is plainly indicated by Michael Scot, who asserted that the Martian "quickly desires (*cupit*) everything that he sees."[122] Dante accordingly gives this generic concept of cupidity prominence in the heaven of Mars by contrasting it with the good will and harmony that characterize his heavenly Martians (*Par.* 15.1–11, cf. 15.146–147). The astrological connection between Mars and cupidity was enough to authorize allusions to all of the seven deadly sins in these cantos, even though the astrologers specifically mention only three of them—wrath, envy, and pride. Wrath has already been treated in the preceding section, and before we consider pride at some length, we may note how Dante touches on the other five capital sins in his Martian cantos.

Alcabitius takes Mars to signify envy (*invidia*),[123] and thus the Pilgrim is cautioned that as an exile he will be tempted to envy his neighbors ("a' tuoi vicini invidie," *Par.* 17.97). Lust is indicated by Dante's allusion to both Sardanapalus (15.107) and Buondelmonte's fatal attraction to a woman more beautiful than his fiancée (16.139–141). Sloth, which earlier in the poem has been defined as a lack of zeal for heavenly goods (*Purg.* 17.130–132), would seem to be the vice alluded to in the prologue to *Paradiso* 16, where it is said that the human appetite is warped "down here where our affections languish" (3). Moreover, the Pilgrim himself is almost weighed down by sullenness, which is one form of *acedia*, or sloth, until his thoughts are redirected by Beatrice (18.1–6).[124] The opposite of sloth, as well as of avarice, will be evidenced in Can Grande by "his caring naught for money or for toils" (17.84). Avarice itself is of course evident in the history of Florence as the motive of those aliens who, according to Cacciaguida, were drawn to immigrate by the city's prosperity (e.g., 16.121–122). Furthermore, avarice is implied in Cacciaguida's frequent and unfavorable references to merchants (e.g., 16.61 and 15.120). Although the astrologers do not explicitly ascribe avarice to Mars, they do describe the Martian as an unscrupulous businessman.[125] Dante, moreover, considered prodigality to be a form of avarice (*Inf.* 7.30, *Purg.* 22.31–45), and Scot repeatedly attributes this quality to Mars.[126]

Although only one astrologer hints that Mars prompts men to gluttony, Dante certainly associated that sin with the fifth planet. Bonatti provided the hint, for he states that the Martian native "eats flesh that is putrid or not well cooked,"[127] but even without this clue, a gluttonous tendency would be indicated by the Martian's generalized greed and lack of restraint (above, n. 122). For whatever reason, Dante undoubtedly worked gluttony into the pattern of these cantos. Florence swollen in size by immigration is compared to a human body overstuffed with food (*Par.* 16.67–69); the city should have "gone fasting" of new neighbors (16.135). Another form of metaphorical gluttony is the greed of the Florentine cathedral chapter, whose canons "fatten themselves" by delaying the election of their next bishop (16.112–114). Such metaphors involving food come readily to Cacciaguida's Martian mind, which is alive to the right as well as the wrong use of nourishment. Thus his long and eager wait for his descendant's arrival in heaven is compared to a fast ("digiuno," 15.49), and the unpleasant truths of the *Commedia* are likened to food that, although disagreeable in taste, still provides "vital nourishment when digested" (17.130–132).

Pride. Six of the seven deadly sins are more or less evident in the Martian cantos, but all are overshadowed by the seventh—pride. Among the astrologers, Scot and Bonatti are the most insistent that Mars signifies pride (*superbia*): "it is the proud planet," Scot asserted, and "it also makes man proud."[128] This, of course, agrees wholly with the magnanimous man's emphasis on honor, which Thomas associates with the Martian virtue of fortitude (above, after n. 26). Dante accordingly incorporates both the vice and virtue of pride into these cantos. Explicitly, *superbia* is mentioned only once by name, when it is used to identify the Uberti family—"quei che son disfatti / per lor superbia!" (*Par.*16.109–110)—by the vice that led to their downfall and which has already had been exemplified in their most famous member, Farinata (*Inf.* 10).[129] Another reference, which clearly indicates the sin without actually naming it, is made by Cacciaguida, who explains his relationship to Dante in terms of his son, Alighiero, "from whom your family has its name and who a hundred years and more has circled the mountain on the first ledge" (15.91–93). He clearly refers to the first circle of Purgatory, where the sin purged is pride (*Purg.* 10–12), the besetting sin of Dante himself (13.136–138). The manner of purgation there requires the penitent, who was once erect with pride, to walk bent under the weight of a great stone, and the Pilgrim himself must bend to converse with the souls there (10.115–116, 130–137, 11.52–53, 73). This form of purgation is itself astrological in origin, for Bonatti states that "Mars gives a man a bent body."[130] Perhaps the astrologer meant this literally, but the poet took it as a metaphor illustrating the principle that every source of pride is potentially the source for an equivalent degree of humiliation. This principle, which is only hinted at in Purgatory, becomes evident in the heaven of Mars when the Pilgrim is told that in his exile "that which shall most weigh your shoulders down (*ti graverà le spalle*) will be the evil and senseless company" of his fellow exiles (*Par.* 17.61–66). To the extent that the exiled Dante prided himself on his good will and good sense, the lack of these qualities on the part of his associates in exile was a burden to him. And because both pride and bent shoulders are effects of Mars, that planet's heaven is the appropriate place to clarify the form of pride's correction in Purgatory.

The effects of pride are evident in more subtle ways as well in the heaven of Mars. Cacciaguida is delighted by his descendant (e.g., *Par.* 15.86–89), while the narrator confesses that in Mars he "gloried (*gloriai*)" in his noble birth, which, he was careful to explain, it was legitimate to do insofar as one could be proud of the family in question (16.1–6). Just as Cacciaguida, Dante's model Martian, is still subject to wrath in the form of righteous indignation, so also he displays legitimate pride, not only in his family but also in his community. He evinces proper civic pride in his satisfaction at having been born "to so reposeful, to so fair a life of citizens, to such a trusty community, to so sweet an abode" (15.130–133); he glories in the virtue and simplicity of the Florence of his time, with "her people so glorious and so just" (16.151–152). Although his pride shows through at many other points, these few examples should suffice to make the point that pride, like wrath, remains a part of his Martian character even in heaven.[131]

Honor, glory, and fame. Traditional astrology recognized that the pride of Mars entailed a "love of glory" and a "desire for honor";[132] both these adjuncts of pride figure prominently in Dante's Martian paradise.

The term *onor* is expressly applied to those chosen to appear in the *Commedia* ("non fa d'onor poco argomento," *Par.* 17.135); similarly, the Amidei affinity group was "onorata" in Cacciaguida's time (16.139). Moreover, the concept of honor is implied by equivalent expressions, such as the citizens who are "illustrious (*illustri*)" (16.90) and those who occupy the "highest seats" or hold civil magistracies (16.27, 108). Glory likewise typifies Florence in her golden age ("glorïoso," 16.151), and the nobly born, including the narrator himself, justifiably "glory" in their condition (16.2, 6). For Dante both these terms are closely linked to *fama*, which describes both the souls he has been shown in the afterworld (17.138) and the great, forgotten Florentines catalogued by Cacciaguida (16.87). Fame is, in effect, the leading characteristic of the great Martians named at the end of the episode, who on earth "were of such great renown (*gran voce*) that every muse would be rich with them" (18.32–33; see above, after n. 62).[133]

FOLLY

The early astrologers were not consistent in their characterization of the Martian mind. Alcabitius, for example, reports that Mars "signifies *calliditas* in all things,"[134] which could be taken in either a good sense ("cleverness") or a bad one ("cunning"). Michael Scot selected a neutral term to express the same quality, characterizing the Martian as "ingenious (*ingeniosus*),"[135] which Dante echoed in his description of the sunshades "which men with skill (*ingegno*) and art contrive" (*Par.* 14.117). The *calliditas* ascribed to Mars by Alcabitius seems incompatible, however, with the mental mediocrity that Haly attributed to the Martian type, who has "moderate understanding and a limited capacity for comprehension."[136] Scot nonetheless found a way to reconcile these opposing views: the native of Mars, he explained, "is a simpleton, or almost so, in doing good, but he is wise, or nearly so, in doing evil."[137] Dante did not follow him in this, for instead he couples simplicity with evil as the attributes of his fellow exiles, who will be "malvagia e scempia" (*Par.* 17.62).[138] In fact, he usually stresses the simple-minded tendencies imparted by Mars, and in doing so he concurs with the majority of astrologers, who picture the Martian as foolish, fickle, importunate, impetuous, and generally lacking in discretion.

Haly, more than any other astrologer, stressed what a fool the Martian could be. The native was in general a "fool (*stultus*)"; specifically he was "ignorant (*nescius*)," "forgetful (*obliviosus*)," and heedless of consequences; his planet in its exaltation signified "foolish people."[139] Albumasar added that the Martian was prone to have a false and foolish sense of security ("stulta securitas"); the *Liber novem iudicum* summed it up in a word—"indiscretus," which in medieval Latin had come to mean "indiscreet," "unwise," or "lacking in judgment."[140] The "foolish people" mentioned by Haly are echoed by Dante's "gente folle," the pagans whose obscure oracles are contrasted with the clear predictions of Cacciaguida (*Par*.17.31–35). Martian folly, however, is most amply exemplified by the Pilgrim himself. His imperfect comprehension of the opening hymn, which came to him "as to one who understands not, but hears" (14.126), certainly qualified him as *nescius*. Even more foolish is the false security that he at first displays when inquiring about his future (17.23–24), though after hearing what is in store for him, he assumes a more prudent attitude, admitting that "such a blow is heaviest to whosoever is most heedless" (17.108).

Folly was too general a term for some astrologers, who preferred instead to describe various specific manifestations. Thus Scot says that Mars "signifies whatever is done impiously (*impie*), madly, and with no sense of discretion."[141] Accordingly Dante characterizes his fellow exiles as "tutta matta ed *empia*" (*Par.* 17.64) in their plotting against Florence, their alma mater; their conduct contrasts with the *pietas* of the Florentine matron whose oft-told tales instilled respect for the progenitors of the Florentine people (15.124–126).[142] Another instance of the Martian's lack of discretion, also noted by Scot, is his poor sense of the appropriate time, for he is "importunate (*inportunum*),"[143] a term that is echoed in the family named "Importuni" (16.133), which Cacciaguida blames for promoting the growth of their neighborhood inopportunely. Finally, the Martian shows his folly in fickleness, for "in matters that require thought," Albumasar states, "he changes his mind."[144] This was indeed the weakness of Buondelmonte, who by jilting his finacée for another, plunged Florence into a century of civil war (16.136–147).

SPEECH

According to Scot, Mars "makes a man talkative (*loquacem*)," and more than that, "eloquent (*eloquens*)."[145] Cacciaguida certainly typifies the first of these Martian qualities, for he speaks more lines in the *Commedia* than any other character, except of course for the Pilgrim's guides. Cacciaguida utters some 299 lines in direct discourse, as well as two speeches that are reported indirectly; the runner-up is Aquinas, with 287 lines of direct discourse and no hint of further communications.[146] Moreover, Cacciaguida is technically eloquent, for he speaks, not in the vernacular, but in Latin. Unlikely though this ability may seem in a simple knight, it is plainly indicated in the text: his first speech is wholly in Latin (*Par.* 15.28–30), and although he subsequently speaks less profoundly (44–45), still it is "not in this our modern speech" (16.33) but "with precise Latin (*con preciso / latin*)" (17.34–35). To be sure, the narrator translates all but the first of these speeches into Italian, but this is to be expected, since he has already done so in the case of Aquinas, who, we are informed, had been speaking Latin (12.144).[147]

Only Scot attributes loquaciousness and eloquence to Mars, but most astrologers remark the planet's affinity for abusive language (*maledictiones*),[148] insults (*contumeliae*),[149] derision,[150] and the like,[151] for the Martian character is rough and bristly (*horridus*).[152] Such tendencies are treated explicitly when Cacciaguida advises the poet to be utterly frank in telling his story, even though his words may seem "harsh (*brusca*)" (*Par.* 17.126) to those sensitive to shame. Indeed, Cacciaguida has been guided by his own advice throughout the interview, for he has relentlessly castigated a good half of Florence's prominent families in terms that would certainly arouse resentment. The Pilgrim handles this bristly old man with kid gloves, plying him with "blandishments" (16.30), so that, for almost twenty lines his speech is comparatively "sweeter and gentler" (16.32); then the Martian harshness surfaces again. Finally, when Martian loquacity is mixed with the violence natural to that planet, the result is an "outcry (*clamor*)."[153] Accordingly, the Pilgrim is warned that he will be blamed by his accusers not in truth but "in outcry—*in grido*" (*Par.* 17.53). Similarly, his poem will be his outcry ("questo tuo grido," 17.133) against the most famous sinners.

A Martian Miscellany

Up to now our concern has been the Martian personality; we have seen it first as typified by the god of war, then by its virtues and vices. In addition to these large, coherent categories, however, the astrologers supplied Dante with a number of apposite details that bear little relation to one another, other than their common association with Mars. I have gathered them together in this section, where they are organized into small, relatively discrete categories, which in turn are grouped only loosely together. First come sex and childbirth, then brothers and boys; next, occupations and animals; followed by the perceived qualities of color and taste, by climate, and finally by various sorts of motion, including violent blows and travel.

Sex. The astrologers available in Latin to Dante associated the planet with only the seamier side of sex. Alcabitius took Mars to signify "the beastliness of coitus," which Bonatti interpreted to mean "an abundance of coitus."[154] The typical Martian is accordingly lustful, Scot explains; he is "a seducer of almost everyone" and specializes in the violation of virgins.[155] Ibn Ezra adds that the planet "promotes pandering."[156]

The *Commedia*'s cantos of Mars faithfully reflect these lusty proclivities, and most memorably when Cacciaguida praises the modesty of early Florence: "Sardanapalus had not yet arrived to show what could be done in the chamber" (*Par.* 15.107–108). Again, Buondelmonte's decision to break his engagement and marry another woman was prompted by lust:

> o Buondelmonte, quanto mal fuggisti
> le nozze süe per li altrui conforti!   (*Par.* 16.140–141)

"O Buondelmonte, how misfortunate you fled from its [the house of Amidei's] nuptials for the comfort of another."

Lust is clearly the motive according to my interpretation of the last phrase, which usually is rendered "at the promptings of another,"[157] namely Buondelmonte's future mother-in-law. But even the traditional understanding of the phrase brings us to the same conclusion, for what caused Buondelmonte to change his mind, if we believe Villani, was the beauty of the Donati girl, which was much greater than that of his Amidei finacée. The would-be mother-in-law effected her purpose simply by promising Buondelmonte her daughter's hand and then letting him see how beautiful her girl was; the devil, Villani says, did the rest.[158] A final instance of lust is the adulterous affair between Queen Guinevere and Lancelot, to which allusion is made at *Paradiso* 16.13–15. Beatrice smiles at the Pilgrim's manifestation of his newborn respect for Cacciaguida, just as the lady of Malehaut coughed knowingly at the moment that Lancelot was about to reveal the origin of his love for Guinevere.[159] This allusion is, of course, underscored by Dante's use of the same episode in the circle of lust (*Inf.* 5.127–138). There the Martian character of the episode is reinforced by Francesca's remark that the book containing this episode brought her and Paolo together just as in the story Gallehault had served as the go-between for Guinevere and Lancelot. Not to put too fine a point on it, then, the episode was a pander—a function that Ibn Ezra has told us is promoted by Mars.

Childbirth. Lusty Mars does not want offspring. Albumasar, Alcabitius, Ibn Ezra, and Bonatti all agree that the planet signifies aborted childbirth, sometimes intentionally induced.[160] Moreover, for Albumasar, Mars indicated a variety of difficulties associated with childbirth: "it is oppressive (*gravis*) to the pregnant woman, harmful to her when she is in labor, and most dangerous to her newborn offspring."[161] This explains why Dante has Cacciaguida dwell on the circumstances of "the birth in which my mother, who now is sainted, was lightened of me with whom she had been burdened (*grave*)" (*Par.* 16.35–36). Not only was the pregnancy burdensome, but the delivery itself was also difficult: "Mary, called on with loud cries, gave me [to Florence]" (15.133). In latter-day Florence, by contrast, daughters are unwanted because costly (15.103–105), and there are even "houses empty of family" because sex is now practiced for pleasure rather than for procreation (106–108). Just how libidinous Florentines contrived to avoid having children is not made explicit, but since artificially induced abortion was known and practiced in thirteenth-century Europe, the passage could readily suggest to the contemporary reader abortive as well as contraceptive measures.[162]

Boyhood and brothers. The astrologers generally agreed in assigning the period of youth, or early manhood (*iuventus*), to the planet Mars. Albumasar disagreed; for him Mars governed the earlier age of adolescence (*adolescentia*).[163] Dante introduced a fleeting allusion to the latter by having the Pilgrim ask, "what were the years that were reckoned in your boyhood (*püerizia*)" (*Par.* 16.23–24).

Brothers are closely associated with boyhood; they are the third event in a person's life, Bonatti explained, coming after conception and birth, just as Mars is the third planet.[164] Most astrologers, however, simply take Mars to signify *fratres* without explanation.[165] It is appropriate to Cacciaguida's planet, therefore, that he should not neglect to name his brothers: "Moronto fu mio frate ed Eliseo" (*Par.* 15.136).

Peaceful occupations. Mars's close connection with iron and fire inevitably put blacksmithing under his control, but the planet signifies other, less predictable arts as well. Although Mars, when joined with the Sun, can signifiy the smithing or minting of gold,[166] by itself the planet signifies the craft of gilding, especially when applied to the accoutrements of war.[167] Accordingly, Dante exemplifies gilding in general by the "balls of gold" in the Lamberti arms (*Par.* 16.110) and its application to the tools of war by Galigaio, who had "the hilt and the pommel in his house already gilded" (16.101–102). Moreover, gilding would seem to be implied by the "mirror of gold" to which Cacciaguida is compared (17.123), although Ibn Ezra offers another possibility by placing "polishers (*expoliatores*)" under the influence of Mars.[168] The latter interpretation would explain the recurrence of mirror imagery in connection with Mars (*Par.* 15.113, 17.41, and 18.2) and is not incompatible with the traditional connection of mirrors with Venus (see above, p. 84), because Bonatti takes Mars to signify the fabrication of women's jewelry and the like when the planet's warlike nature is softened by Venus.[169] It is, of course, just such a softening that Cacciaguida condemns in Florence. In his day the women of a more purely Martian Florence were not overdressed with necklaces, crowns, and other female adornments (15.100–101).

Mars also governs the most humble of occupations. Scot says that the Martian enjoys any work (*ars*) that is "dangerous or difficult, exhausting, contemptible, and low paid."[170] This downscale Martian is surely "the lowliest artisan (*l'ultimo artista*)" of whose purity Cacciaguida boasts (*Par.* 16.51). The least expected Martian occupation, however, is that of chorister, which is noted only by Ibn Ezra.[171] Such, of course, is the heavenly occupation of Cacciaguida himself, whose soul "showed me how great an artist it was among the singers (*i cantor*) of that heaven" (18.50–51).

Animals. Latin astrology routinely associates Mars with sheep because that planet has its day house in the sign of Aries, the ram.[172] This animal species accordingly appears five times in Dante's Martian cantos, usually in the form of a lamb. The shift from ram to lamb was probably suggested by the "Agnel di Dio che le peccata tolle" (*Par.* 17.33), whose sacrifice on the Cross the Pilgrim glimpsed as he entered this heaven (14.104–105). The Martian propensity for bloodshed and violence of course enhances the aptness of the image. The lamb is also linked to the theme of civil life by Cacciaguida's proverbial justification of the small community: "a blind bull falls more headlong than the blind lamb" (16.71). Like the *agnello*, the normal, natural community is not only modest in size but also, in consequence, both nonviolent and innocent of the sins that beset overdeveloped cities, of which latter-day Florence is the type. Even the citizens of a corrupt community can become "mild as a lamb (*agnel*)" when they, like the Adimari, are overawed by threats of violence or simply bribed (16.117). Moreover, sheep also provide the image of citizens as members of a citywide Christian community: thus the Pilgrim calls his city "the sheepfold (*ovil*) of Saint John" (16.25). These civic sheep are under the care of John the Baptist, the patron saint of Florence, whom Dante contrasts with Mars, the pagan patron of the city (*Inf.* 13.143–144; cf. *Par.* 16.47: "tra Marte e 'l Batista"). Like Mars, the Baptist was associated with sheep, for he is usually depicted bearing the Agnus Dei. Thus the image of Florence as a sheepfold is appropriate to both its pagan and its Christian patron. What Florence rejected in changing patrons was the baleful influence of the god of war and his planet; the city, by the astrological doctrine of signatures, still remains under the planet's influence, but that can work for good as well as evil. Thus Dante takes the lamb as a metaphor for the natural community of citizens no less than for the spiritual community of Christians. Finally, the shepherd and his sheep provide yet another Martian image in these cantos, the flock in this case being the whole community of living Christians under the care of their pastors, the popes ("i pastor," 15.144).

"Among the birds," Ibn Ezra declares, the one proper to Mars is "the goshawk, and other such raptors."[173] The narrator accordingly uses an image drawn from falconry to describe how his eye followed the introduction of one hero after another on the cross of Mars: "com' occhio segue suo falcon volando" (*Par.* 18.45). Again, a less mundane raptor is the imperial eagle on the arms of "the great Lombard who bears the holy bird upon the ladder" (17.71–72).

Curiously enough, the wolf is conspicuous by its absence from the Martian cantos. Once might expect it here because it was sacred to the god Mars in Roman mythology.[174] Dante almost certainly knew this tradition, because elsewhere he associates wolves with war and its god. For instance, he repeated the legend that made Romulus, who was suckled by a wolf, the son of Mars (*Purg.* 8.131–132); moreover, he characterizes the preying of wolves on lambs as a war: "lupi chi li danno guerra" (*Purg.* 25.6). But none of the astrologers he could have known in Latin made the connection between Mars and the wolf,[175] so he too avoids it in the heaven of Mars, which, it would therefore seem, draws its imagery from the celestial rather than the legendary Mars.

Colors. Since Mars is the red planet, the astrologers agreed that it governed its natural color.[176] The Pilgrim, of course, observes the planet's proper color—it was "more red (*roggio*) than usual" (*Par.* 14.87)—and the Martian souls also glow with a fiery red ("roggi," 14.94). The poet found other ways to bring red into his Martian cantos: for example, the closing word of canto 16 is "vermiglio," the color of the Guelf lily (16.154). Reddening is also implied in the blushes that are twice imputed to wrongdoers: those that falsify measures ("arrosan," 16.105) and Dante's fellow exiles, who will blush red ("rossa") when their foolish, impious schemes against Florence fail (17.66).[177] Such blushing would be governed by Mars, to whom the astrologers assign the blood vessels (*venae*) of the human body.[178]

As one would expect, Mars "possesses . . . every red stone,"[179] but surprisingly he governs gems of other colors as well. "Pearls are Martian in power," claims the *Liber novem iudicum*,[180] a statement which lends credence to Singleton's suggestion that the gems on a ribbon to which the Martian souls are compared are in fact pearls (*Par.* 15.22).[181] Further possibilities are opened by Mars's association with colors in which red is mixed with yellow. Ibn Ezra lists saffron ("crocus") as a Martian pigment,[182] which Michael Scot offers in diluted form: "Among the colors, [Mars] denotes red or white and citrine (*citrinum*)."[183] Both combinations of red and yellow suggest the color of the gem topaz—to which the Pilgrim compares the glowing soul of Cacciaguida ("vivo topazio," 15.85)—and especially the color citrine, since the semiprecious yellow quartz of that name is otherwise known as "false topaz."[184] Previous studies of Dante's use of gems in the *Commedia* have assumed that Cacciaguida resembled a topaz because the red light natural to Mars was blended with yellow light from the Sun,[185] although this seems unlikely in view of the explicit statement that the souls illuminated by the reflected light of the Sun were remarkable for their redness ("tanto robbi," 14.94). Now it appears that the reference to a topaz was suggested by that gem's specifically Martian color, which made it appropriate to this heaven.[186] The same may be true of the effect created by Cacciaguida who, in moving along the Martian cross, "seemed like fire behind alabaster" (15.24), since alabaster, too, is red-yellow, somewhat more so than ivory.[187] The comparison with alabaster may well have been suggested to Dante by Scot's combination of "white and citrine" as Martian colors.

Bitter tastes. Bitter tastes belong to Mars, declared Alcabitius, and he was echoed by Bonatti, Scot, and John of Seville.[188] Dante works this small detail into his Martian cantos three times. First, the Pilgrim characterizes Hell as "the world bitter (*amaro*) without end" (*Par.* 17.112); a few lines later he fears that for many readers his reports from the afterlife will have an "exceedingly sour (*agrume*) taste" (17.117); and finally, pondering what he has learned from Cacciaguida, he tempers his bitter thoughts ("l'acerbo") with sweet ones (18.3).[189]

Countries and peoples. Ptolemy's system of climatic zones, which had provided Dante with geographic allusions in the heavens of Mercury, Venus, and the Sun, had little to offer the poet for the third climate, which Mars ruled. He was following the division of the *climata* made by Alcoarismi (al-Khwârizmî), probably as he found it in Albertus Magnus, *De natura locorum* 1.9,[190] and consequently he accepted 30° north latitude as the boundary between the third and fourth climates. Hence he was bound to place both Alexandria and Jerusalem in the fourth climate because their accepted latitudes, according to both the Marseilles Tables and the Toledo Tables, were 31° and 32° respectively. Thus we have already seen allusions to Jerusalem and northern Egypt in the heaven of the Sun, which governs the fourth climate (above, p. 120). Had he followed the system of climatic division proposed by Alfraganus, in which the two climates are divided at 33° 22′ north latitude, both cities would have fallen into the third climate. Alcabitius and Bonatti evidently followed Alfraganus in this, inasmuch as both place Jerusalem under the lordship of Mars.[191] Ezra wavered between the two systems and inexplicably split the difference, assigning Israel to the fourth climate and Egypt to the third.[192] Dante, seems to have ignored these deviations from the Albertus-Alcoarismi system,[193] but the system he preferred supplied him with scant material for poetic allusions to the third climate. The Marseilles Tables, for example, would have provided him with the names of four cities in this climate, all of them in Moslem hands, of which only Medina is likely to have been meaningful either to him or his audience.[194]

Since the third climate offered no suitable allusions, Dante turned to Michael Scot, who connected Mars not with places but with certain peoples: "in general Mars lords it over (*dominatur contra*) Saracens and warlike, warfaring peoples."[195] The third climate was included in this formulation, for the Marseilles Tables named only Moslem cities, but Scot's indication was not climate-specific, so Dante was free to allude to Saracens in any climate, not to mention other warlike peoples. The eight heroes pointed out on the cross of Mars were, of course, all famous for their wars. Six of them certainly fought against Saracens: Charlemagne and Roland in Spain; William of Orange and his Saracen-born comrade, Renouard, in southern France; Robert Guiscard in southern Italy and Sicily; and Godfrey of Bouillon, the first Christian king of Jerusalem, in the Holy Land.[196] The other two heroes, Joshua and Judas Maccabaeus, were both Jews who lived before either Christ or Mohammed, and Dante may have loosely associated them with Saracens because they fought against those who, like Semiramis, "held the land that the Sultan rules" (*Inf.* 5.60). Cacciaguida certainly fits the prevalent pattern because of his crusade with the Emperor Conrad "against the iniquity of that law whose people, through fault of the Pastors, usurp your right," namely the Saracens, "that foul folk" who martyred him (*Par.* 15.139–148).

The Saracens were only one of the "warlike, warfaring peoples" ruled by Mars; Alcabitius and, following him, Bonatti, allocated to Mars "the land of the Romans as far west as the setting sun."[197] Although Rome is an ever recurrent theme in the *Commedia*, it is continually woven into the Martian cantos with an unusual density, especially by Cacciaguida— himself perhaps descended from a Roman family[198]—who is fond of contrasting Roman virtue with the vices of latter-day Florence. He mentions Rome twice by name and alludes to it a third time (*Par.* 15.126, 16.10, 15.109–111); he also names such eminent Romans as Cincinnatus and Cornelia (15.19), Julius Caesar (16.58–59), and the Roman emperors Charlemagne (18.43) and Conrad (15.139); moreover, he alludes to the bishops of Rome in general (15.144) and to Popes Boniface VIII and Clement V in particular (17.50–51, 82); finally, Virgil is named by the Pilgrim as his guide (17.19) and is referred to by the narrator as his authority for the reunion of Aeneas and Anchises (15.28). To be sure, attention in the Martian cantos is focussed on Florence rather than Rome, but that stress is also authorized by astrology, for the final item on Alcabitius's list of parts of the world subject to Mars is "the lands of the Tuscans."[199]

MOTION
"Mars signifies mobility (*mobilitatem*) in all things." This generalization by the Greek astrological poet Dorotheus (fl. ca. 100 A.D.) was echoed in one form or another by most astrologers in the Latin-Arabic tradition.[200] Some, like Haly, stress motion as mutability; more typical was Ibn Ezra, who took Mars to signify "motion from place to place."[201] Just such local motion characterizes the blessed souls whom Dante observes in Mars. From the first the narrator emphasizes their movement ("si movien," *Par.* 14.110). Cacciaguida himself moves like a meteor—a star that "changes place (*tramuti loco*)" (15.16)—and this action is subsequently used to characterize him as the soul "who had changed its place (*avea mutato sito*)" (17.6). Eventually, of course, each of the Martian souls moves as it is identified (18.37–51), and verbs twice stress the abstract notion of movement in this connection ("moversi," 18.41; "mota," 49).

Furthermore, Dorotheus ascribed a certain quality of motion to Mars: the planet signified "speedy motion (*festinatio*),"[202] or, as Scot called it, "fast motion (*velocem motum*)."[203] In consequence, Scot says, Mars causes men to be "agile" and to go "nimbly and swiftly."[204] Not only is Cacciaguida himself as swift as a falling star, but his thoughts are also colored by this influence, for he chooses to identify his own birthplace by reference to the course of Florence's annual foot race (16.42). Similarly, the element of speed recurs in these cantos: some of the souls in the cross move quickly ("veloce," 14.113), the slain bull falls faster ("più avaccio," 16.70),[205] and time spurs toward the Pilgrim (17.106). The ultimate refinement of this theme is provided by Albumasar, for whom speedy motion is also "unforeseen,"[206] which is just how the narrator represents the dramatic entrance of Cacciaguida, who appears as unexpectedly "as, through the still and cloudless evening sky a sudden fire shoots from time to time, moving the eyes that were at rest" (15.13–15).

Blows. Martian motion is often violent, since the planet imparts a propensity to violence. Thus Mars "signifies striking (*percutere*)" and the resulting "blows" as well.[207] Both aspects of violent motion are faithfully mirrored by Dante, who uses a calc of the Latin verb ("percuote," *Par.* 17.134) and an equivalent noun ("per colpo," 17.107) to describe the action of the wind and of time respectively.[208] Michael Scot drew on other properties of Mars to further qualify the general concept of "striking blows" that he found in his predecessors: with him the blows become "injurious," and they are one of many ways in which Martians are impelled by their planet "to do evil deeds in public or in private."[209] Cianghella, one of Cacciaguida's examples of scandalous modern conduct, was notorious for just such behavior. Benvenuto of Imola reported that she once caused a riot in church by attacking some women who would not make room for her; at home, he says, "she went through the house . . . with a rod in her hand, now striking the servant, now the cook."[210]

Journeys. Travel constitutes a special kind of local motion, and when it carries one away from one's place of birth, travel could be considered a form of violent rather than natural motion, to use a commonplace distinction of Aristotelian physics.[211] Travel (*peregrinatio*) was associated with Mars by Alcabitius, Bonatti, and Scot.[212] Perhaps Alcabitius had violent motion in mind when he took Mars in itself to signify a particular kind of travel—"peregrinationem extra patriam"—on which Bonatti elaborated, saying that Mars signified "trips outside one's country and birthplace."[213] Cacciaguida's complaint against Florentine merchants who left their wives to travel on business to France, which might prove to be their final resting place (*Par.* 15.118–120), is surely a case in point; another may be the emigrants who left their homelands to settle in Florence, to Cacciaguida's distress (16.49–72). A third, less deplorable, instance of Martian travel is the Second Crusade, which similarly took Cacciaguida himself to a foreign grave (15.139–148). Each case is associated with a recurrent theme in the Martian cantos, but they all are nonetheless overshadowed by the two great *peregrinatio* themes of the *Commedia*, both of which culminate in canto 17, where the Pilgrim learns of his impending exile (44–60) and of the reason for his pilgrimage through the afterworld, which he has been shown in order that he may write of it (112–142).[214]

Revelation. According to Ibn Ezra, Mars "signifies revelation (*revelationem*)," which he later defines as "laying bare whatever is disclosed."[215] Alcabitius chose another word to express the same concept: *apertio*—the act of opening or making a thing accessible.[216] The generality of this concept enabled Dante to apply it widely, both in major themes, such as his exile and mission, and in lesser matters as well. Can Grande's future, for example, is revealed to the Pilgrim, though he is enjoined to conceal it (*Par.* 17.92–96). The Pilgrim's thoughts are revealed ("pandi") in the mirror of the divine mind (15.63), and Cacciaguida himself is "hidden and revealed (*chiuso e parvente*)" by the smiling light of his glory (17.63). Similarly, fortune, like the Moon, "covers and discovers (*cuopre e discuopre*)" the affairs of Florence (16.83). To be sure, the *Paradiso* is filled with revelations, but here in Mars both the narrator and his informant make the reader aware of the process by repeated reference to things hidden and manifest. Fame is hidden by time ("nascosa," 16.87), and Dante's future holds snares that also are hidden ("nascose," 17.96); just so, the mortality of long-lived things is concealed ("celasi," 16.80). All of these occult matters are, of course, revealed to the Pilgrim, who is enjoined to make his vision "manifesta" (17.128) and is assured that he had only been shown famous persons because one does not learn from examples that are not patent ("non paia," 17.142).

The principal revelation that the Pilgrim receives while in Mars is the prophecy of his exile, which had only been alluded to darkly by earlier informants.[217] That he should learn of his impending misfortunes at this stage in his journey is appropriate to the planet that brings "adverse fortune and makes man unhappy in many ways,"[218] often in the form of sudden emergencies with unforeseen results.[219] Although Fortune has already been identified by Virgil as a separate intelligence that controls the distribution of worldly goods (*Inf.* 7.77–81), it would seem that she in turn is influenced by Mars, as one would expect in a cosmic order wherein the higher organs "receive from above and operate downwards" (*Par.* 2.123). Mars's special influence on Fortune accounts for the several references to her in the fifth heaven (*Par.* 15.118, 16.84).[220]

The Malignancy of Mars

At the beginning of this chapter we saw that Dante took a positive view of Mars's influence, referring to it the cardinal virtue of fortitude and its sequelae. Nonetheless we have found as our study progressed that Mars has many negative effects as well, which is only to be expected from Beatrice's assertion that the planets are to be blamed as well as honored for their influence on human conduct (*Par.* 4.58). For the astrologers, however, Mars is far worse than it appears in the Martian cantos of the *Paradiso*. To conclude this study, I propose to confront this apparent disparity and seek to determine whether Dante's view of Mars departs from traditional astrology or can be harmonized with it.

The bad planet. Among the astrologers there is a consensus on the moral nature of Mars. The best generalization is probably that formulated by Michael Scot: "it is a planet . . . harmful to many by its influence," or in one word, "injurious."[221] The elementary handbooks, however, put it more simply: for John of Seville, Mars is "the star of evils (*malorum*)," and for Alcabitius it is just plain "bad (*malus*)."[222] Rabbi Ibn Ezra makes the same point, but with greater force: "it is altogether bad (*malus*) in its entirety [and is] absolutely deprived of good."[223] Still Scot can improve even on this by elaboration: "the planet is also untrue, unlucky, and good for nothing (*nequam*)."[224]

This evil influence consequently endows the Martian man with a host of vices, which the astrologers list, often at great length. For example, Albumasar says that the Martian "says and does evil, and is ill-disposed (*malignus*),"[225] though Scot, as usual, has the most luxuriant list, including such negative qualities as "malicious," "odious," and "diligent in doing evil."[226] Such lists, of which I have given only a sample, can be summed up by a principle provided by Ibn Ezra: "Mars augments turpitude (*turpitudo*)," that is, any shameful, disgraceful, or dishonorable tendency in man.[227]

When one turns to Dante's Martian cantos to look for traces of the planet's evil influences, the first impression is one of surprise, because only a few of the astrologers' key terms are echoed there. Notably absent are the words derived from *malo*, most of which occur frequently elsewhere in the *Commedia: maladizione* (1), *maladetto* (12), *maligno* (6), *malignamente* (1), *malizia* (9), *malizioso* (1), and *malmenare* (1).[228] Nonetheless words related to *malo* do appear in these cantos, and in each case they describe, not undifferentiated evil, but some specific effect of Mars that we have already encountered.

(1)
o Buondelmonte, quanto *mal* fuggisti
le nozze süe per li altrui conforti!   (*Par.* 16.140–141)

"O Buondelmonte, how harmfully you fled from its nuptials through the counsels of another."[229]

Here the stress is on the destructive influence of Mars, which brings harm to the whole city, as the following lines make clear. But these lines also suggest that Buondelmonte acted in this way because of his specifically Martian character, for in rejecting his finacée in favor of another he showed himself to be fickle and foolish. According to Villani, what caused him to change his mind was the sight of a more desirable bride shown to him by her mother, who suggested that her exceedingly beautiful daughter would suit him better. Like a true Martian, who "quickly desires whatever he sees,"[230] Buondelmonte hastened to marry her instead.[231] Impulsive cupidity, then, lay at the root of the matter.

To make the grounds of Buondelmonte's choice clear, Dante would have us understand that it lay between two old Florentine families, both of which claimed descent from the original Roman colonists. The jilted finacée was of the Amidei, a family which Cacciaguida says was in his day "honored, both itself and its consorts" (*Par.* 16.139), while her rival was of the Donati family, equally ancient and proud, but nonetheless ready to marry rich nonnobles (119–120).[232] In consequence, we must gather that social status did not determine Buondelmonte's choice; instead it was based on the relative physical attractions of the two women. Buondelmonte's family, on the other hand, had immigrated from the Val di Greve (66), so no matter which woman he had married, the union would exemplify Cacciaguida's thesis that "the intermingling of people was ever the beginning of harm (*mal*) to the city."

(2)
Sempre la confusion de le persone
principio fu del mal de la cittade.   (*Par.* 16.67–68)

The civil wars that resulted from Buondelmonte's murder by the Amidei, his dishonored, would-be in-laws, were only part of the *mal* inflicted on Florence by immigration; it takes two-thirds of canto 16 for Cacciaguida to develop fully the contrast between the peaceful and honorable city in his day and its degenerate state in Dante's time (*Par.* 16.44–154). The harm is manifested in various ways, many of them recognizable as effects of Mars (e.g., pride, envy, dishonor, civil war), but again the root of it all is cupidity. On the one hand, the Florentines were too eager to enlarge their boundaries (54), while on the other hand the immigrants who swelled the population of the city and upset its static society came to make money. Thus the Caponsacchi came from Fiesole to engage in trade (121–122); another family rose in three generations from being itinerant beggars or peddlers in Semifonte to be Florentine bankers and merchants (61–63); and the Adimari could always be bought off with money (117). In other words, one form of cupidity led to another: through territorial aggrandizement the Florentines created commercial opportunities for newcomers to the city. Again, both the cause—cupidity—and its effects are typically Martian.

(3) The only form of *mal-* in these cantos is *malvagia*, used to characterize Dante's fellow exiles: "the ungrateful (*malvagia*) and simpleminded company with which you shall fall into this vale; which, being wholly ungrateful (*ingrata*), wholly mad and impious (*matta ed empia*) shall come to oppose you."

> . . . la compagnia malvagia e scempia
> con la qual tu cadrai in questa valle;
> che tutta ingrata, tutta matta ed empia
> si farà contr' a te   (*Par.* 17.62–65)

Singleton, following the usual interpretation of this passage, translates instead: "the evil and senseless company with which you shall fall into this vale; which shall then become all ungrateful, all mad and malevolent against you."[233] But it seems far more likely that the object of the exiles' ingratitude is not Dante but rather Florence. Otherwise "empia" has to be taken in the loose sense of "malevolent" because one can hardly suppose that it was "impious" to oppose one of the company's members, whereas the term would properly describe a hostile attitude towards their native city. This would fit the generally received view that Dante probably remained with the exiles while they attempted to negotiate a peaceful return to Florence but disassociated himself from their company when they and the Pistoians launched an attack against Florence from Lastra in 1304.[234] Be that as it may, however one decides to translate "malvagia" in this context, it clearly describes the end product of the degeneration of Florence as traced by Cacciaguida.

To recapitulate our results so far: the "*mal* of the city" had its beginnings in the twelfth century; by the early thirteenth century, the accumulated explosive elements were ignited into civil war when Buondelmonte acted "mal"; and a century later the exiled leaders of one faction are so maddened by their loss that they have become "malvagia"—at least "wicked," and more likely impious and ungrateful enough to attack their native city. Moreover, their conduct is described in terms which we have seen are the proper effects of Mars: not only the generalized evil that *malvagia* suggests, but also more specific qualities such as impiety, folly, and "bestiality (*bestialitate*)" (67), not to mention the propensity to wage war, and especially a fratricidal one. Once again it seems that the poet took special care not to ascribe undifferentiated evil to Mars; when he uses *mal* and *malvagia*, it is in a context that enables the reader to identify the specific forms that he had in mind. Furthermore, his use of *mal* and *malvagia* in these cantos is always associated with Florence, and indeed seems to be deployed in order to provide a conspectus of the baleful effects of Mars on the city's history.

Were *mal* and *malvagia* the only terms indicating generalized badness to appear in these cantos, it might seem unlikely that the poet intended the pattern I am proposing, inasmuch as Florence is the principal subject of these cantos, and so it need not be either remarkable or significant that they all relate to that theme. What convinces me that the pattern is intentional rather than coincidental is the presence of a second group of terms that echo those with which the astrologers describe the badness of Mars, and this second group is also associated with a city—Rome—but one that appears in these cantos infrequently and always in connection with Martian evil.

Montemalo. Moreover, the first of these terms also links Rome with Florence, thus binding the two complexes together. In canto 15 Cacciaguida contrasts the sobriety and chastity of his Florence with the various forms of *luxuria* that were symptomatic of the cupidity of latter-day Florentines (*Par.* 15.97–129). But the contrast has a spatial as well as a temporal dimension, for in the middle of the passage he declares that in his time Florence had not yet surpassed Rome. This declaration is framed in terms that associate each city with sin: for each is designated by the suggestive name of a hill that dominates the northern approach to the city—Uccellatoio for Florence and Montemalo for Rome. The former, which literally means "a site for catching birds," suggests cupidity, that is, the entrapment of desire, since in the *Commedia* desire is frequently represented by avian imagery (explicitly at *Par.* 15.72 and *Purg.* 4.28–29), while the latter hardly requires interpretation: Rome is the "mount of evil"—Monte*malo*. Thus we are assured that Rome participates in the evils that beset Florence. This, of course, comes as no surprise to the reader who recalls Marco Lombardo's explanation of the ills of Italy: essentially it is the "ill-guidance (*mala condotta*)" provided by the papacy, which by its greed for temporal goods had set a bad example for ordinary Christians (*Purg.* 16.100–105).[235]

Traligna and maligna. In fact Cacciaguida expressly blames the Roman curia for the influx of opportunists into Florence. One Florentine commercial family would still be beggars in Semifonte, Cacciaguida asserts, "if the folk who are the most degenerate (*traligna*) in the world had not been a stepmother to Caesar, but like a mother, benignant (*benigna*) to her son" (*Par.* 16.58–60). Although the allusion is obscure in its details,[236] the general sense is clearly that the family made its fortune as a result of one of the thirteenth-century conflicts between pope and emperor ("Cesare," 59), and since the fortune was made no more than three generations before 1300, the emperor in question could only be Frederick II.[237] Cacciaguida was right, for these wars did indeed make many a fortune in Florence, because the papacy borrowed heavily from Florentine merchant bankers to finance its cause.[238] Thus Rome's evil is again linked to the degeneration of Florence, this time with further hints of Martian influence. The papal curia is explicitly termed "*traligna*—degenerate" (98) because the former goodness of the papacy had turned to evil, which corresponds to the tendency, noted by Ibn Ezra, that Mars has of bringing out the worst in anything (above, n. 227). Furthermore, the Romans are implicitly called *maligna* or "ill disposed" as well, though the actual term is avoided by the rhetorical softening device of litotes, whereby they are likened to a stepmother who is *not* "benignant (*benigna*)" (60), that is, its rhyming opposite, "malignant," which Albumasar listed as one of the properties of Mars (above, n. 225).

Turpa and nequizia. The two references to the papacy we have already

examined give added point to a third passage in which the papacy is
mentioned, at the close of canto 15:

> Dietro li andai incontro a la nequizia
>   di quella legge il cui popolo usurpa,
>   per colpa d'i pastor, vostra giustizia.
> Quivi fu' io da quella gente turpa
>   disviluppato dal mondo fallace,
>   lo cui amor molt'anime deturpa. . . .   (*Par.* 15.142–147)

> I went, in his train, against the unrighteousness (*nequizia*) of that
> law whose people, through fault of the Pastors, usurp your right.
> There by that base folk (*turpa gente*) was I released from the
> deceitful world, the love of which debases (*deturpa*) many souls. . . .

Here Cacciaguida extends the contrasts between his world and Dante's to
cover the crusades, which were still a potent force in Christendom when
he accompanied Emperor Conrad III on the Second Crusade in 1147. This,
like the First Crusade, was organized by the papacy, as were subsequent
ones until, after the Sixth Crusade (1228–29), popes showed little concern
for the recovery of the Holy Land. This change of policy causes Cacciaguida to complain here that Moslems hold the Holy Land, which by right
should be Christian, "through fault of the Pastors" (144). It is a complaint
that Dante repeats elsewhere (*Inf.* 27.85–90 and *Par.* 9.125–126), but nowhere does he come closer than in this passage to specifying what he
thought the reason was for this change. Evidently Dante considered papal
disinterest in crusading to be culpable ("per colpa," 144), but as usual the
poet is guarded in his criticisms of the papacy.

What permits us to go beyond the text are the other two references
to the thirteenth-century papacy in these Martian cantos. Both indicate
the preoccupations that diverted papal attention away from the crusades:
at home the Roman curia set the standard for ostentatious luxury (Montemalo) and in Italy its efforts were almost wholly absorbed by Guelf politics. Thus by juxtaposition Dante hints that worldly concerns led the
papacy to neglect the crusades, and consequently its "colpo" can be seen
as an instance of the generalization with which Cacciaguida concludes the
passage: love of the deceitful world debases many souls (146–147). Once
again the power of Mars to bring out the worst is manifested in the pa-

pacy, which we have already seen to be "degenerate (*tralinga*)" (16.58) and which now appears also as "debased (*deturpa*)" (15.147).

Thus the papacy proves to be no better than the Moslems, who in the same sentence are described as "that base (*turpa*) folk" (145). They, too, are under the malignant influence of Mars, as the epithet *turpa* shows, since Ibn Ezra had declared that "Mars augments turpitude" (above, n. 227). At first glance this seems to be nothing more than religious prejudice calling names that lack specific content, but inasmuch as we are assured that the Saracens are "base," we can be certain that they, like the papacy, are an instance of how the deceitful world "debased (*deturpa*)" many souls (146–147). Unlike the papacy, which sinned by deviating from the precepts of Christianity, the Moslems are debased because they have followed a religious system that is characterized by "nequizia" (142). Although many translations have been proposed for the term in this context, ranging from "iniquity" through "perversity" to "depravity,"[239] it seems to me that "unrighteousness" comes closest because here, as elsewhere (*Par.* 4.69 and 6.123), Dante rhymes *nequizia* with, and contrasts it to, *giustizia*, which signifies "righteousness" as well as "justice." All these nuances strive to express what Dante felt was the essential shortcoming of Islam, namely that it debased its adherents by promoting undue love of this world.

Amor iniqua. By an attentive analysis of the vocabulary of Martian badness, we have been able to see that both the papacy and Islam were unduly attracted by "the deceitful world, the love of which debases many souls" (*Par.* 15.146–147). The structure of *Paradiso* 15 suggests that in fact the entire canto illustrates the same theme, for it begins with another generalized statement of the underlying principle, so that in this canto Cacciaguida's references to specific forms of misbehavior are enclosed between two statements of the principles that make these diverse vices proper to Mars. The opening lines of the canto tell how the Martian souls all ceased singing simultaneously, being moved, the narrator assures us, by

> Benigna volontade in che si liqua
>   sempre l'amor che drittamente spira,
>   come cupidità fa ne la iniqua. . . .   (*Par.* 15.1–3)

> Benign will into which the love that aspires rightly always resolves itself, as cupidity does into unjust will.

Into these three lines Dante compresses a summary of the process of moral choice that is already familiar to the reader from Virgil's magisterial discourse on love (*Purg.* 18.19–75) and his preceding explanation of how the organization of Purgatory is based on the various ways in which love can be misused (17.85–139). Once the reader has sorted out the somewhat involute construction of the sentence, Dante's meaning is clear enough: love is of two kinds, one which aspires "rightly (*drittamente*)" and another which does not and is consequently "unjust (*iniqua*)." By the process Virgil described in *Purgatorio* 18, each kind of love leads to the formation of a corresponding kind of will: just or right love results in "benign will," whereas unjust or unrighteous love produces the opposite effect, "cupidity," which hence is now seen to be a synonym for malignant will. Moreover, the poet goes on to define both kinds of love in terms that later will be echoed at the end of the canto.

> Bene è che sanza termine si doglia
>   chi, per amor di cosa che non duri
>   etternalmente, quello amor si spoglia.   (*Par.* 15.10–12)

> Right it is that he should grieve without end who, for the love of what does not endure forever, robs himself of that love [that has been displayed by the souls in Mars].

As we know from *Purgatorio* 18, right love aims primarily at the lasting goods of eternal life but also, secondarily, at the transitory, temporal goods of this life, which are to be desired with due measure. Wrong love, on the other hand, can fail to love one's fellow man (the sins of pride, envy, and wrath), or to love eternal goods enough (sloth), or finally it can love temporal goods too much (avarice, gluttony, and *luxuria*). Evidently only this third category fits the damned soul "who robs himself of that [right] love for the sake of the love of what does not endure forever" (*Par.* 15.11–12). This, of course, is identical with "the love of the deceitful world which debases many souls" (146–147). In summary, these parallels can conveniently be presented in tabular form. This schema enables us to identify the cause of cupidity: it is the excessive love of corruptible things. Such, in fact, is one of the definitions of cupidity approved by Thomas Aquinas: "a certain inclination of corrupt nature to desire corruptible goods inordinately."[240] The role of Mars in producing cupidity also can be clarified

Par. 15	*Cause*	*Result*
1–2	amor che drittamente spira	benigna volontade
3	[amor] iniqua	cupidità [maligna volontade]
11–12	per amore di cose che non duri etternalmente	quello amor si spoglia
146–147	mondo fallace, lo cui amor	molt'anime deturpa

now. The Martian man, as Scot said, "quickly desires everything that he sees."[241] According to Virgil's exposition of how man makes moral decisions, this would seem to refer to the harmless "first intention" by which the uncorrupted soul is naturally attracted to desirable objects (*Purg.* 18.18–75). "This primal will admits no deserving of praise or blame" (59–60) because man has the power of free will, by which he can consider the moral consequences of his desire and then make up his mind whether to pursue the desideratum or not. These "second intentions" are the benign or malign dispositions listed as the results of love in the table above. The formation of cupidity, then, is in accordance with Marco Lombardo's account of the relation between astral influence and free will (*Purg.* 16.67–81). In this case, Mars disposes man to cupidity, but his choice is not inevitable.

The strong assertions of the astrologers about the badness of Mars must be understood in accordance with this theological view of cupidity. The planet's influence can lead men into every kind of evil, so the astrologers' sweeping generalizations are correct as to the potential effects of Mars, but as we have seen, the planet also promotes the cardinal virtue of fortitude, and with it the proper use of money. The noble or magnanimous man wants money only so he can perform things that bring him honor (above, at n. 27). When money is desired either for its own sake or for the sake of things that lead to dishonor, this desire is cupidity, and in fact cupidity of a special kind that Aquinas calls "an inordinate appetite for wealth (*appetitus inordinatus divitiarum*)." This was the species of cupidity that Saint Paul had in mind when he wrote that "the desire of money is the root of all evils—*radix enim omnium malorum est cupiditas*" (1 Tim. 6.10). Aquinas provides the rationale for Paul's dictum:

> For we see that through riches man acquires the ability to commit any sin whatsoever and to fulfill any sinful desire whatsoever because money can help a man to have all kinds of temporal goods, as is said in Ecclesiastes 10.19: "All things obey money."[242]

Although revelation teaches that it is specifically cupidity for money that leads to all other evils, Aquinas admits that the same may be true of the more general kind of cupidity that is an immoderate desire for any corruptible good. In the *Commedia*, Dante uses *cupidigia* in both senses,[243] and although the broader definition is the one expressly formulated in *Paradiso* 15, the complaints against Florentine merchants and bankers show that Dante subsumed monetary cupidity under the larger category.[244]

Dante's position on the malignancy of Mars is finally clear. Because the planet incites human cupidity, it can be blamed for all the evil on earth. In heaven this is only hinted at, for evil is seen through the righteous eyes of Cacciaguida, but his clues are nonetheless veracious; the evil effects of Mars are presumably most fully evident in Hell, where they have already been detected by Rabuse.[245] As usual, Dante has found a suitable symbol to express poetically what we have discovered by historical research, for the wolf, which is his recurrent image of cupidity,[246] was sacred to Mars in Roman mythology.[247]

6. Jupiter

For the pagan astrologers, Jupiter was the best of the seven planets because its influence was thoroughly benign. Moreover, like its namesake the king of the gods, the planet Jupiter ruled the other six planets, albeit with intermittent success, by tempering their qualities for the better. Accordingly, one might suppose that Dante would have had no difficulty in adapting this beneficent planet to his Christian cosmology, but paradoxically its goodness posed almost as many problems for the poet as the malignancy of Mars had. At the heart of the matter lay the materialistic interests of the pagan astrologers (and their clients), which led them to associate Jupiter with an abundance of such goods as food, sons, possessions, and money. These material benefits Dante ignored or deemphasized; instead he selected from the astrologers' lists of properties those that were in accord with his own ideals, notably *iustitia*, which included both moral righteousness and legal justice. In order to show how the poet adapted traditional astrology to his own purposes, this chapter will begin by establishing the fundamental agreement between Dante and the astrologers on the underlying principles that determined the character of Jovian influences; next it will consider some of the ways in which Dante departed from his astrological sources; and finally it will consider the astrological properties he stressed as one form or another of *iustitia*.

Jovian Principles

The astrologers agree that it is Jupiter's nature to be hot (*calida*)[1] and wet (*humida*)[2]. Both the combination and the intensity of these two qualities distinguish Jupiter from the other planets. When heat is combined with dryness, as is the case with both the Sun and Mars, the result is an intense, burning heat; but the wetness of Jupiter tempers its heat, though not as much as when the same pair of qualities are combined in Venus, which is only "tepid and moist."[3] Consequently, the Jovian key note is moderation or temperance, because in the planet and its effects both the hot and the wet are "tempered" (*temperata*).[4] Moreover, this moderating effect is especially exercised on the element air (*aër*), which the Greeks understood to be composed of the qualities wetness and hotness, although the astrologers stress the effects rather than the cause. The most commonly held view was that of Ptolemy, who stated that Jupiter tempers the air, thereby producing an abundance of moist winds that increase the yield of the earth.[5] Jupiter's connection with air and wind was further stressed by Haly, who reported that some philosophers believed that the planet itself had been created out of air and wind;[6] Scot, on the other hand, pointed out that the pagan poets had spoken of Jove as "the airy star, that tempers the winds and other onslaughts."[7] Finally, many astrologers also associated Jupiter with blood, which is the humor that corresponds to air.[8] All these fundamental Jovian properties, with the exception of blood, appear in the *Paradiso*.

Heat. For Dante, the planet is "that jovial torch (*facella*)" composed of sparks that are the Jovian souls (*Par.* 18.70). As they move to form the image of an eagle, they remind the poet of sparks ("faville," 101) sent flying by the striking of a log, but he soon explains that it was God who kindled ("accende," 105) these sparks. In the next canto (19.19–21), the same souls are compared to embers ("brage") that combine to produce a single heat ("calor"). Later, the souls in the Eagle's eye are kindled more ("più acceso") than the others with love (20.85), and finally we are told that when Trajan believed in God he "was kindled (*s'accese*) to such a fire (*foco*) of true love" that he was saved (20.115). Souls on the other planets are similarly illuminated by love, but here the phenomenon is described in terms of sparks and kindling, which are appropriate to the moderate heat generated by Jupiter. Although Dante chiefly stresses the metaphorical heat of Christian love, the poet nonetheless contrives one allusion to the real, but smoldering and hence moderate, heat of an inactive volcano[9] by referring periphrastically to Sicily as "the isle of fire" (19.131).

Wetness. In the *Paradiso*, Jupiter's wetness is acknowledged by extensive water imagery. Metaphorically water is used as an image of divine "grace that wells from a fountain so deep that never did creature thrust eye down to its first wave" (*Par.* 20.118–120). Real water applied to a spiritual use is implicit in three references to baptism (19.76, 20.127, 129), but even more astrologically specific are allusions based on Jupiter's association with rivers and the sea. Ptolemy ascribes to Jupiter "safe navigation of the sea (*maris*) and the tempered flowing of rivers (*fluminum*)"[10] Accordingly, the Eagle's voice reminds the poet of "the murmuring of a river (*fiume*) that falls down clear from rock to rock" (20.19–20). The shore of a river or sea is mentioned three times: the *riva* of the Indus (19.70), the shallows off the *proda* of the sea (19.61), and an indeterminate *riviera* from which birds rise (18.73). The most notable water image of these cantos, however, compares divine justice to the sea: near the shore the human eye can see the bottom, but "in the open sea (*pelago*) it sees it not, and nonetheless it is there, whereas the depth conceals it" (19.58–63).[11] Just possibly this image may have been suggested by Alcabitius, who states that, when the influence of Jupiter is modified by the Moon, "it signifies the science of the management of water and its measurement, as well as that of earth."[12] Such a modification existed at the supposed time of Dante's journey, when Jupiter and the Moon were "square," forming an angle of more or less 90°, which indicates difficulty or relative impossibility.[13] This aspect would fittingly indicate limitations on human ability to plumb the depths of the sea or measure the earth. Thus Dante's image of the depths of the sea that are beyond human knowing is appropriate both to the time and place at which it occurs in the poem.

Air. The element that unites wetness and heat is especially influenced by Jupiter's tempering quality. Dante accordingly gave prominence to air in his Jovian cantos, especially in connection with musical instruments (see below at n. 70). Most notably, he explains that the voice of the Eagle is produced by a murmuring that passes up through the neck as it would through a hollow tube and emerges from the beak "as the sound takes its form at the neck of the bagpipe, and the wind (*vento*) at the vent of the pipe it fills" (*Par.* 20.22–27). In Dante's universe, of course, air was confined to the earth's atmosphere; he assures us that the singing souls there, though comparable to pipes, "were filled only with the breath (*spirto*) of holy thoughts" (20.15). Moreover, since the Latin word *spiritus* refers basically to breath or wind,[14] air is obliquely suggested when the Holy Spirit is twice named ("Spirito Santo," 19.101, 20.38).

Ideally Jupiter tempers the winds, as we have seen, making them beneficial to man by their combination of moderate heat and moisture. A hot and dry wind, which Jupiter has not been able to temper, is called a *fumus* in the technical language of Aristotelian meteorology,[15] and Dante likens human avarice to such an ill wind, "the smoke (*fummo*) that vitiates your ray" (*Par.* 18.120) by obscuring the planet's influence that disposes man to justice and righteousness.[16]

Temperance. Dante introduces Jupiter as "the temperate sixth star—*la temprata stella / sesta*" (*Par.* 18.68–69). He makes no reference to its tempering of heat and moisture, probably because in the *Convivio* he had already adopted another explanation for the temperate quality of Jupiter: "it moves between two heavens which are antagonistic to its excellent temperateness, that is to say, the heaven of Mars and that of Saturn." What is more, he clarifies his assertion by citing Ptolemy's *Quadripartitum*:[17] "Jove's star is of temperate nature, for its path is halfway between Saturn, which makes things cold, and Mars, which makes them boiling hot."[18] In attributing a temperate nature to Jupiter, Dante was in fact following the majority opinion among astrologers.[19] Instances of temperance in his treatment of Jupiter, therefore, may be considered astrological in origin. The only other explicit reference to temperance comes at the moment of transition from Jupiter to Saturn, when Beatrice explains that she is not smiling because, as they ascend, her beauty "is kindled (*s'accende*) the more," so that it would overcome him "if it were not tempered (*temperasse*)" (*Par.* 21.8–10). Thus the Jovian property of temperance is apparently at work tempering the effects of Saturn, just as Ptolemy said it did; hence the passage exemplifies the view of Jupiter's nature that Dante had adopted in the *Convivio*.

Although Dante mentions temperance explicitly only at the beginning and end of the Jupiter episode, the influence of this virtue nonetheless pervades his treatment of the planet, since temperance in a moral context amounts to moderation, and in a legal one to equity.[20] Both of these varieties will be treated at length later in this chapter and need only be mentioned here, but one lesser example of Jovian temperance will serve to illustrate its ubiquity in these cantos. Temperance is a harmonious blending of opposites, for example, an alteration between vocal expression and silence. The Jovian souls at first sing (*Par.* 18.77, 79–81), then speak (19.10–90), sing again (97–99), and are silent (100); again they speak (103–148), become silent (20.9), and break into song (11–12); yet again silence (18), a speech (31–72), and silence (74). The narrator carefully notes the Eagle's intervals of silence, which suggests that they, too, are important, but at last he gives us an image that combines the bird's utterances and silences into a single pattern that leaves no doubt of his intention: as the Eagle falls silent, it is said to be "Like the lark that soars in the air, first singing, then silent, content with the last sweetness that satiates it" (20.73–75). Thus the poet clearly indicates that the holy bird's silences alternate significantly with its songs and speeches; he leaves the reader to infer that this is an instance of temperance.

Muted Joviality

Although Dante agreed with the astrologers on the basic nature of Jupiter, he could not agree with them in detail because their materialism often was inappropriate to a Christian view of the world. For example, Scot saw Jupiter as the source of human happiness: "Indeed this planet . . . [when well placed] makes every person happy (*beatum*) according to his status."[21] What Scot meant, of course, was that Jupiter conferred peace and material prosperity, both of which are benefits that Dante esteemed as part of the "happiness of this life" while acknowledging the existence of a higher "happiness of eternal life" (*Mon.* 3.15.7). Insofar as Dante treats happiness (*beatitudo*) in the Jovian cantos, it is exclusively the higher, heavenly kind—the salvation of Trajan, Ripheus, and the Indian—and in each case it is clear that such happiness comes, not from Jupiter, but from God.[22]

The happiness that Jupiter confers, however, comes from good luck (*fortuna*) rather than from grace. Most astrologers agreed with Ptolemy that Jupiter gives rise to every kind of good fortune in human affairs,[23] but Dante could not agree, at least within the fiction of the *Commedia*, because he had departed from traditional cosmology in raising Fortuna, or Lady Luck, to the rank of an angelic intelligence who effects change in the sublunary sphere (*Inf.* 7.67–96).[24] Still, his simile of the foolish fortune tellers, who augur from the sparks they raise by striking burning logs (*Par.* 18.100–102), may be a dismissive allusion to the *fortuna* of the astrologers.[25]

In general, then, it appears that Dante Christianized the astrologers' view that Jupiter produced human happiness and good fortune. Dante's tendency to discount the material benefits supposedly bestowed by the planet will be even more evident when we examine these gifts in detail.

JOVIALITY

When the narrator calls Jupiter "that jovial torch—*quella giovïal facella*" (*Par.* 18.70), it is tempting to assume, as Sapegno did, that he was speaking "the language of astrology,"[26] whether it was meant simply as the adjectival form of Jove or as an allusion to the "jovial" disposition. In fact, the Latin astrologers I have consulted do not use the adjective *iovialis*; it seems to have been used first by the Christian apologist Arnobius (ca. 300) and later by Martianus Capella and Macrobius (both ca. 400), but not in an astrological sense.[27] Nonetheless it is a convenient, if anachronistic, rubric under which to collect the pleasant qualities that many astrologers ascribed to Jove. The tradition does not extend back to Ptolemy but begins with Albumasar, who takes the Jupiter to signify "joy (*gaudium*)" and "a cheerful and agreeable disposition (*dispositio . . . hilaris, iocundus*)."[28] Alcabitius, with Bonatti following him, takes Jupiter to signify "gladness (*laetitia*)," while Scot combines the two traditions into the formula "delight (*gaudium*) of body and gladness (*laetitia*) of soul."[29] The Jovian has a cheerful, somewhat ingratiating smile on his face for everyone.[30]

Dante echoes the jovial terminology of the astrologers twice, but in each case the context has been transferred from earth to heaven. The Jovian souls are "flowers of the eternal *letizia*" (*Par.* 19.23); their state is a "rejoicing (*gioco*)" (from Latin *iocus*; 20.117).[31] Since *laetitia* can also mean "pleasure," an occurrence of the Italian equivalent, *piacer*, may be tentatively added to these unmistakable echoes: it refers to the sensual pleasure imparted by a well-accompanied song (20.144). This physical sort of pleasure, however, is balanced by an earlier reference in the same canto to "l'etterno piacere," which is to say God's pleasure or will (20.77).

Sweet and pleasant. Albumasar, our earliest source for joviality, considered Jupiter by nature to be "sweet (*dulcis*)," and subsequent astrologers assigned sweet tastes to that planet.[32] Scot provided a rationale by specifying that Jovian flavors are not only sweet but also "pleasant (*suavis*)," which he took to be a mean that avoids the extreme sweetness of wine or sugar. Furthermore, he extended Jove's tempering power to metaphorical as well as literal sweetness: e.g., a man whose replies are sweet.[33] In the heaven of Jupiter, Dante reflects both of Scot's innovations. The Eagle's reprimand is "sweet medicine (*soave medicina*)" (*Par.* 20.141); both the Jovian souls' enjoyment of their condition and their limited knowledge are "dolce" (19.2, 20.136); and the lark is satiated with the "dolcezza" of its song (20.75).

Abundance of Useful Things

Because Jupiter brings good weather for crops and animals, the astrologers regularly associate the planet with "the increase of the necessities of life," as Ptolemy first expressed it.[34] Alcabitius somewhat broadened the scope of this influence to include any "abundance of substance."[35] Other astrologers stressed that Jupiter governed everything that was useful, but none more strongly than Haly: "Only through Jupiter does a deed or thing possess utility (*utilitas*) or any good at all."[36] In his Jovian cantos, Dante alludes to many such things, but "abundance (*ubertà*)" he pointedly refers to God (*Par.* 20.21).

Growth and fruition. Jupiter controls the growth of vegetation[37] and "denotes fructification."[38] Dante incorporates the latter property by borrowing a technical term from theological Latin to express the "enjoyment" of the Jovian souls—their "dolce *frui*" (*Par.* 19.2). Because this Latin term is an evident intruder in the text, the reader is invited to consider it more closely than he would an unobtrusive Italian word. The Latin infinitive *frui*, here used substantively, literally means "to enjoy the fruits," which enables the poet to suggest fruition by the etymological connotation of a word that, in this context, denotes the enjoyment of a goal attained.[39] Later Dante alludes to fruition more accessibly by the rhetorical device of antiphrasis, that is by referring to its opposite, when he writes that Lucifer, "through not awaiting light, fell unripe (*acerbo*)" (19.48).

Nutrition. Another of Jupiter's natural powers is nutrition. According to Scot, when Jupiter's influence is uppermost, it signifies "abundance of foodstuffs such as bread."[40] If strong in a natal horoscope, Jupiter will assure the baby adequate nutrition and will dispose an adult to be a gourmet.[41] Dante adapts these properties and their opposites to his Jovian context. The Pilgrim's desire to understand God's justice is "the great fast which has long held me hungering (*in fame*), not finding any food (*cibo*) for it on earth" (*Par.* 19.25–27, cf. 33). After the Eagle has answered his question, it circles over the Pilgrim "As the stork circles over her nest when she has fed (*pasciuti*) her young," and he is "as the one which she has fed (*pasto*)" (*Par.* 19.91–93). This breakfast is wholly immaterial, as is the spiritual "bread (*pan*)" denied by excommunication (18.129), whereas carnal pleasure is the opposite of nutritious, i.e., "poison (*veleno*)" (19.66).

The astrologers list among Jupiter's properties many crops and trees that are useful to man, but the only one that appears in the Jovian cantos is a "vineyard (*vigna*)" (*Par.* 18.132).[42] They also frequently include in their lists an abundance of children, and especially of sons, as one of Jove's useful gifts.[43] The counterpart in these cantos is the "son (*figlio*)" for whose loss Trajan consoled the widow, and perhaps God's "creatures (*creatura*)" may qualify as well (20.45, 119).

PRECIOUS SUBSTANCES

When Michael Scot listed useful substances, the first that came to his mind was "a supply of money."[44] Generalizing more than most astrologers, he characterized Jupiter as the bringer of benefits, including "wealth, profit, [and] honor." Thus, according to Scot, the Jovian type is predisposed "to have much wealth of movable and immovable things, such as cloaks, towers, honorable houses, beautiful buildings, pleasure gardens with trees and plants that are noble in their fruits and odor."[45] Dante selected only a few of the precious substances for which Jovians had a predilection, but he stressed these few unmistakably.

Money. Other astrologers agreed with Scot that Jove was the planet of money.[46] What the Jovian man chiefly thinks about is how to acquire money; he prefers lucrative occupations, such as "sitting at the tollhouse and changing money there."[47] Hence the narrator prays appropriately that God will substitute justice for "the buying and selling" that now prevails in the Church (*Par.* 18.122)—and both are effects of Jupiter. A few lines later, an unidentified pope is accused of desiring only money, represented by the florin (130–136). Finally, one of the bad rulers condemned by the Eagle had falsified his own country's coinage and another had counterfeited his neighbor's (19.119, 141).

Colors and metals. In the *Convivio,* Dante declares that Jupiter "alone among the stars is white (*bianca*) in appearance, as if covered in silver (*argentata*)."[48] The narrator, too, uses both terms to describe the planet: it possesses the quality of "whiteness (*candor*)" and it "appears silver (*pareva argento*)" in contrast to the golden lights of the Jovian souls (*Par.* 18.68, 96). Curiously, this detail does not come from the astrologers, most of whom do not indicate the planet's own color.[49] Scot, the only one who does, says that Jupiter is "like electrum or copper in color," and moreover he remarks that only in poetic myth is the planet white.[50] In the *Convivio* Dante had accepted the testimony of the poets because he wanted to assimilate Jupiter to geometry, which "is of the purest white in that it is free of any taint of error, and utterly certain both in itself and its ancillary science, called Perspective."[51] Although sometimes in the *Comedy* he was prepared to correct his past errors (e.g., concerning the cause of lunar spots in *Paradiso* 2), in this case poetic fiction evidently still suited his purpose better than scientific fact.

Gems and glass. Scot lists a number of precious substances that the Jovian merchant likes to deal in, among them "jewels (*gemmas*)" and "glassware (*vitreos*)."[52] We have seen that other planets, notably Venus, the Sun, and Mars, have their specific jewels; similarly, Ibn Ezra assigned to Jupiter "every stone (*lapis*) that is white, bright, and useful," e.g., onyx, crystal, white and yellowish sapphire.[53] Our other astrologers, however, associated no gems with Jupiter. Dante apparently ignored these diverse indications and instead took the ruby (*rubinetto*) as Jupiter's gem (*Par.* 19.4, cf. 18.115 and 20.16), perhaps selecting it from some *lapidarium* for its symbolic value.[54] Still Scot's association of glass with Jupiter (above, n. 52) may just possibly have suggested the comparison of the Pilgrim to glass ("vetro," *Par.* 20.80).

Textiles and clothes. Cloth and clothing made from it are the most prominent substances that Dante borrowed from the astrologers. Scot in particular elaborated on the Jovian fondness for luxury fabrics: his *homo Iovinus* "delights in dress that is noble in color, well cut, and made of beautiful materials." Similarly, the *Iovialis* is predisposed to sell luxury dry goods and fancy accessories, such as silk purses.[55] In Jupiter's cantos, Dante has color "clothe (*veste*)" glass (*Par.* 20.80), a metaphor which neatly embodies the Jovian attachment to colored clothing. Moreover, he mentions several specific articles of clothing that the astrologers mention in connection with Jupiter. According to Scot, Jovians enjoy needlework; for example, they like "to make ladies' veils (*vella*)."[56] Dante echoes this in addressing the Eagle, who he is sure does not perceive divine justice through a "veil (*velame*)" (19.30). Other kinds of clothes dear to Jovians are instanced by Ibn Ezra, who says they like "beautiful clothing, such as coats and every sort of fashionable cloak (*clamis*)."[57] Dante alludes to two kinds of the latter in these cantos: the mantle, through a verbal form ("ammanti," 20.13), and the hood ("cappello," 19.34). Scot also mentions luxury fabrics by name (silk, linen, frise),[58] and although Dante is not so specific, in Jupiter's cantos he does allude twice to weaving: the souls are "interwoven (*conserte*)," and the Eagle is "woven (*contesto*) of praises" (19.3, 38). To these unquestionable instances might be added other, less secure ones proper to textile design and needlework,[59] but Dante's reliance on the astrologers, and especially Scot, in this regard is evident enough.

The Eagle

Astrology only hints at the great bird that dominates the cantos of Jupiter. Each planet has birds that are appropriate to it, and according to Ibn Ezra, Jupiter's are ones that eat grain and are useful to man, such as peacocks, chickens, and pigeons.[60] Scot repeats this list but enlarges the definition to include hunting birds, such as falcons and hawks, which his Jovian likes to have around the house as pets.[61] Accordingly Dante does compare his eagle to a falcon ("falcone," *Par.* 19.34), though this is only a minor point of contact. Only one astrologer whom Dante is likely to have known associates the eagle with Jupiter, and the reference is mythological rather than astrological in origin, for the 1491 printed text of Bonatti's list of

Jovian properties is illustrated with a woodcut of Jove's chariot drawn by two eagles.[62] Since it was a commonplace of Roman mythology that the eagle was Jove's bird, it is unlikely that Dante's Eagle was suggested to him by astrology; at most it would appear that the obvious choice was not incompatible with that science.

Once Dante had determined to give prominence to an eagle in his heaven of Jupiter, astrology may have suggested to him the means of representing it as an image formed by the Jovian souls. In Haly he could have found the statement that Jupiter is the planet "of handsome appearance and of a composed person—*composite persone*."[63] Given the context, Haly most likely meant a "tidy person," one whose person was "well ordered," but the Latin adjective *compositus* nonetheless has as its primary meaning something that is "composed of, made from, several parts or ingredients,"[64] which could readily suggest the device of having the Eagle be so formed.

Concord. Any organism composed of many coordinated parts would be an apt emblem of a Jovian trait recognized by most of the astrologers, though they employ various terms to describe it. For Haly, Jupiter is the planet of "community"; for Alcabitius and Bonatti, it promotes "participation"; for Albumasar, it gives rise to "societies of men, living together, comradeship"; and for Ibn Ezra, what Jovian man "chiefly thinks about is . . . to congregate (*congregare*)," i.e., he is gregarious.[65] Thus Dante's Jovian souls act and speak together in such harmony that they collectively speak in the singular (*Par.* 19.10–12). Indeed, the virtue of concord (*concordia*) is instilled by Jupiter, as both Scot and Bonatti remark,[66] and Dante makes it prominent in this heaven by putting it in final place, for the Jovian souls are last glimpsed as two of them quiver in harmony with the Eagle's words "just as the winking of eyes concords—*si concorda*" (*Par.* 20.147).

Etymologically, the Latin word *concordia* is derived from *cor*, "heart," and literally means "a unison of hearts." The same etymon appears in another attribute of the Eagle, *misericors* (*miser* + *cor*), "tender-hearted." These heart-related words are appropriate to Jupiter, which some astrologers said governs the human heart and makes it noble.[67] In addition to another etymological allusion ("mi ricorda," *Par.* 20.145), Dante also makes direct reference to the heart of the Pilgrim, which is waiting to receive the Eagle's words, presumably because it is a noble heart ("core," *Par.* 20.30). It is noteworthy that Dante selected only the heart from the astrologers' long list of those parts of the human body that Jupiter governs: the blood and liver, semen and testicles, arms and hands, and the torso from the breast to the umbilicus, including the ribs, stomach, and intestines, as well as the heart. From this list it is also evident that the parts of the Eagle that Dante does mention—its eye, beak, throat, and wings— have no astrological significance.

Music. The term *concordia* signifies musical as well as social harmony,[68] so it is fitting that the souls who comprise the Eagle express their concord by singing, as well as speaking, in unison (*Par.* 18.79, 97–99; 19.39, 20.11). Their singing is not in itself unusual, since all the souls we have met in Paradise have also sung, but none of the others have made one voice of many. The author in fact provides a rationale for their choral unison: "All that is just is consonant (*consuona*) with" God's will (20.88). These just souls, therefore, are figuratively consonant with the divine will and, as a token of this, they are literally "sounding together" with one another.

Although the concord such singing betokens is proper to Jupiter, singing per se is not; instead, the Jovian man "likes to enjoy the sound of instruments that sound well."[69] Dante's narrator accordingly compares the Eagle's voice to a wide variety of musical instruments: "flutes (*flailli*)," "chimes (*squilli*)," "guitar (*cetra*)," "bagpipe (*sampogna*)," and lute (implied by "citharista").[70] In addition, the reed pipe may be implicit in the poet's invocation to one of the Muses ("O diva Pegasëa," 18.82), who most likely is Euterpe because this heaven was traditionally hers, and her instrument was the *calamus* or *tibiae*.[71] Even if this mythological allusion were not controversial, it does not account for the diversity of instruments Dante names but only enriches it. Astrology rather than mythology shows why so many musical instruments are appropriate to the heaven of Jupiter.

Speeches and books. The Eagle, though neither the most nor the least loquacious of Dante's heavenly informants, speaks a good deal; his speeches in fact total 202 lines.[72] This, too, is appropriate, because the astrologers assure us that "speeches" are an effect of Jupiter. Moreover, Jovians like "to talk not a little"; they do so "rhetorically," and they are "grave in speech."[73] Without belaboring the matter, it should be evident that the Eagle's component souls conform to the Jovian pattern in all these respects.

The native of Jupiter is also a connoisseur of rhetoric. Specifically, he likes "to hear orators," and especially to hear them relate "the deeds done long ago (*gesta antiquorum*)."[74] Hence it is appropriate to Jupiter that the Eagle complains about wicked men who honor the memory of the Jovian saints in word but not in deed: "they recommend it but do not follow the story (*storia*)" (*Par.* 19.18). Their reaction to history, then, is aesthetic rather than ethical.

Scot characterizes Jovian occupations as "honorable, good, light work," including not only merchandising and money changing but especially "the knowledge of letters, e.g., grammar, medicine, law, astrology, natural science."[75] Alcabitius, in a similar list, takes Jupiter to signify "the knowledge . . . of writing (*scribendi*)."[76] In Jupiter's heaven, Dante avoids references to the higher branches of learning and concentrates instead on the basics of literacy—grammar and writing. The most obvious example is the motto that the souls spell out letter by letter (*Par.* 18.88–93); the narrator draws on the technical terminology of grammar to describe its progress: vowels and consonants (89), a verb and a noun (92), and a vocable (94). Scribal activity is a recurrent theme: the popes "only write to cancel" (18.130); "never did ink record" anything like the Eagle (19.8); the Bible is "la Scrittura"; the Pilgrim "wrote" the Eagle's words on his heart (20.30). This scribal imagery culminates, however, with "that open volume" (113) in which the sins of bad rulers "are written" (114) with a quill pen (116) and shall be displayed at the Last Judgment (19.106–148). The metaphor is elaborated in terms of medieval scribal practice: the text can be compressed using abbreviation by truncation ("lettere mozze," 134) and the Roman numerals I and M quantify good and bad deeds respectively (127–129).

It is clear, then, that the profusion of scribal imagery in these cantos is authorized by astrology; but the occupational indications given by Scot and Alcabitius (above, nn. 75–76) do not explain why Dante chose to emphasize writing to the exclusion of the other honorable arts that those astrologers assigned to Jupiter. It may be because, at the moment the Pilgrim visited Jupiter, the planet was in the "first face" (i.e., the first five degrees) of Taurus, where Haly said it would confer "the knowledge of judging what is good and of writing."[77] But Haly offers another possibility, for the Jovian born when Jupiter is in the first face of Gemini "busies himself with writing, reading, and knowing books about good habits and philosophy."[78] This would apply aptly to Dante himself if, as I have argued elsewhere, his birthday fell on 8 June.[79] As the Jovian display, like all his planetary encounters, was adequated to the Pilgrim, it would naturally stress those properties that were indicated by his natal horoscope.

Both of Haly's formulas can be applied to the blessed Jovians as well as to the Pilgrim. They, too, are scribes who copy out a text of ethical import: the opening verse of the biblical book of Wisdom that is their motto (*Par.* 18.91–93). Since that text is inspired by God, those souls are literally copying the word of God and, more specifically, his injunction that earthly rulers should cherish justice. Thus in heaven they display literally the same tendency that figuratively characterized their excellence on earth, where they modelled their judgments on God's, which is to say they took him as the exemplar that they copied. This concept is reinforced by the choice of David as the most prominent soul, who, as the pupil of the Eagle's eye, looks most directly at God, just as a real eagle was supposed to look at the Sun (20.31–32).[80] The text clearly indicates the sense in which David can be said to have looked more directly on God than the others: "he was the singer of the Holy Spirit" (38) because he wrote the Psalms as God's scribe. Now he is being rewarded for transcribing God's text (40–42). The same idea emerges most clearly as the Book of Judgment, in which God's judgments are recorded. As in the other cases, God is the exemplar which is copied by a scribe—in this case, presumably a recording angel, though Dante does not say so.

The Eagle itself is of course the copy rather than the copyist; that its body is transformed from the final letter of a biblical text (*Par.* 18.94–114) suggests that it, too, is derived from God. The Eagle, like the letters which preceded it, is also significant: it is the "sign that made the Romans reverend to the world (*segno / che fé i Romani al mondo reverendi*)" (101–102), which is to say that it made them "worthy of reverence,"[81] or more precisely (to paraphrase Dante's own definition of *reverenza*), worthy of the world's due subjection confessed by a manifest sign.[82] And what, then, made the Romans *worthy* to be duly acknowledged as ruler of the world? Of Dante's answer there can be no doubt, for he devoted the second book of his *Monarchia* to proving that the Roman Empire existed "de iure," and he argued specifically that the Roman people, by seeking the common welfare, intended the goal of *ius* and therefore acted "cum iure" in subjecting the whole world to its rule (*Mon.* 2.5). In other words, the Romans conformed to the Jovian motto and cherished *iustitia*. Hence the Eagle is the sign of justice.[83] This virtue and its ramifications will be our chief concern for the rest of the present chapter.

Justice and Righteousness

Jupiter's moderate nature, derived from its intermediate course between the heat of Mars and the cold of Saturn, was a fundamental given for all the astrologers. As they elaborated Ptolemy's bare indications, it was a short step from moderation to equality, and then from equality to justice;[84] thus Albumasar added equality to the planet's natural attributes,[85] and Alcabitius found that one of the qualities of the human soul signified by Jupiter was "iustitia."[86] For Ibn Ezra, the planet instilled justice into the human soul, and hence it signified just men and "discourse concerning justice and equity."[87]

In the *Paradiso*, no theme is introduced with more spectacular effects than the justice of Jupiter, which is literally spelled out in lights by the Jovian souls: "*DILIGITE IUSTITIAM*" (*Par.* 18.91). Directly following this display, the narrator delivers a commentary on Jovian justice from his enlightened standpoint, which may therefore be considered Dante's definitive statement on the subject.

> O dolce stella, quali e quante gemme
>   mi dimostraro che nostra giustizia
>   effetto sia del ciel che tu ingemme!   (*Par.* 18.115–117)

> O sweet star, how many and how bright were the gems which made it plain to me that our justice is the effect of the heaven which you engem!

At first glance, this statement seems to endorse the view of the astrologers that Jupiter's influence produces human justice; but a closer reading shows that Dante has distanced himself from the astrologers' world-view. For Dante, human justice is an effect, not of the planet Jupiter, but of the heavenly sphere that carries it on its course, or rather, to be even more precise, of the angelic intelligences that animate that sphere. The enlightened narrator has profited from the Pilgrim's education, for he prudently claims only "our justice," that is human justice here on earth, as an effect of the heaven of Jupiter. The Pilgrim had already learned from Cunizza that the Thrones, the angelic intelligences that govern the heaven of Saturn, reflect God's judgments ("Dio giudicante," *Par.* 9.61–63). Accordingly, the Pilgrim assures the Eagle that he is aware that "divine justice—*la divina giustizia*" is reflected from another heaven, though he assumes (correctly) that the Eagle, like Cunizza, can perceive this reflection accurately (19.28–30). Thus, even at the outset of the episode, the Pilgrim is aware that the justice dispensed to men by Jupiter is not inherent in the nature of the planet, as the astrologers asserted, but instead comes to it from God via Saturn.

The Pilgrim has another lesson to learn from the Eagle, however, because he conceives justice to be an abstract quality distinct from God, so that in his mind he asks, "Where is this justice (*questa giustizia*) that condemns" a righteous man who is ignorant of Christianity? (*Par.* 19.77). The Eagle's answer is simply that whatever God wills is ipso facto just and good, and that no creature can completely understand the mind of the Creator (19.40–90). God is justice "everlasting (*sempiterna*)" and "everliving (*viva*)"; he is the measure of all that is "just (*giusto*)" (58, 68, 88). Hence God is not the source of justice in the sense that he made something distinct from himself; rather, he *is* justice. Consequently, the Saturnine Thrones are "mirrors" that receive God's judgments from above and transmit them to the lower heavens, including that of Jupiter. Thus Dante relocates astrology in a Christian context. The heaven is the mediate cause of human justice, but the ultimate cause is God because he is justice itself. The theocentric tendency of Dante's astrology is indeed hinted in the motto "*DILIGITE IUSTITIAM*" itself, inasmuch as it is a text drawn from the Latin Vulgate Bible (Sap. 1.1).

Judges and judgment. The motto was addressed to human judges: "*QUI IUDICATIS TERRAM—*you who judge the earth" (*Par.* 18.93). Astrologically, this too is appropriate to "the star of judges" and "judgments," for Jovians like to be judges, lawyers, notaries, and rulers at every level of society, and what is more, they make good judges because their planet gives them "discretion," which enables them "to judge justly."[88] Like the astrologers, Dante in the Jovian cantos associates judgment with justice: it is presumptuous for any man "to judge (*giudicar*)" the case of the righteous but ignorant Indian (19.80); man cannot understand God's judgment ("il giudicio etterno," 99) and will be surprised by it at the Last Judgment ("in giudicio," 107); "the eternal judgment" can be postponed but not altered (20.52); men should exercise restraint in judging ("a giudicar," 134).

From these passages, it is evident that Dante takes a broader view of judgment than the astrologers do, for they limit judgment to matters of human law, while Dante is concerned rather with the occult judgments of the Almighty and man's inability to form accurate opinions about them.[89] Nonetheless, he includes the narrower theme of legal justice and judgment within his broader framework. The few Jovians named in the Eagle's eye were all rulers, but as we shall see presently (below, after n. 165), only King William the Good represents good rulership per se.

Dante similarly deemphasizes legal themes that are given prominence by the astrologers: for example, human laws are mentioned only once ("*leggi*," *Par.* 20.54)[90]

RIGHTEOUSNESS

But what is *iustitia*? For Aquinas, it is the virtue that governs relations between individuals, and he defines it in Aristotelian terms as giving everyone his due.[91] The Bible, however, offers an alternative to this restricted, philosophic concept of justice. The broader, biblical sense of *iustitia* is often translated as "righteousness" or "moral rectitude": for instance, "Love righteousness (*iustitiam*), ye that be judges of the earth" (Sap. 1.1a, Authorized Version).[92] Although there are many traces of the narrower sort of justice in Dante's works, he preferred to use the more general sense when he defined the term: "The eleventh [virtue] is justice, which disposes us to love righteousness (*drittura*) and to exercise it in every thing."[93] In the Jovian cantos, this definition is exemplified in the case of the Indian who was ignorant of Christ:

> e tutti suoi voleri et atti buoni
>   sono, quanto ragione umana vede,
>   sanza peccato in vita o in sermoni.   (*Par.* 19.73–75)

and all his wishes and acts are good, as far as human reason sees, without sin in life or in speech.

And again Ripheus the Trojan "set all his love down below on righteousness (*drittura*)" (20.121). In both cases we are dealing with justice as it is perceived by human reason unaided by revelation (19.74), and so we may suppose it should have been perceived by the astrologers, whose science was based exclusively on reason. In fact, it is righteousness, rather than justice in Aquinas's strict sense, that the astrologers do stress as the peculiar property of Jupiter.

The planet of goodness. Jupiter, Haly says simply, "signifies goodness (*bonitatem*)." "For it is the planet the nature of which is good," Scot explains, "and its property is . . . every influence of good."[94] Hence he calls the planet "benign," and moreover he claims that it always indicates "good to everyone and never evil."[95] Haly took it to signify "betterment (*melioratio*)," which Ibn Ezra paraphrased as "increase of every good."[96]

The astrologers left no doubt that Jupiter produced good morals no less than good crops and good luck. Most commonly they summed up its moral influence as *honestas*, "moral rectitude";[97] occasional alternatives were "virtue," "good habits," and "a good way of life both in deed and word."[98] With a variety of formulas they stressed that the planet disposed one's intentions towards good and away from evil: "diligens bonum et odiens malum" (Ibn Ezra).[99] Furthermore, the planet itself was "the benevolent star" that imparted *benevolentia* to men.[100] This may be echoed in the Eagle's mention of "buon voler," the good will to which the damned never return (*Par.* 20.107), which I take to be "the good of the intellect" that they have lost (*Inf.* 3.18).

The rational man. The rectitude of Jovian man is closely allied to his reason. Of anything that comes to his attention he "quickly desires to hear what is good and reasonable (*rationabilia*)"; conversely, he detests whatever "lacks reason."[101] "Understanding (*intellectus*)" is generally given as one of the astrological properties of Jupiter,[102] and consequently it is also the "planet of wisdom (*sapientiae*)," and indeed of "sound wisdom" and "the fruit of wisdom," namely "every precept that is good, beautiful, and precious" and generally "praiseworthy."[103] Scot sums it up by taking Jupiter to signify "the rational soul" in general.[104] Moreover, several astrologers are remarkably optimistic about rational inquiry. Albumasar says the planet stands for "certitude," while for Scot it signifies not only "explanation (*solutio*)" but also "perfect understanding."[105]

Dante, too, associates human reason with Jupiter, only to stress its limitations. God is "the first reason," or cause, which man can know only imperfectly ("cagion," *Par.* 20.132; cf. 19.90). Man's rational capacity is acknowledged in references to his ability to speak (*ragionare*, 19.71, 20.50), but doubting and questioning are more in evidence in these cantos than certitude (19.33, 69, 84, 20.79). The Pilgrim, in framing his hypothetical case about the Indian, only asserts that the man is without sin "insofar as human reason sees" (19.74), not absolutely. Later the Pilgrim, in his inability to understand how Trajan and Ripheus can be in heaven, exemplifies human reason unable to proceed unaided (20.88–93). Men cannot understand God's judgments any more than the Pilgrim can comprehend the Eagle's "notes" (19.97–99). And finally, with heavy anaphora, the Eagle points out how each of the six souls that make up his eye has greater understanding now than he had while living ("ora conosce," 20.40, 46, 52, 58, 64, 70). Clearly Dante has borrowed the theme of human understanding from the astrologers, thus acknowledging that the planet does produce human rationality, but he Christianizes the theme by stressing various shortcomings of human reason.[106]

Jovian Virtues

The astrologers' Jovian man might well take as his own the Socratic motto "Knowledge is virtue," for through reason he has acquired wisdom; consequently he cherishes righteousness and accordingly leads a virtuous life. Since the moral virtues are acquired by the cultivation of good habits, the influence of Jupiter is summed up by the role assigned it in the casting of lots: it indicated "the progress of habit (*habitudinis profectus*)."[107] The narrator marks the ascent into Jupiter with a simile based on this theme: "from feeling more delight in doing well, a man from day to day becomes aware that his virtue makes progress."

> . . . per sentir più dilettanza
> bene operando, l'uom di giorno in giorno
> s'accorge che la sua virtute avanza . . . .   (*Par.* 18.58–60)

Here the exhortation "*DILIGITE IUSTITIAM*," echoed in the man's "dilettanza," clearly applies to *iustitia* in the sense of moral rectitude, "la sua virtute." Although Jupiter would thus seem to promote every virtue, the astrologers singled out several that especially characterized the Jovian, and these must be briefly noted insofar as Dante made use of them.

The virtues of moderation. Since Jupiter is the planet that instills moderation, it presumably promotes all the Aristotelian virtues that are a mean between two extremes, but the astrologers single out only a few. Temperance, of course, is the leading one (above, nn. 17–19); the Eagle would seem to be recommending it when he warns mortals to "keep yourselves restrained in judging" (*Par.* 20.133–134). Generosity (*liberalitas*) for Aristotle is a mean,[108] and accordingly the astrologers often associate it with moderate Jupiter;[109] only Albumasar, however, mentions large-scale generosity (*magnificentia*), which is also a mean.[110] Although Dante does not mention either form of generosity by name here, the greater kind is surely implied by the Donation of Constantine (20.55–60). As early as Ptolemy, astrologers ascribed magnanimity to Jupiter, and Dante remarks the absence of this Aristotelian virtue in King Wenceslas II, "him of Bohemia, who never knew valor (*valor*) nor wished it" (19.125–126).[111] Aristotle treats modesty (*verecundia*) in his discussion of the mean, although strictly speaking it is a passion rather than a virtue,[112] so it too appears as an astrological property of Jupiter.[113] Thus in *Paradiso* the passage from the reddish heaven of Mars to the whiteness of Jupiter is compared to the change of color of a pale woman "when her face frees itself from a burden of modest shame (*vergogna*)" (18.65–66). Finally, the astrologers attribute to Jupiter the virtue of "patience (*patientia*),"[114] which Aquinas defines as "the tolerance of tribulations with a certain equanimity."[115] Such patience is implicit in the Eagle's exclamation: "O happy Hungary, if she did not allow herself to be maltreated any more" (19.142–143).

Theological virtues. One astrologer places charity among the Jovian virtues and another adds hope,[116] but faith is mentioned with great frequency. Sometimes *fides* is given without qualification or the Jovian is said to be *fidelis*.[117] Sometimes faith is a moral rather than a theological virtue, e.g., fidelity as a friend, as a witness, or as a custodian;[118] but religious belief is certainly intended by John of Seville, for whom Jupiter was "the star of the expositors of the faith," and probably also by Albumasar, for whom it indicated "true faith."[119]

It is not surprising that all three theological virtues are mentioned in Dante's heaven of Jupiter (*Par.* 20.127), but it can hardly be a coincidence that, as with the astrologers, the emphasis on hope is slight (20.108–109) even though both kinds of faith are stressed. In a nonreligious sense, the Pilgrim believes that Ripheus is saved although that seems incredible (20.67–69, 80), and several of the bad rulers were not faithful to their marriage vows, either figuratively or literally (19.138–139).[120] But Trajan and Ripheus eventually had faith as a theological virtue, while the hypothetical Indian lacked it (20.104, 114, 19.76).

PITY AND PIETY

The Eagle, speaking collectively for all its component souls, declares that they have been raised up to the heaven of Jupiter "for being just and *pio*" (*Par.* 19.13). The medieval commentators understood *pio* to mean "merciful," "compassionate," or "showing pity," so that these souls, like God himself, proceeded with mercy as well as justice.[121] Although this interpretation is still widely accepted, some modern scholars—notably Chimenz and Mattalia—insist that in this context *pio* means simply "pious," that is, "devoted" or "obedient" to God's will, which is the foundation of all true justice. In this view, Dante linked justice with piety in the phrase "giusto e pio" in order to stress the close relationship between the two, since devotion to God entails devotion to justice, of which he is the source.[122]

Pity. The astrologers lend support to both interpretations. Michael

Scot provides strong support for the traditional one, for he maintains that the planet itself is "*pius* to all," which could hardly be translated "pious." Elsewhere he is more explicit: "to every living thing, the planet is *pius* and clement, merciful, helpful, and benign." When he sums it up in a word, he says that the Jovian is "*misericors*—merciful."[123] Scot also gives numerous examples of the Jovian's mercy: he raises up the fallen, comforts others in misery, sorrows for the poor, gives alms.[124] Although Dante is more concerned with God's mercy than man's, such human works of mercy are recalled in Trajan, who comforted the poor woman out of *pietà* (*Purg.* 10.74–93).

Piety. There is even wider astrological support for the second interpretation, however, for the astrologers commonly take Jupiter to signify "religio."[125] That the term is not limited to the monastic life is indicated by its equivalents, "fearing God" and "worshiping God."[126] But one hesitates to assert that the souls exhibited in Jupiter are typical of the religious life, for which Dante could have found unmistakable exemplars in such rulers as Edward the Confessor, Saint Louis of France, or the Emperor Henry II. True, the blessed in Jupiter are said to be "pio" (*Par.* 19.13), but the sense in which that was meant is one of the poem's obscurities (n. 122, above), which we shall attempt to clarify in the final section of this chapter. For the moment let us note that conventional religious practices are present, but sparsely, in these cantos: King Hezekiah prays a "worthy prayer (*degno preco*)" to God for longer life (20.53) and Pope Gregory—himself not apparently a Jovian—makes hopeful "prayers (*prieghi*)" for Trajan's resurrection (20.109).[127]

Religion, as the astrologers conceived it, was by no means monolithic, however. Alcabitius wrote that Jupiter's significance concerning sects was "plurality and simulation," which Scot intensified to "the greatest plurality and simulation" in those things that have to be done, and moreover he made it clear that these sects were "divisions of faith."[128] Since Jupiter therefore signifies hypocrisy (*simulatio*), it is appropriate that the narrator declares: "many cry 'Christ, Christ,' who, at the Judgment, shall be far less near to Him than he who knows not Christ" (*Par.* 19.106–108). There are, as the Pilgrim learns in this heaven, unconventional ways to salvation (again Trajan, Ripheus, and the Indian), and these departures from the norm would seem to exemplify the astrologers' "plurality" of religion.

Religious pluralism suggests heretics, but Dante avoids treating them in this heaven; at most, in his persona as narrator he hopes that God may again be indignant "at the buying and selling in the temple (*templo*) that made its walls of miracles and martyrdoms" (*Par.* 18.122–123). Here again his starting place was astrology, which considered "temples (*templa*)" and "the place of divine worship" to be among Jupiter's properties.[129] But what Dante is deploring is the desecration, not of a building, but of Christ's Church on earth. He avoids the distinction, which would have been suspect of heresy, between an *ecclesia carnalis* and an *ecclesia spiritualis*;[130] instead, his image is of one true Church, the *ecclesia universalis*, that is presently filled with the smoke of avarice generated by a corrupt papacy.

Since Jupiter induces men to show both pity and piety, the ambiguity of Dante's *pio* may be more than verbal: he may have used the term with the knowledge, derived from the astrologers, that either meaning would be suitable to this heaven. The final section of this chapter will attempt to determine more precisely the sense of "giusto e pio" at *Paradiso* 19.13.

Success

For the astrologers, virtue is not its own reward; instead Jupiter brings victory, fame, and honor. For Dante these themes are appropriate to every planetary heaven because all the blessed souls have their reward, but in the heaven of Jupiter he is nonetheless careful to offer a Christian version of these themes.

Victory. Jupiter signifies "victory." Moreover, "what [the Jovian] thinks about especially," says Ibn Ezra, "is to conquer (*vincere*) in all things, provided that he wins fairly (*iure*)."[131] The kingdom of heaven, of course, is what the Christian chiefly thinks of winning, and Dante offers a string of cryptic observations on the process in which forms of the verb *vincere* occur six times. The glory of the Jovians "cannot be conquered by desire" (*Par.* 19.15),[132] and the divine will cannot be conquered "as man overcomes man"; instead, God's will is conquered by love and hope because it wills to be conquered, and in turn God's will conquers the human will with his goodness (20.94–99). It would be beside the point to explicate these lines, for it is enough for our purpose to recognize that they are built around the theme of conquest, which the poet apparently borrowed from the astrologers because it was appropriate to Jupiter and applied to salvation.

Reward. Similarly, Dante echoes an astrologer when he terms David's reward "lo remunerar" (*Par.* 20.42), for the Latin translation of Ptolemy states that Jove's "proper effect on men is . . . recompense (*remunerationes*) and rewards (*praemia*) from kings, and also the increase of royal things, a famous name, and magnanimity."[133] Justice is implied, since the primary meaning of *remuneratio* is "repayment." Dante likewise suggests just compensation with the term *mercede*, which has the basic sense of "wages" (20.108).

Fame and glory. In addition to due recompense of a material kind, Jupiter promised men fame (*fama*), according to Ptolemy, John of Seville, Ibn Ezra, and Michael Scot.[134] For Scot, this meant "praise (*laudem*) of a good life," which Jovians especially desire.[135] Such praise, Dante implies, is empty unless one follows the good example one praises (*Par.* 19.18), as the souls in the Eagle imitate the justice and mercy of God to whom they not only give "praises (*laude*)" in heaven (19.37) but even applaud, since the Eagle flaps his wings ("*si plaude,*" 19.35). Dante substitutes *gloria* for *fama*: successful poets become "glorïosi" for ages on earth (18.83), but the better glory is the eternal kind to which the Jovians, and Trajan in particular, have been exalted (19.14, 20.112).

Dignity. Jupiter presaged "high rank" according to Ptolemy and "dignities (*dignitates*)" according to Albumasar. Scot repeated the latter and glossed *dignitas* as "lordship (*dominium*)."[136] Dante had defined *dignitas*, the quality of being "worthy" (Latin *dignus*, Italian *degno*) as "the effect or goal of merits,"[137] and in the heaven of Jupiter he accordingly stresses the moral rather than the material aspect of the concept: Trajan was "degno" to go to heaven (*Par.* 20.117), Hezekiah's prayer was "worthy" (20.53), and David did not stand on his dignity when he danced and sang while escorting the Ark (20.39; cf. *Purg.* 10.55–72).

Rulers. The persons named or alluded to in the heaven of Jupiter are predominantly rulers. Two emperors and three kings adorn the Eagle's eye and eyebrow, each said to be representative of the highest degree of his grade of beatitude (*Par.* 20.36). Moreover, the Eagle more or less identifies fifteen contemporary Christian kings whose names will appear among the damned in the Book of Judgment (19.115–148), and he mentions four other states.[138] Previously the narrator had condemned the venal judgments of avaricious popes (18.130–136) and had praised the Roman Empire (19.102), while the Eagle mentions Lucifer (46–48), "the king of Hell" (*Inf.* 34.1).

In no other heaven does Dante refer so frequently to kings, kingdoms, and sovereign states. The reason for this concentration on kingship is in part mythological, of course, for Jupiter was the king of the gods; but the mythographers had a smattering of astrology, for they recognized

that Jove's star is especially dominant—"multum dominatrix."[139] Consequently, the Jovian, according to Scot, "desires to have lordship or dignity
(*dominium seu dignitatem*).[140] Albumasar delimited with precision the political effects of this urge for power: it results in "political preeminence
(*principatus*)" and "kingdoms (*regna*)"; typical Jovians include those men
who possess great power ("magnates") and those who are placed in authority over others ("prelati").[141] These categories include both kings and
kingdoms, but they allow not only for greater rulers, such as emperors,
but also for a nonruler, such as Ripheus, who as a Trojan hero could be
accounted a magnate.

   Bad rulers. How Jovian are the Christian rulers against whom the
Eagle directs his invective? As a group, they have not "cherished righteousness," and so they merit not praise but dispraise ("dispregi," *Par.* 19.114).
To this extent they are not Jovian, but in other respects they do fall under
Jupiter's influence, because they all are rulers, and also because many of
them are driven to commit injustices by the desire to increase their lordship, which is likewise an effect of Jupiter. The Eagle is often unclear about
the nature of specific offenses—for instance, the offense of Dinaz of Portugal is unknown—and even the identity of certain sovereigns—e.g., "he
of Norway" (19.139); although in other cases the sinner and/or the sin is
explicitly identified. It is noteworthy that in many instances where Dante
is specific, he does so to introduce an allusion to some property of Jupiter.
Thus "lust (*lussuria*)," which Dante attributes to the kings of Spain and
Bohemia (124–125), was reckoned by the astrologers to be an effect of
Jupiter. It was prompted by a sanguine temperament but also accorded
with the legendary lechery of the king of the gods, which also rendered
appropriate an allusion to cuckoldry (138).[142] Philip the Fair provided the
occasion for three Jovian reminiscences at *Par.* 19.118–120: first, his cognomen, "the Fair (*Pulcher*)," refers to a Jovian property, inasmuch as both
the planet and its natives are "fair (*pulcher*) in appearance";[143] next, his
debasement of the coinage is proper to "the planet of money" (see above,
at n. 46); and finally, he died while riding and hunting, both of which are
Jovian activities.[144]

   Dante's reliance on astrology in his characterization of the unjust
kings appears most clearly in the well-known acrostic that runs through
their lines: "LLLLVVVVEEEE," spelling out *lue*, "plague" or "pest"
(*Par.* 19.115–139). The astrologers, for their part, insisted that Jupiter
brought health,[145] and Haly was more specific: by Jupiter's influence "the
infirmities of an epidemic (*epidimie*) are diminished."[146] Once again, the

literal materialism of the astrologers has been transmuted into its metaphorical equivalent: the unjust rulers are a plague for which Jupiter's *iustitia* is the sovereign cure.

Six Degrees of Justice

Little more remains to be said about Dante's use of astrology in the heaven of Jupiter. Despite an abundance of parallels, astrology has contributed less to the understanding of this heaven than any other. This should not be surprising, for after the Pilgrim passed beyond Venus and the shadow of the earth, the role of traditional astrology in the poem has diminished. Some traditional interpretations the poet simply ignores, others he retains entire, and many he transposes into a higher, specifically Christian, context, thus creating his own Christian astrology. In Jupiter the inadequacy of earthly, materialistic interpretations has been particularly apparent. By comparing the astrologers and Dante in this heaven, we have repeatedly found the poet soaring beyond their meaning while retaining their vocabulary. Thus, on the one hand Dante acknowledges that the stars do influence human affairs, but on the other he accords only a limited value to the astrologers' interpretation of these influences. His own modifications suggest that he was convinced that the science of astrology, which was the work of unaided human reason, could comprehend astral influences more fully with the aid of revelation.

In this chapter we have been able to determine the extent of Dante's debt to traditional astrology, but we have not turned to revelation to discover the sources of the Christian elements in Dante's own system of astrology. To do so in detail would be a long story, for *iustitia* is a major theme in scholastic theology: for example, a good third of Aquinas's treatment of the virtues is devoted to varieties of this one.[147] Nonetheless, we can attempt a brief foray into the Christian sources of Dante's astrology that will at least indicate where the missing pieces of the puzzle can be found.

Let us begin with an open question proposed by the text. As the Eagle is about to point out the six spirits that compose its eye, he informs us that, of all the souls in the Eagle, these six "are the highest of all their degrees (*e' di tutti lor gradi son li sommi*)" (*Par.* 20.36). Since all these souls are in this heaven "for being just and pious/pitying—*Per esser giusto e pio*" (19.13), it follows that there are degrees or grades ("gradi") of justice and/

or *pietá* according to which the blessed Jovians are ranked. The reader, then, is being shown only what Dante considers to be the uppermost levels ("li sommi") of six kinds of justice and/or *pietá*; presumably there are many lower forms as well. Leaving aside for the moment the ambiguous term *pio* (see above, at nn. 121–22), this accords well with Aquinas's treatment of justice, which distinguishes justice into a bewildering number of varieties and associated virtues. The problem, then, amounts simply to this: What virtues are exemplified in these six cases?

David. When the Eagle identifies the souls that make up his eye, he begins with David, the light that stands for his pupil. As that part is unquestionably nobler than the eyebrow, we may plausibly conjecture that David represents justice in its highest form. What, then, is the highest form of justice? Aquinas is ready with a possible answer—*religio.* According to the *Summa theologiae*, religion is a part of justice; furthermore, Aquinas says that religion is the outstanding moral virtue.[148] If Dante agreed with Aquinas that religion is the highest form of justice, we would expect it to be exemplified in David, the most prominent part of the Eagle's eye. To test this, we have but to ask how well it fits Dante's description of David.

> Colui che luce in mezzo per pupilla,
>   fu il cantor de lo Spirito Santo,
>   che l'arca traslatò di villa in villa:
> ora conosce il merto del suo canto,
>   in quanto effetto fu del suo consiglio,
>   per lo remunerar ch'è altrettanto.   (*Par.* 20.37–42)

He who shines midmost, as the pupil, was the singer of the Holy Spirit, who translated the ark from town to town: now he knows the merit of his song, so far as it was the effect of his own counsel, through the recompense that is equivalent.

David is represented, not as a king, but as a singer. Although the text does allude to his singing before the Ark (*Purg.* 10.58–69), is David being rewarded for that song alone? It seems more likely that this is only one instance of his many songs, which as the Book of Psalms were all held to have been inspired by the Holy Spirit because they were part of Holy Scripture. We have, therefore, an intertextual reference to the Psalms; accordingly, we must ask whether they show their author to have been "religious" in Aquinas's sense of the term. Aquinas says that the object of religion is to show reverence to God "insofar as he is the first principle of creation and of the government of all things."[149] A substantial number of David's psalms do just that.[150] For example, David praises God as creator in Psalm 103, saying: "How great are thy works, O Lord? thou hast made all things in wisdom: the earth is filled with thy riches."[151] The Psalmist also praises God as ruler of all things in Psalm 97: "he cometh to judge the earth. He shall judge the world with justice and the people with equity."[152] Moreover, God's *iustitia* is mentioned by name more often in the Psalms than in any other book of the Bible. Dante, therefore, had ample justification for according David the highest place in his heaven of Justice.

Trajan. After David, who obviously exemplifies a higher kind of justice than the souls in the eyebrow, the Eagle passes on to Trajan. What virtue does he represent? Although he does justice as a ruler, it is unlikely that he exemplifies political, or legal, justice, since that, we shall see, is the only virtue that William the Good can exemplify. Again, the text points the way:

> Dei cinque che mi fan cerchio per ciglio,
>   colui che più al becco mi s'accosta,
>   la vedovella consolò del figlio:
> ora conosce quanto caro costa
>   non seguir Cristo, per l'esperïenza
>   di questa dolce vita e de l'opposta.   (*Par.* 20.43–48)

Of the five who make a circle for my brow, the one who is nearest to my beak consoled the poor widow for her son. Now he knows, by experience of this sweet life and its opposite, how dear it costs not to follow Christ.

What the Eagle stresses is that Trajan's act "consoled the poor widow"; it was, then, an act of mercy (*misericordia*), because it was done to a widow, one of the *miserabiles personae* whose condition especially requires mercy.[153] Thus, according to Aquinas, "injuries become worse when they are done to widows and orphans . . . because such injuries are more opposed to mercy." Trajan's rank order in the Eagle's eye is justified by Aquinas's discussion of the question, "Whether mercy is the greatest of the virtues" (*Summa theologiae* II-II q.30 a.4). The proposition is true in the abstract, Thomas admits, but in fact it applies only to God because only God has no superior. Mercy is always done by a superior to an inferior, because in such an act one must be more powerful than the other in order that the stronger can supply what the weaker lacks. God in his omnipotence can be completely merciful, but even the most powerful human being is inferior to God. The greatest virtue for man, Thomas argues, is to be joined to God in love, so as a human virtue *misericordia* is outranked by *caritas*. Just so, David outranks Trajan in the Eagle's eye. Nonetheless, it is significant that in Dante's view an emperor had no superior save God,[154] and consequently Trajan is the best human example of mercy.

There is, however, a grave objection to the view that in the Eagle's eye Trajan exemplifies mercy. We know that consoling the widow was not enough to win salvation for the pagan emperor, for at first he went to Hell and was only saved when Pope Gregory's prayers earned him a chance to believe in Christ.

> ora conosce quanto caro costa
>   non seguir Cristo, per l'esperïenza
>   di questa dolce vita e de l'opposta.   (*Par.* 20.46–48)

Now he knows, by experience of this sweet life and of the opposite how dear it costs not to follow Christ.

Accordingly, we must wonder how an act of mercy that was insufficient to gain salvation for a pagan was converted into an exemplary act after Trajan's conversion. The answer would seem to be that for Christians, an act of mercy is also an act of piety. Thus, in Jesus' parable of the Last Judgment, the good discover that their merciful treatment of those who were homeless, or hungry, or thirsty, or naked, or in prison has earned them a place in heaven because, as Christ the Judge explains, "as long as you did it to one of these my least brethren, you did it to me" (Matt. 25.40). Saint Augustine notes that "by popular usage the word [*pietas*] is frequently used of works of mercy. This has happened, I believe, because God especially enjoins the performance of works of this kind and assures us that they are pleasing to him in place of or in preference to sacrifice."[155] Hence for a Christian, an act of mercy to the miserable is also an act of piety to

God.[156] Thus it would appear that Trajan exemplifies not mercy per se but rather Christian mercy-as-piety.

Furthermore, we may wonder whether Trajan's pious mercy can be subsumed under justice. In his younger days, Thomas taught in his commentary on the *Sentences* that mercy as a moral virtue is a species of justice, although in the *Summa theologiae* he treated it as one of the effects of the theological virtue of charity, and since the two views are not mutually exclusive, some Thomists would have it both ways.[157] Thus Dante could plausibly take Trajan's mercy to exemplify one kind of justice. Similarly, the emperor is a type of justice if one views his treatment of the widow as an act of piety, because the *Summa theologiae* includes piety as part of justice.[158] Hence it appears that Trajan, like the other souls in the Eagle's eye, is the supreme example of a certain kind of justice.[159]

Hezekiah. Now we know that the Eagle is listing the souls in descending rank order, so Hezekiah must typify the third highest kind of *iustitia*. The three biblical versions of his miraculous cure offer a number of possibilities (4 Reg. 20.1–6, 1 Par. 32.24–26, and Isa. 38.1–22), but once again Dante's text enables us to single out the salient features:

> E quel che segue in la circunferenza
>   di che ragiono, per l'arco superno,
>   morte indugiò per vera penitenza:
> ora conosce che 'l giudicio etterno
>   non si trasmuta, quando degno preco
>   fa crastino là de l'odïerno.   (*Par.* 20.49–54)

And he who follows on the circumference whereof I speak, upon the upward arc, by true penitence delayed death. Now he knows that the eternal judgment is not changed when worthy prayer there makes today's into tomorrow's.

The Eagle, the veracious spokesman, assures us that Hezekiah's life was prolonged by his "true penitence." If this is not overly evident in the Bible, we must accept the Eagle's word for it.[160] Consequently, our question must be whether true repentance typifies some kind of justice, and again Aquinas has the answer: "insofar as penitence is a virtue, it is a part of justice."[161] He also explains how "worthy prayer" can affect the implementation of something God has ordained. God cannot be persuaded "to change his mind," but insofar as his will is carried out by secondary causes, such as nature, those can be altered.[162] Since the functioning of Hezekiah's body plainly belongs to the realm of nature, it would be subject to prolongation by competent prayer.[163]

Constantine. In the case of Constantine (*Par.* 20.55–60), the question is whether the Donation of Constantine—the emperor's act of giving the Latin West to Pope Silvester I—can in itself be considered some form of *iustitia.* In Aquinas's terms, such a gift, made by a layman to a cleric, is called an "offering" or *oblatio.* According to Aquinas's classification, offering an oblation is a kind of religious act, which in turn is a form of *iustitia.*[164] Constantine's gift, made under the influence of Jupiter, was a magnificent one, as we have seen (above, at n. 110). God has rewarded his generosity, which was just because his intention was just.[165]

William of Sicily. The fifth degree of justice is that exemplified by William II, king of Sicily (1166–1189), who is generally called "William the Good."

> E quel che vedi ne l'arco declivo,
>   Guiglielmo fu, cui quella terra plora
>   che piagne Carlo e Federigo vivo:
> ora conosce come s'innamora
>   lo ciel del giusto rege, e al sembiante
>   del suo fulgore il fa vedere ancora.   (*Par.* 20.61–66)

And him you see in the downward arc was William, whom that land laments that deplores the living Charles and Frederick. Now he knows how heaven is enamored of the just king, and he also makes this plain by the radiance of his appearance.

The grade of justice typified by William is explicitly identified in the text: he is "the just king." It is in his official capacity that he is contrasted with his successors as rulers of the kingdom of Sicily; indeed, his public life stands in marked contrast to his private one, which was that of a pleasure-loving oriental potentate.[166] The four higher degrees of justice have also been exemplified by kings, but not *qua* kings, since religion and piety are by no means a royal prerogative. William, then, is the only king in the Eagle to be there because he was a good king, i.e., a just one. Aquinas calls William's form of justice "legal justice (*iustitia legalis*)," which is so called because the righteous acts of individuals are directed to a common good by the laws enacted and enforced by rulers. Thus legal justice is primarily the virtue of a ruler, who ordains the laws, and only secondarily is the virtue of subjects, who observe them.[167]

Legal justice is what is commonly meant by justice today, and outside academic circles it was what was meant by justice in the Middle Ages as well. The point of Dante's graded classification of *iustitia* is, I think, that religion and piety are higher forms of justice than is good government, much though he valued the latter. By understanding these higher forms of *iustitia*, the ordinary reader will broaden his concept of justice.

Ripheus. The Eagle's series concludes with the revelation that Ripheus the Trojan was a Christian before the birth of Christ (*Par.* 20.67–72). How that could be is presently explained: Ripheus "set all his love down there [on earth] on righteousness (*drittura*)" (121), and consequently with the help of God's grace he eventually came to believe that mankind would be redeemed by Christ and openly repudiated his paganism. The whole process might be explicated in Thomistic terms,[168] but the point that chiefly concerns us is whether his love of *drittura* is a species of justice. The answer is a foregone conclusion because Dante had stated in the *Convivio* that justice disposes us to love righteousness, or "*drittura*" (above, n. 93), and we may note, moreover, that Aquinas concurs.[169] Since Ripheus is ranked last among the souls in the Eagle's eye, it follows that Dante considered ethical righteousness to be the lowest of the six top grades of justice.

This analysis enables us to resolve the controversial interpretation of "giusto e pio" at *Par.* 19.13. Both senses of *pio* are exemplified in the Eagle's eye, but piety is the primary and more general sense, which manifestly characterizes David and Hezekiah, whereas pity applies only to Trajan. It would seem, therefore, that Dante retained the ambiguity of *pio*, so that some of his Jovians were pious and others were compassionate. Just as many of his readers would understand justice in its narrow, legal sense, so they would take *pio* to signify mercy. In neither case would they be completely wrong, for both are exemplified in the Eagle's eye; but the more discerning reader will be led to discover broader meanings: to be just is essentially to be righteous, while to be *pio* implies a religious devotion and obedience to what is right, which ultimately is God. Hence both pity and piety can be subsumed under justice.

I have sketched the outlines of a thesis that could be greatly elaborated and refined, but several important conclusions can be drawn even from this rough approximation. (1) Dante's concept of justice includes acts of reverence, pious mercy, penitence, and oblation, all of which the ordinary reader would not associate with either legal justice or even upright ethical conduct. (2) Dante gives the six degrees a rank order, in which religious and pious varieties of justice take precedence over the strictly secular forms exemplified by William and Ripheus. (3) The theology of Thomas Aquinas appears to be the poet's primary source for this scheme. (4) Using unaided human reason, the astrologers nonetheless did glimpse most of these truths, albeit imperfectly, for among Jupiter's properties they listed religion, mercy, generosity, concord and judgment, and righteousness (above, nn. 66, 88, 97–99, 109, 123, 125), which leaves only Hezekiah's penitence without a parallel in astrology. Dante has used their astrological indications selectively, and in many cases theology seems to have provided him with the principles of selection; nonetheless, in many matters of detail he accepts the authority of astrology as sufficient in itself and therefore appropriates astrological properties simply because they typify the influence of Jupiter. To remind us that for Dante astrology often does have independent value, here is one final parallel.

Peoples and places. Ibn Ezra, who assigns one of the seven climates to each of the planets, pairs Jupiter with the second climate.[170] Armed with this equation, Dante must have again sought more information in Alfraganus's textbook of astronomy, which would have told him that the second climate begins in the east, and after crossing China, "it goes across the regions of India, and next through the regions of Acint, and the city of Almansora, i.e., Adumata, is in it."[171] The regions of India are in the north, since Alfraganus had explained in the previous paragraph that the first climate passes through the southern part of India. *Acint* is "as-Sind," the valley of the Indus River, which the Moslems conquered in the early eighth century; they secured their conquest by building the strong city of al-Mansûra (= "Almansora," Mansurah) on the banks of the Indus.[172] Thus the second climate includes the home of Dante's hypothetical man who was "born on the bank of the Indus (*nasce a la riva / de l'Indo*)" (*Par.* 19.70–71). Furthermore, Ibn Ezra adds that Jupiter governs the peoples of Babylonia and Persia, and their countries are listed as Jovian regions by Alcabitius and Bonatti.[173] This explains why Dante chose the Persians as a non-Christian people that might reproach the unjust Christian kings on judgment day: "Che poran dir li Perse a' vostri regi . . . ?" (*Par.* 19.112).[174]

7. Saturn

Of all the seven planets, Saturn presented the greatest challenge to Dante because in his view it was closest to God, and hence most godlike, while for the astrologers it was the worst of all planets—the greater malefic. Dante had faced a similar problem in the case of Mars, which he solved by offsetting the planet's bad qualities with good ones that he borrowed from Thomistic theology. In the case of Saturn, however, his solution was more direct: he selected a number of astrological properties that appeared to be misfortunes to the worldly astrologers but which could be regarded as virtues from an otherworldly point of view. For example, the astrologers thought Saturn unlucky because it brought exile, famine, impotence, and poverty; for Dante these became the virtues of men who withdrew from this world and as monks embraced a life of fasting, chastity, and apostolic poverty. This simple inversion of values, which was inherent in Christianity, enabled Dante to retain a great many of the traditional astrological properties of Saturn in his Christian astrology.

Just as Dante had used mythology as well as astrology to construct his lower planetary heavens, so in the highest one he stressed Saturn's association with the Golden Age, when mankind was most nearly perfect. Similarly, Dante's heaven of Saturn approaches perfection more closely than the other planets because, according to the poem's cosmology, it is the true God himself who can be seen there as in a mirror (*Par.* 9.61–62, 19.28–30). Although Dante seemingly ignores other aspects of Saturn's legend, nonetheless the Saturn of the mythographers influenced the poem through astrology, which in antiquity had drawn on classical myth to shape the astrological meanings of the planet.[1] Because Saturn takes over twenty-nine years to complete an apparent orbit around the earth (actually, of course, around the Sun), it is the slowest of the planets; hence it was associated with old age and equated first with Kronos, the father of Zeus, and eventually with his Roman counterpart, Saturn, as well. Once the planet was identified with Kronos-Saturn, the former acquired certain mythical properties of the latter. For example, just as the god had gone into exile, so the planet indicated long journeys from home. Similarly, as he had lost his kingdom, it signified poverty; and as he was castrated, it brought impotence. By the second century of our era, the basic properties of Saturn were fixed, and astrologers had already lost sight of the myths on which they were based. None of the astrologers used in this study refers to the mythical antecedents of Saturnine properties, not even Michael Scot, who usually does report the opinions of the mythographers. Dante followed their example, perhaps, as suggested above, because this suited his own cosmology.

In the heaven of Saturn, as in the lower heavens, the Pilgrim sees an emblem that symbolizes the planet's beneficent influence and then interviews representative natives. In the case of Saturn, the emblem is Jacob's ladder, and the natives all are monks. In this chapter we will consider these two phenomena separately, but before doing so we will first consider the basic properties of the planet and their utilization in allusions to inanimate phenomena. Our second major concern will be the planet's effects on humans, and especially on monks but to a lesser extent on the secular clergy and laity as well; then, in conclusion, I will offer an astrological interpretation of Jacob's ladder.

Saturnine Astrophysics

Dante's astrologers based their interpretations of Saturn's powers on what they understood to be the physical nature of the planet. They all agreed that one of Saturn's qualities was cold (*frigus*), and almost all of them paired this with the quality of dryness (*siccitas*).[2] The exception was Ptolemy, who explicitly mentioned only the coldness of the planet, not its dryness; in fact, in his elaboration of the effects of Saturnine cold, he tends to favor combinations of cold and wet.[3] This ambivalence about whether Saturn was dry or wet in nature was one of long standing in Greek astrology. From Babylonian astrology the Greeks learned that Saturn's nature was dry, but in their own mythology Kronos was a rain god or a sea god, and hence his planet's nature should be wet.[4] This ambivalence was passed on to the Arabs, who resolved the difficulty by declaring that Saturn's essential qualities were cold and dryness, although "sometimes accidentally it was wet."[5] The coldness of Saturn, however, was undisputed and was explained by the planet's distance from the Sun, just as Mars's proximity to the Sun made it hot and Jupiter's intermediate location gave it a moderate temperature.

Dante acknowledged the coldness of Saturn in two passages. Peter Damian recalls that in his mountaintop hermitage he endured "frosts (*geli*)" (*Par.* 21.116). Again, the narrator compares the gathering of souls at a certain step on Jacob's ladder to the way daws "move about together, at the beginning of the day, to warm their cold (*fredde*) feathers" (21.35–36). The poet does not, however, refer directly to either the planet's essential dryness or its accidental wetness, though both are implied by references to the elements earth (dry + cold) and water (wet + cold) (see below, at nn. 8–14). Another indirect allusion to Saturnine dryness may be the repeated references to thunder (21.12, 107, 142), which Aristotelian meteorology attributed to clouds colliding with dry exhalations.[6]

Although Dante followed the astrologers in taking cold to be a natural quality of Saturn, he laid far greater stress on the opposite quality of heat in his Saturnine cantos. Usually heat in these passages is a spiritual rather than a physical quality, but even the literal "frosts" that Damian suffered in his hermitage are counterbalanced by "heats (*caldi*)" (*Par.* 21.116). Dante's justification for this departure from what he regarded as scientific fact would ultimately be revealed in *Paradiso* 28, where the Pilgrim sees an alternative, spiritual or supranatural model of the universe, in which God is a point of light at the center, around which the angelic intelligences of each sphere circle at varying speeds that are proportioned to their understanding and hence love. The Thrones that animate Saturn are expressly mentioned in third place from the center (28.103–105), and they move faster than any of the other planetary intelligences. The reader has long been prepared for this principle, however, by the beauty of Beatrice, which has grown greater in each successive heaven, as she reminds the Pilgrim just as they are entering the heaven of Saturn (21.7–8). She explains the increase in heat-related terms, for she says her beauty has been progressively "kindled (*s'accende*)" (21.8).

The superior spiritual heat of Saturn should suffice to explain the high frequency of heat-related language in the Saturnine cantos, but Dante reinforced this with an alternate, natural explanation. In the same speech, Beatrice goes on to state that the planet Saturn "rays downwards its power now mixed beneath the breast of the burning Lion" (*Par.* 21.14–15). Accordingly, we must understand that the natural coldness of Saturn is at that moment being mingled with the hotness of the constellation Leo, under which the planet is presently passing.[7]

The poet therefore has provided a natural and a supernatural explanation that both justify the abundance of fire imagery in these cantos. The souls he sees there are "fires" (*Par.* 22.46) or "flamelets" (21.136); they are "kindled" by the "heat" of love (22.32, 47) with which they "burn" (21.68). Peter Damian is a "flame" that is "aflame" with joy (21.90, 88); the Pilgrim perceives Benedict's "ardors" (22.54) and is himself filled with "hot desire" (21.51). Finally, still greater "flaming" can be seen (21.69) in the fixed stars above Saturn.

ELEMENTS

Since Saturn has in effect three qualities, one of which is constant, these can combine to produce two elements. Either the element earth is formed from the union of coldness with dryness, or if dryness is replaced by wetness, water results instead. The astrologers ascribe both elements to Saturn, and Dante accordingly makes use of both earth and water.

Earth. Michael Scot ascribes all the characteristics of the element earth to Saturn: "The nature of Saturn is cold and dry in the highest degree; it is bad, hard, heavy, harmful, weighty, hard to move, and cruel; hence he is called the god of earth."[8] Alcabitius extends Saturn's dominion over *terra* to include "lands or all that is associated with them—*terras vel res terrarum.*" Dante uses "terra" once in the sense of the ground we walk on (*Par.* 22.74) and again to refer more broadly to the whole sublunar world: Christ "brought to earth (*terra*) that truth which so uplifts us" (22.41).[9]

Dante was well aware that earth is the heaviest of the four elements, for this fact occasioned his *Questio de aqua et terra.* Michael Scot, in the passage quoted above, describes earth as being both "heavy (*gravis*)," and "weighty (*ponderosa*)," and the other astrologers frequently assign both of these characteristics to Saturn.[10] In particular, according to Bonatti, "Saturn makes men heavy" and "signifies heaviness of body."[11] For Dante, heaviness is one of the evil effects of Saturn, which he uses to satirize "the modern pastors." Whereas Saints Peter and Paul went "lean and barefoot (*magri et scalzi*)" (*Par.* 21.128), their modern counterparts, the popes and cardinals, "are so heavy (*tanto son gravi*)" that they require attendants to lead them and to prop them up on either side (21.130–132).

Water. Dante has only one direct reference to bodies of water in connection with Saturn: "Jordan driven back, and the [Red] sea fleeing when God willed" are less likely miracles than God's reform of the Church (*Par.* 22.94–96). Why did Dante select these out of all the miracles available in the Bible? Perhaps because they were appropriate to Saturn, to which Ptolemy attributed "diminutions and augmentations of the sea" and "excessive flooding in rivers."[12] Another allusion to water is suggested by Guido Bonatti, who lists among the crafts proper to Saturn both "work involving water or that is done near water" and "the building of houses, and especially the houses of monks who wear black habits."[13] Peter Damian's hermitage on the eastern slope of Mount Catria (*Par.* 21.109–110) was a religious house, although the habit of the hermits was white, and it took its name from a nearby spring among the pine trees—Fonte Avellana.[14] Inasmuch as Dante suppressed the name of the house, however, it would seem that he did not wish to stress this connection with Saturn; as we shall see, he had quite other astrological reasons for associating a famous hermitage with Saturn.

HUMORS

Each element had its corresponding humor, so Saturn was associated accordingly with two of the humors or complexions. From its essential qualities of cold and dry came both earth and melancholy, but when the planet was cold and wet, it gave rise to the phlegmatic disposition and to water.

Melancholy. Most astrologers agreed that Saturn causes melancholy.[15] This temperament disposes men to be miserable and especially to "a life of mental misery."[16] Saturn's children are at least inclined to be gloomy and habitually unhappy (*tristis*),[17] if they are not reduced to actual sorrow (*dolor*)[18] and lamentation.[19] Bonatti says that "Saturn causes a man to laugh never, or hardly ever," and Scot declares that the Saturnine man "rarely laughs, and when he does, his laughter is a long time coming, so he rarely seems to be cheerful."[20]

Superficially, melancholy seems to be the prevalent mood in Dante's heaven of Saturn, for Beatrice does not smile on the Pilgrim, and the blessed souls, unlike their lower counterparts, do not sing. But in fact, the souls are filled with joy: Peter Damian refers to "the joy (*allegrezza*) with which I am aflame" (*Par.* 21.88), which the Pilgrim had already described as "la tua letizia" (21.56). Beatrice carefully explains that she does not smile in this heaven because her beauty, which is enhanced in each succeeding heaven, would now be so great that the Pilgrim could not stand it (21.4–12). Later, Peter Damian adds that the Saturnine spirits are not singing for a similar reason, namely that the Pilgrim's mortal hearing could not bear the sound (21.61–63). Finally, the Pilgrim is given a small sample of Saturnine sound, which only terrifies him, thereby proving that his mortal senses are not ready for the exalted effects of this heaven (21.140–142, 22.1–12).

In this case Dante used melancholy, the best-known property of Saturn, to distinguish his Christian cosmological system from that of conventional astrology. We may be sure this was intentional both because he gave the point primacy of place and because he later twice elaborated and reiterated it. In Dante's universe, the highest planet has more joy than the others, just as it burns with more ardor. This, of course, does not preclude the possibility that Saturn can induce melancholy in men, as indeed we may suspect it does for Dante, since he leaves no doubt that the planet's spiritual heat does not impede its affinity for the element earth.[21]

Swift and slow. We have seen that sometimes Saturn produces water rather than earth, and it follows that it makes men phlegmatic as well as melancholy. Although Alcabitius asserted this boldly,[22] Bonatti, who usually followed him slavishly, was less certain: "Among the complexions of the body," he wrote, Saturn "signifies melancholy, and perhaps that melancholy will be mixed with phlegm and with the weight and heaviness of the native's body so that he will neither walk or jump lightly nor will he learn to swim or do other things that are done to display lightness of body."[23] Evidently Bonatti had no doubt that Saturnians lack lightness of body, and while he is inclined to attribute this to a natural heaviness, which, like melancholy, would be a consequence of their affinity for earth, he allows for the possibility that the cause may be an admixture of phlegm in the temperament. Other astrologers were content to assert that "Saturn signifies slowness (*tarditatem*)" and that its children were slow in moving, thinking, and speaking, just as the star itself moved slowly in its orbit.[24]

Dante's Saturnians show no trace of slowness. Indeed, slowness is only mentioned in these cantos to deny it, as when Benedict answers the Pilgrim's thought "lest you, by waiting, be delayed (*non tarde*)" (*Par.* 22.34),[25] or when he asserts that God's sword "cuts not in haste nor slowly (*tardo*)" (22.16). Furthermore, movements in this heaven are rapid rather than the reverse. Beatrice reassures the Pilgrim like a mother who comforts her son "quickly (*sùbito*)" (22.5); their ascent up Jacob's ladder is "swift (*ratto*)" (22.104); Peter Damian is "quick (*presta*)" to obey God's will (21.67) and, what is more, he expresses his heightened joy by spinning around "like a rapid (*veloce*) millstone" (21.81). The last instance perhaps justifies the others, for in Dante's theocentric model of the universe, the angelic orders, which are endowed with greater vision and love, also have greater velocity, so that Saturn in this nonphysical sense is the swiftest rather than the slowest of the planets (*Par.* 28.34–36). Once again, Dante, by reversing the traditional characteristics of Saturn, indicates that the true nature of the planet is determined, not by its crystalline body, but by the angelic intelligences that animate that body.

Aspects of Earth

For Dante, the higher, spiritual nature of Saturn was superadded to that lower, physical one known to the astrologers. That Dante did justice to both is readily apparent from his allusions to the element earth, which he made sparingly but unmistakably while in Saturn's sphere. An interesting pair occurs in connection with Saints Peter and Paul, whom he describes obliquely as "Cephas" and "the great vessel of the Holy Spirit" (*Par.* 21.125–126). "Cephas" is an Aramaic word meaning "rock man," which was glossed in the Gospel of John by its Greek equivalent, *Petros*, and translated in the Latin Vulgate as *Petrus* (John 1.42)—both being the masculine form of *petra*, a rock, boulder, or building stone. By using the original form of Peter's name, Dante drew attention to its etymology, which made it appropriate to Saturn, the planet that signified "stones."[26] Once Peter, stones, and Saturn have been linked together, one can appreciate why Dante chose Peter Damian as one of his typical Saturnians (called "Pietro" at 21.121–122).[27] Paul, the other apostle referred to, is also associated with Saturn, but by periphrasis rather than etymology. "The vessel (*vasello*) of the Holy Spirit" (21.127) is appropriate to this planet because, according to Michael Scot, the Saturnian is naturally gifted in working with earth, including terra cotta and potter's clay: he delights in making ceramics, tiles, bricks, clay forms for smelting and founding metals, and terra cotta jars.[28] Finally, either bricks or stones are suggested by Benedict's mention of abbey "walls (*mura*)" (*Par.* 22.76).

Millstones. Saturnians work with stones in many forms, including the millstone (*mola*). Scot remarks that they like "to turn a *mola* for whetting some iron tool," and Bonatti says they are apt to build mills (*molendina*).[29] Thus it is appropriate that when Peter Damian whirls like a top to express his joy, the narrator likens this movement to a "swift millstone (*mola*)" (*Par.* 21.81), which is a simile appropriate to the place. In passing, it may be noted in this connection that there is no astrological basis for the extraordinary prominence of spheres, circles, and circular motion in these cantos.[30]

Mountains. Both Benedict and Peter Damian tell the Pilgrim about their mountains, respectively "that mountain on whose slope Cassino lies" (*Par.* 22.37) and "a hump whose name is Catria" (21.109). Both, of course, are masses of stone, and indeed the poet goes out of his way to remind the reader that Catria is made of "rocks (*sassi*)" (21.106). Although the former, being surrounded by towns (22.44), was relatively civilized,[31] the latter is described as a wild place, high above the thunder and subject to extremes of temperature (21.108, 116). According to Scot, such a wild and savage landscape suits Saturn, which is *silvaticus.*[32]

Agriculture. Even before the Latin god Saturnus became associated with a planet, he presided over agriculture, and for most astrologers that remained his province, which was also indicated by his influence over elementary earth.[33] Saturnians were typically farmers, which in the predominantly agricultural economy of the Middle Ages made up perhaps as much as ninety percent of the population.[34] Scot, who was much given to elaboration, represented agrarian life in a series of vivid vignettes by listing every agricultural activity he knew.[35] Dante's narrator reflects this rustic mood as he tells us that Beatrice was "the pasture (*pastura*) of my sight" (*Par.* 21.19–20). A more extended agricultural metaphor comes readily to the lips of that typical Saturnian Peter Damian as he deplores the decline of Fonte Avellana: "That cloister used to yield abundantly (*fertilemente*) to these heavens, and now it is become so barren (*vano*) that soon it needs must be revealed" (21.118–120).

Caves and concavities. "The places that belong to Saturn are concavities," Ibn Ezra declared, and as examples he listed "cesspools, wells, prisons, and every dark, inhabited place, and graveyards."[36] Other astrologers mention many of his examples but do not generalize from them."[37] Dante follows this and gives another example of a "dark, inhabited place" when he has Benedict complain that "the walls, which used to be an abbey, have become dens (*spelonche*)" (*Par.* 22.77). This is generally understood as an intertextual reference to the biblical "den of thieves (*speluncam latronum*),"[38] but it is nonetheless astrologically appropriate. Moreover, since a *spelunca* is primarily a cave, which may or may not be used as a den or lair, the subtext is Benedict's own early life as a hermit who lived in the *Sacro Speco* at Subiaco.[39] Thus the latter-day degeneration of his order is implicitly contrasted with its austere beginnings. In the same speech, Benedict also complains that nowadays "the cowls are sacks full of foul meal"

(*Par.* 22.77–78). Perhaps this rather strange metaphor may have been suggested by Saturn's general lordship over concavities. A Freudian would not hesitate to swell the list with references to an "abyss" and a "hat" (21.94, 125).

Prisons and restraints. "Prisons (*carceres*)" were listed as one kind of concavity by Ibn Ezra. They had long been associated with Saturn because of Kronos's legendary imprisonment, and by extension many astrologers mention other forms of captivity as well, such as physical restraint by shackles, manacles, and chains.[40] Thus Dante suggests bondage faintly but distinctly several times in his Saturnine cantos. At one point, Peter Damian's words "restrained" or "bridled" the Pilgrim ("prescisser," *Par.* 21.103); at another Beatrice bids him to "release" his burning desire ("solvi," 21.51). More generally, the Church is a custodian that "guards" or "has in keeping" the property entrusted to it ("guarda," 22.82). Finally, we pass from physical to moral restraint as the narrator compares the Pilgrim to one who "restrains himself (*sé repreme*)" from fear of excess (22.25–27).

The first climate. Although the sublunar world is called "earth" from its predominant element, only one part of it falls under Saturn's influence, which is the zone that Ptolemy called "the first climate." We have seen that Dante has usually followed the system found in Ibn Ezra, who assigned each climate to a planet,[41] but in the case of Saturn he pointedly ignores the opaque geographical indications provided by the astrologers[42] and instead picks out an intelligible detail from Alfraganus, who described the first zone, starting from China: it passes westward across southern India, "and next the climate crosses the Red Sea, goes into the region of the Ethiopians, and crosses Egypt's Nile."[43] This authorized Dante's reference to the opening of the Red Sea: "e 'l mar fuggir, quando Dio volse" (*Par.* 22.95).[44] The accompanying reference to the crossing of Jordan (22.94) may well have been suggested by the pairing of the two crossings in Psalm 113 (114), "In exitu Israel de Aegypto. . . . Mare vidit, et fugit: Jordanis conversus et retrorsum" (verses 1a, 3), since Dante was particularly familiar with that psalm, which he had expounded as his specimen text in the *Epistle to Can Grande.*

Saturn and Monasticism

Saint Benedict informs the Pilgrim that the spirits in the group from which he and Peter Damian came "were all contemplative men (*contem-*

planti)" (*Par.* 22.46), so presumably the same is true of the Pilgrim's interlocutors. But the poet does not explain why contemplatives are proper to
this particular planet. The reader can surmise that it is appropriate that the
planet closest to God should rule the lives of those who sought to be
closest to God. No doubt this is part of the answer, but to to be more
correct we must add that astrologers had already associated monks with
Saturn, and for other reasons.

The most basic of these reasons was probably the Saturnian love of
solitude. "He does not wish society," wrote Haly; "he wishes to be alone
and separate. . . . He is not comfortable with anyone nor anyone with
him."[45] Benedict and the souls identified by name in this heaven—Peter
Damian, Macarius, and Romuald (*Par.* 21.121, 22.49)—all withdrew from
secular society and lived as hermits, though that did not preclude living
with other like-minded men.[46] Damian, in fact, repeatedly wrote in praise
of solitude[47] and exemplified it in his life as well when he resigned the
office of cardinal to return to the eremitical life.

Although Saturnian solitude fits the religious impulse to live apart
from secular society, the astrologers did not make the connection explicitly. Bonatti did mention monks expressly, however, in connection with the
black robes that are the Benedictine habit. Since black is Saturn's characteristic color, Alcabitius had taken the planet to indicate black clothing,[48] and
Bonatti applied this specifically to monks: Saturn "signifies black clothing
and those who naturally use black garments, including both members of
religious or cloistered communities and others as well."[49]

Bonatti mentions Black Monks again in connection with building,
an activity over which Saturn also had lordship: "Among the crafts it
signifies . . . the building of houses and most especially of the houses of
monks wearing black robes."[50] Dante would seem to have regarded Saturn
as the planet of religious houses in general, since in these cantos he refers
to a "hermitage (*ermo*)" as well as monasteries properly speaking, which
are termed "cloister (*chiostro*)," "house (*casa*)," and "abbey (*badia*)," not
to mention the Franciscan "*convento*" (*Par.* 21.110, 118, 22.50, 76, 122, 90).

SERVICE AND SENIORITY

Dante's decision to populate the heaven of Saturn with monks and other
religious represents a fusion of astrological indications with his own cosmology. Once the basic decision was made, astrology offered the poet
many other parallels between Saturnine properties and monasticism. For
instance, astrologers agreed that Saturnians were inclined to be *servi*, i.e.

functionally servile, whether legally slaves, serfs, or simply wage-earning servants.[51] Moreover, these *servi* typically engaged in what are politely termed humble occupations, although some astrologers use stronger language: Ibn Ezra qualifies *servi* as "despicable"; Bonatti links them with "eunuchs and vile persons," Scot with "handmaidens (*ancillas*)."[52] This dishonorable, Saturnian service is precisely the kind that Peter Damian attributes to himself and God's other servants when he declares that love "makes us prompt servants (*serve*)" of divine providence (*Par.* 21.70–71), for by substituting the derogatory form *serva* for the more neutral *servo*, Damian implies that their services are domestic and degrading.[53] Furthermore, he himself rendered such service not only in heaven but also on earth, for at Fonte Avellana he was steadfast "al servigio di Dio" (21.114). The *dominus-servus* relationship is, of course, a biblical commonplace for the respective roles of God and man, but in the thirteenth century both Roman and canon lawyers elucidated the legal status of monks by equating it with that of *servi* in Justinian's *Corpus iuris civilis*.[54] Consequently, in the medieval culture of Dante's time there was a special reason for regarding the monk as a *servus*, and astrology recognized both monk and *servus* as appropriate to the heaven of Saturn.

Elders. Dante's representative Saturnians were all in religious orders, but they were not just ordinary monks. Cacciaguida's principle, that the *Comedy* should contain only famous persons (*Par.* 17.136–138), justifies their fame, but the nature of Saturn also played a part in their selection. What they have in common beyond simple membership in a religious order is that each was the *head* of his order. Benedict, Macarius, and Romuald founded their own orders as well, but Damian merely reformed the one he had joined.[55] Seniority, then, characterized the position of each within his order. And Saturn signifies elders, especially in familial relationships. Thus John of Seville generalized that Saturn "signifies a father, a grandfather, and all elders."[56] Most astrologers specified at least "fathers (*patres*)," many added "grandfathers (*avi*)," and the list was occasionally extended to include "great-grandfathers (*proavi*)" and "elder brothers (*fratres maiores/longaeviores*)" as well.[57]

Dante frequently makes use of these familial roles in connection with Saturn. The Pilgrim addresses Benedict as "father (*padre*)" and in return is called "brother (*frate*)," as are faithful monks in general (*Par.* 22.58, 61, 50). The theme of paternity is extended by allusion to Dante's "fatherland (*patria*)" and to Jacob "the patriarch (*patriarca*)" (21.107, 22.70). Although most astrologers either ignored senior female relatives or even excluded them from Saturn's influence, Dante suggested a broader view by comparing Beatrice's reassurance of the Pilgrim to the way in which a "mother (*madre*)" comforts her son (22.1–6).[58] Finally, the monk's spiritual family is contrasted with his physical one in Benedict's complaint against the misappropriation of monastic property to "relatives (*parenti*)" (22.84).

Elder relatives were associated with Saturn because the god was represented as "a tired old man" and signified old age, decrepitude, and the end of life in general.[59] This aspect of Saturn is reflected in Peter Damian's account of his elevation to the cardinalate, when "little mortal life was left to me" (*Par.* 21.124). Similarly, the Pilgrim is told that he will see God punish the papal curia "before you die" (22.15). Indeed, mortality is a common theme in these cantos, which refer to "mortal powers," "mortal hearing as well as vision," and "the flesh of mortals" (21.11, 61, 22.85). This consciousness of death is appropriate to Saturn, which signified not only the last stage of life but death itself.[60] The poet in fact alludes to Saturn's association with death when he says that, while the god Saturn ruled the earth, "every wickedness lay dead (*morta*)" (21.27).

The Saturnine Ascetic

In *Paradiso* 22, Benedict's chief function is to discuss the problem of religious institutions. After Benedict has identified himself, the Pilgrim is curious to see him, but the saint explains that he will be visible only in the Empyrean, the highest heaven, where everything finds its perfection, including the soul, which will be united there with its body (*Par.* 22.52–67). Although the Pilgrim's question has been answered, Benedict's speech proceeds by association to consider the problem of attaining perfection in heaven. One must climb "our ladder (*nostra scala*)" (68), he says, which he equates with the ladder that Jacob saw in a dream (70–72; cf. Gen. 28.12). Dantists generally understand "our ladder" to refer to the one seen in this heaven (*Par.* 21.29–30), but the pronoun is ambivalent because the historical Saint Benedict had made Jacob's ladder peculiarly his own by using it in his *Rule* as a metaphor for the twelve steps of humility.[61] This subtle intertextual reference prepares the alert reader for an overt one several lines later, when Benedict announces that "my rule—*la regola mia*—remains as pages wasted" (22.75).[62]

Benedict does not dwell on the substance of his *Rule*; the references to it are enough to take it as read. Instead, for the rest of the speech he complains about the degeneration of observance among his successors and those of Peter and Francis (*Par.* 22.76–96). He especially contrasts the pristine ideals of each founder with their latter-day corruption, and he anticipates an eventual reformation. Benedict's *Rule* stands at the core of this speech, tacitly paralleled by those of Damian, Macarius, and Romuald, who were also monastic innovators, either by establishing or reforming the rules of their respective orders. At the periphery are *nonmonastic* ecclesiastical institutions that are dealt with more extensively elsewhere in the *Paradiso*: Francis and the mendicants earlier (cantos 11–12) and Peter and the Roman church later (canto 27). The focus in this passage is accordingly on the *Regula Benedicti*.

Astrology offers many reasons why Benedict's *Rule* is appropriate to this heaven. First, it was one of the "ancient and durable things" proper to Saturn, the planet of old age and inheritances.[63] Benedict, in worrying about the fate of his work, shows himself to be a true Saturnian, who "considers and cogitates on ancient things."[64] Furthermore, the material on which such a document was written was typically parchment, and all forms of leather belong to Saturn.[65] Thus Dante draws attention to the physical pages ("carte") on which the *Rule* was written (*Par.* 22.75).[66] And finally, astrologers provided an apt description of the *Rule*'s historic role as the unifying force in western monasticism: for religious sects, Alcabitius declared, Saturn signifies "one that professes unifying doctrines (*unitates*)."[67]

In the course of his Saturnine cantos, Dante touches on a number of monastic virtues, practices, and themes, most of which became part of Latin monasticism though the diffusion of the *Regula Benedicti* (= *RB*). Like the *Rule* itself, they are properties of Saturn. For example, Benedict had no use for monks who wandered from one spiritual master to another; he insisted that his monks, in contrast to these *gyrovagi*, pledge themselves to "stability (*stabilitas*)," i.e., remaining in the monastery where they made their vows (*RB* 1, 61.5). Similarly, Saturn tends to be immobile and governs "fortitude and stability."[68] Thus Peter Damian was "steadfast (*fermo*)" in his discipline at Fonte Avellana and had to be dragged away to Rome (*Par.* 21.114, 125). Likewise, Benedict identifies the Saturnine monks as "my brethren who stayed their feet within the cloisters and kept a steadfast heart (*cor saldo*)" (22.50–51).

Silence is enjoined by Benedict on his monks (*RB* 7), and astrologically Saturn signifies "a multitude of silence."[69] This taciturn disposition is not only reflected in the silence that the Pilgrim finds in Saturn, but also in his own silence ("il tacer mio") when Damian appears (*Par.* 21.47, 49).

Benedict's *Rule* also made elaborate provision for the liturgical life of the monastic community (*RB* 8–20). It specified, for instance, the hours at which the divine office was to be celebrated, the number of psalms to be said at each, and the seasons in which an Alleluia is to be said with them. In making these provisions, Benedict was typically the Saturnian who, Ibn Ezra noted, is "wise in the worship of God."[70] Dante's Benedict in fact singles out fasting and prayer ("orazione") as the original features of his order (*Par.* 22.89). Similarly, Fonte Avellana "was once given wholly to worship (*latria*)," the outraged souls cry out for vengeance in their "prayers (*prieghi*)," and the Pilgrim frames his request to Benedict as a prayer (21.111; 22.13, 58). Finally, Dante even speaks of the pagans' "impious cult" (22.45), perhaps because he had read that Saturnians were also given to impiety.[71]

Chastity is a Saturnian virtue that Scot attributes to the planet's frigidity, although the more common opinion traced it back to the castration of Kronos.[72] Benedict apparently assumed that monks were by definition chaste; his *Rule* says nothing more than that the monk is "to love chastity (*castitatem amare*)" (*RB* 4.64). Dante imitates Benedict rather than the astrologers in this regard and omits sex altogether from the Saturnine cantos, in which the only seduction mentioned is spiritual (*Par.* 22.45).[73]

Work and poverty. Bonatti remarked that the life of many Saturnians is one of work and poverty,[74] but Dante stressed only the latter, even though most of his astrologers associated Saturn with labor[75] and Benedict's *Rule* prescribed daily manual labor for the monks (*RB* 48).[76] On the other hand, the Benedictine *Rule* did not embrace poverty as a good in itself. Private ownership of property was forbidden to individual monks (*RB* 33) and was instead vested in the community as a whole and administered by the abbot, who provided for each monk according to his needs (*RB* 34). When the *Rule* mentions *pauperes*, they are destitute persons outside the monastic community;[77] it is possible that the monastery itself can be poor (*RB* 48.7), but this condition is not represented as either normal or desirable. Instead, Benedictine monks are required to help the poor: "Great care and concern are to be shown in receiving poor people and pilgrims, because in them more particularly Christ is received."[78] Accordingly, Dante's Benedict deplores monks who misuse their income, "for whatsoever the Church has in keeping is all for the folk that ask it in God's name" (*Par.* 22.82–83). But in Fonte Avellana, Dante has given us an example of a community in which monks do adopt the lifestyle of the poor, for there Peter Damian lived on a meager diet with little protection from the elements (21.115–116). This is the Saturnian poverty of the astrologers.[79] Dante works poverty into these cantos in yet a third way, by referring to Saint Francis as the one who began his order "with humility (*umilmente*)" (90), which the reader, from what he already has been told of Francis (11.74), can gloss as poverty. This intertextual reference to Francis does in fact comment on the limited poverty of Benedict and Damian, for Bonaventure, speaking with the guaranteed veracity of the blessed, had said that no one between Christ and Francis had embraced Poverty (11.64–66). Hence Dante evidently held that poverty per se was not a monastic ideal until Francis made it so. Neither Benedict nor Damian considered poverty to be good in itself; the one helped the poor for Christ's sake and the other mortified his flesh with some of the hardships that accompany poverty.[80]

Food. Peter Damian's subsistence diet followed the example of Benedict, whose order was founded on the principle of "fasting (*digiuno*)" (*Par.* 22.89). In this both saints were Saturnian because that planet brought famine and caused its native to be "a man of little food and less drink."[81] So were the Apostles Peter and Paul, who like Saturn himself were "lean (*magra*)" (*Par.* 21.128).[82] Food is important to Saturn's children, perhaps because he has lordship over the stomach[83] and "produces men who consume much at a meal."[84] Though Dante's Saturnians are ascetics, they are nonetheless prone to use food-related language in their figures of speech: both good works and ecclesiastical revenues are "fruits (*frutti*)" (22.48, 80); spiritual vision is "milked (*munta*)" from God (21.87); and Damian says "I embelly myself" in light—"io m'inventro" (21.84).

Dante also alludes in these cantos to several foods that belong to Saturn. The "acorn (*ghianda*)" (*Par.* 22.87) he himself had already associated with Saturn, whose Golden Age "made acorns savory with hunger" (*Purg.* 22.149). Ibn Ezra confirms that this association is astrological as well as literary, for he assigns to Saturn "every tree of nuts (*glandium*)."[85] Hence Fonte Avellana is also appropriate to Saturn, because in Latin and Italian, *avellana* means "hazel nut." Finally, Dante alludes to "bad flour (*farina ria*)" (22.78), which reflects Saturn's reputation as the planet that ruins foodstuffs by coagulating oil, thickening honey, generating worms in vegetables, and producing putrefaction in general.[86]

Contemplation and cogitation. Since Dante took such care to paint his picture of monasticism with Saturnian pigments, we cannot be surprised to find that contemplation, which was for him that institution's central feature, should be painted with the same brush. Benedict defined his colleagues as "all contemplatives (*tutti contemplanti*)," and Peter Damian was one too, for his contentment at Fonte Avellana consisted in "contemplative thoughts" (*Par.* 22.46, 21.117). In the heaven of the contemplatives, the Pilgrim shows himself to be under the spell of the place when, as he contemplates Beatrice's face, he withdraws his mind from all else (21.1–3). The connection between Saturn and contemplation was made most clearly by Ibn Ezra, who declared that Saturn's "part of human nature or custom is meditation—*meditatio*."[87] This propensity arises from Saturn's identification with man's power of thought ("cogitationis vis"), an equivalence which originated with the Neoplatonists, notably Macrobius, and was a commonplace with subsequent astrologers.[88] Dante may have commemorated Saturn's general lordship over the human intellect with incidental allusions to thought and reason (21.57; 22.33, 36), but he is more specifically Saturnian in his weighing of one thought against another ("contrapesando," 21.24), which amounts to the quality of "deliberation (*deliberatio*)" that Albumasar ascribed to the planet.[89] The malefic capacity of Saturn could also cause human thought to malfunction,[90] of which Dante gives several instances: the Pilgrim hears the saints cry out but does not understand what they say ("né io lo 'ntesi," 21.142); the human mind, which is clouded on earth, has its limitations even in heaven (21.97–102).

Occasionally astrology provides the *raison d'être* for otherwise puzzling passages in the poem. One such is the Pilgrim's insistent desire to know why "the counsel (*consiglio*) that governs the world" singled out one particular soul, whose identity is as yet undisclosed, to greet him; to which the reply is that only God knows (*Par.* 21.71, 73–102). Why should this point be made in the heaven of Saturn? Simply because the planet, which mirrors God, signified "profundity of counsel."[91]

Biographical subtexts. As Dante's prime examples of the ascetic life, Benedict and Peter Damian have been our constant companions in the foregoing discussion of monasticism. Before passing on to consider corrupt servants of God, let us pause briefly to observe that the lives of both these saints provided Dante with subtexts that contain astrological references. I do not want to insist overly on these correspondences between astrology and extratextual evidence, but some are sufficiently striking to deserve mention in passing.

In Christian iconography, Saint Benedict is commonly accompanied by the raven that his biographer, Gregory the Great, says "regularly came from a nearby wood at the saint's mealtime and received bread from his hand."[92] Black birds are astrologically proper to Saturn, and Dante in fact

alludes to them in these cantos (see below, n. 157). Another incident re-
counted by Gregory also has Saturnian affinities. After living by himself
for some years, Benedict was persuaded to assume the headship of an ex-
isting monastic community at Vicovaro, but "the brothers under his guidance raged like madmen" because he enforced their rule strictly. To get rid
of their unwanted abbot, the monks plotted to kill Benedict and accordingly "mixed poison in his wine," but the fatal glass cup was shattered
when the saint blessed it.[93] This incident can certainly be considered a
family quarrel, between the father/abbot and the brothers/monks, and
hence it is proper to Saturn, which signifies "discord between family members."[94] Furthermore, the assassins' *modus operandi* was Saturnian, since
that planet indicates poison.[95]

The *Life* of Peter Damian, by his disciple John of Lodi, presents even
more Saturnian parallels.[96] First of all, Peter was raised in poverty,[97] which
we have already seen is an effect of Saturn (above, n. 79). When young,
the saint was forced to work as a swineherd,[98] and pigs also belong to
Saturn.[99] He was, however, a clever boy,[100] which is an endowment from
Saturn.[101] Damian, his elder brother, therefore, sent him off to school to
get a liberal education, and in gratitude Peter assumed the surname "*Damiani* (Damian's)."[102] And Saturn, as already mentioned, does signify "elder brothers" (above, n. 57). Finally, Saturn even favored Peter's celebrated
career as a papal legate, because Haly says that the native likes "to build,
to sow, to plant," which echoes the verse of Jeremiah (1:10) that was incorporated into the papal formula for appointing a legate.[103]

Damian's double. Subtextual allusions by their nature must necessarily
be nothing more than suggestive, but astrology can offer more positive
assistance in the controversy over the significance of the obscure assertion:

> In quel loco fu' io Pietro Damiano,
>   e Pietro Peccator fu [?fu'] ne la casa
> di Nostra Donna in sul lito adriano.   (*Par.* 21.121–123)

In that place was I Peter Damian, and Peter the Sinner was [?I] in
the house of Our Lady on the Adriatic shore.[104]

Commentators for centuries have disputed whether Dante meant to
equate the two Peters or to distinguish between them. The latter view was
held by Jacopo di Dante, Lana, and the Ottimo, and still has its adher-

ents.[105] If this position is correct, however, it would seem that the poet had inserted this tercet simply to dispel some confusion current among his contemporaries. Since Dante generally avoided irrelevant pedantry, at least in his poetry, this simple and obvious explanation has seemed doubtful to many. But astrology can remove this doubt, inasmuch as Michael Scot declared that Saturn "also signifies . . . false rumors."[106] Hence it would be entirely appropriate for the poet to deal with such a rumor in this heaven. Peter Damian, then, is dispelling a false rumor, to the effect that he was the Peter the Sinner who was associated with "the house of Our Lady" on the shore of the Adriatic.

Corrupt Servants of God

In astrology, Saturn was the greater malefic, "whose property it is to signify everything evil to friends and enemies."[107] Evil, however, is a broad and flexible concept. For example, occupations that were not honorable, such as working in the Moslem equivalent of a massage parlor, or that were simply dirty work, such as fulling cloth, were considered evil because they were "vile," or as we would say, demeaning.[108] Sometimes the astrologers regarded evil privatively, as the absence of good or utility,[109] but more often they represented it as positively "harmful."[110] Most commonly, astrologers simply ascribed to Saturn every bad quality that occurred to them. Albumasar, for instance, characterized Saturn's child by "malice of every kind, iniquity, and violence," not to mention "envy and hatred of everything good."[111]

Dante's use of Saturn is accordingly often paradoxical. In the preceding section, we have seen how his Christian viewpoint frequently found spiritual virtue in what the worldly astrologers thought to be disadvantages. Thus for old age Dante stresses not so much the decline of the body as the soul's approach to God;[112] patriarchs, founding fathers, and elders in general deserve respect rather than the reverse. If Saturn's children are prone to lead lives of destitution, starvation, and impotence, they have a special aptitude for monastic poverty, fasting, and chastity. Their dishonorable condition of menial servitude is glorified when it becomes the service of God. Michael Scot glimpsed the possibilities for converting Saturnian vices into virtues when he wrote that "the Saturnine man . . . is the worst kind of all, unless he is inspired by God."[113] Perhaps this remark even suggested to Dante how he might bring the greater malefic into line with his theocentric world view; at any rate, it encapsulates his essential strategy.

Although in the heaven of Saturn Dante stressed the planet's power to effect good, he nonetheless did not deny its evil influence. A few scattered references in these cantos acknowledge Saturnine forms of evil in a generalized way: the pagans of Monte Cassino were "*mal disposta* (perverse)";[114] ecclesiastical revenues should not be diverted to nepotism or to some other use that is "*più brutto* (filthier)";[115] the cardinals go "from bad to worse—*di male in peggio*" (*Par.* 22.39, 84; 21.126). But for the most part Dante presents Saturnian evil more specifically as the perversion of the same impulses that produce Saturnian saints. In this section we will see how Saturn can corrupt as well as create servants of God.

Monks. Benedict's complaint about the neglect of his *Rule*, which is the dominating feature of *Paradiso* 22, is astrologically appropriate for several interrelated reasons. Saturn governs "inheritances and old, durable things,"[116] and by 1300, the ideal date of the poem, the *Rule*, which was Benedict's legacy, had endured for more than eight centuries.[117] Moreover, Saturn often signifies change,[118] especially for the worse, such as by loss, destruction, dissipation,[119] or—most significantly—the deformation of old things.[120] Thus the slackening of devotion at Fonte Avellana (21.111), no less than the neglectful Benedictines, betrays the baleful influence of Saturn. Dante emphasizes the element of change at Fonte Avellana by comparing it to a once fertile field that now has become barren (21.118–119), which alludes to the sterility Saturn brings.[121]

Dante's complaints against corrupt monks can be reduced to a single cause, namely their failure to keep their monastic vows. This offense is no less Saturnian than the monastic impulse itself, for that planet's natives are given to "holding back a promise"; they are facile liars who excel at fraud, deception, perfidy, and treason.[122] With good will, which for Dante is love of the good, their Saturnian nature would have made them good monks, but when the will is inclined to evil, Saturn conditions their defects, making them into false monks who do not observe the rule to which they are pledged.

Dante is specific about the way in which Saturn afflicts monks: their income "makes the heart of monks so mad (*folle*)" (*Par.* 22.81), and both folly and insanity belong to Saturn.[123] Saturn also defines the object of their desire, which is wealth, especially that which is derived from legacies.[124] Saturn's children, however, are prone to the sin of avarice in many forms: they are misers and mercenaries;[125] they are retentive in general and apt to possess much;[126] they are forgetful of benefits received[127] and, when something has been given to them as security for a loan, they do not want to return it.[128] Dante alludes to the last two traits when usury is said to compare favorably to the malversation of monastic revenues (22.79–84), for it is surely ingratitude to ignore a donor's intention.

Cardinals. Although corrupt monks are the primary target for Dante's satire in these Saturnian cantos, the cardinals of the Roman curia are brought in for their share of abuse by Peter Damian (*Par.* 21.130–135). Damian's own reluctant career as a cardinal provides the pretext for including the cardinals at this point, and the topic is also artistically justified because it foreshadows Peter's denunciation of his recent successors in the next heaven (*Purg.* 26.19–66). But it was probably from astrology that Dante first got the idea of connecting cardinals with Saturn, because that planet signified "those who supervise work," i.e., *praelati* or prelates, especially those appointed by rulers.[129] Furthermore, Saturn accounts for the chief faults of one to whom high authority is delegated. Michael Scot wrote that, when a Saturnian receives

> prelacy and lordship over others, he is not properly grateful, and accordingly he conducts himself badly towards them and tends to interfere in any thing that requires discretion on the part of his subordinates. Thus the good that was done to him [by raising him to high office] is lost and, once it is conferred, that good is almost smothered by ingratitude. Hence it must be said that the Saturnine man, i.e., one born under Saturn, is the worst of all unless he be inspired by God.[130]

Dante comments on the "modern pastors" by comparing their corrupt lifestyle with that of their prototypes, the Apostles Peter and Paul. The first pastors were humble in their dress to the point of going barefoot, took their food wherever they could find it, and so were lean; by contrast, their well-fed and well-dressed modern counterparts travel in style on horseback with attendants on every side. The sins of pride and gluttony are clearly implied by this contrast,[131] but also ingratitude, inasmuch as the cardinals, like the corrupt monks, are abusing their legacy.

Damian's companions respond to his denunciation with a great cry for vengeance (*Par.* 21.136–142, 22.12–15), which is in character, for Saturn denotes "*conclamatio*—crying together."[132] They are prompted by Damian's exclamation, "O patience, that do endure so much" (21.135), which betrays the impatience that typifies a Saturnian: "He has little tolerance," Haly remarked, "because he cannot bear evil."[133] Nonetheless, he is also capable of harboring wrath for a long time, as Dante's Saturnians have to do.[134] The poet prudently avoids almost any express value judgments on the behavior of these modern cardinals, although astrology suggests not a few, for Saturn signifies conduct that is infamous, detestable, degrading, and disgraceful.[135]

Leather. Dante has only one bad name for contemporary cardinals: "beasts (*bestie*)." "They cover their palfreys with their mantles, so that two beasts go under one hide (*pelle*)" (*Par.* 21.133–134).[136] Although the astrologers consulted by Dante do not associate horses with Saturn, several of them do link that planet with hides of beasts, for it is the "star of leatherworkers," including those whose work is "stitching the hides of wild beasts together to make garments."[137] Thus it was appropriate that Damian should compare the cardinals' rich trappings to hides, which a Saturnian would naturally think of, just as Venusians are apt to speak in terms of luxury goods.

The Saturnine Mind

For the psychiatric researcher, Saturn would be the most rewarding planet, for its natives more than any others display the better known symptoms of neurosis. In addition to melancholy, they are also afflicted with fear and anxiety, doubt and hesitation, arrogant presumption, and an affinity for the occult, to mention only the astrological properties that Dante echoed in the *Paradiso*. These psychological traits are more frequently exemplified in the Pilgrim than in his interlocutors.

Fear and anxiety. For example, the Pilgrim resembles one who "fears to exceed" (*Par.* 22.27) and the guilty await God's vengeance "in fear (*temendo*)" (22.18). In addition to these overt references to fear, it is implied elsewhere. On hearing the outcry for vengeance, the Pilgrim turns to Beatrice as a child "runs back to where it has most confidence" (22.3); presently he announces that Benedict's evident good will towards him "has expanded my confidence as the sun does the rose when it opens to its fullest bloom" (22.55–56). When his confidence is shaken, he wants reassurance (22.6), and even when he is self-confident he desires greater assurance (22.58). Not only does the Pilgrim hesitate to speak on two occasions, but on the former, he even takes his cue from Beatrice, who "pauses (*si sta*)" (21.47; 22.25–27). Finally, the narrator remarks how the Pilgrim is divided between the pleasure of contemplating Beatrice and that of obeying her, and there is a note of anxiety in his description of the second alternative as "another care—*altra cura*" (21.21). All of these psychological states are properly Saturnian. From Ptolemy on, astrologers declared that the planet "will generate fears,"[138] from which flow anxiety, doubt, and consequently hesitation, especially in speaking.[139]

Boldness and indiscretion. With nice psychological perception, Dante has his Pilgrim swing from one emotional extreme to another, so that twice he is presumptuous and overbold. The first time, he presses Peter Damian to explain why Providence had predestined the saint to meet him (*Par.* 21.73–78) and has to be told that such questions are presumptuous, even in heaven (21.97–102). Later, brimming with self-confidence, he requests the favor of seeing Saint Benedict in the flesh (22.52–60) and is told that that is only possible in the Empyrean, where this "high desire" will be fulfilled (22.61–63). Such behavior also belongs to Saturn, which signifies "audacity" and makes its natives "indiscreet."[140]

Stupor and secrets. Since Saturn signifies any "affliction of the mind," its province includes not only anxieties and indiscretions, but also states in which the mind is confused and disabled. Scot ascribed to Saturn "confusion of sense" in any animal, and particularly "obscurity of intellect" in man; Ptolemy had summed it up in one word—*stupores*.[141] This is precisely the condition of the Pilgrim when he is overwhelmed by the indignant outcry of the Saturnian saints: he is "oppressed with *stupore*" (*Par.* 22.1).[142] Indeed, the human mind on earth is at best "smoky (*fumma*)" (21.100).[143]

But according to Albumasar, Saturn gives the mind "a high understanding of secrets" and "unlimited esoteric wisdom (*occulta sapientia*) concerning the innermost secrets," both of which he loosely linked with both magic and laconic speech.[144] Dante ignores the magical element and instead stresses Saturn's affinity for things that are hidden or concealed. Damian's soul is "hidden (*nascosta*)" from the Pilgrim, who later is curious to see Benedict's "uncovered (*scoverta*)" (21.55, 22.60). Both, of course, are secrets at this point, though they will be revealed in the highest heaven. Another secret soon to be revealed is Fonte Avellana's decline (21.120), but some never will be, for the Pilgrim also learns that not even the highest creature can discover God's secret reasons for predestination (21.83–102). Thus Dante retains Saturn's significance for secret things, but for him it is not the magus but God who understands the ultimate secrets. Jacob's ladder, "rising up so high that my sight might not follow it" (21.29–30) makes the same point symbolically.

Jacob's Ladder

The heaven of Saturn has as its distinctive symbol a golden ladder that stretches from earth to the highest heaven. Astrology contributed little or nothing to the making of this symbol,[145] which is primarily biblical, as the poem explicitly states (*Par.* 22.70–71), although a classical parallel has been detected on the border of Philosophy's mantle, where it symbolizes the ascent from practical to speculative philosophy.[146] Astrology does, however, contribute a few suggestive details to the poet's descriptions of this ladder. For instance, because the ladder reaches to the highest heaven, which exists outside of space, the Pilgrim cannot see its upper end. The poet expresses this conclusion with an odd turn of speech—"it steals itself (*s'invola*) from your sight" (22.69)—which enables him to introduce from astrology the theme of theft, for Saturnians are natural-born thieves.[147] In one detail, however, the ladder is the antithesis of Saturn; it is "uno scaleo *eretto*" (21.29), whereas the *homo Saturninus* is just the reverse of erect: "when he walks he usually looks at the ground"; he is "stooped over (*recurvus*)."[148] Perhaps, as Singleton suggested, the ladder is golden (21.28) because this color is appropriate to the god Saturn, who reigned during the Golden Age.[149]

Exiles from eternity. Jacob's ladder differs from the symbols displayed in the lower heavens. The circles in the Sun, the cross in Mars, and the eagle in Jupiter all were composed of the blessed spirits themselves, whereas in Saturn they are seen passing up and down the ladder (*Par.* 21.29–33), so it would seem to possess a reality of its own distinct from that of those who use it. What that might be is suggested by a discrepancy between the biblical and Saturnine ladders. In Jacob's dream the ladder was filled with angels rather than human souls: "angelos quoque Dei ascendentes et descendentes per eam" (Gen. 28.12b). Dante does not discard Jacob's angels altogether; instead, they are deferred until the end, when they are seen "descending" and "reascending" (31.10–11) in the great ray of light that emanates downwards from God to the Primum Mobile (30.106–108). Since the reader has been assured that Jacob's ladder extends up out of sight into the Empyrean, it is reasonable to infer that when we encounter Jacob's angels there, we are also seeing the upper end of their ladder, namely the *raggio* or ray. Indeed, the color of the ladder in its lower reaches is that of "gold on which a ray (*raggio*) shines" (21.28), so the poet gave us a hint of the ladder's nature when he first introduced it. Saturn is a mirror that reflects heaven, and just so, the ladder with its saints is the counterpart of the ray with its angels.

What the Pilgrim sees at first is a throng of "many splendors descending along the steps" (*Par.* 21.31–32); presently some will return upwards, some will proceed downward, and some will stay in the Pilgrim's vicinity on Saturn. But at first, they all descend. Since they are all blessed souls, it would seem that what the Pilgrim sees here is the return of souls to their stars, which Beatrice had explained to him early in their ascent (4.22–63, esp. 37–39). Astrologically it is fitting that this process be recapitulated in Saturn because that planet signifies "the separation of journeys" from home, especially difficult or perilous ones,[150] and particularly "exile."[151] The literal journeys that the astrologers had in mind are transposed by Dante into the medieval commonplace that we are wayfaring pilgrims on earth and heaven is our home. The homeless wandering of Peter and Paul was of this type (21). But, believing as he did that man can be happy on earth as well (*Mon.* 3.15.6), Dante provides the example of Peter Damian, who was forced to descend from his hermitage on Mount Catria and go into spiritual exile at the papal curia (21.124–126). References to the return of the Jews from their exile in Egypt are similarly appropriate (22.94–96) and are made specific to exile by echoing Psalm 113 (see above, after n. 44).

The astrologers stress that Saturnian journeys are difficult (see n. 150), as indeed they would be for anyone under that planet's influence, for when the native walks, "he proceeds ponderously, shuffling along with his eyes glued to the ground."[152] Dante accordingly associates footwork with difficult or perilous journeys. For Benedict, good monks "stayed their feet (*li piedi*) within the cloisters" (*Par.* 22.50–51) and thus avoided the spiritual dangers attendant on a journey through the secular world.[153] Metaphorically, the attempt to understand God's reasons for predestination is a difficult journey, and indeed an impossible one, as Damian would have the Pilgrim make clear to "the mortal world . . . so that it may no longer presume to move its feet (*li piedi*) toward so great a goal" (21.97–99). Finally, the monastic life is a journey towards God. The historical Benedict represented this journey as the ascent of Jacob's ladder, the steps of which are the twelve grades of humility (*Regula Benedicti* 7). Dante's Benedict complains that "no one now lifts his feet (*i piedi*) from earth to ascend it" (22.73–74).

Black and bright. Saturn's appropriate color is black in a variety of shades, which range from plain black through "dark" and "dusty" to simply "obscure."[154] Dante incorporates this character in a number of images, but with an implied contrast to light. Thus Beatrice's smile on Saturn would devastate the Pilgrim just as Semele was turned to "ashes (*cener*)" by seeing Jupiter in all his glory (*Par.* 21.6). Again, the mind of mortal men is "smoky (*fumma*)" (21.100), whereas the saints see with greater, though not perfect, clarity. The contrast is drawn most sharply by Benedict, whose image of monastic corruption is "white made dark (*bruno*)" (22.93). References to things dark in these cantos are, moreover, amply counterbalanced by the brightness of the ladder and the lights that pass along it, not to mention explicit allusions to clarity (21.44, 89–91).

Just so the black daws contrast with the bright souls on the ladder of whom they are an image (*Par.* 21.35–42).[155] But the daws are appropriately Saturnian in other ways as well. If, as is commonly understood, the movements of the souls on the ladder represent three types of the contemplative or monastic life, then the black birds can be compared to monks, whose habits often were of dark colors (black for the Benedictines, but white for the hermits of Fonte Avellana). Benvenuto extends the comparison, pointing out that daws, like contemplatives, prefer solitary places and are plain and simple, all of which would also be Saturnian enough.[156] But perhaps the primary justification for the simile is simply that, as Ibn Ezra declares, "every bird of black color" belongs to Saturn.[157] Here, as elsewhere in the *Comedy*, birds are symbolic, for they fly "with the swift wings and the plumes of great desire" (*Purg.* 4.28–29). And it is with just such wings that the Pilgrim himself mounts the ladder at the end of the episode ("ala," *Par.* 22.105).

Conclusion

I have scouted out Dante's planetary heavens for traces of astrology and now must return my report. The primary purpose of the expedition, as set forth in the Introduction, was to determine whether, and to what extent, Dante made use of the properties of planets in the first twenty-two cantos of the *Paradiso*. This is the sort of matter-of-fact problem on which philological positivism thrives; it is susceptible of a definite answer. But beyond the main problem lies another, broader question to which no definitive answer can be given: What does it all mean? This explorer's report will address both questions, first by assessing the positive results of this investigation and then by considering their significance.

I

Dante's use of astrology is evidenced most strikingly in the major features of these cantos. For example, it provides the most specific rationale for his choice of inconstant nuns as the Moon's appropriate "sign (*segno*)" (*Par.* 4.37–39). Similarly, Romeo exemplifies a complex of Mercurial properties in being an effective administrator and clever counsellor who preferred poverty to dishonor. Likewise, Carlo Martello, as a princely connoisseur of rhetorical elegance with a penchant for a luxurious lifestyle, embodies a cluster of Venusian traits that are indicated by astrology but would not have been suggested by mythology. In short, astrology is most abundantly reflected in Dante's characters, which is scarcely surprising, since his explicit statements about astrology, which we reviewed in the Introduction, chiefly concern the influence of the stars on human character.

Often astrology provides the link between a discourse and the heaven in which it is delivered. Thus a Solarian affinity for fattening foods prompted Dante's Aquinas to describe undeviating Dominicans as "fattening themselves well" (*Par.* 10.96), which in turn led him, and then Bonaventure, to describe the Mendicant mission in *Paradiso* 11 and 12. Similarly, the Martian propensity for prophecy justifies the revelations in *Paradiso* 17 about Dante's future, the Jovian attributes of *religio* and *misericoria* are exemplified in the Eagle's eye, and Bonatti suggested Carlo Martello's corollary.

The influence of astrology is by no means limited to such major features, however; indeed, it permeates the planetary cantos in literally hundreds of details. Each heaven exerts its influence not only on the blessed souls who appear there but also on Beatrice and the Pilgrim, not to mention the narrator himself, so that all the voices heard in a given heaven are filled with astral allusions appropriate to that planet. To recall only one such cluster, everyone in the heaven of Venus refers to luxury goods: mirrors, jewels, crowns, garlands, and textiles. These passing references to planetary properties enable the poet to saturate his text with astrological echoes. One such allusion might be dismissed as nothing more than a coincidence, but these hundreds of parallels indicate the systematic exploitation of astrological sources. Taken together with the more striking cases mentioned above, they place Dante's use of astrology in these cantos beyond doubt.

Thus we have attained the principal goal of this study. Now it is clear that Dante's respect for astrology was in fact matched by his use of it in the *Paradiso*. To put it bluntly, Dante's debt to the astrologers deserves to be acknowledged in the *apparatus fontium* to the poem. Such bluntness is necessary nowadays. A century ago, when the search for Dante's sources was at its height, such a discovery would have been recognized as a positive contribution to knowledge and warmly welcomed; today, when few new facts about the *Commedia* are forthcoming, most Dante studies tend to be appreciated as more or less ingenious interpretations rather than judged for their objective truth. Although the present study has its share of subjective, interpretive insights, still I must insist, at the risk of seeming old fashioned, that at its core lies a new body of solid fact.

At the beginning of this study, I identified nine astrologers whom Dante was likely to have consulted. Now we are in a position to see the extent to which he made use of them. I have counted the number of times each one was used to establish a point; if several passages from the same astrologer were cited to establish the same point, they were lumped together into a single "item." In other words, each item is the first citation

Relative Use of Nine Astrologers in *Paradiso* 1–22
(in descending order of frequency)

Text	Items	Percent
Michael Scot	374	26
Guido Bonatti	210	15
Alcabitius	187	13
Ibn Ezra	183	13
Albumasar	179	13
Haly	118	8
John of Seville	79	6
Ptolemy, *Quadpartitum*	62	4
Liber novem iudicium	39	2
Total	1431	100

of that text in a note. The accompanying table presents the results. As we suspected from the start, Dante made most frequent use of Scot and Bonatti, the two astrologers whom he identified as such in the *Comedy* (*Inf.* 20.115–118). Their preponderance is perhaps to be expected because both these texts are far longer than the others and hence provided more details. Scot, whose list of properties is the longer of the two, was particularly repetitious, so that in a given note he is often cited two or three times to the same effect. Beyond doubt Michael Scot was Dante's favorite astrologer.

The runners up form a tight cluster of texts that each supplied 13–15 percent of the items; combined they account for 54 percent of the total. Of the four, it should be remembered that Bonatti incorporated most of Alcabitius's text into his own, so it is not certain that Dante knew Alcabitius directly. The last four, low-scoring texts, which collectively amount to only 20 percent of the total, are all relatively short and consequently tend to be more general than the others; hence Dante found less in them that he could use. With the exception of the *Liber novem iudicum*, he seems to have consulted all these shorter sources and drawn on them occasionally. Almost certainly he would have used Ptolemy, both because he was a standard author in the university curriculum and because he is the only astrologer other than Scot and Bonatti to be named in the *Comedy* (*Inf.* 4.142). Ptolemy is cited seldom simply because his lists of properties are the briefest. In sum, Dante took more from the longer lists because they had more to offer. With the exception of the *Liber novem iudicum*, he seems to have consulted all these sources and taken as much as they had to offer.

II

But what does it all mean? The bare facts are not enough for most of us; we want significant facts, facts that have been interpreted. This leads us onto shaky ground, for it is far easier to establish a fact than to understand its significance. Nonetheless, I will endeavor to give some reasons why this discovery seems important for our appreciation of the *Divine Comedy*, but in doing so I am aware that what I say must necessarily be tentative, suggestive, and incomplete. Especially incomplete, because this is the first attempt to assess a newly discovered body of facts, which doubtless will be appreciated more fully from perspectives other than my own.

Let us begin with the question that the modern reader is most likely to ask when confronted with the fact that Dante made extensive use of astrology: but why did Dante do it? The question generally proceeds from a sense of dismay that Dante was apparently steeped in superstition. The answer, of course, is that Dante was a man of his own time, when intellectuals accepted astral influence as a scientific fact. We moderns may prefer to admire those facets of his poem that we still consider respectable, such as philosophy, theology, and rhetoric, but if we are ever to appreciate the poem in its entirety—as the poet conceived it—we must view it from his perspective, not ours.

Once we are prepared to bridge the gap between modern and medieval culture, there is no difficulty in ascertaining Dante's reasons for using astrological materials. He expressed them himself, explicitly, unambiguously, and often, as we have seen in the Introduction. He was convinced that "it is without doubt within the capacity of human understanding to comprehend the mover of the heaven and his will by means of the motion of the heavens" (*Ep.* 5.8.23). In other words, unaided human reason could discover God's will through astrology. Given this conviction, it would be strange if Dante did not exemplify it in his *Commedia*, especially since the relation of reason to revelation is a major theme of the poem. He wanted to show, by concrete examples, how the several planets influenced human character in accordance with God's will. *Paradiso* offered the best opportunity for this exemplification, not only because there the effects of each planet could be observed at the point of origin, but also because in Paradise everyone speaks the truth, so the message would be unambiguous.

How, then, did Dante use astrology? This is a deeper, more complex question with countless ramifications. Let us begin with the problem of practicability, for once it appears that Dante commanded a wide range of astrological learning, one may well wonder how he attained it. The question can, of course, be shrugged off with the observation that Dante evidently acquired a considerable knowledge in many fields, so it is not difficult to accept his command of yet another medieval discipline. But the sheer quantity of the correspondences we have amassed, not to mention the subtle quality of many of them, perhaps suggests a breadth and depth of familiarity that may seem implausible. The mastery implied by our discoveries is not, however, particularly difficult to attain. The astrological texts that list the properties of planets rarely run to over a page per planet, so for Dante's purposes it would hardly take more than a day to read all the sources for one planet. Committing these lists to memory or to writing would certainly require more time, but not an inordinate amount. Indeed, I would estimate that all the properties Dante needed for one planet could have been recorded on a single folio page, so that a quire of four leaves would have sufficed for his entire astrological apparatus. I am not sure, however, that he would have needed to keep a written record, because memorization was not only a commonplace skill practised by medieval litterati[1] but also one for which Dante himself was remarkable. One anecdote in Boccaccio's *Life of Dante* recalls how Dante consulted an unfamiliar book at an apothecary's shop in Siena. It took him over three hours to get what he wanted from the book, and all the time he was lying face down on a bench, a circumstance which surely indicates that he was relying on his memory rather than on written notes. Even though the tale may be legendary, Boccaccio clearly believed that it illustrated an outstanding trait of his subject, for immediately after relating this story, he goes on to praise the poet's exceptionally tenacious memory ("memoria tenenissima").[2] He may well have memorized the planetary properties that interested him, then, but however he collected these materials, my point is that the task could not have been particularly difficult.

PROPERTIES INTO POETRY
The challenge, of course, was to turn a list of properties into poetry. Ideally, the effects of the planets should be blended into the poem as they

were into life, unobtrusively, but in such a way that they would still be accessible to human reason. Evidently Dante was equal to the challenge, for the presence of these properties in the poem has been overlooked for centuries. Now that they have been detected, however, they afford the critic a unique opportunity to observe the poet at work, because the parameters of the problem he set for himself are, in this case, clearly defined. He wished to exemplify the effects of each planet in its proper heaven; for this purpose he had collected lists of planetary properties from the astrologers. The artistic problem was how to incorporate this raw material into his story. Because for once we know precisely what he wanted to do and just what he had to work with, we are in a position to appreciate the poet's ingenuity from a new perspective.

No doubt he was guided by the principles of rhetoric, and it would be instructive to determine how figures of speech, such as metaphor, metonomy, or periphrasis, were used to bring properties into the poem. But this would be a study in itself; here I only want to draw together a few observations that have been made in passing during the foregoing study in order to show the different *ways* in which Dante made use of planetary properties.

Although many properties were introduced as a sort of ornamental appliqué, others are more fundamental and thus deserve to be stressed at the outset of our classification. Most notably, astrology evidently governed the choice of characters that were to appear in each heaven. Thus nuns who left the convent are appropriate to the Moon; clever stewards proud of their *virtù* fit Mercury; a courtly patron, poet, and lover belong to Venus; exemplars of wisdom and knowledge are proper to the Sun; an indignant and truly noble knight suits Mars; a composite person made up of gregarious souls who were just and pious embodies Jovian properties; and in a variety of ways Peter Damian exemplifies Saturn's influence, but especially in his preference for a life of solitude and meditation. The poet must have selected his representative characters while the cantos in which they appear were in the planning stage, and the fact that all the major characters are astrologically appropriate indicates beyond doubt that astrology was a guiding, organizing principle, though not necessarily the only one. Indeed, one advantage of having the Pilgrim pass through the several planetary heavens, rather than rise directly to the Empyrean "heaven of the theologians," was the opportunity it afforded the poet to exemplify the properties of the planets.

Dante also have must taken astrology into account while he was inventing discourses that would be appropriate to each planet. Thus the lordship of Venus over seed and the generative process suggested the problem of how good seed can produce bad offspring, and Bonatti's exhortation that each person should develop the talents conferred by the stars similarly suggested Carlo Martello's corollary. Again, Aquinas's discourses are both prompted by astrological properties of the Sun—the first by fat and the second by prudence. And finally, because Saturn signifies "profundity of counsel," Dante has the Pilgrim attempt to discover God's unfathomable reason for sending Peter Damian to meet him.

In addition to the basic traits that qualified a character to exemplify his heaven, Dante added many others. Characterization was certainly the most natural way to use astrological properties, and the one to which Dante was most inclined, because both he and the astrologers were primarily interested in the influences the planets exerted on human character. Dante endowed his characters with a variety of appropriate traits, which usually are presented through characteristic speeches. The luxury goods proper to Venus, for instance, come readily to the lips of all four natives, who speak of mirrors, jewels, crowns, garlands, and textiles. Similarly, references to desire keep cropping up in their speeches. Again, Justinian shows himself to be a clever, vain Mercurian by flaunting his familiarity with the seven liberal arts. Or again, the Jovian tendencies to speak gravely and at length are both exemplified in the long, dignified speeches Dante gave to the Eagle, while Saturn's lordship over the stomach prompts Peter Damian to devise a strange metaphor: "I embelly myself in light" (*Par.* 21.84).

Elsewhere in the *Comedy* actions often speak louder than words, but they rarely have a chance to express character in Paradise, where the encounters are static and the transitions instantaneous. Nonetheless Dante contrived a few occasions for significant motion, as when Cacciaguida speeds along the bands of the cross, exemplifying Martian swiftness and mobility. Even more dramatically, the Jovians act out their propensity for scribal activity by forming the letters of the planet's motto.

The influence of each planet is also exemplified by the Pilgrim. For example, on Venus, the planet of good will, he is well disposed to an unknown soul (*Par.* 8.44–45), while on Mars he manifests the influence of the planet in his audacity and elation (16.17–18). Beatrice, too, exhibits the influence of the place, e.g., when on Mercury, the planet of good counsel, she offers the Pilgrim "mio infallibile avviso" (7.19). These manifestations are obviously appropriate because the travellers have fallen under the spell of the planet they are visiting, but it is less clear how the narrator, who is writing after the event, can also be influenced by each planet as he writes about it. The most likely explanation is simply that, since the narrator is the poet himself, he can consciously incorporate astrological references that are appropriate to the planet he is writing about. Whatever his rationale, Dante frequently uses the voice of the narrator to introduce planetary properties into the poem. For instance, in the heaven of Mars, which inclines one to make false accusations, the narrator accuses himself falsely (14.136–137).

The astrological elements in the speeches of the Pilgrim, Beatrice, and the narrator are, of course, pure fiction. For the most part, the same is true of the other characters as well. Known biographical facts, such as Justinian's vainglorious self regard, probably suggested the suitability of an historical personage to exemplify the effects of a given planet, but once the poet had selected his cast of characters, he was largely free to invent speeches for them that were astrologically appropriate but had no basis in historical fact. He could hardly have known whether Cacciaguida was testy or Aquinas prone to pastoral imagery. Accordingly, the poet was not greatly constrained by biography; instead, the task of incorporating astrological properties into his planetary cantos was an artistic and intellectual challenge. The disparity between his world view and that of the astrologers presented an intellectual problem, which he resolved by devising a Christian astrological system of his own, largely by spiritualizing the traditional planetary properties. When he agreed with the astrologers, the multitude of properties they supplied had to be worked into the poem aptly and unobtrusively, and the poet displayed remarkable ingenuity in solving this artistic problem. In the following paragraphs, I will classify his allusions in order to illustrate the variety of solutions the poet found for both problems.

Broadly speaking, Dante's allusions to planetary properties are either direct or indirect. The direct allusions, which we shall treat first, are the easiest to recognize, because they either echo an astrological text or exemplify it. Thus the Jovian virtue of concord is unmistakably indicated by a verbal allusion to the winking of eyes in concord ("si concorda," *Par.* 20.147). Astrological properties are sometimes echoed in proper names, for example Solar gold in "Crisostomo" and "Cieldauro" and Saturnian nuts in "Fonte Avellana." Such verbal echoes are the most direct kind of allusion, because the abstract language of the astrologers is simply repeated in the poem.

Exemplification moves one step further, from the abstract to the concrete, from the general to the specific. For instance, because Jupiter governs musical instruments Dante names five kinds of instruments in the corresponding cantos. Similarly, because Mars indicates the gilding of weapons, Dante alludes to a gilded sword hilt and gilding on a coat of arms (16.101–102, 110). Often the relevant quality is exemplified by a notorious event, such as the bloodshed for which the bishop of Feltre was responsible or the fraudulent measures employed by a Florentine salt merchant, which respectively exemplify blood and fraud (9.56, 16.105). On occasion the event is a future one foretold to the Pilgrim, most notably when his own exile and pilgrimage, which both belong to Mars, are prophesied in canto 17.

Dante frequently draws his astrologically appropriate examples from other texts rather than from events or things that are common knowledge. So the biblical story of the Red Sea exemplifies "augmentation and diminution of the sea" (*Par.* 22.94–96), and perfidy is typified by a classical parallel (17.47). Although the Bible and the Latin classics are Dante's favorite sources for such intertextual allusions, he uses vernacular ones as well, e.g., one of his own *canzoni* exemplifies song (8.37), and the Lancelot romance alludes to lust (16.13–15). The most extensive instance of exemplification by intertextual reference is the *Rule of Saint Benedict*, which embodies many Saturnian characteristics.

Dante's allusions to astrological properties are not always immediately apparent, because, instead of an explicit reference, he often finds some way to suggest it indirectly. Most commonly, he conceals the property by implication. Thus at *Par.* 19.131, an inactive volcano implies the moderate heat that is characteristic of Jupiter. Usually such indirect allusions by implication rely on common knowledge, such as the nature of snow, which instantiates the Lunar properties of white and cold (2.108). Similarly a sword is implied when Cacciaguida recalls that the emperor "girt me with his knighthood" (15.140). But sometimes the allusion can be grasped only by the learned, as when "abundance of substance" is implied by the Latin verb *frui*, "to enjoy the fruits" (19.2). The series of allusions based on the seven *climata* is the most elaborate use of specialized knowledge to refer to astral properties.

In the allusions we have examined so far, Dante accepted the astrologers' properties at face value and referred to them either directly or indirectly. But often he goes beyond their worldly materialism to suggest a broader application of the property in question. For example, in astrology Mars signified blood, death, and destruction; Dante extends the application of each of these terms, exemplifying them by "nobility of blood" (*Par.* 16.1), by Cacciaguida's martyrdom, and by the destruction of Florentine families. In each of these cases, Dante has moved beyond the obvious instance to one that would not have occurred to the astrologers. Perhaps the best illustration of this tendency is the way he broadened the concept of "ruler" in the heaven of the Sun to include not only kings and emperors but also the ecclesiastical hierarchy and God himself, not to mention spiritual self-mastery.

Frequently the poet transcends the literal sense of a property by using it figuratively. Thus the "noble cloth" proper to Solarians becomes their "garment of light" (*Par.* 14.37–38). By metaphor, Dante can convert the material sense to a spiritual one, as when physical food is turned into spiritual sustenance, e.g., "the bread of angels" (2.10–12; cf. 19.91–93). Often Dante takes a cliché, such as the heart that burns with ardor, and by elaboration reminds us of the literal sense that otherwise would pass unnoticed (14.88–89). Many of Dante's extended metaphors would seem to have been suggested by astrological properties. A case in point is the Solar propensity for making books, which prompted the poet to liken the Franciscan order to a book that is being written by the lives of its members (12.121–126).

Sometimes Dante admits an astrological property into his poem only with qualification. Melancholy, for example, was a familiar effect of Saturn, but when Beatrice fails to smile there, she does so only because it would be too intense for the Pilgrim to bear. Thus Dante alludes to melancholy but apparently rejects it as a property of Saturn. On the other hand, he accepts Saturn's association with cold in theory but offsets it in practice by placing the planet under the warmth of the constellation Leo. Most often, however, he accepts the astrologers' observations but rejects their interpretation of the observed effects of a planet. Saturn, for instance, causes famine, poverty, and exile, which for the astrologers made it the planet of misfortune, but Dante places a different interpretation on the same effects; for him fasting, apostolic poverty, and withdrawal from the world are all praiseworthy monastic virtues.

Since astrology relies on human reason, it must, in Dante's view, be necessarily imperfect; consequently, on occasion he significantly modified astrological doctrine. Thus the concept of *iustitia* he presents in Jupiter is more concerned with Bible-based righteousness than with legal justice. His greatest departure from the astrologers is his insistence that planetary properties ultimately come from God, not from the planets, which are only God's instruments. Thus, although prudence is treated in the heaven of the Sun, which is its proper source according to the astrologers, in the same place Dante stresses that God is the ultimate source of all good counsel (*Par.* 11.29; 12.75; 13.141).

Although Dante's astrological allusions could be studied in far greater detail, the foregoing examples should suffice to show the poet's ingenuity in working planetary properties into his text. By varying the means of allusion, a surprising amount of astrological material was incorporated into the poem, for the most part unobtrusively. I say "for the most part" because every reader of the poem is nonetheless struck with the originality, and even oddness, of the poet's metaphors. It seems odd, for instance, to compare the Franciscan order to a book that is being written (*Par.* 12.121–126), and indeed the analogy is obscure or even inexact in some respects. (What in the order corresponds to a folio? To a page?) One senses that the poet must have some reason for developing this comparison, and the discovery of his hidden agenda provides the explanation. He set himself the complicated task of inventing metaphors that were often astrologically appropriate. Now that we know his self-imposed limits, puzzlement gives way to appreciation.

DANTE'S CHRISTIAN ASTROLOGY

As our study progressed through Dante's seven planetary heavens, we noted that his treatment of astrology became increasingly deeper and more complex. In part this progression is the poet's usual practice of introducing the reader to the first member of a series in a straightforward manner and then, once the principle has been grasped, of gradually challenging his understanding by varying the treatment and by posing problems. Thus the neutrals in Ante-Hell and the proud in Purgatory provide paradigms for their respective *cantiche*; subsequent complications culminate in the enigmatic cantos of the thieves in Hell and the gluttons in Purgatory, which remain unsolved cruxes in the interpretation of the poem. Progressively raising the level of difficulty is Dante's version of programmed learning. One way of progressive complication is to restrict the astrological allusions in the earlier heavens and concentrate instead on basics, and then to increase the density of allusions gradually in subsequent heavens. The accompanying table, which is based on the same data tabulated above, shows the distribution of allusions in the seven heavens.

In the planetary heavens of *Paradiso* there is also a qualitative change in the character of the allusions, for the power of the planets that are

Distribution of Astrological Allusions in *Paradiso* 1–22

Heaven	Items	Percent
Moon	106	7.4
Mercury	135	9.3
Venus	184	12.9
Sun	185	13.0
Mars	296	20.7
Jupiter	252	17.6
Saturn	273	19.0
Total	1431	100.0

within the scope of earth's shadow is more material, while the benefits conferred by the higher planets are increasingly more spiritual, the closer they are to God. We have already seen these patterns piecemeal; now let us seek to draw the pieces together into a connected account.

In the Moon, Dante reduced his use of astrology to the bare essentials. Two parallel cases of the same effect are presented, so one is encouraged to generalize and ascribe the inconstancy of both nuns to the influence of the Moon, and an astrological explanation is suggested because both souls are women, who were notoriously subject to Lunar influence. Piccarda, the only speaker, also exemplifies a few other Lunar qualities, such as anxiety, moderation, piety, and a love of peace, but beyond this the poet restrains his astrological allusions to a few examples that are but tokens of the profusion yet to come. The result is an uncluttered introduction that presents the essentials without confusing complications. Furthermore, by concentrating on the distinction between the absolute and the conditioned will, the poet reminds the reader that, as Marco Lombardo had already observed, although the stars do exert an influence on humankind, this can be overcome by the habitual exercise of reason and free will. The Moon disposed Piccarda to be fearful and to passively accept change, which is to say that it shaped her conditioned will, but it had no power over her absolute will to remain in the convent. Thus the limits of astral influence are established at the outset.

Things are not so simple as we move on to Mercury. The pair of Lunar women are paralleled by two Mercurial men, who both ambitiously pursued fame and honor, but now the two cases are different and invite comparison. We begin to learn at this stage that a planet can produce a diversity of effects, and accordingly the allusions to planetary properties are more various and numerous, although they continue, as before, to refer chiefly to the principal characters. The scheme of the seven *climata* is phased in at this point, from which the discerning reader learns that astral influence varies in relation to geography.

The level of difficulty increases sharply in the heaven of Venus. There are now four main characters, three of whom speak, and the reader is left to figure out for himself how they exemplify the planet's influence. As in Mercury, each case turns out to be different, but the the treatment is more complex because the number of characters has doubled. From the fact that Rahab enjoys a higher degreee of bliss than some Venusians, we learn for the first time that all natives of a planet are not equally blessed. The riddle posed by Rahab's superiority serves to clarify the role of the stars in human salvation: Venus disposed her to be faithful, but presumably only an infusion of divine grace led her (and Folco) to turn from worldly love to love of God. In other words, the nature conferred by the stars can be perfected by grace. And hence astrology at best affords only partial insight into human behavior. (The point is reinforced by the answer to the riddle of Rahab, to which the Bible contributes as much as astrology.) Astrological allusions in this heaven are somewhat more numerous than before, but they are distinctly more noticeable because many of them are more concrete, especially those referring to Venusian artifacts, such as mirrors, jewels, crowns and garlands.

Further complexities appear in the heaven of the Sun. We are introduced to no less than twenty-four souls—the most named in any heaven—so the central planet is seen to have the most diverse effects. Moreover, the materialism of the astrologers subtly begins to be spiritualized by using the planetary properties in a figurative sense. Thus Solarians speak fittingly of shepherds and sheep, but not literally; they refer instead to Christian flocks, or congregations. The Sun imprints man with the image of God in his threefold aspect: its power to produce light and heat corresponds to the generation of understanding and love in the human mind and heart. Dante is careful to show that the Sun is only the intermediary between God and man. The density of allusion for the whole heaven is the same as for Venus, although Dante allotted more than twice as many lines to the former.

In the heaven of Mars, Dante continued to interpret the material properties of planets, which he found in traditional astrology, giving them a figurative, spiritual sense. But Mars required a more radical departure from the astrological tradition because, according to Dante's cosmology, Mars, being closer to God, should confer a higher grade of goodness than the planets beneath it, whereas traditionally it had been viewed as basically bad. Dante consequently developed his own Christian astrology, which was based on Thomistic angelology. By equating the fifth planet with the fifth order of angels, he was able to attribute fortitude, their distinctive virtue, to the planet moved by these angelic intelligences. Because Aquinas subsumes many lesser virtues under the cardinal virtue of fortitude, Dante could associate them with Mars as well. Thus nobility and magnanimity are major Martian themes for Dante. In this way the poet was able to emphasize the positive gifts of Mars while retaining but minimizing its traditional negative properties, such as war, bloodshed, anger, and pride. With Mars, the first of the higher planets, the number of astrological allusions rises markedly, attaining in fact its highest level. In part this is due to the large number of allusions to malevolent effects, which are stressed here more than in the other heavens. If allowance is made for this difference in treatment, Mars takes its place in the pattern of progressively richer allusion. The diversification of effects also continues, but not by exemplification; instead, a single speaker provides examples, largely drawn from Florentine affairs, while the eight Martian souls who are named apparently all epitomize one thing—the highest form of Martian virtue.

Canto for canto, the allusions to astrology are more frequent in the heaven of Jupiter than in Mars. This does not mean, however, that Dante relies on the astrologers more than ever. Quite the reverse is true, for although he largely agrees with them on what the effects of Jupiter are, he regularly reinterprets these data. Some properties that the astrologers thought desirable, such as having lots of money, Dante regards as baleful. In general, he continues to counter their materialism by substituting spiritual, and specifically Christian, values for their worldly ones. This process of desecularization is more striking in Jupiter because, unlike Mars, its properties were generally held to be beneficial, and so the discerning reader is repeatedly challenged to expand and redefine his cherished positive values. Only an astrologer would be upset to learn that Mars was in fact a beneficent planet, but every man should be troubled to learn that the benefits bestowed by Jupiter are not the material advantages he supposed them to be. Desecularization is Dante's principal way of reconciling planetary properties with his Christian world-view; it enables him to incorporate them into his text by the score. But in Jupiter his critique of astrology runs deeper, because the burden of these cantos is that the astrologers, and the philosophers they followed, only succeeded in discovering a small part of *iustitia*. The astrologers only perceived the politico-legal sense of the term; to discover its broader sense of righteousness as duty to God, one must turn to revelation. The result is a new science of astrology that, though still rational, is guided by revelation—in short, a Christian astrology.

The Christianization of astrology culminates in Saturn. The challenge was to convert "the greater malefic" into the most beneficent of planets. Again Dante relied heavily on desecularization, but with a special twist. Conditions that the astrologers considered to be misfortunes become virtues when viewed from a Christian perspective. Servitude as the world knows it is a misfortune, but the service of God brings the highest form of human happiness. Thus the monk, whose practices are largely properties of Saturn, such as fasting and poverty, is the model Saturnian. This tactic of value inversion differs from the poet's solution to the maleficence of Mars, which he largely accepted but counterbalanced with beneficial effects suggested by Aquinas and Aristotle. The reader has by now become accustomed to the spiritualization of particular properties, but the scale of this wholesale transvaluation is unprecedented. The maneuver is all the more effective because it is firmly based on fundamental Christian ideals that were, moreover, well known to be practiced widely in monastic communities. As with Jupiter, Dante accepts the astrologers' data while qualifying much of their interpretation. The density of astral allusions in the two cantos of Saturn is higher than in any other planetary heaven, so his commitment to astrology is affirmed, and made most evident, even as he is rejecting the traditional astrological values and replacing them with Christian ones.

III

We have made a good beginning. The initial hunch that astrology might have been one of Dante's sources is now amply justified. But this has been only a reconnaissance in force, not a conquest, for this study raises new questions that must be left unanswered here. Still, they can fittingly be asked at the end of our investigation, lest it be taken as definitive rather than preliminary.

The most obvious question is whether Dante employed these astral properties throughout the poem. An affirmative answer is strongly indicated because Beatrice has assured us that, in a sense, the planets can be blamed as well as honored for the differences in human character (*Par.* 4.58–60). Moreover, this expectation has already been confirmed by Georg Rabuse's discovery of Martian properties in both the *Inferno* and the *Purgatorio*.[3] But it remains to ascertain the traces of the other planets, and the task will be more difficult than ours has been. In the present study, one had but to compare the properties of one planet with Dante's text, but when the task is not defined by the seven heavens, one must proceed on the assumption that a given canto may contain allusions to all seven planets. Consequently, it would be extremely laborious, though by no means impossible, to extend the methodical approach of the present study to the extraplanetary cantos. The next step would probably be to examine one canto of the *Inferno* throughly for allusions to any and all planets. But perhaps there are shortcuts, for the planetary cantos provide many cross references to earlier material that suggest places where soundings may profitably be taken. For example, the allusion to the Lancelot romance (*Par.* 16.14–15) is reminiscent of the book that Francesca and Paolo were reading (*Inf.* 5.133–138), so one should search for other Martian properties in the latter place. After a few cantos have been thoroughly surveyed for planetary properties, it should become evident whether the properties are mixed in the extraplanetary cantos. I would be surprised if they were, however, because Beatrice, in the passage cited above, assumes that every soul has an affinity for only one star.

Another question will occur to adepts in astrology. Planetary properties are only a small part of that complicated discipline. As explained in my Introduction, I have concentrated on them in this preliminary study because they lend themselves readily to verbal and conceptual comparison. But now that it has been established that Dante made abundant use of astrology, one should look for more sophisticated applications of that discipline in the poem, similar to his elaborate use of the doctrine of *climata*. In this study, I have suggested a few in passing, such as the placement of a planet in relation to a sign of the zodiac (dignity, especially by rulership or domicile) and to another planet (aspect, especially conjunction), and I would be surprised if many more were not found. In short, someone needs to do for Dante what J. D. North has done for Chaucer.[4]

The attentive reader will have noted that some properties are attributed to more than one planet. Sometimes I have been able to perceive a distinction that justified the duplication, but in many cases I have simply reported the opinions of the astrologers and have shown how Dante followed them. I would not expect our nine astrologers to be mutually consistent, but I do find it hard to believe that Dante would have incorporated their inconsistencies into his poem without good reason. The problem, then, is why he alluded to certain properties—for example, water, nutrition, agriculture, animal husbandry—in more than one heaven. His astrological sources certainly authorized the repetition, but I suspect that Dante attached some further significance to the recurrence of these themes. Tentatively, I will suggest the possibility that these recurrent properties exemplify the descent of divine goodness as it is "mirrored, as it were, in nine subsistences" (*Par.* 13.59). Dante's Aquinas, in his sketch of emanation, is tantalizingly vague about how the process works in detail, and perhaps the variations Dante rings on these recurrent themes was intended to show how the ideas in the divine mind are progressively differentiated.

I have hesitated to develop this line of inquiry because no firm conclusions can be drawn until we have a better understanding of Dante's cosmology. Specifically, it is still unclear, to me at least, what role he assigns to the angels in the diffusion of divine goodness. They are present in the ray that strikes the *primum mobile*, and the analogous image of Jacob's ladder (see above, pp. 240–41) suggests that they function diversely as divine goodness descends through the heavens, but just how Dante thought it all worked remains to be determined.[5] If we could reconstruct Dante's cosmological model more precisely, I think we would be in a better position to appreciate the importance he attached to astrology. As it is, we cannot at present be certain just how he thought the stars received, exerted, and passed on their powers. In other words, we do not know exactly how astrology is related to cosmology in Dante's thought.

Nonetheless we can be sure that for Dante the two were closely integrated. Astrology for him was not divorced from science, as it has been since the seventeenth century. Instead, the operation of universal Nature through the stars was a doctrine that was generally recognized in medieval philosophy and theology. Because astrology is no longer a reputable study in the modern world, Dantists have probably been disinclined to emphasize its importance in the *Commedia*. But if we attempt to reconstruct Dante's world-view in its totality, we will not only assign a major role to astrology but will also be necessarily led back to philosophy and theology in order to gain a better understanding of how God operates through the stars.

Appendix 1:
Biobibliography

This appendix provides fuller information on the astrological sources used in the foregoing study (see list in the Introduction, p. 14). To avoid lengthy, repetitive citations, most of them have been cited in the text and footnotes simply by name. Full bibliographical information on each text is given below, together with a brief sketch of the author and/or work and select references. The presentation is ordered chronologically.

Ptolemy

Claudius Ptolemaeus is the only astrologer that Dante noticed in the Noble Castle (*Inf.* 4.142: "Tolomeo"), where his position between the geometer Euclid and the physician Hippocrates suggests that Dante considered him worthy of honor as an astrologer, not just as an astronomer, since Ptolemy himself regarded astrology as the science that provides medicine with mathematical explanations (*Quad.* 1.3; Tester, p. 63). To be sure, Dante and his contemporaries also honored Ptolemy as the preeminent authority on astronomy, especially for his *Almagest*, the treatise that expounded the mathematical foundations of the Ptolemaic world-system, but his four-book exposition of astrology—the *Tetrabiblos* or *Quadripartitum*—was in fact more widely used as a university textbook than the *Almagest*, which was replaced by simpler expositions expressly written for instructional purposes (see above, Introduction, n. 4). In short, Ptolemy's contributions to astrology were as well regarded in scholastic circles as his achievements in astronomy.

Surprisingly little is known about the life of the greatest Greek astronomer (ca. 100 to ca. 170 A.D.). About all one can gather from his works is that he flourished in Alexandria around the middle of the second century A.D. He wrote in Greek on a variety of mathematical sciences, most notably astronomy, but also geography, optics, and astrology. Ptolemy brought clarity, system, and order to each field that he mastered. When the work of his predecessors was consistent with the system he adopted, he incorporated it with due acknowledgement, but sometimes he had to introduce adjustments and more often simply attempt new, even brilliant, solutions to unsolved problems, e.g., the mathematical models he devised to account for the observed motion of the planets other than the Sun and Moon (*Almagest* 9–11).

Quadripartitum. Having provided predictive models that accounted for the motion of the heavenly bodies in the *Almagest*, Ptolemy undertook the parallel task of showing how the influence of these bodies on things terrestrial could likewise be predicted. The most recent editors of this second treatise entitle it *Apotelesmatica* ("Astrological Influences"), although traditionally and more commonly it has been known by the title *Mathêmatikês tetrabiblou suntaxeôs* ("Mathematical Treatise in Four Books"), or more briefly, *Tetrabiblos* in Greek and *Quadripartitum* in Latin. The four books treat: (1) basic astrological concepts, (2) astral influences in general, (3) influences on individuals before and at birth, and (4) influences on individuals after birth.

To produce this treatise, Ptolemy surveyed the mass of astrological writings that were available to him at Alexandria, including the work of Babylonian and Egyptian, as well as Greek, astrologers. When these different traditions were not compatible, as was most frequently the case, he opted for the one that was simpler and more amenable to mathematical treatment. As he believed that astral influences were natural, physical phenomena, he tended to exclude those elements of earlier astrology that could not be justified by reason; indeed, no other astrologer, either before or after Ptolemy, was as ready to offer explanations for the underlying causes of astral influence. In other words, he sought to make astrology respectable in terms of Greek philosophy, which is to say natural science.

Text. The standard critical edition of the Greek text is now that prepared by F. Boll and A. Boer for *Claudii Ptolemaei opera quae extant omnia*, vol. 3, part 1: Ἀποτελεσματικά (Leipzig: Teubner, 1957). An earlier edition with English translation by F. E. Robbins is readily available in the Loeb Classical Library: Ptolemy, *Tetrabiblos* (Cambridge: Harvard University Press, 1940). The original Greek text is largely irrelevant to a study of Dante, however, since he and his contemporaries knew the *Quadripartitum* in Latin translations. I have used the one that Plato of Tivoli made from an Arabic translation in 1138, because this one has been printed; I cite the text as it was printed at Basel in 1551 by Joannes Hervagius along with other astrological works, the first of which is Firmicus Maternus, *Astrono-micon* (each separately paged; copy at the University of Wisconsin). It is possible, however, that Dante used the more common but unprinted translation by Aegidius de Tebaldis (1256), or even one of the four other thirteenth-century translations noted by Carmody (pp. 18–19).

Planetary properties. Unlike later writers, Ptolemy draws up two lists of planetary properties. The first is placed at the beginning of his exposition of the basic concepts of astrology (*Quad.* 1.6). This introductory list concentrates on essentials: the quality of the planet (hot, wet, etc.) and its consequent effect on the sublunary world (heating, humidifying, etc.), to which Ptolemy adds brief explanations of the physical basis for the influence in question. This list treats the Sun and Moon first and then proceeds from Saturn downward to Mercury. The other list (*Quad.* 2.8) omits the Sun and Moon but otherwise more closely resembles later lists of planetary properties that classify the effects of each planet. Ptolemy's categories include human illnesses, calamities, and benefits; animals, weather, crops, and rivers and seas. Explanations are infrequent in this second presentation, which probably was compiled from previous writers.

Bibliography. For a recent, critical account of Ptolemy's life and works, see G. J. Toomer, "Ptolemy," *Dictionary of Scientific Biography* 11 : 186–206. The *Quadripartitum* is presented in its cultural context and sympathetically analyzed by S. J. Tester, *A History of Western Astrology* (Woodbridge, Suffolk: Boydell Press, 1987), pp. 57–88. Scholarship has justly ignored William J. Tucker, *Ptolemaic Astrology: A Complete Commentary on the "Tetrabiblos" of Claudius Ptolemy* (Sideup, Kent: Pythagorean Publications, 1962). Technicalities can often be clarified by A. Bouché-Leclercq, *L'Astrologie grecque* (Paris, 1899; rpt. Brussels: Culture et Civilisation, 1963); properties, pp. 311–326. Francis J. Carmody, *Arabic Astronomical and Astrological Sciences in Latin Translations: A Critical Bibliography* (Berkeley and Los Angeles: University of California Press, 1956), pp. 15–21. *Enciclopedia dantesca*, s.v. "Tolomeo," 5 : 620–621.

Albumasar

Abû Ma'shar al-Balkhî, Ja'far ibn Muhammad (787–886), known in the Latin West as Albumasar, was the foremost astrologer of the Moslem world. A prolific writer (Pingree lists 42 works), Albumasar was remembered as "the teacher of the people of Islam concerning the influences of

the stars" (Ibn al-Qiftî, before 1248). He earned this reputation by combining earlier astrological doctrines into a single system that provided the
foundation for subsequent Arabic astrology. He was not the first to attempt such a synthesis, for he drew so heavily on earlier works that he was
rightly accused of plagiarism, but his work was more comprehensive and
influential than his predecessors'.

Albumasar's background predisposed him to syncretism. He grew
up in Balkh, in Khurasan (northern Afghanistan today), where the old
Persian learning was still honored, including a traditional blend of Greek,
Indian, and Iranian astrology. When he moved to Baghdad and took up
astrology, Albumasar studied these Persian sources, though not in the
original Pahlavi but rather in Arabic translations; similarly, he consulted
his Greek and Syriac sources in translation. He did not realize that all of
his far-flung authorities had been tinged with Greek astrology; instead,
their similarity convinced him that the truth of astrology had been revealed progressively to divers peoples by a series of prophets, beginning
with Hermes Trismegistus, the prophet of the "Sabaean" star-worshipers
of Harrân. This conviction authorized Albumasar to draw freely on all the
astrological traditions known to him; the result was an eclectic, often inconsistent, synthesis.

Unlike most astrologers, Albumasar elaborated a philosophical justification for his system, which is mostly Aristotelian but includes significant Neoplatonic elements. Since this doctrine is expounded in the same
work that Dante used for the properties of planets, Albumasar is a possible source for Dante's cosmology. Dante cited Albumasar by name in
Conv. 2.13.22, but his immediate source was evidently Albertus Magnus,
De meteoris 1.4.9.

Text. Albumasar's principal work is the *Kitâb al-madkhal al-kabîr 'alâ
'ilm ahkâm al-nujûm*, "The Great Introduction to the Science of Astrology," which he wrote in Baghdad ca. 850 A.D. It is called "great" to distinguish it from a shorter version, which he also wrote. The longer work was
twice translated into Latin, first by John of Seville in 1133, then again by
Hermann of Carinthia in 1140. The second translation has been printed
several times: by Erhard Ratdolt at Augsburg (1489, 1495), then by Sessa
at Venice (1506) with the title: *Introductorium in astronomiam Albumasaris
Abalachi octo continens libros partiales.* I have used a microfilm of the Vatican
copy of the 1506 edition, which is available as: Saint Louis University Library, "Microfilms of Rare and Out-of-Print Books," List 6 (1959), no. 4
(106 pages; colophon: "Venetiis: mandato & expensis Merchionis Sessa:
per Jacobum Pentium Leucensem, 1506").

Planetary properties. The text used for the present study is *Introductorium*, liber 7, capitulum 9: "*De naturis stellarum septem et proprietatibus ducatum per universa rerum genera.* Postremo est universi stellarum ducatus ...—... per diversa tempora colliguntur*" (ed. Venice, 1506, fols. g5v through g7r). The order of presentation is from Saturn downwards to the Moon. Each planet is illustrated with a woodcut in which the god or goddess is represented as enthroned, bearing a symbolic implement, and wearing an appropriate headdress; two medallions indicate the planet's domiciles in the zodiac. The list of properties is relatively brief: about twenty lines are devoted to each planet.

Bibliography. David Pingree is the leading authority on Albumasar; the best summary treatment is his article "Abû Ma'shar" in the *Dictionary of Scientific Biography*, 1:32–39. For the Latin translations of Albumasar and their supposed impact on scholastic philosophy, see Richard Lemay, *Abû Ma'shar and Latin Aristotelianism in the Twelfth Century*, Publications of the Faculty of Arts and Sciences, Oriental Series, no. 38 (Beirut: American University of Beirut, 1962). J. M. Millàs, "Abû Ma'shar," *The Encyclopaedia of Islam*, 2nd ed., 1:139–140. Francis J. Carmody, *Arabic Astronomical and Astrological Sciences in Latin Translations: A Critical Bibliography* (Berkeley and Los Angeles: University of California Press, 1956), pp. 88–101, lists manuscripts and editions. *Enciclopedia dantesca*, 1:109–110. S. J. Tester, *A History of Western Astrology* (Woodbridge, Suffolk: Boydell Press, 1987), uses Albumasar to typify Arabic astrology (pp. 157–172) but, to judge from the number of surviving manuscripts, overrates his popularity in the West.

Alcabitius

Abû al-Saqr 'Abd al-'Azîz ibn 'Uthmân ibn 'Alî was generally known as al-Qabîsî (Latin: Alcabitius, Alchabitius) from his birthplace, Quabîsa, a village in Iraq, probably the one of that name near Mosul, where he studied astronomy. He flourished about the year 950 in Aleppo (Syria) at the court of its ruler, Sayf al-Dawla, to whom several of his works are dedicated.

Not an original thinker, Alcabitius is nonetheless an important figure in the history of astrology because his introduction to natal astrology (genethialogy) was widely used, in both the Muslim world and the Latin West. This book, *Al-madkhal ilâ sinâ'at ahkâm al-nujûm* ("Introduction to the Art of Astrology") is organized into five sections (*differentia*): (1) basic definitions, (2) the nature of the seven planets, (3) ways in which the powers of these planets are modified, (4) definitions of more advanced technical terms, and (5) the so-called Arabian parts.

The *Madkhal* was translated into Latin by John of Seville (*Hispalensis*) in the mid-twelfth century under the title *Opus isagogicum* or *Liber introductorius*. In this form it had a long life as a university textbook and was therefore frequently printed (editions most reliably listed by Pingree). The edition I cite is: *Preclarum summi in astrorum scientia principis Alchabitii Opus ad scrutanda stellarum magisteria isagogicum*, ed. Antonius de Fantis of Treviso (Venice: Petrus Liechtenstein, 1521), fols. 2v–21v. I worked from a microfilm of the Vatican copy, which is available as: Saint Louis University Library, "Microfilms of Rare and Out-of-Print Books," List 6 (1959), no. 2. No. 1 of the same list is another edition (Venice: Sessa, 1512), which I have occasionally consulted for variant readings.

Commentaries. Because the *Opus isagogicum* was a text for university lectures (e.g., at Paris, Bologna, and Montpellier), Latin commentaries grew up around it. The edition of Venice 1521 gives that of Johannes Danko, of Saxony, who lectured at Paris in 1331 (fols. 23r–63v). Since Dante could not have known this, having died ten years earlier, I have used it sparingly. Dante's contemporary, the ill-fated occultist Cecco d'Ascoli (Francesco Stabili, 1269–1327) also commented on Alcabitius: *Il Commento di Cecco d'Ascoli all'Alcabizzo*, ed. Giuseppe Boffito, Pubblicazioni dell'Osservatorio del Collegio della querce 1 (Florence: Olschki, 1905). But this, too, is not relevant to the present study because Cecco's commentary unfortunately breaks off in the middle of the first *differentia*, never reaching Alcabitius's discussion of planetary properties in the second *differentia*.

Planetary properties. Alcabitius devotes the second *differentia* to "the natures of the seven planets, both what is proper to them and what they signify concerning the essence of things" (fols. 9r–12v). He procedes downward from Saturn planet by planet. For each planet he first gives a traditional list of properties that is, if anything, shorter than Albumasar's, but the presentation is more readily intelligible because he makes clear the rationale by which he groups certain qualities together. To this traditional material he regularly appends a long list of the ways in which one planet's nature can be affected by the others, and finally he reports extratraditional views, e.g., of Messehalla and Dorotheus. Alcabitius's list of properties became the basic repertory for Latin astrologers, if only because it was the one they learned first at the university. Bonatti incorporates much of it verbatim.

Bibliography. David Pingree gives the most recent and careful account in *The Encyclopaedia of Islam*, 2nd ed, 4 : 340–341, s.v. "al-Kabîsî"; a less technical version appears in the *Dictionary of Scientific Biography*, 11 : 226, s.v. "al-Qabîsî." Francis J. Carmody, *Arabic Astronomical and Astrological Sciences in Latin Translations: A Critical Bibliography* (Berkeley and Los Angeles: University of California Press, 1956), pp. 144–150, must be used with caution. A commentary on Alcabitius can be gleaned from J. D. North, *Chaucer's Universe* (New York: Oxford University Press, 1988), who uses a Middle English translation unnoted by Carmody and Pingree.

Haly Abenragel

In the Latin West, this astrologer's name, Abu 'l-Hasan 'Alî ibn abi 'l-Ridjâl, was occasionally given in full as "Albohazen Haly filius Abenragel," but more frequently he was designated by one or more of its constituent parts: Albohazen (Alboacen), Haly Abenragel, Abenragel, or simply Haly. In his youth he may have witnessed astronomical observations in Baghdad (988), but most of his career was spent in Tunisia at the capital of the Zirid dynasty in Kairawan. There he tutored the prince al-Mu'izz ibn Bâdîs (1016–1062) and played a leading part in his government. The date of his death is uncertain because, although his tombstone was reportedly dated 1034/5, his own works refer to at least one later event (1037), and modern scholars often give 1040 as a *terminus post quem*.

Haly's principal work is an astrological compilation in eight books that is entitled *Kitâb al-Bâri' fi ahkâm al-nudjûm*, "The Distinguished Book on Horoscopes from the Constellations." The scale is much more generous than the writers described above, the Latin text filling 196 folio pages in the Venice edition of 1503. In part, the bulk is greater because the scope is wider, including not only natal astrology but also interrogations, forecasts of enterprises, and applications to politics and history.

Although quite popular in the Moslem world (two dozen manuscripts), this work was a latecomer to the Latin West, where it was translated about a century after Albumasar and Alcabitius. Oddly enough, it was first translated from Arabic, not into Latin, but into Old Castilian for Alfonso the Wise by a Jew, Judah ben Moses (Yehûda ben Môshê), who completed his work in 1256. Subsequently, the Castilian version was translated into Latin by Aegidius de Tebaldis with the assistance of Petrus de Regio; this is the text used for the present study. Eventually the work was translated into Portuguese, French, English, Hebrew, and even Latin again.

Text. The Latin translation by Aegidius de Tebaldis (made after 1256) was first printed in 1485, but I have used a later edition: *Preclarissimus in iudiciis astrorum Albohazen Haly filius Abenragel* (Venice: J. B. Sessa, 1503), which I know from the Vatican copy reproduced as: Saint Louis University Library, "Microfilms of Rare and Out-of-Print Books," List 43 (1963), no. 4 (98 numbered folios with double columns).

Planetary properties. Haly takes a practical approach to astrology: he devotes one of the earliest of his introductory chapters to the powers of the planets (book 1, chapter 4 *in naturis planetarum*; ed. Venice, 1503, fols. 3r–4v). He treats the Sun and Moon first, then descends from Saturn to Mercury. Although he writes more about each planet than either Albumasar or Alcabitius, less of what he says is relevant to the present study because he deals with the absolute nature of the planet in a cursory fashion and then elaborates at length on what it signifies in relation to each of the other planets and each of the signs of the zodiac. This treatment doubtless simplified interpretation for beginners, as it still does in many modern manuals of astrology, but it provided less grist for Dante's mill.

Bibliography. Summary, rather skimpy, article by David Pingree, *The Encyclopaedia of Islam*, 2nd ed., 3:688, s.v. "Ibn abi 'l-Ridjâl." The older notices are collected and criticized by A. R. Nykl, "Libro conplido en los juizios de las estrellas," *Speculum* 29 (1954), 85–99; cf. the reply of G. Hilty, "El Libro conplido en los iudizios de las estrellas," *Al-Andalus* 20 (1955), 1–74. Francis J. Carmody, *Arabic Astronomical and Astrological Sciences in Latin Translations: A Critical Bibliography* (Berkeley and Los Angeles: University of California Press, 1956), pp. 150–154.

John of Seville

Among other introductions to astrology, Albertus Magnus recommended one by "John of Seville, which begins *Cinctura firmamenti*" (*Speculum astromoniae* 6). The author flourished in Spain as a translator from Arabic into Latin from 1133 until at least 1142; the work in question is his *Isagoge*. In saying more, one must proceed with caution because there has been much confusion among modern scholars about both the man and his work. The biographical difficulties were largely clarified in 1959 by Lynn Thorndike. John, as his name indicates, originated in Seville, which in his lifetime was under Moslem control. His career, however, was in Christian Spain, and chiefly in Toledo, which had been conquered from the Moslems in 1085 and which became a center for Latin translations from the Arabic under the patronage of Archbishop Raymond I (1125–1151). Some of John's work, however, was done in the Galician district of Limia, and he dedicated one work to the wife of the ruler of the adjacent county of Portugal, Tharasia, who died in 1130. Thus in all probability he was originally a Mozarab, i.e., a Christian who had assimilated Moselm culture, and moved north to Christian Spain, where there was a demand for his services as a translator.

As a translator, John of Seville specialized in astrology. For example, in previous entries of the present biobibliography I have noted his translations of Albumasar's *Introductorium* and Alcabitius's *Opus isagogicum*; in addition he translated perhaps another dozen works. Consequently, he played a key role in the transmission of Arabic learning to the Latin West, for which he is principally remembered today.

After translating two Arabic introductions to astrology, John wrote one of his own, which he called the *Isagoge*. The basic concepts of astrology are treated under 29 heads (*capita*). It is not immediately apparent, however, that this is the introduction to which Albertus Magnus referred, because Albertus did not quote the incipit accurately. The correct form, given by Carmody, is: "Zodiacus [vel cinctura firmamenti] dividitur in duodecim signa. . . ." Some texts, including the edition of 1548, omit the phrase in brackets; Albert, on the other hand, omitted the first two words, "Zodiacus vel").

As a sequel to his *Isagoge*, John of Seville also wrote a more advanced treatise, which in the edition of 1548 is entitled: *Libri quatuor de iudiciis astrologicis*. Because this treatise is divided into four books or parts, it is often called the *Quadripartitum*. The titles of the four parts are: (1) *De gentibus, regibus, divitatibus, aeris mutatione, fame, et mortalitates*; (2) *De nativitatibus*; (3) *De interrogationibus*; (4) *De electionibus*. The text of the treatise begins with the words: "Considerandum est quod signum. . . ." The *Quadripartitum* concludes with a colophon that dates it A.D. 1142.

Although the *Isagoge* and the *Quadripartitum* are distinct works, they have often been confused (e.g., by Carmody). Probably John of Seville conceived them as a sequence; certainly they appear together in many manuscripts, but as far as I can tell, they were only given a common title in the mid-sixteenth century: *Epitome totius astrologiae, conscripta a Iohanne Hispalensi Hispano astrologo celeberrimo, ante annos quadringentos, ac nunc primum in lucem edita. Cum praefatione Ioachimi Helleri Leucopetraei, contra astrologiae adversarios* (Nuremberg: Johannes Montanus and Ulricus Neuber, 1548), 175 unnumbered octavo pages. Of four recorded copies in the United States, I have used a microfilm of the one at the University of Chicago. A subsequent octavo edition, lacking the title page (144 pp.), held by the John Crerar Library, Chicago, is listed in the *National Union Catalog, Pre-1956 Imprints*, 281:94, no. 106287.

Planetary properties. In the *Isagoge*, the list of properties forms a series of seven *capita*, beginning: "Caput XIII. De naturis septem planetarum, ac de Sole primum," followed by the Moon, and then the other five from Saturn downward to Mercury (cap. 13–19, fols. D1 recto through D2 verso). The treatment is extremely brief—about 15 lines per planet—and the properties can be found elsewhere almost without exception, though John's phrasing can occasionally clarify an obscure concept.

Bibliography. Lynn Thorndike, "John of Seville," *Speculum* 34 (1959), 20–38, presents a mass of evidence that is only partially digested. Earlier notices (e.g., Sarton) must be used with caution. Francis J. Carmody, *Arabic Astronomical and Astrological Sciences in Latin Translations: A Critical Bibliography* (Berkeley and Los Angeles: University of California Press, 1956), pp. 168–170. John and other Spanish translators are briefly discussed, with useful references, in *Science in the Middle Ages*, ed. David C. Lindberg (Chicago: University of Chicago Press, 1978), pp. 62–66.

Ibn Ezra

Like Ptolemy, Abraham Ibn Ezra is an astrologer who is much better known today for his contributions to other fields. Browning's poem "Rabbi ben Ezra" has made him a commonplace figure, so much so that Sarton used the same form of his name to mark a new epoch in the history of science. He was born circa 1090 at Tudela, then part of the Moselm emirate of Saragossa but about a day's journey from the Christian kingdoms of Castile, Navarre, and Aragon; his birthplace was conquered by Navarre in 1114. Thus he was well placed to appreciate the cultural crisis of Sephardic Jews, who in the twelfth century were progressively being cut off from the Arabic world that had provided them with their secular culture, Hebrew being for them a sacred language reserved for religious purposes. His first fifty years were spent in Moslem Spain and North Africa, but in 1140 he began a 21-year tour of Jewish communities in Italy, France, and even England: first Rome, then Salerno, Mantua, Verona, Lucca, Narbonne, Béziers, Rouen, Dreux, and London, finally returning to settle down in Calahorra, not far from his birthplace; he died circa 1065. Ibn Ezra preferred to live simply, without either wealth or possessions, except for an astrolabe.

During his travels Ibn Ezra wrote biblical commentaries, probably on all the books of the Old Testament, though not all have survived. He adopted a new exegetical method, which aimed to establish the literal meaning of the text while hinting at esoteric truths, often based on astrology, numerology, and Neoplatonic philosophy. He made an exception in the case of the legislative parts of the Pentateuch, however, which he interpreted traditionally in accordance with the Talmud. These commentaries are the most influential of his works, having elicited over fifty supercommentaries.

The most distinctive feature of his secular writings is that they are in Hebrew. Evidently he was determined to make Hebrew the language of secular learning in Jewish communities where the knowledge of Arabic was nonexistent. Thus he desacralized Hebrew in his poetry, which often employed the forms and nonreligious themes cultivated by Arabic poets in Spain. (Esepcially notable is a prose poem, *Hai ben Mekiz*, in which a mysterious figure guides the hero, representing philosophic reason, through "mystical worlds," including the seven planetary heavens.) When he found that Italian Jews had only a passive knowledge of Hebrew, he wrote and translated elementary grammatical treatises that would enable them to write and speak the language. Similarly, he made the elements of Arabic arithmetic available in Hebrew, including a decimal system, and he provided instructions for the application of arithmetic to the calendar, to astronomical tables, and to the astrolabe. Ibn Ezra's mathematical interests culminated in astrology. He not only translated two astrological treatises of Messehalla but also composed a great many short ones of his own (ten in the 1507 edition, although Steinschneider lists fifty).

Text. The treatise with which we are concerned is *Reshit Hokmah*, "The Beginning of Wisdom," a brief introduction to astrology, which he wrote at Lucca in 1148. In 1273, a Flemish scholastic, Henry Bate of Malines (1246—ca. 1310), commissioned a French translation of this and other astrological works by Ibn Ezra. One Hagin (Hayyim) the Jew dictated his translation to a scribe, Obert of Montdidier. Bate apparently meant to translate the French into Latin himself, and did eventually produce his own Latin version of the *Initium sapientiae* at Orvieto in 1292. Shortly thereafter, the French version came to the attention of that great physician and astrologer, Pietro d'Abano, who in 1293 again translated Ibn Ezra's introduction as the *Introductorium quod dicitur Principium sapientiae*. Pietro explains that he has corrected Hagin's errors and has somewhat rearranged the text of this work, though Levy's collation (1927) found little improvement and few substantial changes. In all he translated and/or revised ten treatises by Ibn Ezra (in some cases using Bate's Latin version), which were printed first at Venice in 1485 and again as: *Abrahe Avenaris Judei astrologi peritissimi in re iudiciali opera, ab excellentissimo philosopho Petro de Abano post accuratam castigationem in Latinum traducta* (Venice: Petrus Liechtenstein, 1507), fols. 1r–31v. I have worked from the Vatican copy as reproduced in Saint Louis University Library, "Microfilms of Rare and Out-of-Print Books," List 6 (1959), no. 3.

Planetary properties. Not surprisingly, Ibn Ezra's introduction to astrology was not among those recommended by Albertus Magnus (above, Introduction, n. 31), because the *Principium sapientiae* was not translated into Latin until after Albert's death in 1280. I have not hesitated to use it, however, since Dante is likely to have known the translation by Pietro d'Abano. Ibn Ezra collected an extensive list of properties, which in the printed edition amounts to about a quarto page per planet: *Introductorium quod dicitur Principium sapientiae*, chapter 4: "In natura septem planetarum et earum potestate et in omni eo quod significant" (ed. 1507, fols. 18v–22r). Ibn Ezra's list resembles that of al-Biruni in treating such categories as climates, peoples, metals and stones, plants and animals; he is singular in assigning certain Hebrew letters (and hence numbers) to each planet.

Bibliography. Martin Levey, "Ibn Ezra, Abraham ben Meir," *Dictionary of Scientific Biography*, 4:502–503. Emmanuel Poulle, "Henry Bate of Malines," *ibid.*, 6:272–275. "Ibn Ezra, Abraham," *Encyclopaedia Judaica*, 8:1163–1170, by various authors. Lynn Thorndike, *A History of Magic and Experimental Science*, vol. 2 (New York: Columbia University Press, 1923), pp. 926–930. Raphael Levy, *The Astrological Works of Ibn Ezra* (Baltimore: Johns Hopkins University Press, 1927). George Sarton, *Introduction to the History of Science*, vol. 2, part 1 (Baltimore: published for the Carnegie Institution of Washington by Williams & Wilkens, 1931), pp.187–189. The French text has been edited by Raphael Levy, *The Beginning of Wisdom: An Astrological Tract by Abraham Ibn Ezra*, Johns Hopkins Studies in Romance Languages and Literatures, extra vol. 14 (Baltimore: Johns Hopkins

University Press, 1939), but I have preferred the Latin version because, being the one made in Italy, it is more likely to be the one with which Dante was familiar. The Hebrew text was edited by Francisco Cantera in the same volume, and Levy provided an English translation of it (pp. 152–235; chap. 4, pp. 193–202).

Liber novem iudicum

The last title recommended by Albertus Magnus as an introduction to judicial astrology was a *Liber novem iudicum* that begins with the words "Caelestis circuli" (*Speculum astronomiae* 6). Of the two works with this title, designated I and II by Carmody, Albertus's incipit corresponds exactly to the first, which is, moreover, the only one relevant to this study because it contains a long section on planetary properties.

The work is called "The Book of the Nine Judges" because it is an anthology of nine authorities on judicial astrology. The anonymous compiler's method is simple: he divided his subject into topics and under each heading he noted what each of his authorities had to say on the subject. The source of each extract is usually identified in an initial rubric.

Carmody noted that the Latin prose style was consistent throughout the work and concluded that it was therefore a translation from the Arabic. But Burnett has discovered that three of the "judges" are quoted from translations that were made in northern Spain around the middle of the twelfth century. The apparent consistency that deceived Carmody is due to the compiler's habit of abbreviating and paraphrasing his sources.

The date and provenance of the compilation are unknown. The compiler's use of Spanish translations might indicate Spain as the place of origin, but given the widespread and rapid diffusion of many Spanish scientific translations, this hypothesis would only be tenable if it could be shown that at least one of the sources of the *Liber novem iudicum* was unknown outside of Spain. Burnett's projected study of the compiler's sources may make possible a more precise determination of provenance. The date can be fixed only within broad limits: the book must be later than the mid-twelfth century translations it contains, and it must be earlier than Michael Scot's *Liber introductorius*, which made use of it; but Scot's work cannot be dated more precisely than 1235, the date when he died after probably having worked on it for many years (see next entry below).

Since the compilation now seems to have been assembled from Latin sources, we must regard as spurious the statement found in a fourteenth-century manuscript to the effect that the *Liber novem iudicum* was sent by the sultan of Babylon to Emperor Frederick II at the same time that the caliph sent Master Theodore (of Antioch) to him (British Library, MS. Royal 12 G. VIII, fol. 1r; quoted by Burnett 1984, p. 155).

Text. Carmody lists nine manuscripts, which vary in length from 11 to 269 folios, but whether from abridgment, interpolation, or truncation is not always evident. I have used the only one that he examined, simply because it was evident from his description that it contained a section on planetary properties: Oxford, Bodleian Library, MS. Digby 149, fols. 210r–212v (14th century, according to Carmody). I have worked from prints made from a microfilm master by the Oxford University printer.

Planetary properties. These appear in an untitled section that Carmody numbers XIII. Each of the seven planets is treated separately, from Saturn downwards to the Moon. Three of the nine "judges" apparently had nothing to say about the nature of the planets, but the compiler extracts the other six, always following the same order: Albumasar, Aomar/Tiberias, Jergis, Aristotle, Messahalla, and Alkindi (omitted are Abendaiat, Dorotheus, and Zahel). I transcribed the chapter on the Moon and ascertained that I already knew most of the properties from other sources, so in gathering materials for subsequent planets, I read through the *Liber novem iudicum* after I had taken notes from all my other sources and then selected relevant items that had not occurred elsewhere. I am not convinced that Dante used this source.

Bibliography. Francis J. Carmody, *Arabic Astronomical and Astrological Sciences in Latin Translations: A Critical Bibliography* (Berkeley and Los Angeles: University of California Press, 1956), pp. 103–107. C. S. F. Burnett, "An Aprocryphal Letter from the Arabic Philosopher al-Kindi to Theodore, Frederick II's Astrologer, concerning Gog and Magog, the Enclosed Nations, and the Scourge of the Mongols," *Viator* 15 (1984), 150–167. Idem, "A Group of Arabic-Latin Translators Working in Northern Spain in the Mid-12th Century," *Journal of the Royal Asiatic Society* (1977), pp. 62–108, esp. 65–66. On *Lib. nov. iud. II*, see Carmody, *Latin Translations*, pp. 107–112, and the printed edition, *Liber novem iudicum in iudiciis astrorum* (Venice: Liechtenstein, 1509); a microfilm of the Vatican copy is available as: Saint Louis University Library, "Microfilms of Rare and Out-of-Print Books," List 10 (1959), no. 34 (204 pp.). Version II is an abbreviation of I (Burnett, 1977, p. 73, n. 34).

Michael Scot

Albertus Magnus omitted Michael Scot from his list of recommended authorities on judicial astrology, and little wonder, because elsewhere Albertus dismissed him as a charlatan. Dante, of course, placed Scot in Hell among the diviners, remarking that he "truly knew the game of magic frauds" (*Inferno* 20.115–117), but, as I have argued elsewhere, Dante did not consider the science of astrology in itself to be one of those frauds. The common sin of the diviners, I maintain, was the belief that, having discovered the will of God from their study of the heavens, they attempted to evade it. Michael, moreover, mixed in a good deal of white magic with his astrology and indeed was long remembered as a magician in popular legend. Both these faults are departures from astrology proper, so Dante would have no difficulty in using Scot's technical exposition of astrology while condemning his misuse of it. Therefore I have included Scot in my list of authors, and the correctness of this decision has been confirmed by the discovery that about a quarter of Dante's astrological allusions were derived from this, apparently his favorite astrological authority.

Michael's surname, "Scot," has suggested that he was born in Scotland, but this is not certain because in the Middle Ages the term included natives of Ireland as well. This ambiguity seems to have misled the pope into conferring the archbishopric of Cashel on Michael Scot in 1224, but Michael immediately resigned on the pretext that he did not know Gaelic, and instead he was well content to receive a number of ecclesiastical benefices in Scotland and England. Since benefices were preferably conferred on natives, this exchange strongly suggests that Michael's roots were in Scotland and England. In the course of the present study, I noted that Michael uses a number of Latin words that have only been attested from British and Irish sources (documented from Latham in the footnotes), which suggests that wherever he was born, he perfected his Latin in England. Nothing more is known of his early education.

Scot first emerges into the light of history in Toledo on 18 August 1217, when he completed a Latin translation of al-Bitrûji's Arabic treatise *De motibus caelorum* with the aid of a Jewish collaborator. As he then styled himself *magister*, he had already taken a higher degree at some university, probably in the faculty of arts. Apparently Scot had then gone to Spain and learned enough Arabic to translate this and a number of other scientific works; he soon dispensed with the services of a collaborator. As a sequel to al-Bitrûji's defense of the Aristotelian system of concentric spheres, Scot translated the Arabic version of Aristotle's *De caelo* together with Averroës's major commentary on it. In addition, he produced the first Latin translation of Aristotle's *History of Animals* and several related biological works. These translations give him an important place in the transmission of Greek thought to the Latin West. Although better translations of Aristotle from the original Greek became available later in the century, Scot's versions were the ones used by the thirteenth-century scholastics. His fame as a translator caused many other translations to be attributed to him (conveniently listed by Minio-Paluello), but only the ones mentioned in this notice are definitely his work.

By 1220 Scot was in Italy, where he remained until his death, probably in 1235. At first he was living in Bologna, and he maintained cordial relations with that city: in 1231 he forecast the future of Bologna and its allies at the request of the city officials. As already noted, through papal patronage he received a series of English and Scottish benefices in 1224–1227, which presumably supported him for the rest of his life; he was a nonresident priest.

Michael's most famous Italian patron was Emperor Frederick II Hohenstaufen, to whom he dedicated a translation of Avicenna's *De animalibus* in or about 1232, as well as other undated works. Although a later generation remembered him as "astrologer to the emperor" (Salimbene), there is no contemporary evidence that this was an official position or even that he forecast events for the emperor. What is clear from Michael's own writings is that he and Frederick occasionally discussed a variety of questions concerning natural phenomena and cosmology—just the sort of questions that a curious amateur might might put to an acknowledged authority on astronomy and natural history.

Out of these conversations grew Michael Scot's most ambitious major work, an untitled trilogy that he dedicated to Frederick. The first book, the *Liber introductorius*, is a rambling introduction to astrology that is addressed to novices with more interest than background in natural science. Scot fleshes out the dry bones of professional astrology with a wealth of examples, digressions, and encyclopedic information that make his treatment more lively and engaging, though less useful, than its predecessors. The second book, the *Liber particularis*, addresses more advanced questions, including a number that were specifically posed by Frederick. The third book, the *Liber physionomiae*, deals with living creatures, notably mankind, and shows especially how human character can be deduced from physical signs. An abridged version of the last book was immensely popular in the Renaissance, when it was printed about forty times, but the rest of the trilogy remains unpublished, except for the introduction to the first book, which has been edited by Glenn Edwards. The trilogy is incomplete insofar as Scot apparently never supplied the general epilogue that he had promised in his introduction, but the author seems to have regarded each of the component books as complete because he sent each of them separately to Frederick with a preface addressed to him. Probably the epilogue was never composed because Scot never had occasion to combine the three books into a single codex. The trilogy is a vast work that must have been many years in the writing, but it cannot be dated any more precisely than to Michael Scot's fifteen years in Italy (ca. 1220–1235).

   Liber introductorius. More details on this part of Scot's trilogy are in order because it contains his list of planetary properties. Although the work includes the sort of astrological information found in other introductions to astrology, it was never so popular because it was impractically prolix (about 425,000 words). Serious astrologers did not require the elaboration that pleased Frederick, and consequently only four manuscripts survive. The work has been most intensively studied by Glenn Edwards, who is preparing a critical edition. He generously loaned me his transcript of Oxford, Bodleian library, MS. Bodley 266, fols. 150v–158r, which he had collated with Munich, Bayerische Staatsbibliothek, MS. Clm 10268, fols. 100r–105r. (The other two manuscripts, most fully described by Thorndike, are both considerably shorter.) The older of the two main manuscripts is the Munich codex (M), which is written in a north Italian hand of the first half of the fourteenth century, probably at Padua. Astronomical tables for the year 1320 have been added in a later hand on fol. 76va, which suggests that the text itself was in fact written no later than that date. The Munich manuscript, therefore, is close to Dante both in time and place. The Bodleian manuscript (B), on the other hand, was written in the fifteenth century by three hands, two Italian and one English. Although Haskins and Edwards maintain that M was the exemplar of B, Thorndike has pointed out that each text has passages not found in the other, which indicates that B is dependent on another exemplar. I found neither manuscript to be textually superior to the other; sometimes one had the better reading, sometimes the other.

   Although Edwards kindly authorized me to use his transcription of the section "De notitia planetarum" (pp. 1692–1752 of his typescript), he also advised me to use M as my base text and control it from B (the reverse of his procedure). Encouraged by the Dantesque provenance of M, I accordingly secured photocopies of both texts and followed his advice. In 1992 I collated my transcript, made from photographs, against the original manuscript of M in Munich. I am therefore responsible for the Latin text quoted in this study, but I gratefully acknowledge that Edwards's transcript facilitated my task. A critical edition of Scot's text requires an apparatus that would be out of place in the notes of the present work, so here I offer nothing more than a working text, which is based on M but with frequent tacit corrections from a photocopy of B, as well as a few emendations of my own that are indicated by <broken brackets>.

Planetary properties. Scot's treatment of planetary properties runs to about 14,000 words, which makes it by far the longest of our texts. It forms a single chapter, "De notitia planetarum" (*Liber introductorius*, distinctio 1, unnumbered chapter 3), with its own introduction in which Scot states his purpose and method: "in order to help students who are novices in this art and have a bad memory, we have gone to the trouble of collecting together everything about the form of the planets and their nature and what is proper to them both generally and specifically, to the best of our ability and to the extent of our personal experience of individual cases" (M, 100ra). After a few more preliminaries, he devotes a section to each planet, proceeding downward from Saturn to the Moon. Each section follows the same general plan: the first and larger part considers the planet in itself, while the second part describes the native of the planet.

Part one begins with physical information on the planet (location, substance, shape, color, weight) and provides a brief list of its inherent astrological qualities (Saturn is proud, cruel, sterile, etc.), after which he gives the planet's astrological symbol and names the spirit who rules the planet. Next comes a less concise discussion of the ways in which the planet is affected by other planets. Finally he turns to the significance of the planet and begins to list properties in earnest. The discussion is divided into categories, some of which are clear and traditional (e.g., colors and tastes, human ages, occupations, traits of character, religious sects), while others are vague and overlapping. For example, Jupiter signifies such things as "friendship and new friends"; it is the *significator* of movable property, with many examples; it has certain tempering effects on the elements. For most of part one, the organization is neither better nor worse than earlier lists, although harder to follow because of the length of Scot's lists, but towards the end he tends to repeat himself, for instance in yet another discussion of the nature of Jupiter. Probably these repetitions are undigested addenda; certainly they confuse the reader and justify Scot's reputation for disorganization. Towards the end of part one he regularly gives a conventional representation of the planet as a seven-rayed star; the transition to part two is further marked by a rubric, e.g., "De transumptione Iovis in hominem viventem et qualiter eum format moribus et figura corporis" (M, 101ra). As announced, the second part describes the planet's natives with special attention to moral and physical character traits. Here Scot is treating astrological influences not as causes but as symptoms that can be observed; it is the same distinctive approach that led him to append the *Liber physionomiae* to his two books on astrology proper. The second section repeats much that had already been said in the first section, but the repetition is deliberate, methodical, and rationally justifiable.

Bibliography. Lorenzo Minio-Paluello, "Michael Scot," *Dictionary of Scientific Biography* 9:361–365, gives an excellent critical summary and extensive bibliography. The best longer treatment is still Charles Homer Haskins, *Studies in the History of Mediaeval Science*, Harvard Historical Studies no. 27 (Cambridge, Mass.: Harvard University Press, 1924), pp. 272–298. Lynn Thorndike, *Michael Scot* (London: Nelson, 1965), is detailed but diffuse; more useful is his article, "Manuscripts of Michael Scot's *Liber Introductorius*," in *Didascaliae: Studies in Honor of Anselm M. Albareda*, ed. Sesto Prete (New York: Bernard M. Rosenthal, 1961), pp. 425–447. On the text, see Glenn M. Edwards, "The *Liber introductorius* of Michael Scot" (Ph.D. diss., University of Southern California, 1978) and Piero Morpurgo, "Il *Liber introductorius* di Michele Scoto: Prime indicazioni interpretative," *Atti della Accademia nazionale dei Lincei, Rendiconti della classe di scienze morali, storiche e filologiche* ser. 8, vol. 34 (1979), 151–161. Ulrike Bauer, *Der "Liber introductorius" des Michael Scotus in der Abschrift Clm 10268 der Bayerischen SB München* (Munich: Tuduv Verlagsgesellschaft, 1983). R. Kay, "The Spare Ribs of Dante's Michael Scot," *Dante Studies* 103 (1985), 1–14.

Guido Bonatti

"I saw Guido Bonatti," Dante says, immediately after mentioning Michael Scot (*Inf.* 20.118). Each wrote an extensive introduction to astrology, and I have included both works among my sources for this study even though they were ignored by Albertus Magnus. Results justified this decision, for Bonatti yielded 15 percent of the relevant allusions, taking second place only to Scot.

Bonatti's life can be documented more fully than any other astrologer used for this study, but the materials are still little more than anecdotal glimpses and autobiographical asides, both of which are difficult to piece together into a coherent whole. Quite a few reconstructions have been attempted only to be more or less demolished. Probably the safest approach is that taken by Cesare Vasoli, who has reviewed the evidence scrap by scrap, but I shall attempt yet another synthesis, which for the most part will be based on the firmer facts.

Guido Bonatti was born in Forlì and, except for brief absences, lived there all his life. He was a landowner and played a prominent part in local politics, engineering the downfall of one city boss, Simone Mestaguerra (1255–1257), and serving as the the chief adviser to another, Guido da Montefeltro (1275–1283). He was born around 1210, give or take as much as a decade, and died circa 1297, give or take a year.

Bonatti practiced medicine as well as the closely allied discipline of astrology, but where he received his training is not certain. From his own account of the revivalist John of Vicenza, we know that Bonatti was in Bologna in 1233. At that time Bologna was the university town closest to Forlì, and it was already a center for physicians and medical students, even though formal academic instruction and degrees in medicine only appear there a generation later. These facts suggest that most likely he learned both his medicine and astrology in Bologna.

As an astrologer, he attached himself exclusively to patrons who were Ghibellines. An admirer of Frederick II, Guido warned him in 1246 by letter from Forlì of a plot he had discovered in the stars, but he was never an intimate of the emperor as Michael Scot was. As far as we know, his career as a courtier was limited to three consecutive years beginning in 1259, when he was with Ezzelino da Romano at Brescia and witnessed his downfall and death at the hands of the Guelfs. Soon thereafter he joined the entourage of Guido Novello I dei conti Guidi, the Ghibelline leader in Tuscany, whom he accompanied at the battle of Montaperti (September 1260) and on a raid against Lucca (September 1261). In the meantime, the triumphant Ghibellines employed him as "astrologer of the commune of Florence," which he represented in the conclusion of a treaty with Siena in November 1260.

By 1264, Guido was back at Forlì, where he remained for over thirty years. There he was well placed to serve the Ghibelline cause again, however, for Guido da Montefeltro made Forlì the party's stronghold in the Romagna from 1275 until 1283, and Guido Bonatti was his right-hand man. He devoted his last years to the completion of his masterpiece, the *Liber astronomicus*, which can be dated after 1277 by an internal reference to the battle of Valbona. He was still living in 1296, when a document named him as one of the leading citizens of Forlì, but he was dead when his former patron, Guido da Montefeltro, died in September 1298.

Liber astronomicus. This is a comprehensive treatise on astrology, comparable to similar works by Albumasar, Haly, John of Seville, and Michael Scot, but longer than most (424 folio-size pages in the 1550 edition). It is addressed to beginners—ostensibly to the author's nephew, Bonatto—in terms so clear that a chronicler of Forlì observed that "it seemed as if he wanted to teach astrology to women." Like his predecessors, Bonatti began with an introduction to the elements of the subject (books 1–4); he went on to treat judicial astrology, first in general (book 5) and then in each of its parts (interrogations, elections, revolutions, and nativities, in books 6–9), with a final book on weather prediction (10). Much of the work consists of extracts from earlier authorities: e.g., almost all of Alcabitius's planetary properties are repeated verbatim, often with explanatory phrases by Bonatti interpolated. His greatest virtue is clarity, which he achieves by glossing his sources and by illustrating them with examples. The author had little new to say about astrological theory, but he was able to offer much practical advice based on his forty years of experience. The most original part of the work is book 5, which presents 146 general *considerationes* to keep in mind when forming astrological judgments: it was translated into English by William Lilly (1676).

The result was the most successful Latin treatise on astrology of the period. Bonatti's approach was more professional than Scot's, because he limited himself to technical astrology, and accordingly he found a wider audience. His book did not replace the Arabic treatises on which it was based, but it was valued because it showed how their principles could be applied to the needs of a Christian society (e.g., Bonatti explains how to predict not only whether a querent will attain high ecclesiastical office but also which one—bishop, abbot, cardinal, pope, and so on). He himself was a layman who repeatedly expressed his hostility to the clergy, and especially the Mendicants. Nonetheless, by bridging the gap between Moslem and Christian culture, Bonatti was particularly useful to Dante.

The *Liber astronomicus* has been printed four times: Augsburg, 1491; Venice, 1506; and Basel, 1530 and 1550. The *editio princeps* is available in the microcard series, "Landmarks of Science" (New York: Readex, 1974), but I have worked from a microfilm of the copy of the 1550 text at Harvard University.

Planetary properties. Bonatti devotes the whole of his third book to the planets and begins with their properties: *Liber introductorius*, tractatus 3, chapters 1–7 (ed. 1550, cols. 97–119). The scope of the treatment is elaborated in the title: "On the seven planets, and what is proper to them, and what the planet signifies concerning the essence of every thing in accordance with its own essence and with the nature of things, and what the planets imprint on things beneath them according to the diverse quality of their motions" (col. 91). Altogether these seven chapters run to about 9300 words, which is a third shorter than Scot's treatment but still is considerably longer than any of the other lists. Alcabitius supplied Bonatti with his basic material and organization.

Bibliography. Cesare Vasoli, "Bonatti, Guido," *Dizionario biografico degli Italiani*, vol. 11 (Rome: Istituto della Enciclopedia italiana, 1969), pp. 603–608, surveys the evidence but is occasionally careless. Augusto Vasina, "Bonatti, Guido," *Enciclopedia dantesca*, 1:668–669, especially for Bonatti at Forlì and for Dantists' studies of him. Lynn Thorndike, *A History of Magic and Experimental Science*, vol. 2 (New York: Columbia University Press, 1923), pp. 825–835, for an analysis of the *Liber astronomiae*. Francis J. Carmody, *Arabic Astronomical and Astrological Sciences in Latin Translations: A Critical Bibliography* (Berkeley and Los Angeles: University of California Press, 1956), p. 172.

Appendix 2:
Planetary Positions for Paradiso

The influence of a given planet can be modified by its position either in the zodiac or in relation to another planet. To explore Dante's possible use of these relative values one must accordingly know where each of the seven planets was placed in the zodiac at the ideal date of the *Paradiso*. This determination requires some assumptions. First, we must decide what tables of planetary positions to consult. Modern ones, such as those compiled by Bryant Tuckerman, are precise but do not agree with the ones available to Dante. I have adopted the set prepared by Profatius (Jacob ben Machir ben Tibbon), edited by J. Boffito and C. Melzi d'Eril as *Almanach Dantis Aligherii, sive Profhacii Judaei Montispessulani "Almanach perpetuum" ad annum 1300 inchoatum* (Florence: Olschki, 1908).

From these tables one can calculate the planetary positions for a given day and year. I use 14 April 1300 as the date when the Pilgrim was in Paradise, in accordance with G. Buti and R. Bertagni, *Commento astronomico della "Divina Commedia"* (Florence: Sandron, 1966), table I. For this date Profatius (ed. cit., p. 130) gives the positions listed in the accompanying figure. Like all Profatius's data, these are calculated as of noon at the meridian of Montpellier (3° 53′ E. Long.). If we were constructing a horoscope, which would show the positions relative to another place and/or time on earth, these figures would have to be adjusted accordingly. But since in Paradise Beatrice and the Pilgrim are not on earth but instead move from planet to planet, the unadjusted figures for noon at Montpellier suffice to show the relative positions of the planets and signs on 14 April 1300. The resultant relationships between planets and signs can most readily be appreciated by plotting the positions on a chart of the ecliptic, as in the accompanying figure.

The most striking feature of the chart is the conjunction of four planets in Taurus—Jupiter, Venus, Mercury, and the Sun. Although Venus is about 10° distant from the others, and hence not strictly in conjunction according to many astrologers, yet Alcabitius reckoned all planets in the

PLANETARY POSITIONS FOR 14 APRIL 1300

Saturn	♄	126°	6° 49' 30"
Jupiter	♃	32°	2° 58' 30"
Mars	♂	8°	8° 53' 9"
Sun	☉	32°	2° 8' 33"
Venus	♀	42°	12° 49' 12"
Mercury	☿	32°	2° 24' 0" retrograde
Moon	☽	316°	16° 41' 13"

♈ Aries	♌ Leo	♐ Sagittarius
♉ Taurus	♍ Virgo	♑ Capricorn
♊ Gemini	♎ Libra	♒ Aquarius
♋ Cancer	♏ Scorpio	♓ Pisces

same sign to be in conjunction (ed. 1521, f. 4r). This cluster of conjunct planets forms a square (*tetragon*) with both Saturn and the Moon, which are in direct opposition to one another. Mars, the malignant planet, stands largely apart from the others, although it is "trine" to—that is, more or less 120° from Saturn—an aspect Alcabitius says is one "of concord and perfect affection—*concordie et dilectionis perfecte*" (ibidem).

The astrological interpretation of this chart and its application to the *Commedia* would be a study in itself, and not an easy one, because astrologers differed as to what constituted a significant aspect. See, for example, J. D. North, *Chaucer's Universe* (New York: Oxford University Press, 1988), pp. 208–213. The chart here is given chiefly as a convienient reference, but it it is worth observing that the striking symmetry of this planetary configuration, which is by no means common, may have played its part in Dante's choice of an ideal date for the *Comedy*. Those who would place the *Comedy* in 1301 on astronomical grounds will find that the corresponding day in Paradise that year (31 March) is far less significant astrologically speaking (data in Profatius, ed. cit., p. 131).

Notes

Introduction

1. *Conv.* 2.13.8, 28–29; 2.3.4, 6; 4.15–16, trans. Jackson here and throughout this chapter.

2. *Speculum astronomiae* 1.3, ed. August Borgnet, *Opera*, 10 (Paris: Vivès, 1891), 630, 633.

3. Roy J. Deferrari, *A Latin-English Dictionary of St. Thomas Aquinas* (Boston: St. Paul Editions, 1960), s.v. "astrologus" and "astronomia."

4. Lynn Thorndike, *University Records and Life in the Middle Ages*, Records of Civilization—Sources and Studies, no. 38 (New York: Columbia University Press, 1944; rpt., New York: Norton, 1971), pp. 281–282. In general, see Richard Lemay, "The Teaching of Astronomy in Medieval Universities, Principally at Paris in the Fourteenth Century," *Manuscripta* 20 (1976), 197–217.

5. *Speculum astronomiae* 1: "De divisione magnae sapientae astronomiae in theoricam scilicet, et practicam" (ed. Borgnet, 10:630).

6. *Speculum astronomiae* 3: "doceat nos qualiter mundanorum ad hoc et ad illud mutatio, coelestium fiat corporum mutatione" (ed. Borgnet, 10:633).

7. Busnelli and Vandelli, 2:190–191 ad *Conv.* 2.13.5.

8. Thus Grandgent, Sapegno, and Singleton, as well as Toynbee, s.v. "Serse."

9. Before this process can be effective, the will itself must be trained, and thus Marco goes on to explain how law serves as a bridle to the will (*Purg.* 16.85–96).

10. *Ep.* 5.8.23. ed. P. Toynbee, *Dantis Alagherii Epistolae; The Letters of Dante* (Oxford: Clarendon Press, 1920), pp. 55, 61: "simpliciter interest humanae apprehensioni, ut per motum coeli motorem intelligamus et eius velle."

11. *Rime* 43 (100) in *Opere minore*, 1.1, ed. D. De Robertis and G. Contini, La Letteratura italiana: Storia e testi (Milan: Ricciardi, 1984); no. 77 in K. Foster and P. Boyde, *Dante's Lyric Poetry* (Oxford: Clarendon Press, 1967). The astrological allusions have been most fully recognized by Robert M. Durling, "'Io son venuto': Seneca, Plato, and the Microcosm," *Dante Studies* 93 (1975), 95–129, esp. pp. 112–113 and n. 41, pp. 126–127. The investigation begun in Durling's essay has subsequently been richly elaborated in Robert M. Durling and Ronald L. Martinez, *Time and the Crystal: Studies in Dante's "Rime petrose"* (Berkeley: University of California Press, 1990), pp. 71–108.

12. Apparently cited from Albertus *De meteoris* 1.4.9, according to Paget

Toynbee, *Dante Studies and Researches* (London, 1902; rpt., Port Washington, N.Y.: Kennikat Press, 1971), pp. 39–40.

13. Correctly translated by Vinay and by Nardi; wrongly by Vianello, Meozzi, Wicksteed, Schneider, and Nicholl. See *Monarchia*, ed. Gustavo Vinay (Florence: Sansoni, 1950), pp. 284–286.

14. *Enciclopedia dantesca*, 1:427–431, s.v. "astrologia," by I. Capasso and G. Tabarroni.

15. Edward Moore, *Studies in Dante: Third Series* (Oxford: Clarendon Press, 1903; rpt. New York: Greenwood Press, 1968), pp. 1–106, with astrology at pp. 19–21.

16. Patrick Boyde, *Dante Philomythes and Philosopher: Man in the Cosmos* (Cambridge: Cambridge University Press, 1981), pp. 132–171, 250–253.

17. M. A. Orr, *Dante and the Early Astronomers* (London, 1913; 2nd ed., Port Washington, N.Y.: Kennikat Press, 1956).

18. I. Capasso, *L'Astronomia nella Divina Commedia* (Pisa: Domus Galilaeana, 1967).

19. C. Gizzi, *L'Astronomia nel Poema sacro*, 2 vols. (Naples: Loffredo, 1974).

20. Paolo Pecoraro, *Le Stelle di Dante: Saggio d'interpretazione di riferimenti astronomici e cosmografici della Divina Commedia* (Rome: Bulzoni, 1987).

21. G. Buti and R. Bertagni, *Commento astronomico della Divina Commedia* (Florence: Sandron, 1966).

22. R. Piccoli, *Astrologia dantesca* (Florence: Aldino, 1909); A. Barzon, "L'Astrologia in Dante," in *Miscellanea dantesca pubblicato a cura del Comitato cattolico padovano per il VI° centenario dalla morte del poeta* (Padua: Tipografia del Seminario, 1922); and E. Pasteris, "Astrologia e libertà nella Divina Commedia," *La Scuola cattolica* 14 (1929), 348–358; ibid. 15 (1930), 38–56, 433–455; and ibid. 16 (1930), 93–118. Dante's use of astrology was also explored by Rudolf Palgen, *Dantes Sternglaube* (Heidelberg: Winter, 1940), with particular attention to Firmicus Maternus and Macrobius; this limited range of astrological authors was not expanded in his subsequent studies, which instead stressed Neoplatonic parallels to Plato, Plotinus, and Avicenna: e.g., his *Werden und Wesen der Komödie Dantes* (Graz: Styria, 1955). See also Georg Rabuse, *Der kosmische Aufbau der Jenseitsreiche Dantes* (Graz: Böhlaus, 1958) and his collected studies, *Gesammelte Aufsätze zu Dante*, ed. Erika Kanduth, F. P. Kirsch, and S. Löwe (Vienna: Braumüller, 1976).

23. For example, Aristotle is one of the authors who is regularly extracted in the astrological anthology, the *Liber novem iudicum* (Oxford, Bodleian Library, MS Digby 149).

24. See above, n. 4. At the University of Paris both works were studied in 1358, when Master Robert the Norman was authorized to lecture on these texts in his home on feast days: Guy Beaujouan, "Motives and Opportunities for Science in the Medieval Universities," in *Scientific Change*, ed. A. C. Crombie (New York: Basic Books, 1963), pp. 219–236, at p. 222.

25. Richard Kay, "Dante's Double Damnation of Manto," *Res Publica Litterarum* 1 (1978), 113–128, at p. 123.

26. The earliest form of the story is given by Ricobaldo of Ferrara (fl. 1298), *Historia imperatorum* sub an. 1233, ed. L. Muratori, *Rerum Italicarum scriptores* 9

(Milan: Societas palatina, 1726), 128; Dantists know it in the later version related by Benvenuto of Imola.

27. *Liber phisionomie magistri Michaelis Scoti* (Venice: I. B. Sessa, 1503), c. 88. This interpretation is developed in my article, "The Spare Ribs of Dante's Michael Scot," *Dante Studies* 103 (1985), 1–14.

28. J. D. North, *Chaucer's Universe* (New York: Oxford University Press, 1988) and J. Michael Richardson, *Astrological Symbolism in Spenser's "The Shepheardes Calender": The Cultural Background of a Literary Text*, Studies in Renaissance Literature 1 (Lewiston, N.Y.: Mellen Press, 1989).

29. Al-Biruni, *The Book of Instruction in the Elements of the Art of Astrology*, trans. R. R. Wright (London: Luzac, 1934), pp. 240–254, §§ 396–435. In the following sample, I have paraphrased and slightly regrouped the rubrics of Wright's translation.

30. *Enciclopedia dantesca*, 1:102.

31. *Speculum astronomiae* 6 (ed. Borgnet, 10:636). The properties of planets are treated in the preceding chapter.

32. Francis J. Carmody, *Arabic Astronomical and Astrological Sciences in Latin Translation: A Critical Bibliography* (Berkeley and Los Angeles: University of California Press, 1956).

33. Zahel (Sahl), *Introductorium*, in the untitled astrological omnibus printed by Bonetus Locatellus (Venice, 1493), fols. 122v-138r (Carmody, pp. 13, 40–41; copy in library of the College of Physicians, Philadelphia); this treats some aspects of judicial astrology but not the properties. Ptolemy, *De iudiciis ad Aristonem*, in the omnibus printed by Petrus Liechtenstein (Venice, 1509), fols. 1–14 (Carmody, pp. 13, 17; copies at the University of Chicago and Lehigh University); this does treat planetary properties, but only very briefly (fol. 3v); it was discarded because it added nothing new or different.

34. Exceptions: Ptolemy is cited in the usual classical form; manuscript sources are identified by a siglum followed by a folio reference; column numbers are indicated for Bonatti's work, which is much longer than the others.

35. To be more precise, I made out about six thousand cards and retained about two thousand of them.

36. Edward Moore, *Studies in Dante: First Series* (Oxford: Clarendon Press, 1896; rpt. New York: Greenwood Press, 1968).

Chapter 1: The Moon

1. See above, Introduction, pp. 2, 4–7.

2. Ptolemy, *Quadripartitum* 1.6. John of Seville: "Est foeminina stella." Scot: "Genus eius est feminina" (M, 104rb), and similarly Alcabitius and Bonatti. Ibn Ezra says the Moon signifies "mulieres."

3. Albumasar: "parum venerea."

4. Alcabitius and Bonatti. For Scot, the Moon signifies "honestatem" in general (M, 104rb).

5. Albumasar: "maioresque sorores." John of Seville: "sororibus maiori-bus." Ibn Ezra: "sorores et sororum maiores." *Lib. nov. iud.*: "sorores maiores" (B, 212rb).

6. "Matres" in Albumasar, Alcabitius, John of Seville, Ibn Ezra, and Bonatti.

7. *Lib. nov. iud.*: "amitas" (B, 212rb). According to Alcabitius, the Moon signifies maternal aunts (*materteras*).

8. To be sure, the connection has long been recognized in a general, and usually not specifically astrological, way: e.g., Victoria Kirkham, "A Canon of Women in Dante's 'Commedia,' *Annali d'Italianistica* 7 (1989), 16–41, at p. 28: "Costanza, and Piccarda (whose cloister name was said to be also Costanza) dwell in a planet of mutability and inconstancy."

9. *The Catholic Encyclopedia*, 12:253.

10. *Enciclopedia dantesca*, 2:565, citing Ezio Levi, *Piccarda e Gentucca* (Bologna: Zanichelli, 1921).

11. According to Omar, the Lunar type of slave dealer is one who traffics in virgins: "vendunt de hominibus virgines." Quoted in *Lib. nov. iud.* (B, 212rb).

12. Albumasar: "intentio in scientias, legem, altorumque contemplationem, tam et carminum."

13. *Lib. nov. iud.*: "cogitationi anime rursum affectione" (B, 212ra).

14. Alcabitius: "Et ex fide, [Luna significat] religionem." *Lib. nov. iud.* similarly associates the Moon with "religiones" (B, 212ra).

15. Scot: "Ex sectis fidei significat vitam sanctam et asperam ut heremita, religionem ut plus feminarum quam virorum" (M, 104rb).

16. She is said to have been the first to take the veil at her father's newly founded Basilian nunnery of St. Savior's in Palermo: Lynn T. White, jr., *Latin Monasticism in Norman Sicily*, Mediaeval Academy of America Publication 31 (Cambridge, Mass.: Mediaeval Academy of America, 1938), pp. 43, 125.

17. *The Oxford Dictionary of the Christian Church*, ed. F. L. Cross (London: Oxford University Press, 1957), p. 254. The poverty of the Poor Clares is consonant with the Moon's association with the poor ("pauperes"): Scot (M, 104rb).

18. L. Di Fonzo locates Clare "forse nel terzultimo cielo (Saturno), quello dei santi di vita contemplativa": *Enciclopedia dantesca*, 1:954.

19. *RB 1980: The Rule of St. Benedict in Latin and English with Notes*, ed. Timothy Fry et al. (Collegeville, Minn.: Liturgical Press, 1981), pp. 464–465.

20. Possibily Dante may have viewed Clare as a female follower of Benedict's *Rule* because the Tuscan form of the Poor Clares' rule was explicitly derived from that of Benedict. First adopted in 1219 at the same convent of Monticello near Florence where Piccarda professed, this rule in its primitive form began: "Regulam beatissimi Benedicti vobis tradimus observandam . . ." (*Catholic Encyclopedia*, 12:252).

21. On the distinction between the absolute and conditioned will, see *Par.* 4.64–111, esp. 109–111.

22. Bonatti: "Et ex fide significat religionem, quoniam lunares ut multum fiunt religiosi, et maxime in iuventute: tamen aliquando non bene servant promissa deo: et raro bene perseverant in religionibus: et fiunt exinde fabule vulgi."

23. *Enciclopedia dantesca*, 2:240, 565.

24. Bonatti: "Et habet significare indumenta nigra, et eos qui naturaliter nigris vestibus utuntur tam religiosos seu claustrales, quam alios."

25. Ptolemy, *Quad.* 1.4: "Its [chief] action therefore is precisely this, to soften and cause putrefaction in bodies" (trans. Robbins, p. 35).

26. Albumasar: "Omnibus motibus accomodata et accepta nihilominus."

27. Haly: "nec est firmus in aliqua re: nec amorem habet nec amicitiam completam."

28. Ibn Ezra: "et universaliter ad omnes est conversiva naturas."

29. Scot: "signficant res . . . brevis perseverantis dum advenerit. Causa est quia parum perseverat in signo, et mutatio signo mutatur influentia" (M, 104rb).

30. Scot: "Est levis, et ideo levia significat futuorum cum brevitate perseverantie" (M, 104rb).

31. Scot: "In genere est planeta femininus . . . sepe falax, cito convertibilius ad utrumque, et quod significatione promittat cito perficit, et illud parum durat" (M, 104va).

32. Scot: "Hic quidem planeta semper alteri promittit quodlibet cum dubietate et parva perseverantia rei ut timorem, paupertatem, laborem et cetera. Unde luna semper significat personam simplicem, vanam, cito convertabilem ad·utrumque" (M, 104va).

33. Scot: "In etate [Luna] est ut forma puelle formose cuius promissio est plena dubietate, ut spes viri propter puellam quam diligit et peroptat propter effectum sui ipsium, quia modo crescit, modo decrescit; et cum quis credit quod ipsa faciat bonum, tempus facit contrarium vel e contrario. Et sic de aliis per tempora et etates sui. Planeta femininus est et ideo dicitur esse debilis, timidus, pauci fortitudinis, brevis potentie, et dicitur dea fortune per causam" (M, 104rb).

34. Scot: "proprietas est motus, instabilitas, et facilitas conversionis a re in rem, ut de bono in malum et econtro" (M, 104rb).

35. Scot: "Significatio fame: . . . facile convertibilis" (M, 105rv).

36. Scot: "significat res . . . de quibus non est diu sperandum longa stabilitate, ut roris, pluvie, algoris, planctus viatoris naute, et cetera (M, 104rb).

37. See e.g., the commentaries of Sapegno and of Singleton to *Par.* 4.100–114.

38. Latin translation of *Nic. Eth.* 3.1, 1110a4 as printed in Thomas Aquinas, *In decem libros Ethicorum Aristotelis ad Nicomachum expositio*, ed. R. M. Spiazzi, 3rd ed. (Turin: Marietti, 1964), p. 111, text no. 243.

39. Ibn Ezra: "timorosus . . . minime magnanimus."

40. Scot: "significat res debiles et que fiunt cum timore et cum parva virtute" (M, 104rb).

41. Scot: "Ex facili est pavidus, quietus, ubique satis obediens et servicialis alteri, multum vanus in volendo rem et nolendo" (M, 104vb). Cf. "timidus," above, n. 33.

42. Scot: "Potentia . . . eius est debilis," and "Sensus eius est . . . simplex et fatigabilis" (M, 105rv).

43. Albumasar: "corporum saluti studiosa."

44. Scot: "Que vita eius est . . . pacifica de omni" (M, 105rv).

45. Scot: "Gratia in altero: . . . pia, condolens, et servitialis" (M, 105rv).

46. *RB 1980*, p. 465. In medieval Latin, the term *servitus* signified both serfdom and the monastic life: *Revised Medieval Latin Word-List from British and Irish Sources*, ed. R. E. Latham (London: published for the British Academy by the Oxford University Press, 1965), p. 436.

47. According to the *Lib. nov. iud.* (B, 212rb), another Lunar role by consanguinity is paternal aunt; see n. 7, above.

48. Albumasar: "matrone, coniugia, gravide, nutritura; et nutrices, matres." Only "coniugia" in *Lib. nov. iud.* (B, 212rb).

49. John of Seville: "uxore."

50. Albumasar: "eius [Lunae] sunt . . . parum venerea."

51. In passing it should be noted that Dante seems to have made little use here of the doctrine of the four temperaments, according to which the cold and moist qualities of the Moon combined to produce the phlegmatic temperament or complexion. In this he seems to have been following his astrological authorities, who considered the presence of phlegm to be a medical condition that did not produce psychological side-effects. The *Lib. nov. iud.* lists a series of Lunar traits, including "frigida et humida, flegmatica" (B, 212ra), which does nothing more than describe the composition of phlegm. Ibn Ezra mentions phlegm clearly only in connection with sickness: "Morbique illius [Lunae] sunt omnes ex flegmatis superexcrescentia contingentes." Alcabitius distinguishes the tempered phlegm of the Moon from the colder phlegm of Saturn, and he is followed in this by Robertus Anglicus in his commentary on Alcabitius, ed. Lynn Thorndike, *The "Sphere" of Sacrobosco and Its Commentators* (Chicago: University of Chicago Press, 1949), p. 156. Bonatti repeats Alcabitius on this point, but otherwise he mentions Lunar phlegm only in connection with sickness: "ex egritudinibus frigidis et humidis, ut flegmaticis." Likewise for Scot the Moon's phlegm appears only in medical contexts: "Luna tenet naturaliter in persona cerebrum, fleugma, pulmonem" (M, 104va), and "Que [planetae, sc. Lunae] infirmitas [est] . . . flegmatis" (M, 105rv). On the incomplete assimilation of humor psychology to Arabic astrology and its direct Latin descendants, see R. Klibansky, E. Panofsky, and F. Saxl, *Saturn and Melancholy: Studies in the History of Natural Philosophy, Religion, and Art* (New York: Basic Books, 1964), pp. 127–133, esp. n. 10.

52. The ultimate source is Messehalla's indications *de figuris hominum*; as quoted by Alcabitius, the Moon gives one a "pulcrum statum." The remark is repeated verbatim by Robertus Anglicus (ed. Thorndike [n. 51, above], p. 156) and by Bonatti. The 1521 edition of Alcabitius garbles it to "pulchram staturam" (12r). According to Scot, the *Lunaris* is beautiful in appearance: "Parissibilitas: pulcher, convenienter pinguis" (M, 105rv).

53. Chiefly because they do not regularly give indications as to jewels. Al-Biruni, an Arabic astrologer unknown to the Latin West, does assign pearls to the Moon in his list of the astrological affinities of jewels: *The Book of Instruction in the Elements of the Art of Astrology*, trans. R. R. Wright (London: Luzac, 1934), p. 243.

54. Scot: "Ex figuris hominum significat hominem . . . in pelle album vel quasi brunum cum pauco colore vel quasi nullo" (M, 104va), and "Luna facit naturaliter hominem . . . faciem quasi sine colore" (M, 104vb). Scot is here conflating

two traditions. On the one hand, al-Biruni (n. 53, above) took the Moon's color to be white (p. 240), so it gave a "clear white complexion" (p. 249); on the other, Moon colors for Ibn Ezra were dusty and green as well as white ("Colorum albus et pulverulentus ac viridis"), so for him the Lunar complexion was accordingly dusky: "aspectu albus, modice glaucedini admixtus."

55. Scot: "Hic quidem planeta [Luna] in eius promissione est valde falax" (M, 104rb).

56. Scot: "modum cito credendi alteri que audi dici, sepe falacia proposita faciendi" (M, 104rb), and "Testimonio alteri est . . . sepe falsidica" (M, 105rv). Cf. Albumasar: "mendacium delatio."

57. Scot: "Moralitas eius est . . . mediocriter in laude et vituperatio" (M, 105rv).

58. Albumasar: "tenuis memoria." Ibn Ezra: "plurimum obliviosus." Scot: "facilem oblivionem mentis" (M, 104rb).

59. Bonatti: "Et cum fuerit sub radiis Solis, significat secreta et occulta: significat etiam occultanda: unde tunc est bonum tractare et facere ea quae occultanda sunt, illa scilicet quae volumus populo latere, antequam separetur a Sole. Illa vero quae volumus occultari ad tempus postquam fuerit separata a Sole antequam exeat de sub radiis Solis. . . . Et ab hora separationis suae a Sole significat apertationem exitus ab occultatione." Scot has a more precise formulation: the Moon signifies secrets only when it is in combustion, i.e., within 15° of the Sun (M, 104va). Bonatti's basic conception comes from Alcabitius: "Et cum fuerit [Luna] sub radiis Solis, significat secreta et res occultas."

60. According to the ecclesiastical calendar, the Moon was full, and hence in opposition to the Sun, during the night Dante spent in the *Selva oscura* (*Inf.* 20.127), and consequently it had been on the wane for five nights at the time of Dante's visit to the Moon. It was still "full," however, since medieval astrologers and modern almanacs alike consider the Moon to be full during the seven days it takes to pass through the 90° from opposition to the third quarter: e.g., Bonatti, cols. 117–118. On the real new Moon (5 April 1300) versus the calendar one (7 April), see Edward Moore, *The Time-References in the "Divina Commedia"* (London: Nutt, 1887), pp. 16–19, 34–41.

61. Scot: "Luna semper significat personam simplicem"; "Ex figuris hominum [Luna] significat hominem . . . plus simplicem quam bene sapientem"; "Simplicior est quam sapiens per se" (M, 104va). For Bonatti, the Moon "significat . . . cogitationem . . . et debilitatem ingenii atque sensus."

62. Scot: "Luna operatur frigitatem et humiditatem, et significat naturaliter dominium omnium frigidorum et humidorum, quorum est omnino significatrix, ut feminarum, maris, et flegmatis" (M, 104rb). The tradition goes back to Ptolemy, *Quad.* 1.4, and is echoed by Bonatti, citing Albumasar and Alcabitius.

63. Scot: "Ex substantia [Luna] significat . . . aquam" (M, 104rb).

64. Scot: "roris, pluvie" (M, 104rb) and "maris" (above, n. 62). Ibn Ezra adds rivers: "Et ipsius est flumina, maria. . . ."

65. Scot: "et omne opus quod fit cum aqua" (M, 104rb), e.g., "nauta, marinarius . . . piscator" (M, 104vb; mariners also on 104rb). Ibn Ezra associates the Moon with fishmarkets ("piscarie"). Alcabitius simply states that the Moon "ex

operibus habet . . . opera aquarum" without giving specific examples, and Bonatti follows him. Cf. *Lib. nov. iud.*: "Et que ad terram et aquas negotia pertinent" (B, 212ra).

66. Without inconsistency Dante adds: "e scalda sì, che più e più m'avviva" (*Par.* 4.120), since water can be warm. Albumasar expressly notes that the Moon is not necessarily cold but can sometimes be warm: "frigida accidentaliter, interdum calida." Ptolemy had already said that the Moon "shares moderately in heating power because of the light which it receives from the sun" (*Quad.* 1.4, trans. Robbins, p. 35). The vivifying effect ("m'avviva") could also have been suggested by Ibn Ezra's assertion that the Moon could ripen fruit when in opposition to the Sun, as was the case at the ideal time of the poem (see n. 60, above): "Et cum in solis oppositione fuerit fructus omnes maturat. Et in ipsius parte est nature vigor." *Lib. nov. iud.* may be following Albumasar: "Luna . . . frigida et humida, flegmatica, accidentaliter calida" (B, 212ra).

67. For nurses, see above, n. 48. Cf. Bonatti: "[Luna] significat matres et materteras et praebetrices ciborum: sciet enim natus praebere cibaria aliis."

68. Albumasar: "substantia cum victualibus."

69. Alcabitius: "nutritiones parvulorum . . . et preparationes ciborum."

70. Haly: "Omnis fructus aque aperitur per eam [Lunam]. . . . Luna est unus trium planetarum pluvias facientium, et per applicationem et demonstrationem ipsius scietur habundantia vel charistia precii panis."

71. *Dictionary of Philosophy*, ed. Dagobert D. Runes (Ames, Iowa: University of Iowa Press, 1955), p. 42.

72. John of Seville: "Est eius [Lunae] argentum, vaccae, pecudes."

73. Ibn Ezra: "Animalium: muli, asini, ovile, lupus, et pisces."

74. Ibn Ezra: "Et avium omnis alba, et serpientium omne album."

75. Scot: "Hic quidem homo [Lunaris] naturaliter se delectabitur in arte levi et gravi, id est mediocritatis unius, cuiusque tam laboris magni quam parvi, et perdite quam lucri, et ideo fragili et vili, ut est esse . . . pastor gregis . . ." (M, 104vb).

76. See above, n. 32.

77. For Ibn Ezra, the color of the Moon attracts birds and creeping things of that color to it (n. 74, above), and perhaps salt is there for the same reason as well. *Lib. nov. iud.* takes the Moon to indicate white clothing ("de vestibus candidas," B, 212rb).

78. Scot: "Color eius . . . argenti puri" (M, 105rv), and "Planeta . . . cuius color est ut argenti boni et purissimi lustratera" (M, 104ra–b).

79. Silver is categorized as a metal by Ibn Ezra and as a substance by Alcabitius and Bonatti. *Lib. nov. iud.* refers silver merchants to the Moon (B, 212rb).

80. Above, n. 66.

81. Alcabitius: "Et ex operibus [Luna] habet legationes et mandata." Bonatti quotes him to this effect.

82. Albumasar: "eius sunt . . . nuncii, mandata." Ibn Ezra mentions only "nuncii."

83. Scot: "[Luna] significat . . . legationes, . . . precepta, nuntios" (M, 104rb).

84. Aquinas, *Summa theologiae* I q.108 a.5 resp. and ad 1 and 4.

85. Scot: "Gabriel rector in suo celo" (M, 104rb), and "Rector in spera [Lunae] est . . . Gabriel" (M, 105rv).

86. *Enciclopedia dantesca*, 1:269–270.

87. Alcabitius: "Et significat ex viris oculum sinistrum, et ex mulieribus dextrum." Repeated by Bonatti, who attributes it to "Toz Graecus et Albumasar," and by *Lib. nov. iud.* with no citation (B, 212rb).

88. Bonatti: "Et autem alternatio maior oculis, aut est per oculum percussus. Et dixit [Sacerdos] quod [Lunaris] est vir strabo vel omnino altior orbis oculum. Et ut breviter tibi verum fatear, alter oculorum nullatenus vicio carebit." Previously he had reported that the Moon could signify an "impedimentum oculi" as a birth defect.

89. *Lib. nov. iud.*, extracting Aristotle: "Vix tandem aut nunquam potest accidere oculum utrumque vel saltem alterum vicio carere colorem" (B, 212rb).

90. Alcabitius: "Et dixit Mesceala quod significat de figuris hominum hominem album confectum rubore, iunctis superciliis, benivolum, habentem oculos non ex toto nigros, faciem rotundam, pulchram staturam, et in facie eius signum." Bonatti repeats the description but with this significant variant: "habentem oculos non ex toto *magnos*."

91. See David C. Lindberg, *Theories of Vision from al-Kindi to Kepler*, University of Chicago History of Science and Medicine (Chicago: University of Chicago Press, 1976), index s.v. "Extramission theory of vision" (p. 315).

92. *Lib. nov. ius.*: "lumen, namque a sole mutuans, [Luna] portendit gaudium" (B, 212ra). For further discussion of the Moon as the "oculus mundi" in relation to *Par.* 2.142–144, see Robert M. Durling and Ronald M. Martinez, *Time and the Crystal: Studies in Dante's "Rime petrose"* (Berkeley: University of California Press, 1990), pp. 224–232.

Chapter 2: Mercury

1. Albumasar: "fama, rumores, ambitio magis glorie cause." Similarly, Ibn Ezra: "In omne opere, ingens desiderium."

2. Scot: "[homo] multum curat habere bonam famam in gentibus" (M, 104ra).

3. Scot: "Ex qualitate animi [Mercurius] significat . . . cupiditatem sciendi omnia que sunt utilitatis et fame" (M, 103va).

4. Scot: "Significatio fame [Mercurii]: . . . in bono et malo communis" (M, 105rv).

5. Alcabitius: "[Mercurius] significat etiam . . . honorem."

6. Scot: "semper cupit pervenire ad magna et utilia grandis honoris et divitiarum" (M, 104ra).

7. Scot: "Hic quidem homo naturaliter delectatur in arte . . . honorabili" (M, 104ra).

8. Scot: "amat honestatem" (M, 103vb); "ex qualitate animi significat [Mercurius] . . . honestatem" (M, 103va).

9. Scot: "Que vita eius est . . . honesta et pacifica" (M, 105rv).

10. Scot: "operari res ingenii et subtilitatis, que alteri placent et laudantur incignamento cooperante" (M, 104ra).

11. Scot: "vanagloriosus est sue scientie seu rei alterius quam habeat convenienter" (M, 103vb); cf. "ex qualitate animi [Mercurius] significat . . . parum invidie et vanaglorie" (M, 103va).

12. Alcabitius: "[Mercurius] significat etiam . . . opus."

13. Scot: "[Mercurius] cuius proprietas est . . . labor" (M, 103va), and "quid [Mercurius] notificat: . . . labor" (M, 105rv).

14. Ptolemy, *Quad.* 1.6.

15. Scot: "In genere est planeta plus masculinus quam femininus" (M, 103va), and "Genus eius [Mercurii] . . . masculinis plusquam femininus" (M, 105rv).

16. Robertus Anglicus: "Mercurius est masculinus." In *The "Sphere" of Sacrobosco and Its Commentators*, ed. Lynn Thorndike (Chicago: University of Chicago Press, 1949), p. 156.

17. For a detailed analysis, see text at pp. 101–107.

18. Ptolemy, *Quad.* 2.8: "[homines] forte erunt etiam in hoc, quod agere voluerint subtilis ingenii" (ed. 1551, p. 31).

19. Alcabitius: "et ex operibus, opera que generant cogitationem." Thus Scot: "[homo] est multe cogitationis" (M, 104ra); and Bonatti: "significat Mercurius . . . cogitationem."

20. Scot: "Sensus eius est . . . sagax et sapiens" (M, 105rv).

21. Scot: "Set quanto sit quis plus mercurialis tanto magis est subtilis spiritus, ad contemplandum ingeniosus, et ad reperiendum subtilitates et bene seu perfecte laborandum et in laborerio perseverandum satis. Reperitur etiam quod est planeta . . . cuius proprietas est vox, sciencia, ingenium, eloquentia, labor, cogitatio, immisso sciendi et operandi omnia que sunt et fiunt ingenio subtilitatis animi et arte pulcra" (M, 103va). "Unde dicitur planeta ingenii et deus scientiarum, eloquens, sapiens, ingeniosus, sagax, officiosus ac magisterialis eorum que sunt subtilitatis et ingenii animi" (M, 103vb).

22. John of Seville: "Significatum habet in anima rationi, grammatica, et omni scientia, sculptoribus, scriptoribus. . . ."

23. E.g., Albumasar: "Tum divinitatis fides, prophetie, sermone discipline, doctores cum discipulis ingenium, ratio, eloquentia, percepta eorumque observatio, plena sapientia, sana doctrina, salubris exhortatio, arguta deceptio, probabiles indu[c]tiones, necessarii sylogismi, philosophie ac poetrie studium, plurimumque in mathematica: arismetrica, geometrie, et astronomie, nec sine metrica et richmica."

24. Haly: "Per eum [Mercurium] . . . in nati[vi]tatibus scietur loquela nati vel si est mutus, et scietur si est expeditus in ratione sua vel non."

25. John of Seville: "Eius est . . . lingua."

26. Ibn Ezra: "verborum sine manuum immissione contentio."

27. Haly: "Mercurius est planeta . . . computationum," and the Mercurian "diligit . . . computationes."

28. Alcabitius: "et ex operibus . . . opus numeri maxime."

29. *Lib nov. iud.*: "habet . . . artes liberales" (B, 212vb), and "ea scilicet que trivii vel quadrivii secuntur origionem" (B, 212ra).

30. Scot: "Significat enim . . . studium litterarum," and "significat . . . plenitudinem scientie liberalis subtilitatis" (M, 103va).

31. As Mariotti has pointed out, Dante was following Huguccio of Pisa's mistaken definition of *cincinnatus* as "crinis qui prolixe dependet" (*Enciclopedia dantesca*, 2:4).

32. William Harris Stahl, *The Quadrivium of Martianus Capella* in his *Martianus Capella and the Seven Liberal Arts*, vol. 1, Records of Civilization: Sources and Studies 84 (New York: Columbia University Press, 1971), pp. 126–127.

33. Alcabitius: "et ex operibus, opera que generant . . . negociationes et extimationem," and "ex partibus, habet partem negociationis."

34. Albumasar: "mercature partiens negociationes."

35. Ibn Ezra: "Hominum quoque . . . mercatores . . . et in his prelati." And "ipsius [Mercurii] quidem sunt mercatorum mansiones."

36. Bonatti: "Et habet Mercurius significare . . . scientiam negociationis, et sciet disponere negotia multa, et de multis se intromittet, et sciet illa ducere ad effectum."

37. Bonatti: "Et ex partibus habet partem negociationis, quoniam habet significare negociatores propter nimiam solictudinis aestuationem, quam significat, et propter nimium studium quod viget in eo in inquirendo diversa."

38. The phrase *assegnare ragione* was a term of art in medieval accounting: M. Barbi, *Problemi di critica dantesca: Prima serie (1893–1918)* (Florence: Sansoni, 1934), p. 251.

39. Alcabitius: "et significat servos."

40. Albumasar: "servitus."

41. Ibn Ezra: "Ipsius quidem sunt . . . loca omnium ministeriorum."

42. Albumasar: "obedientia cum summa intentione."

43. Scot: "Servit secundum eius facultatem. . . . Est homo magne consciencie dum pervenit ad perfectionem etatis licet herret ut ceteri" (M, 104ra); "libenter studet servire alteri et legaliter"; Mercury the god is "officiosum" (M, 103vb).

44. Scot: "[Homo] utilis amicis, et fideliter sibi servit dum incipit ponere amorem in aliquo. . . . Aliena facta fideliter percurat postquam incipit in societate alterutrorum" (M, 104ra).

45. Ptolemy, *Quad.* 2.8: "Est etiam . . . officii divini" (ed. 1551, p. 31); "He is the cause of events taking place which concern . . . the worship of the gods" (trans. Robbins, p. 187).

46. Haly: "In revolutionibus annorum mundi, habet [Mercurius] magnam et veridicam significationem super tenentes officia domini et regni."

47. F. M. Powicke, "Dante's Romeo," in his *Ways of Medieval Life and Thought: Essays and Addresses* (Boston: Beacon Press, 1951; rpt. New York: Crowell, 1971), p. 247, citing V. L. Bourrilly and R. Busquet, *La Provence au Moyen Age* (Marseilles: Barlatier, 1924).

48. The early commentators took *baiulo* in its literal sense of "bearer" to mean that Augustus was the standard-bearer of the imperial eagle, but Dante's other uses of the term have inclined modern scholars such as Sapegno to take the term in its common medieval sense, of one who bears a burden of responsibility entrusted to him. See *Enciclopedia dantesca*, 1:495.

49. *Enciclopedia dantesca*, 1:1033.

50. John of Seville: "Mercurii sydus nunc masculinum, nunc foemininum, nunc diei, nunc noctis, nunc fortuna, nunc infortuna, permutatur ratione Circuli. . . ."

51. Haly: "Mercurius est planeta . . . convertibilis: masculinus cum masculis, femininus cum femininis, fortuna cum fortuna, infortuna cum infortuna."

52. Ptolemy, *Quad.* 2.8 (trans. Robbins, p. 187; ed. 1551, p. 31): "Mercurius . . . ipse generaliter sicut caeterarum stellarum commiscebitur, ipsius naturae assimilabitur." Ibn Ezra: "Mercurius est mixtus, mutabilis, mutatur enim secundum illorum planetarum naturam."

53. Scot: "Hic quidem planeta in opere valde est debilis, inutilis, et varii influentie, cum omnia quasi tribuat secundum quod alter planeta tribuit cui applicatur" (M, 103rb).

54. Scot: "in complexione [Mercurius est] communis, id est commixtus, cum bonis est bonus, cum malis est malus" (M, 103rb). Bonatti: "Et si ille cum quo iungitur fuerit bene dispositus, significat bonam qualitatem animae."

55. Bonatti: "Quod si iungatur ei Luna, signifcat quod natus sciet servire in curiis regum, magnatum, nobilium, et aliorum, sicut est ponere fercula coram discumbentibus, incidere panem et carnes coram eis, et similia."

56. Haly: "Status eius versus solem est status scriptoris: agilis, morigeratus, et sapiens in ratiocinando et scribendo res sui regni."

57. Alcabitius: "Si Sol complectitur [Mercurio] significat preesse numero regum et substantiae domorum."

58. Scot: "Si [complectitur] Soli, significat numerum regum, domorum, et proprie monasterium, et hominum prelature" (M, 103va).

59. B. Tuckerman, *Planetary, Lunar and Solar Positions A.D. 2 to A.D. 1649 at Five-Day and Ten-Day Intervals*, Memoirs of the American Philosophical Society 59 (Philadelphia: American Philosophical Society, 1964), p. 668: during the months of February, April, June, and September.

60. Alcabitius: "Si [complectitur Mercurio] Jupiter, significat numerum psallendi et numerum librorum divinorum."

61. Scot: "Si Iovi significat numerum psallendi scandendo pedes versuum, ut librorum, et legendi abbacum incantu, cum non possit fieri nisi per ellevationem vocis sursum vel deponentis deorsum" (M, 103va).

62. Bonatti: "Quod si iungatur Iovi, significat opus numerandi et faciendi melodias librorum ecclesiarum, et alios cantus sciet indifferenter, et saltus ludorum, et similia."

63. Haly: "Particeps est cum Iove in sapientia, documento, scientia et intellectu suo."

64. Albumasar: "tributaria aera."

65. Bonatti: "Quod si iungatur Soli, significat eum praeesse numero regum, et substantiae dominorum, magnatum et nobilium et divitum, sciet enim disponere facta ipsorum, et regere familias eorum, et producere ipsorum familiaria facta."

66. Albumasar: "providum consilium."

67. Scot: "Hic quidem homo . . . est . . . recti consilii, magne providentie in agendis, in respondendo alteri veredicus, in factis suis sagax et convenienter secretus" (M, 103vb–104ra).

68. Villani, *Croniche fiorentine* 6.91.

69. Albumasar: "furta, fraudulentia, malivolentia, ignavia, inimicitie"; Haly: "traditor, et sapiens et subtilis in motibus fraudulentiis."

70. Ibn Ezra: "Omnis species cal[l]iditatis et deceptionis, et falsorum instrumentorum scriptura."

71. Haly: "In omnibus partibus Capricorni, pauper, diminutus, denudatus, fatigatus, infirmus, damnatus membris de palatino malo et palatina voluntate."

72. Scot: "Significat . . . paucitatem divitarum magne consolationis corpori" (M, 103va); "non divitias temporales ad gaudendum" (103vb); "paupertate aliorum per tempora ut pecunie et cetera" (103rb).

73. Scot: "multos recipit de futuros ab illis quibus magis servivit, propter more scorpionis, qui primo blanditur et prepugnit blanditum, alteri est fortuna, et ideo habet bonum in contrarium alteri" (M, 104ra).

74. Scot: "[Homo] crudam fortunam habet in propinquis, et est sic abstinens, quod multum se temperat in suis iniuriis, quas recepit ex maiori parte sine culpa sui, cum libenter alteri proficiat, et non multum curat nocere" (M, 104ra).

75. "[Homo] est fortis ire et longe dedignationis" (M, 104ra).

76. A parallel of questionable significance is presented by Dante's description of Romeo as a pilgrim ("peregrina," *Par.* 6.135). Astrologers associated Mercury with any color that is "commixtum et variatum" (Alcabitius and Bonatti; cf. Ibn Ezra and John of Seville). Scot terms such a color "peregrinum, id est sic commixtum quod non sit certitudo plus unius quam alterius" (M, 103va). "Peregrina" is also reminiscent of the peregrine falcon, though it is unlikely that Dante could have known this sense of the term.

77. Ibn Ezra: "pietas."

78. Scot: "Gratia in altero . . . mediocriter pius et impius" (M, 105rv); "reperitur etiam quod est planeta mediocris . . . in operando pietatem et impietatem" (M, 103va).

79. Bonatti: "Et dixit Alchabicius quod significat ex sectis culturam unitatis verae, atque legum rationabilium, et horum similium; et illud significat cum hypocrisi atque simulatione, fingens se meliorem esse quam sit, non tamen cum haeresi."

80. Scot: "Significat etiam cultum divinitatis, videlicet tam publicum quam privatum" (M, 103va). Bonatti: "Et significat Mercurius . . . dilectionis Dei, quantum est ex conscientia sua, licet alias sit lascivus in non licitis." Alcabitius had already noted Mercurians' weakness for lewd women ("dilectionem concubinarum"), and although it is tempting to a modern familiar with the *Anecdota* of Procopius to apply this quality to Justinian's courtship of the notorious prostitute Theodora, Dante certainly could not have known this work, which survived in a single Greek manuscript that was only published in 1623, and it is unlikely that he knew her as anything less than the imposing patroness she appears to be in the famous mosaic in San Vitale, which would have been familiar to him from his years in·Ravenna.

81. Alcabitius: "significat etiam . . . credulitatem." *Lib. nov. iud.*: "credulos" (B, 211vb).

82. Albumasar: "divinitatis fides."

83. Scot: "Ex qualitate animi significat . . . velocis credibilitatis auditorum: (M, 103va).

84. Scot: "Ex figuris hominum significat hominem . . . se cito convertendo pro prece vel consilio alterorum" (M, 103vb).

85. Ibn Ezra: "aversio a malo." Scot: "quantum facile convertibilis est ad utrumque, et tamen plus cito inclinatur ad bonum quam ad malum" (M, 103vb).

86. Bonatti: "et bonam habebit credulitatem, et devote morabitur in templis et aliis oraculis ecclesiarum, et erit bonae fidei et catholicae opinionis."

87. Ptolemy, *Quad.* 2.8: "Est etiam . . . eorum quae futura sunt in haereditatibus domorum orationis" (ed. 1551, p. 31). Actually he was referring to royal revenues, but the medieval translator mistook the civil basilica for an ecclesiastical one.

88. Ibn Ezra: "est ipsium [planetae] . . . scire orationes."

89. Scot: "Significat etiam . . . officium ecclesiasticum sicut missam et cetera, orationes, ieiunia, clericos et prelatos, propheta et prophetias, evangelia, epistolas, ordinem religionem cuiuslibet" (M, 103va).

90. Alcabitius: "Et ex operibus, opera que generant . . . predicationem et rhetoricam." Scot: "Et ex magisteriis hominum significat predicatione" (M, 103va).

91. Bonatti: "Et si fuerit effectus clericus, erit bonus et placabilis praedicator."

92. *Mon.* 3.15.10 (trans. Nicholl, p. 93): "scilicet summo Pontifice, qui secundum revelata humanum genus perduceret ad vitam ecternam, et Imperatore, qui secundum phylosophica documenta genus humanum ad temporalem felicitatem dirigeret."

93. *Mon.* 3.15.18 (trans. Nicholl, p. 94): "Illa igitur reverentia Cesar utatur ad Petrum qua primogenitus filius debet uti ad patrem: ut luce paterne gratie illustratus virtuosius orbem terre irradiet, cui ab Illo solo prefectus est, qui est omnium spiritualium et temporalium gubernator." On this passage, see Timothy G. Sistrunk, "Obligations of the Emperor as the Reverent Son in Dante's *Monarchia*," *Dante Studies* 105 (1987), 95–112.

94. Scot: "Significat . . . ordinem personarum" (M, 103va).

95. Ptolemy, *Quad.* 2.8: "Est . . . variationis morum et legum quandoque secundum ipsius commixtionem cum caeteris stellis" (ed. 1551, p. 31).

96. Albumasar: "legis observatio, verax causata."

97. Haly: "In omnibus partibus Geminorum concupiscit litigationes. . . . In omnibus partibus Sagitarii est . . . preparatus ad litigandum."

98. Scot: "ex sectis fidei, significat unanimos diei et noctis cultu studenti artis scripture seu doctorum, ut gramaticam, loycam, leges, physicam, astronomiam, experimenta et operationem perfectionis cuiuslibet artis subtilitatis" (M, 103va).

99. Scot: "Item [homo] delectatur proprie in astronomia, physica scilicet natura, legibus, et divinitate" (M, 104ra). He describes the Mercurian as one who is "*legalis* per voluntate" (M, 104ra) and who strives to serve another "*legaliter*" (M, 103vb), but both terms are used in their medieval sense of "loyal" and "loyally" respectively.

100. Scot: "ut sunt ea que fiunt studio . . . librorum" (M, 103rb).

101. Haly: "puer diligit libros et computationes, . . . romantii versificare libri ac sci<r>e."

102. Bonatti, citing "Sacerdos" as his source: "Est autem sapiens, lectioni libenter vacans."

103. Albumasar: "scribe eorumque [librorum] officium." Ibn Ezra: "hominum quoque . . . scribe."

104. Haly: "Mercurius est planeta . . . documentorum, scribante, computationum, et scientiarum."

105. Albumasar: "tum libri commenta."

106. Scot: "Significat enim . . . compilationem librorum" (M, 103va).

107. Bonatti: "Et dixit Afla [Jâbir ibn Aflah] quod significat . . . scripturam, et proverbia: erit bonus, moralis." Cf. Alcabitius: "Et ex operibus, opera que generant . . . proverbia et scripturam."

108. Scot: "Dominatur etenim [deus scientiarum] contra Romanos et proprie Lombardos et omnes doctos natura et arte in scientiis nobilibus et magnis" (M, 103vb).

109. Albumasar: "ingenium, ratio, eloquentia, precepta eorumque observatio." Haly: "Mercurius est planeta . . . bene rationatus, bene loquens."

110. *Conv.* 4.9.9 (trans. Jackson, p. 223): "A questa scrivere, mostrare e commandare, è questo officiale posto di cui si parla, cioè lo Imperadore. . . ." On this passage, see R. Kay, *Dante's Swift and Strong* (Lawrence, Kan.: Regents Press of Kansas, 1978), pp. 55–57.

111. Justinian's seven prefatory decrees will be cited hereafter by incipit; the full citations for both text and translation are given here. The three constitutions prefatory to the *Code* (inc. *Haec, Summa rei publicae,* and *Cordi nobis*) are printed in *Corpus iuris civilis,* vol. 2: *Codex Iustinianus,* ed. Paul Krueger, 2nd ed. (Berlin: Weidmann, 1880), pp. 1–4; the three relating to the *Digest* (inc. *Deo auctore* [= *Cod.* 1.17.1], *Omnem rei publicae,* and *Tanta,* [= *Cod.* 1.17.2] in *Corpus iuris civilis,* vol. 1: *Digesta,* ed. T. Mommsen, 3rd ed. (Berlin: Weidmann, 1882), pp. xii–xxix; the same volume contains the *Institutiones,* ed. P. Krueger and separately paged: the constitution *Imperatorium* on p. 2. All these decrees were glossed in the Bolognese *Glossa ordinaria* and hence would be known to all students of Roman law in Dante's time. The whole *Corpus iuris civilis* was translated into English by Samuel P. Scott, *The Civil Law,* 17 vols. (Cincinnati: Central Trust Co., 1932): the prefaces to the *Code* in 12:3–8, to the *Digest* in 2:179–207 (of the two versions of *Tanta* on pp. 189–207, I use the first), and to the *Institutes* in 2:3–4.

112. *Cordi nobis* 1: "omneque ius antiquum supervacua prolixitate liberum." *Deo auctore* 1: "et omni supervacua similitudine et iniquissima discordia absolutae." Further references to superfluous matter in *Haec* 2 ("supervacuis"), *Cordi nobis* 3 ("constitutiones . . . superfluas"). *Deo auctore* 7 ("aliquod superfluum vel minus perfectum, supervacua longitudine semota"), and *Tanta* 10 ("supervacuum").

113. Positions detailed in *Enciclopedia dantesca,* 5:881, by A. Bufano, who advances the third solution, based on *Novella* 7 pr. (ed. G. Kroll [Berlin: Weidmann, 1895], p. 48).

114. *Imperatorium* 3: "nihil inutile nihilque perperam."

115. *Cordi nobis* 3: "constitutiones vero superfluas vel ex posterioribus sanctionibus nostris iam vacuatas." The sense is the same as the decree cited by Bufano (above, n. 113).

116. *Deo auctore* 4: "nulla . . . discordia derelicta." *Tanta* pr.: "nihil . . . contrarium" and § 1: "nullo seditioso."

117. Scot: "Inveniet multa noviter a se ipso que sunt magne utilitatis" (M, 104ra).

118. *Tanta* pr.: "quod nemo ante nostrum imperium umquam speravit neque humano ingenio possibile esse penitus existimavit." Cf. *Haec* pr.

119. Alcabitius: "Et ex operibus, opera que generant . . . dispositionem rei."

120. Ibn Ezra: "organizare."

121. *Haec* 2: "colligentes vero in unam sanctionem, quae in variis constitutionibus dispersa sunt."

122. *Tanta* pr.: "in unam reducere consonantiam."

123. *Tanta* 1–8.

124. Scot: "spiritus perfectionem alicuius artis" (M, 103vb). Albumasar: "perfectio confidenti omnium professione."

125. *Cordi nobis* pr.: "ut nihil a nobis coeptum imperfectum relinquatur."

126. *Tanta* 13 (14): "sed primum quidem inbecillitati humanae, quae naturaliter inest, hoc inscribat"; § 18: "quia divinae quidem res perfectissimae sunt"; cf. §§ 10, 16.

127. *Cod.* 1.1.1: "*De summa Trinitate et de fide catholica et ut nemo de ea publice contendere audeat.*"

128. Bonatti: "Et dixit Iaphar, quod Mercurius . . . a statione sua secunda usque ad coniunctionem Solis corporalem, significat . . . concordiam et eius inquisitionem."

129. *Imperatorium* 2: "sacratissimas constitutiones antea confusas in luculentam ereximus consonantium."

130. *Imperatorium* 1: "omnes vero populi legibus iam a nobis vel promulgatis vel compositis reguntur." Cf. *Summa* pr. and *Tanta* pr.

131. *Tanta* 9.

132. *Imperatorium* 6: "et legimus et cognovimus."

133. *Tanta* pr.: "nostra quoque maiestas semper investigando et perscrutando ea quae ab his componebantur, quidquid dubium et incertum inveniebatur, hoc numine caelesti erecta emendabat et in competentem formam redigebat."

134. Albumasar: "ambitio magis glorie causae deinde questiones."

135. Albumasar: "dubii atque involuti affectus."

136. Scot: "sed ullo studio notare questiones magnas et solutiones velle scire quasi omnia" (M, 104ra).

137. *Deo auctore* 2: "immo magis impossibilis."

138. *Tanta* pr., referring back to *Deo auctore*: "et summo numine invocato deum auctorem et totius operis praesulem fieri optavimus."

139. *Tanta* pr.: "quod caelesti fulgore et summae trinitatis favore confectum est secundum nostra mandata. . . . omnia igitur confecta sunt domino et deo nostro Ihesu Christo possibilitatem tam nobis quam nostris in hoc satellitibus praestante."

140. *Tanta* 12.

141. *Deo auctore* 14: "deique omnipotentis providentiae argumentum."

142. *Deo auctore* 5: "haec materia summa numinis liberalitate collecta fuerit."

143. *Deo auctore* 7: "sed totam nostram esse volumus." Cf. *Tanta* 10.

144. *Deo auctore* 6: "ut omnes qui relati fuerint in hunc codicem prudentissimi viri habeant auctoritatem tam, quasi et eorum studia ex principalibus constitutionibus profecta et a nostro divino fuerant ore profusa."

145. *Imperatorium* 3: "hoc vos a primordio ingrediamini digni tanto honore tantaque reperti felicitate, ut et initium vobis et finis legum [sc. the *Institutes* and the *Code*] a voce principali procedat."

146. *Imperatorium* 3: "ut liceat vobis prima legum cunabula . . . ab imperiali splendore appetere."

147. *Omnem* 2: "Iustinianos novos nuncupari."

148. *Haec* pr.: "uno autem codice sub felici nostri nominis vocabulo componendo." Cf. *Haec* 3, *Summa* 1, and *Deo auctore* 2.

149. *Cordi nobis* 4: "memoratus Iustinianus codex"; cf. § 5.

150. Alcabitius: "significat etiam . . . orationem," and "ex operibus, opera que generant . . . rhetoricam."

151. Scot: "deus scientiarum, eloquens" (M, 103vb), listing among the properties of the planet "vox" and "eloquentia" (M, 103va). Ibn Ezra: "Hominis nature qualitatis sermo est ipsius."

152. Scot: "in loquendo est placidus et suavis, bene componens verba suorum sermonum" (M, 103vb). Cf. Bonatti: "erit enim ordinatus in sua loquela."

153. Ibn Ezra: "Avium sturnus, apes, et omne agiliter volans."

154. Haly: "puer . . . alacer, mobilis in omnibus suis rebus."

155. Jer. 4.13: "velociores aquilis equi illius"; Thren. 4.19 and 2 Reg. 1.23.

156. *Mon.* 2.11.7 (trans. Nicholl, p. 59): "romanum populum sibi de iure orbis Imperium ascivisse."

157. Alcabitius: "[Mercurius] qui si in natura sua fuerit et nullus planeta ei complectitur significat res terreas et rerum augmentationem crescendo." Bonatti: "Et dixit Alchabicius, quod significat [etc.] . . . crescendo."

158. Alcabitius and Bonatti: "Et significat [Mercurius] timorem et infestationem et bellum et inimicitias et seditiones [seductiones *Alc.*] et contrarietates."

159. *Mon.* 2.7. See my discussion of Dante's typology of divine judgment in *Dante's Swift and Strong*, pp. 165–167.

160. Haly: "Mercurius est planeta maleficiorum et violentiarum."

161. Haly: "Quando fuerit in omnibus partibus Arietis est interfector, rixator, contrariator et vociferator. . . . In omnibus partibus Leonis miles valoris, et interfector per vim et victoriam res perquirit. . . . In omnibus partibus Virginis valens tractor baliste; arma tenet bestias, equos, milites et homines ac pedites et bona munimenta. . . . In omnibus partibus Sagittarii est interfector; tenet armorum munimenta."

162. Scot: "Si [complectitur] Marti significat numerum flagellorum et clavarum percutientium ac bellantium ut in exercitu et cetera" (M, 103va). Bonatti: "Quod si iungatur Marti, significat quod natus cui fuerit significator, sciet producere exercitum," elaborating on all the duties of generalship.

163. Bonatti: "Et dixit Guelius, quod significat alezeminium, qui est quidam color similis colori lilii agrestis." Alcabitius: "et ex coloribus habet omnem colorem commixtum atque variatum, et alem menium, qui est color floris lilii agrestis."

164. Thorndike summarizes and discusses the literature on the *climata* in *The*

"Sphere" of Sacrobosco, pp. 16–18, n. 88. The various systems are correlated in a convenient table by John K. Wright, *The Geographical Lore of the Time of the Crusades*, American Geographical Society Research Series 15 (New York: American Geographical Society, 1925), pp. 454–455.

165. *Enciclopedia dantesca*, 2:43, s.v. "clima."

166. Ibn Ezra: "Climatum vero habet [Mercurius] sextum" In this he was following an Arabic system found, e.g., in al-Biruni (trans. Wright, p. 241).

167. Alfraganus (al-Farghani), *Differentie scientie astrorum* 8, trans. John of Seville (1137), ed. Francis J. Carmody (Berkeley: n. p., 1943), p. 15. Idem (Alfragano), *Il "Libro dell' aggregazione delle stelle,"* trans. Gerard of Cremona (ca. 1175), ed. R. Campani (Città di Castello: Lapi, 1910), pp. 88, 92. In *Enciclopedia dantesca*, 2:43, G. Buti and R. Bertagni describe only this system; cf. their *Commento astronomico dell "Divina Commedia"* (Florence, 1966), pp. 192–196.

168. Francis J. Carmody, *Arabic Astronomical and Astrological Sciences in Latin Translation: A Critical Bibliography* (Berkeley and Los Angeles: University of California Press, 1956), pp. 46–47.

169. *Opera omnia*, ed. A. Borgnet, vol. 9 (Paris, 1910), p. 548.

170. Busnelli and Vandelli, 1:309–310, ad *Conv.* 3.5.12.

171. John K. Wright, "Notes on the Knowledge of Latitudes and Longitudes in the Middle Ages," *Isis* 5 (1923), 88, citing both the *Marseilles Tables* and the *Toledo Tables*; "Alconstantina" is no. 54 in his list.

172. Alfragnaus, *Differentie* 9, ed. Carmody, p. 19; cf. ed. Campani, p. 101.

173. Wright, "Latitudes and Longitudes," p. 91, n. 2, and p. 93.

174. Wright, *Geographic Lore*, p. 454.

175. Ptolemy's latitude for Constantinople is given in a North Italian manuscript written ca. 1475, which J. D. North prints with commentary in Appendix 2 of his *Horoscopes and History*, Warburg Institute Surveys and Texts 13 (London: University of London, Warburg Institute, 1986), p. 193. I have refrained from using this list in the present study because, at least in its present form, it was compiled over 150 years after Dante's death, and although it may incorporate earlier material, this has yet to be identified.

176. Alcabitius: "significat etiam deitatem."

177. On Mercurian ambivalence, see above p. 47. Cf. *Par.* 7.21: "pensier miso."

178. Haly: "Mercurius est planeta . . . composite persone."

179. Ernst H. Kantorowicz, *The King's Two Bodies: A Study in Mediaeval Political Theology* (Princeton, N. J.: Princeton University Press, 1957), pp. 42–52, for the fundamental conception.

180. *Tanta* pr.: "Tanta circa nos divinae humanitatis est providentia. . . ."

181. *Tanta* 14, 16, 18; see above at n. 126.

182. Just as the planet brightens because Beatrice is "so glad (*lieta*)," (*Par.* 5.94), so also the joy (*letizia*) of the shades increases the brightness (107–108) that issues from their eyes (125). This relative deficiency of joy is to be expected in Mercury, whose joys are rare and whose disposition is moderately melancholy, according to Albumasar ("rarum gaudium, rare delicie, tenuis voluptas") and Scot: "Que infirmitas . . . plus melancholia quam flegmate" (M, 105rv).

Chapter 3: Venus

1. *Enciclopedia dantesca*, 4:1026, with no mention of her third marriage to a "gentleman of Verona" and with some doubt about the fourth, to Salione Buzzacarini of Padua, her brother's court astrologer. All four are noted by Toynbee-Singleton, p. 208.

2. *Enciclopedia dantesca*, 2:954–956.

3. Alcabitius: "Et ex sectis culturam idolorum, et eos in quibus maxime exercentur comestiones atque potationes."

4. Scot: "Ex sectis fidei, significat cultum ydolorum, ut sacrificia, orationes, experimenta" (M, 102vb–103ra).

5. Bonatti: "Et ex sectis significat idolatriam, et eas . . ." etc., as in Alcabitius, above, n. 3.

6. Ibn Ezra: "Et ipsius anima existit appetitiva, generativa, et augmentativa," and "Ex hominis natura . . . in omnibus appetitus immensitas."

7. Scot: "Etiam Veneris lumbos, renes, ventrem, umbilicum, et vulvam cum matrice, ac partes extremas epatis, ut eius humanitatem qua quis movetur ad amorem non sui set alterius" (M, 103ra). Bonatti: "habet significare . . . umbilicum et ventrem, vulvam quoque atque matricem." Ibn Ezra: "Et morbi sui sunt omnes . . . pudendis" and "epar." Alcabitius assigns ailments of the genitals to Venus; Bonatti repeats this and adds "vel circa illa et similia." The illnesses Scot lists are "in mamis, genitalibus, et cetera" (M, 102vb).

8. Alcabitius: "Et habet ex partibus, partem desiderii." Repeated by Bonatti.

9. Bonatti: "Et erit ille cuius Venus fuerit significatrix vivens in ocio." Albumasar: "eius est . . . ocia preter studia." Alcabitius: "Et ex magisteriis . . . [s]altationes et ocia." *Lib. nov. iud.*: "ociosi" (B, 211va).

10. Scot: "est pacificus et quietus in convictu" (M, 103ra), "significat hominem . . . in actibus pacificum" (M, 103ra), and "treugua, concordia, pax" (M, 102vb).

11. Scot: "faciem placidam ut angeli" (M, 103ra), and "placidus facit onmia et satis velociter" (M, 103ra).

12. Scot: "Ex humoribus significat flegmata dulce" (M, 103ra), and "Que infirmitas [eius est] . . . plus flegmate quam sanguinis" (M, 105rv).

13. Albumasar: "gaudia loci." Alcabitius: "risus et gaudium." Haly: "hilaris, gaudiosa." Ibn Ezra: "ex hominis natura . . . irrisio, gaudium." Scot: "Cuius proprietas est gaudium" (M, 102vb), and "Quid notificat . . . gaudium" (M, 105rv). Bonatti: "Venus est planeta delectationis et gaudii."

14. Scot: "signum . . . rerum vilium ac solitarum velud est fieri inter gentes letitia" (M, 102vb).

15. Scot: "auxiliatrix, adiuvatrix, et iuvatilis (*var.* servitialis B) omnibus deprecantibus eam presentia" (M, 102vb).

16. Albumasar: "eius est . . . amor." Alcabitius: "significat . . . amorem." Haly: "significatrix . . . amoris." Ibn Ezra: "Ex hominis natura . . . amor." Scot: "cuius proprietas est . . . amor" (M, 102vb). Bonatti: "Et habet Venus significare . . . amorem."

17. There is a hint of madness, or better obsession, in Bonatti's description

of the fornicator: "he shall abound in coition so that sometimes for this reason his nature shall be driven out" ("abundabit in coitu, ita quod aliquando exterminabitur natura ipsius illa de causa").

18. Albumasar: "eius est . . . lascivia . . . luxuria." John of Seville: "significat in . . . lascivia."

19. Scot: "cuius proprietas est . . . libido" (M, 102vb).

20. Albumasar: "eius est . . . fornicatio omneque id genus tam naturalis usus quam contra naturam in utrolibet sexu tamque legitimi quam illiciti. . . ." Alcabitius: "et ex magisteriis . . . fornicationes. . . ."

21. Alcabitius: "multitudinem coitus." Scot: "cuius proprietas est coytus" (M, 102vb). Bonatti: "et significat . . . coitus et similia."

22. Haly: "mulierum significatrix, et iacendi cum eis." Ibn Ezra: "Ex hominis natura . . . mulierum concubitus."

23. Scot: "Ex qualitate animi, significat . . . amplexus, baxia, coytum, blanditias" (M, 102vb). In the same column he again mentions *amplexus* three times, *baxia* twice, and *blanditiae* once. For Bonatti, see n. 21, above.

24. Villani, *Croniche fiorentine* 7.61, trans. R. Selfe, *Villani's Chronicle* (London: Constable, 1906), p. 267.

25. *Par.* 9.142. An oblique reference to adultery may be seen in Cunizza's prophecy of the assassination of Rizzardo da Camino (*Par.* 9.49–51), who was killed by an outraged cuckold: see Singleton ad loc., p. 166.

26. See above, n. 10.

27. Alcabitius: "significat . . . coniunctiones masculorum."

28. Bonatti: "Et significat . . . coniunctionem masculorum ad invicem, per modum turpem et prohibitum, atque nepharium et abhorrendum."

29. Ibn Ezra: "Ex hominis natura . . . concubitum appetere naturale sive fuerit aut extra; amare pu[e]ros."

30. Haly: "significatrix . . . amicitie." Alcabitius: "significat amicitiam," repeated by Scot (M, 102vb) and Bonatti. John of Seville: "significat in . . . amicitia."

31. Scot: "Est etiam planeta significatione . . . amicus" (M, 102vb).

32. Haly: "Significatrix . . . amicitie et societatis."

33. Scot: "cuius coniunctio quandoque contingit fieri est signum . . . rerum vilium ac solitarum velud est fieri inter gentes, leticia, solatium, tractatus, nuptiarum, convivium, rixus, amplexus, ballatio, treuga, concordia, pax, et cetera" (M, 102vb).

34. Haly: "Venus est bone voluntatis." Scot: "stella . . . benivola, cuius benignitate amatores et amatrices eam pie deprecantur" (M, 103ra) and "est etiam planeta significatione . . . benignus" (M, 102vb). Bonatti: "Et dixit [Dorotheus] quod . . . ostendit benevolentiam."

35. In *Par.* 8.120 Carlo is undoubtedly referring to Aristotle's dictum that "homo natura civile animal est" in *Politica* 1.2, 1253a2, text no. 19 in R. M. Spiazzi's edition of Aquinas, *In octo libros Politicorum Aristotelis expositio* (Turin: Marietti, 1951, rpt. 1966), p. 5. Civil society, Aristotle concludes, is natural and is based on justice (1253a37, text no. 41, p. 6), and he then goes on to consider what justice is in the simplest human relationship, between master and slave, ultimately deciding that those who identify justice with good will ("iis quidem benevolentia iustum

esse," 1255a16–17, text no. 46, p. 22) are describing the natural form of that relation, which is based on friendship and common interest: "Propter quod et expediens aliquid est, et amicitia servo et domino ad invicem, iis qui natura tales dignificantur" (1255b12–14, text no. 53, p. 23).

36. Sapegno ad loc., pp. 892–893.

37. Albumasar: "eius est . . . charitas."

38. Albumasar: "eius est mulierum genus." Haly: "mulierum significatrix." Alcabitius: "est significatrix mulierum."

39. Alcabitius: "est significatrix mulierum et uxorum ac matrum si fuerit nativitas diurna." Bonatti: "Venus . . . habet signifcare mulieres et uxores. Et si fuerit nativitas diurna, ut ait Alchabicius, significat matres." Bonatti also says that in natal horoscopes Venus signifies "quid accidat ei [nato] a mulieribus, matre scilicet vel uxoribus vel sororibus minoribus, et similia." John of Seville mentions only mothers ("significat in matribus"), as does Ibn Ezra also ("et denotat . . . matres").

40. Enzo Petrucci considers at length the problem of which Clemence Dante had in mind and decides in favor of the wife (*Enciclopedia dantesca*, 2:40–42). However, the poet seems to be addressing a living person who does not share the foreknowledge of the future with which the dead in the *Commedia* are endowed, and this would exclude the wife, who died in 1295.

41. Ptolemy, *Quad.* 2.8, trans. Robbins, p. 185; ed. 1551: "filorum multitudo."

42. Bonatti: "Et est significatrix filorum naturaliter, quoniam filii significantur per quintam domum, et Venus est quintus planeta a Saturno . . ." (cols. 108–109). The Latin term *filii*, of course, can refer to descendants of both sexes.

43. Haly: "In omnibus partibus Tauri [Venus est] multum nobilis et alta, magni nominis et fame, et alti status circa reges et suos filios, et circa nobiles altos et dominatores."

44. Albumasar: "eius est . . . minoresque sorores." Ibn Ezra: "et denotat . . . sororum minores." *Lib. nov. iud.*: "sorores minimas" (B, 211va). Bonatti: "Et si fuerit nativitas diurna . . . ut ait Sacerdos significat sorores minores." John of Seville differs, however: "significat in . . . sororibus maioribus aetate."

45. *Enciclopedia dantesca*. 4:1026.

46. Alcabitius: "filios fornicationis." Albumasar: "eius est . . . omni prole illegali." Bonatti says that a Venusian native "erit . . . filius fornicationis."

47. Haly: "Recipit [Venus] Martem per naturam fornicationis et limpidamentum quod habet in eo; abhorret ipsum propter contrarietate nature sue, que est caliditas et siccitas; separat se ab eo, et malum et infortunium eius retrahit a se ipsa propter mansuetudinem, bona verba, solatium bonum, et mansuetam loquelam."

48. Alcabitius: "et dixerunt quidam quod significat . . . sperma." *Lib. nov. iud.*: "de homine, costas, sperma" (B, 211ra, 211va). Bonatti: "Et dixerunt Guellius et Cancaph quod significat de corpore hominis . . . sperma, et eius decursum." Scot: "Venus naturaliter in persona tenet . . . sperma utriusque sexus, et principalius mulierum quam virorum sicut Iupiter virorum continent" (M, 103ra).

49. The sense is supplied by *Conv.* 4.21.4, according to *Enciclopedia dantesca*, 5:126.

50. Bonatti: "Ista erunt officia illius cuius Venus fuerit significatrix, et quae magis approximabuntur ei, et quae ipse melius sciet facere si voluerit se intromittere de eis, et si intromiserit se de aliis, non addiscet, nec sciet ita bene sicut ista. . . . Et sciet operari . . . si adhaeserit illis magisteriis. Et istud est quod non permittit aliquando quosdam pervenire ad perfectionem suorum magisteriorum seu officiorum, quoniam utuntur scilicet artibus et officiis que non sunt ipsorum naturaliter, et ipsi nunquam perfecte addiscunt illa, et cum labore addiscunt quicquid capiunt ex eis, sed illa quae pertinent ad eos naturaliter, addiscunt leviter et bene."

51. Alcabitius: "ex etate habet iuventutem vel adolescentiam."

52. Scot: "Planeta est . . . in etate similis adolescenti significans principium iuventutis" (M, 102vb), and "Dominatur enim Venus contra omnes feminas, iuvenes, et pueros, non senex" (M, 103ra). In his summary table, however, he simply states: "Qualitas etatis: . . . iuvenis" (M, 105rv).

53. Bonatti: "Et habet significare similiter ex aetate hominis adolescentiam et maxime in mera iuventute, quae est a 14. anno usque ad 22." Thus Ibn Ezra: "etatum autem eius est post 13. annos pueritita." Elsewhere Ibn Ezra is less definite: "et hominum partus pueros possidet et eunuchos."

54. Chronology as given in *Enciclopedia dantesca*, 4:1026. My statements of age are based on the assumption that "Cunizza naque al fine de sec. XII, forse nel 1198."

55. Ptolemy, *Quad.* 2.8: "applicatio ad reges" (ed. 1551, p. 31).

56. Haly: "In omnibus partibus Piscium [homo Venereus] est rex doctus et sapiens. . . ." Alcabitius: "Si [complectitur Veneri] Sol, significat sonum ligni [sic] quo cantatur coram regibus et nobilibus."

57. Villani, *Croniche* 8.13, trans. Selfe, p. 316.

58. Toynbee-Singleton, p. 286.

59. Most commentators take "milizia" (*Par.* 8.83) to refer to "court-officials" or "dignitari e funzionari di corte": Singleton ad loc. and *Enciclopedia dantesca*, 3:956.

60. Bonatti: "Et erit ille cuius Venus fuerit significatrix vivens in ocio, et melius sciet ducere vitam suam, et delicatius vivere et curialius quam alius qui sit valde deterior eo."

61. Scot: "Item [homo] delectatur vivere delicate si posset facere et sine magno labore, ut est stare pro famulo alicuius domini vel domine, nolendo laborare, et causa melius comedendi et bibendi, amplexari, osculari, coyre sepe, fabulari, ballare, letari cognitamina et tristitiam refutare, ac ludere ludibriis puerorum et puellarum, vel ottiosari" (M, 103rb).

62. Chess may be an exception: when the adulterer Rizzardo da Camino was murdered, he was playing this game, the Venusian fondness for which is noted by Alcabitius, *Lib. nov. iud.* (B, 211va), and Scot (M, 102vb).

63. Alcabitius: "significat magisterium omnium sonorum veluti musicam etc." Albumasar: "eius est . . . amor musice."

64. Scot: "Ex magisteriis hominum, significat quod natus sub ea sciat uti et facere ac sonare faciat priusquam moriatur instrumenta sonabilia" (M, 102vb). Bonatti mentions only this kind of music in connection with Venus.

65. Scot: "cuius proprietas est . . . cantus"; "ex qualitate animi, significat . . . cantum"; and "ex magisteriis hominum . . . cantum" (M, 102vb).

66. Scot: "Hic quidem homo naturaliter delectabitur in arte levi, pulcra, sepe fallaci, vana, pauci lucri, et multi motus, velud est facere . . . cantiones, libenter adiscere et eas cantare . . . stare ad audiendum instrumenta pulsare et cantabiles cantiones" (M, 103rb). Cf. the list in Haly: "Eius magisteria et sapientie sunt in faciendo cantus, concordando sonos, tangendo instrumenta, tamburum, tubas, et his similia."

67. Sapegno draws the inference ad loc. (p. 890).

68. Haly: "[Venus] retrahit a se [Marte] propter mansuetudinem, bona verba, solatium bonum, et mansuetam loquelam," and "Venus est . . . saporosorum verborum libera."

69. Bonatti: "Homo autem venereus dulcia et mollia effundit verba; per omnia dulciflua habet eloquia." This verbal sweetness is a particular manifestation of a more general Venusian penchant for *suavitas*, the quality of being sweet or pleasant. Thus Bonatti, echoing Alcabitius: "Et ex qualitate animi significat suavitatem." Scot says Venusians acquire their fame for such things: "Significatio fame [homini Venereo] . . . omnibus suavis et bona" (M, 105rv). The Venusian taste for sweetness is reflected in Carlo's remark that "a little quiet will not be less sweet (*dolce*) to us" (*Par.* 8.39).

70. *Enciclopedia dantesca*, 5 : 325, 4 : 1026.

71. Scot: "Ex magisteriis hominum . . . convivium" (M, 102vb), and "signum . . . rerum vilium ac solitarum, velud est fieri inter gentes . . . convivium" (M, 102vb).

72. Alcabitius: "ex qualitate animi . . . comestionem," and (repeated by Bonatti) "ex sectis culturam idolorum et eos in quibus maxime exercentur comestiones atque potationes." Haly: "diligat . . . comestiones, potationes." Ibn Ezra: "et denotat comestionem et cupiditatem comestionis et potationis." John of Seville simply calls this impulse gluttony: "significat in . . . ingluvie."

73. Bonatti: "et libenter utuntur comestiones et potationibus in societatibus."

74. Alcabitius: "universa genera luxuriae."

75. Albumasar: "eius est . . . omnis voluptas divitie, et oblectamenta, eorumque studiosa inquisitio."

76. Alcabitius: "ex substantia significat eam que acquiritur propter pulcritudinem, ut sunt ornamenta mulierum, et vestimenta earum, margaritas, atque picturas." Scot: "cuius proprietas est . . . decoratio," and "ex qualitate animi, significat . . . adhornationem sui corporis" (M, 102vb).

77. Alcabitius: "ex magisteriis . . . ornamenta quoque, et figuras pulchras . . . et pulcritudinem ac mundiciam, vestimenta etiam, et ornamenta." Bonatti: "Et significat quod natus erit aptus ad sciendum aptare atque praeparare ea quae spectant ad pulchritudinem, sicut sunt pallia, vestimenta mulierum, et earum ornamenta, et que pinguntur in ornamentis cum auro, margaritis, frisiis, et similibus."

78. Scot: "Hic quidem homo naturaliter delectabitur . . . cum arti [sic] laborare ut . . . specula componere" (M, 103rb).

79. Ibn Ezra: "et eius metallorum est . . . omnia iocalia ac ornamenta et

multi anuli." Scot: "Ex magisteriis hominum . . . gemmas, margaritas, annulos" (M, 102vb).

80. The term *gioia* ("joy/jewel") is repeatedly applied to blessed souls (e.g., *Par.* 10.71, 15.86, 24.89), but it is appropriate that this is first done here in the heaven that governs jewelry.

81. *Enciclopedia dantesca*, 4:149.

82. Alcabitius: "ex magisteriis . . . compositiones coronarum et usus earum." Cf. *Lib. nov. iud.*: "coronas omnia" (B, 211va).

83. Bonatti: "et sciet componere coronas et serta."

84. Scot: "Ex magisteriis hominum, significat quod natus sub ea [Venere] sciat uti et facere . . . serta florum" (M, 102vb) and "serta florum facere ac portare vel vendere, aut donare" (M, 103rb).

85. *Oxford Latin Dictionary*, ed. P. G. W. Glare (Oxford: Clarendon Press, 1982), p. 447, s.v. "corollarium."

86. Scot: "ex qualitate animi, significat . . . iocum," and "cuius proprietas est . . . iocus" (M, 102vb). Bonatti: "et significat . . . ludum."

87. Ibn Ezra: "artificiorum omne consuitionis [sic] et tincture." Albumasar: "eius est . . . subtilia mirandaque artificia, ut egregie picture atque [s]uture cum suis artificibus."

88. *Enciclopedia dantesca*, 1:213.

89. Bonatti: "pallia"; see n. 77, above, for the context.

90. Ibn Ezra: "aranea" and "ludus quo movetur rete." Scot: "texere bindas, tavellas, frixia, retia" (M, 103rb).

91. *Lib. nov. iud.*: "de vestibus, sericas" (B, 211va, citing Jergis); "cerici venditores significat" (B, 211va, citing Omar); and "vestes sericas" (B, 211vb, citing al-Kindi). Cf. Scot: "eius significatio sit brevis perseverantie, ut in virgine mundiciem, in lino et *bombice* albedinem, in lacte dulcedinem, et cetera" (M, 102vb).

92. Alcabitius: "habet ex coloribus albedinem." Ibn Ezra: "et colorum est eius albus parumper in viridem conterminans." Scot: "ex coloribus significat album" (M, 103ra). Bonatti: "ex coloribus habet album." Scot also says it can be white like tin (M, 102vb, 105rv).

93. Haly: "Venus est . . . apparentie bone, persona limpidata limpida, formosa," and "Recipit [Venus] Martem per naturam fornicationis et limpidamentum quod habet in eo."

94. Ibn Ezra: "Et eius metallorum est omne terre visceribus inexistens: ut cuprum, citrinum, et lacuram, magnesia, marethach, enussedar, lohage qui modi tincture existunt." His concept of *metallus* evidently includes minerals, since citrine is a stone.

95. John Read, *Prelude to Chemistry: An Outline of Alchemy, Its Literature and Relationships* (London: Bell, 1936; rpt. Cambridge, Mass.: MIT Press, 1966), pp. 17–18, 24.

96. Read, *Prelude*, p. 54, and pp. 51–55 on the history of the text. Dante could have learned of the tablet from Albertus, *De rebus metallicis et mineralibus*.

97. The only astrologer who specifically associates the emerald with Venus is al-Biruni, *The Book of Instruction in the Elements of the Art of Astrology*, trans. R. R. Wright (London: Luzac, 1934), p. 243, whose work was apparently unknown in the Latin West.

98. Ibn Ezra: "Climatum vero ipsius est quintum, ut Hyspania, et partium una terre Edon."

99. John K. Wright, *The Geographical Lore of the Time of the Crusades*, American Geographical Society Research Series 15 (New York: American Geographical Society, 1925), pp. 454–455.

100. John K. Wright, "Notes on the Knowledge of Latitudes and Longitudes in the Middle Ages," *Isis* 5 (1923), 88, no. 38: "Malta," from the *Marseilles Tables*.

101. Wright, "Latitudes and Longitudes," p. 88: The *Marseilles Tables* list "Roma" at 41° 50' north latitude (no. 34) and "Insula sicilie" at 39° (no. 37); in an appendix to the *Toledo Tables*, Naples is at 42° 38' north latitude (pp. 91, 93).

102. Ibn Ezra: "Gentium quidem illius sunt Arabes et omnes sarracenorum fidem testantes."

103. Alcabitius: "et habet ex partibus mundi albiget al alicmen et terras arabum."

104. Bonatti: "et habet ex regionibus Alhegem et Alyemen, et totam terram Arabum, quoniam eius significata magis apparent in illis partibus quam in aliis."

105. Singleton ad loc. (p. 167). For its clarity, see *Enciclopedia dantesca*, 1 : 495–496.

106. Ptolemy, *Quad.* 2.8 (trans. Robbins, p. 185; ed. 1551, p. 31): "Sed in aëris qualitatibus venti cum temperie et humiditate contingent. . . . Quae vero, quae res oriri iuvant, et pluviae quamplures erunt. . . . Flumina augmentabuntur et implebuntur."

107. Haly: "Status Veneris cum statu solis est similis statui mulieris versus virum: quia quando iacet cum ea eiicit humiditatem suam, et per hanc rationem est ipsa significatrix pluviarum, nubium, et himbrium."

108. Scot: "Dominatur enim Venus . . . contra provincias Tuscie, Fori iulii, et cetera sibi consimiles in natura calidas et humidas, quare tales naturaliter delectantur cantu cantionum, coitu, et circumstantiis horum, ut mundicie, ornatu, et cetera" (M, 103ra).

109. Scot: "tepida et multum humida" (M, 102vb, repeated *mutatis mutandis* at 103ra and twice at 105rv). Most other astrologers held Venus to be cold and wet, and hence phlegmatic in temperament like the Moon: thus Albumasar ("frigida et humida temperata"), Alcabitius, Haly, John of Seville, Bonatti, and even Scot himself (above, n. 12). Venus was considered to be warm and wet by the *Liber Aristotelis de CCLV Indorum voluminibus*, quoted in *Saturn and Melancholy: Studies in the History of Natural Philosophy, Religion, and Art*, by R. Klibansky, E. Panofsky, and F. Saxl (New York: Basic Books, 1964), p. 129.

110. Since the marches of Treviso and Friuli were adjacent, and the boundary between them was fluid, Scot's dictum (n. 108) could readily be extended to include Treviso as well.

111. Actually Folco was born in Genoa: *Enciclopedia dantesca*, 3 : 843, 2 : 954–955.

112. For Scot, Venus signifies "rixus," which is one of its properties and at which its natives are masters (M, 102vb). Bonatti is more specific: the native of Venus badly aspected can expect marital discord: "et semper erunt rixae atque discordiae inter eos [natum et uxorem]." Cf. the "dulces querele" of lovers mentioned by Albumasar.

113. Haly: "In omnibus partibus Scorpionis amat interfectiones, rixas, et maleficia; petit res suas per vim quam facit tenentibus eas."

114. Scot: "est vanus et cito credit omnia que audit dici, facile convertitur ad utrumque" (M, 103ra), and again "significat hominem . . . cito audita credentem, . . . ad utrumque convertibilem" (M, 103ra). Thus Alcabitius: "credit omnibus."

115. Bonatti: "et confidunt de aliis, et saep[e] decipiuntur ab eis."

116. *Enciclopedia dantesca*, 4:1028.

117. Albumasar: "eius [Veneris] est . . . fallacia, frequens mendacium ac periuria . . . facilis crudelitas, voluntaria receptio."

118. Alcabitius: "largitatem quoque significat." Scot: "ex qualitate animi, significat largitatem" (M, 102vb). Bonatti: "et habet Venus significare . . . largitatem."

119. Ptolemy, *Quad*. 2.8 (ed. 1551, p. 31): "cuius opus proprium particulare in hominibus est . . . honores . . . meliorationes status . . . augmentationes substantiae."

120. Giulio Salvadori, *Sulla Vita giovanile di Dante* (Rome: Dante Alighieri, 1907), pp. 153–154. Grandgent repeated this speculative reconstruction as if it were an established fact (pp. 721–722).

121. Haly: "Plerumque significat pulchre scribere si Mercurius cum ea participat in aliqua re, quia Mercuri est scribania, et Veneris figurare et picturare et manus subtilitatis et magisterii."

122. Ptolemy, *Quad*. 2.8 (ed. 1551, p. 31): "potentum consanguineitas." Scot: "tractatus nuptiarum" and "contractio nuptiarum" (M, 102vb).

123. For biographical details, *Enciclopedia dantesca*, 4:1026, and above, n. 1.

124. Ptolemy, *Quad*. 2.8 (ed. 1551, p. 31): "coniugii bonitas" and "commoditates omnium rerum coniugialium." Albumasar: "eius est . . . sponse cum sponsalibus, ac thalamis cum triplici iure coniugii simil[iter]."

125. Alcabitius: "Si Mercurius sonum qui exercetur in compositionem versuum." Scot: "si [Venus complectitur] Mercurio, sonum qui fit in scansione pedum metrorum" (M, 102vb). Bonatti: "et si iungatur ei Mercurius, significat sonos quibus fiunt melodiae et componuntur versus, sicut sunt lirae et similia." The conjunction specified is, of course, the case in *Paradiso* (see below, Appendix 2).

126. Scot: "cuius proprietas est . . . gloria" (M, 102vb).

127. Thus Sapegno ad loc. (p. 896).

128. Scot: "dulciter loquitur et cum timore inchoat sua verba" (M, 103ra) and "in extraneis vehementer verecundum et timidum" (103ra); "est multo verecundus et pavidus in persona" (103ra).

129. Alcabitius: "significat . . . domos orationis."

130. Ibn Ezra: "ex hominis natura . . . universaliter adoptare iustitiam et dei cultum."

131. Scot: "ex qualitate animi, significat . . . pietatem" (M, 102vb), with 3 more references on fol. 102vb, 2 on 103ra, and 1 on 105rv. Albumasar: "eius est . . . pietas." Haly: "In omnibus partibus Geminorum, bone voluntatis pietosa; bonum procurat hominibus; intromittit se facere bonum debilibus pauperibus et anxiis."

132. Bonatti: "Si autem iungatur cum Iove, significat quod natus erit doctus in sonis lectionum et cantilenarum ecclesiasticarum, et in omni cantu spectante ad

clericos et religiosos, et utentes in domibus orationis, et altaria et laudem domini
Iesu Christi." Cf. his source, Alcabitius: "Et si complectitur ei Jupiter, significat
sonum lectionum vel cantationum quibus utuntur domini sectarum in altaribus et
locis orationis eorum in laudem dei omnipotentis." Also Scot: "si [Venus complec-
titur] Iovi, cantum ecclesiasticum ante altare" (M, 102vb).

133. *Lyrics of the Troubadours and Trouvères*, ed. and trans. Frederick Goldin
(Garden City, N.Y.: Doubleday, Anchor Books, 1973), pp. 278–279.

134. Cicero, *De natura deorum* 2.53: "stella Veneris, quae Φωσφόρος Graece
lucifer Latine dicitur cum antegreditur solum." Dante had reminded the reader at
Par. 8.12 that Venus is a day star when it precedes the Sun.

135. *Glossa ordinaria*, in marg., ad verba "In calignoso loco" (2 Pet. 1.19): "*et
lucifer*: id est clarus intellectus noster, vel ipse Christus oriatur *in cordibus nostris*."
Printed in *Textus biblie cum Glosa ordinaria, Nicolai de Lyra Postilla . . .* , 6 vols.
(Lyon: Jacques Maréchal, 1520), vol. 6, fol. 224va.

136. Folco's involute presentation is disentangled to this effect by Sapegno ad
loc. (p. 899).

137. Scot: "et est omni satis fidelis" (M, 103rb).

138. Bonatti: "et conversantur in domibus orationis venerei, ut appareant
quod non sunt, et retineant fidem."

139. Alcabitius: "seque credit omnibus; largitatem quoque significat, et dilectionem, diligentiam, et amorem, iusticiam, et domos orationis, retinet quoque
fidem."

140. *Glossa ordinaria*, interlinearis, ad verbum "meretricis" [Jos. 2.1]: "ecclesie,
scilicet de gentibus congregate, que ante in desideriis carnis fornicabatur cum
idolis, unde: 'Meretrices precedent vos in regno celorum' [Matt. 21.31]." Printed in
Textus biblie, vol. 2, fol. 5v.

Chapter 4: The Sun

1. Although the apparent diameter of the Sun is the same as that of the
Moon, the actual diameter is more than 18 times greater, according to Alfraganus,
who was Dante's authority on the dimensions of celestial bodies. See M. A. Orr,
Dante and the Early Astronomers (London: Gall & Inglis, 1913; rpt. Port Washington, N.Y.: Kennikat Press, 1969), pp. 137–138, 309–310.

2. *Conv.* 2.13.15, 3.12.7; *Par.* 20.1.

3. Ptolemy, *Quad.* 1.1; see also above, Introduction, pp. 1–2.

4. Ptolemy, *Quad.* 1.2, trans. Robbins, p. 7.

5. *Enciclopedia dantesca*, 2:283–285, s.v. "cuore" and 1:357, "ardore."

6. Aquinas, *Summa theologiae* I q.108 a.5 resp. and ad 5. I have analyzed
Dante's complex treatment of the interrelated virtues of the two circles in *Dante's
Swift and Strong* (Lawrence, Kan.: Regents Press of Kansas, 1978), pp. 181–186.

7. Haly: "Scito quod sol est lumen et candela celi."

8. Scot: "Princeps est omnium planetarum, et ideo locatus est in quarto
loco, tantum illuminans superius quantum inferius" (M, 102ra).

9. Alcabitius: "si fuerit nativitas in die significat [Sol] . . . lumen." Bonatti: "habet [Sol] significare lumen."

10. Scot: "operatur calorem, siccitatem, et splendorem" (M, 102rb).

11. Scot: "Ex magisteriis hominum significat . . . lumen splendidum" (M, 102rb).

12. Alcabitius: "si fuerit nativitas in die significat . . . splendorem." Bonatti: "habet significare . . . splendorem."

13. John of Seville: "est . . . coloris albi." Ibn Ezra: "Colorum quidem rubeus temperatus et croceus." Scot: "cuius color est ut auri splendidi" (M, 102ra), and "Ex coloribus significat croceum ut aureum vel ruffum" (102rb). Alcabitius: "Et habet ex coloribus quicquid videtur peregrino colore." Bonatti: "Et ex coloribus habet colorem aemulum, qui videtur participare cum omni colore, et secundum quosdam significat colorem album."

14. *Summa theologiae* I q.108 a.8.

15. Alcabitius: "operatur caliditatem et siccitatem." John of Seville: "temperate calidus et siccus." Ibn Ezra: "est calidus et siccus temperate." Scot: "sibi attribuitur calida et sicca," "operatur calorem, siccitatem, et splendorem" (M, 102rb), and "Natura eius est . . . callida et sicca multum" (105rv). Bonatti: "operatur calorem et siccitatem per naturam suam."

16. Albumasar: "Sol natura igneus temperatus."

17. Haly: "Per solem fit decursus aquarum." He also mentions the heating action of the Sun on ground water ("in decoctione aquarum in ventre terre"), but Dante makes no use of this effect.

18. *Oxford Latin Dictionary*, ed. P. G. W. Glare (Oxford: Clarendon Press, 1982), s.v. "decursus."

19. On the cherubic diffusion of divine light, see text above at n. 6.

20. *Oxford Latin Dictionary*, s.v. "decursus."

21. Haly: "Per eum nascuntur nubes et veniunt pluvie."

22. Downpouring water is also implied in the tears shed when Mary "wept with Christ upon the Cross" (*Par.* 11.72) and also in the Flood that Noah survived (12.18).

23. Alcabitius: "et significat . . . ex substantia . . . universas species substantie." Repeated with attribution by Bonatti.

24. Scot: "Ex substantiis, significat res magni valumenti ut aurum, drapos ad aurum, tapeta, gemmas, aromata, et cetera" (M, 102rb), and "cuius proprietas est . . . delectus omnium que sunt magni valumenti" (M, 102rb).

25. Albumasar: "multaque auri cupiditas." Alcabitius: "ex substantia aurum plurimum." John of Seville: "Eius sunt . . . aurum regni acquirendi suspitio." Ibn Ezra: "metallorum terre aurum." Scot: "Ex substantiis, significat res magni valumenti ut aurum" (M, 102rb). Bonatti: "ex substantia significat aurum plurimum, et maxime rude."

26. Ibn Ezra: "Metallorum . . . itidem preciosi lapides, sicut dyamas."

27. Scot: "placent sibi [homini Solari] pulcra vestimenta colore" (M, 102va), and "Hic enim homo naturaliter delectatur in . . . nobiles drapos lana et colore, etiam syricum, purpuram, tapeta, cortinas, bursas, filum auri" (M, 102va).

28. Scot: "cuius proprietas est . . . copia divitiarum" (M, 102ra); "Dominatur

enim contra . . . divites et beneficatos" (M, 102rb); "Verum est quod habet significare concepto et nato dignitatem honoris et copiam divitiarum" (M, 102ra).

29. Translation and interpolations quoted from Singleton, ad *Par.* 10.107 (6:187). See also my discussion of Peter Lombard in *Dante's Swift and Strong*, pp. 191–197.

30. Scot: "cuius proprietas est vita" (M, 102ra).

31. John of Seville: "habet vim in anima et vita."

32. Alcabitius: "si fuerit nativitas in die significat [Sol] . . . animam vitalem." Albumasar: "eius est omnis eorum . . . vita, caput animantis, cum animali spiritu."

33. Ibn Ezra: "Et secundum ipsius quantitatem vigoris quod ipsius est nature imprimit."

34. Haly: "natura et facta sua apparent in omnibus rebus et cunctis animatis et in animatis existentibus in terra."

35. Haly: "per eum nascitur omnis res nascens, crescit omnis res crescens, crescit omne folium et maturatur omnis fructus."

36. Ibn Ezra: "et eius sunt rosa, alebia, atque siricum."

37. Ibn Ezra: "Ex arboribus dactilorum lignum, vinee, olive, pomaria, celsi ceresarie, fici."

38. Ibn Ezra: "Viventium autem homo, equi, leones, et arietes maxime ultramarini."

39. Scot lists both affinities in his table of properties (M, 105rv; cf. 102rb); Alcabitius notes these affinities at the beginning of his *Isagogicus* (1.2–3, ed. Venice, 1521, fols. 3v–4r), and astrologers today still make use of them.

40. A stronger case can be made for sheep as Solar animals, but from sources Dante is less likely to have known. Ibn Ezra's original Hebrew text also included sheep: "of the living beings, man, horses, lions, big sheep, lambs" (trans. Levy, p. 198). The Old French translation rendered the last two items as "les moutons grans, les carim," the latter being the Hebrew for lambs (ed. Levy, p. 88). Henry Bate, the first Latin translator of the French, turned "the big sheep" into rams and conflated them with the lambs: "arietes magni qui vocantur tarim transmarini scilicet" (ibid.). The second Latin translator, Pietro d'Abano, followed Bate and simplified his text (above, n. 38). On the translations, see below, Appendix 1, s.v. "Ibn Ezra."

41. Scot: "in facie [Sol] est formosus et pinguis" (M, 102ra); "Dominatur enim contra . . . pingues" (102rb); "Sol naturaliter facit hominem in asta grossum et pinguem" (102va); "Parissibilitas . . . pulcher et pinguis" (105rv).

42. Scot: "Hic quidem homo tales habet moralitates quoniam . . . bene comedit et bibit" (M, 102va).

43. Ibn Ezra: "Viventium autem homo. . . ."

44. Scot: "Sol naturaliter in persona tenet cor" (M, 102va). Alcabitius: "Et dixerunt quidam quod habet cor." John of Seville: "Habet vim . . . in corde." Ibn Ezra: "Et ipsius corporis est pars cor." Bonatti: "Et dixerunt Ben et Alboali quod significat ex membris cor."

45. Bonatti: "Et virtus eius et potestas maxime est in capite." Albumasar: "eius est . . . caput animantis." Alcabitius: "Potestas eius est in capite." Scot: "Sol naturaliter in persona tenet . . . caput." Haly attributes the relationship to the Sun's

exaltation in Aries, which in turn rules the head: "Et significat [Sol] de corpore hominis quia sua exaltatio est in Ariete id quod est in sui partitione de homine et est caput."

46. Alcabitius: "Et dixerunt quidam quod Sol significat imaginem vultus hominis." Bonatti repeats this but identifies the sources as "Guellius et Atabari."

47. Thus Sapegno, Singleton, and Grandgent ad loc.

48. Alcabitius: "Et ex infirmitatibus comestionem carnium in ore, et deterimentum oris proprie." Ibn Ezra: "Et ipsius sunt infirmitates omnes in ore contingentes." Bonatti: "Et ex infirmitatibus illas quae fiunt in ore, sicut sunt canceres et aliae quae comedunt carnes oris, et omne detrimentum oris."

49. John of Seville: "est . . . saporis dulcis." Alcabitius: "et habet . . . ex saporibus acrem." Ibn Ezra: "saporum pungitivus." Bonatti: "Et ex saporibus habet acutum." Scot: "Ex saporibus significat mediocrem scilicet inter dulcem et acutum" (M, 102rb).

50. See above, n. 15.

51. Albumasar: "eius est . . . oculo dextro."

52. John of Seville: "habet vim . . . in . . . oculo dextro in die, et sinistro in nocte." Ibn Ezra: "Et ipsius corporis est pars . . . oculus dexter in die, in nocte vero econtrario."

53. Alcabitius: "Ex dixerunt quidam quod Sol significat . . . proprie ex viris oculum dextrum, et ex mulieribus oculum sinistrum." Bonatti: "Et dixerunt Guellius et Atabari quod Sol significat . . . proprie ex viris oculum dextrum et ex mulieribus sinistrum." Scot: "In viris proprie significat [Sol] totam partem corporis lateris dextri et oculum dextrum etc., sicut luna significat partem sinistram, et proprie in mulieribus" (M, 102rb).

54. The Sun's control of the right-hand side of the body may be reflected in Bonaventure's description of himself as one "who in the great offices always put the left-hand care (*la sinistra cura*) behind" (*Par.* 12.128–129). Scot modifies his rule (above, n. 53): "In die sol dominatur omni terre super dexteram partem corporis cuiuslibet animalis et in nocte super sinistram ad contrarium lune de omni" (M, 102rb). Two astrologers preferred the broader formulation—John of Seville ("habet vim . . . in dextro parte corporis tota") and Ibn Ezra ("Et ipsius corporis est pars . . . medietas corporis dextra").

55. If the movement of St. Francis's eyebrows ("ciglia," *Par.* 11.88), which were not weighted down by dejection, is not clearly an ocular allusion, it at least is also proper to the Sun as a facial expression.

56. On the emendation, which does not affect the present interpretation of the passage, see below, n. 136.

57. Scot: "Sol naturaliter in persona tenet . . . medullas" (M, 102va). Bonatti: "Et dixerunt Ben et Alboali quod significat ex membris . . . medulla." Alcabitius: "medullam." John of Seville: "habet vim . . . in . . . cerebro." Ibn Ezra: "Et ipsius corporis est pars . . . capitis cerebrum."

58. Alcabitius: "et significat . . . ex qualitate ipsius animi . . . prolixitatem mentis." Repeated by Bonatti.

59. Ibn Ezra: "De hominis <natura> autem esse eius est scientia." Alcabitius and Bonatti: "est significator . . . scientiarum." Scot: "Sensus eius est . . . sciens, tandem quasi simplex" (M, 105rv).

60. Alcabitius and Bonatti: "est significator . . . spiritus sapientiae." *Lib. nov. iud.*: "significat sensum, intellectum, et sapientiam" (B, 211rb). Scot: "cum [Sol] est in linea solstiali reddit etiam gentes fortes sapientiores quam essent" (M, 102ra), although the *homo Solaris* "se reputat sapientiorem quam est" (M, 102va).

61. Scot: "multum diligit [homo Solaris] sibi dici veritatem et odit mendacia" (M, 102va).

62. Scot: "Ex sectis fidei significat cultum boni actus, ut . . . veritatem" (M, 102rb).

63. Scot: "Hic quidem homo tales habet moralitates quoniam apparet . . . in audiendo attentus" (M, 102va).

64. Scot: "Ex sectis fidei significat cultum boni actus ut . . . studium placide doctrine" (M, 102rb).

65. Scot: "Insuper [hic homo] delectatur adiscere doctrinam honoris et laudis, ut leges et physicam seu naturam" (M, 102va). But he is "in adiscendo mediocris capacitatis" (M, 102va).

66. Scot: "Si Mercurio [complectitur Sol] significat . . . opus librorum et picture" (M, 102rb). Bonatti: "Si vero iungatur ei Mercurius, significat consultores regum et incultores [*sic*] librorum et magnorum operum haereditatum."

67. Albumasar: "iudicia," "opinio," "habitudo bona existimatio," "concilia et cetus hominum."

68. Alcabitius: "et significat . . . ex qualitate ipsius animi . . . prudentiam."

69. Grandgent (p. 915) claims that Aquinas in *Summa theologiae* I q.108 ascribes the function of "judgment" to the Powers, the angelic order proper to the Sun; but in fact Aquinas says that their purpose is to ordain how the precepts or judgments of the higher orders are to implemented: "Tertium est autem est ordinare qualiter ea quae praecepta vel definita sunt, impleri possint, ut aliqui exequantur: et hoc pertinet ad Potestates" (ed Caramello, p. 514, a.6 resp.). Therefore Dante's stress on judgment in the Sun would seem to come from astrology rather than from theology.

70. *Lib. nov. iud.*: "habet . . . linguam" and "eloquentiam" (B, 211rv). Scot: "Hic quidem homo tales habet moralitates quoniam apparet . . . mundus eloquens" (M, 102va).

71. Scot: "Hic quidem homo tales habet moralitates quoniam apparet . . . vanagloriosus sui et suorum magnanimus . . . ; in loquendo baronizat" (M, 102va), and "Ex qualitate animi significat . . . vanagloriam cordis . . . et laudem sui" (M, 102rb).

72. Albumasar: "grave eloquium vicinis noxius, remotis contra; sicque inter hec nunc commodus eiusque hic sublimatio, illic degradatio."

73. Alcabitius: "Sol est significator fidei"; repeated by Bonatti. According to Scot, leadership in faith is signified by the Sun joined with Jupiter: "Si Iovi [complectitur Sol] significat principatum fidei ut prelaturam grandem" (M, 102rb). Since Jupiter in this compound represents rulership, it may be inferred that Scot, too, connected the Sun with faith. Bonatti makes the same connection: "Et si iungatur [Sol] cum Iove, significat principatum in fide atque religione."

74. Albumasar: "summe divinitatis contemplatio."

75. Alcabitius: "Et ex partibus habet partem futurorum, i.e., partem divinationis." Bonatti glosses instead "partem futurorum et divinationis."

76. Ptolemy, *Quad.* 1.6. Alcabitius and John of Seville: "est masculus." Scot (M, 102rb) and Bonatti: "est masculinus."

77. Albumasar: "habet . . . patres." Haly: "Ipse significator est patrum." Alcabitius: "est significator patrum." John of Seville: "habet vim in patre." Ibn Ezra: "De hominis autem esse eius est . . . patres." Scot: "significat etiam patres" (M, 102rb). Bonatti: "Et est significator patrum naturaliter" (twice).

78. Haly: "assimilatur patribus in formis et factis suis."

79. Haly: "gubernator mundi" and "planeta magni dominii."

80. Haly: "Locus suus in celo est quarto, scilicet medius septem planetarum, sicut rex sapiens qui per sensum manutenet regnum suum et per considerationem ponit sedem suam in medio regni sui, ut per omnia latera attingat." Bonatti elaborates: the Sun signifies kings and lay lords "quoniam ipse est positus in medio aliorum, tanquam rex, et alii stant iuxta ipsum, quidam ab una parte, quidam ab alia, superiores scilicet a dextra eius, inferiores a sinistra."

81. Alcabitius: "Et ex magisteriis regimen et principatum" and, for those born by day, "regnum maximum." Cf. Bonatti: "Et habet ex magisteriis regnum, regimina, principatum."

82. Alcabitius: "Si [Soli complectitur Venus] significat regnum per mulieres et per obsequium potentum," and "Si Mercurio, significat consultores regum." Similarly Scot (M, 102rb). Haly takes the Sun to signify a king in each of the twelve signs.

83. Scot: "Princeps est omnium planetarum et ideo locatus est in quarto loco" (M, 102ra). See also n. 80 above.

84. Scot: "Significat patres et magnates, ut papam, imperatorem, reges, et alios barones" (M, 102rb). Albumasar: "regimen imperiale."

85. He addressed Emperor Henry VII as "Cesaris et Augusti successor" (*Ep.* 7.5) and termed Julius Caesar "primo prencipe sommo" (*Conv.* 4.5.12).

86. John of Seville: "est stella regum et potestatum." Albumasar: "reges et primates." Ibn Ezra: "Ex hominibus reges, principes, consules" and "regum pallatia." Scot: "Significat patres et magnates, ut papam, imperatorem, reges, et alios barones" (M, 102rb). Bonatti: "Et significat etiam regnum magnum, et omnes alias dignitates laicales tam magnatum quam aliorum." *Lib. nov. iud.*: "significat . . . quoque reges, primates, nobiles, item et potentes" (B, 211rb); "De hominibus, reges" (211rv); "Solis equidem significatio de regibus, sublimes et potentissimos eorum" (211rv).

87. Ibn Ezra: "Ex climatibus ipsius est quartum, velut babylonie terra, et alaerach terra, et israel."

88. Albumasar: "medium zone habitabilis."

89. Scot: "Significat patres et magnates, ut papam, imperatorem, reges, et alios barones ut soldanum Babilonie et cetera" (M, 102rb).

90. Scot: "Dominatur enim contra Saracenos, omnes Yndos et Yopes" (M, 102rb). The Ganges river, mentioned at *Par.* 11.51, may thus be an astrological allusion.

91. Bonatti argues that the Moon can eclipse the Sun just as the Roman Empire is superior to the caliphate of Baghdad: "Et [Luna] significat naturaliter regem Romanorum, qui habet potentiam super regem Babyloniae de iure, cuius

Sol est significator naturaliter." "Et [Sol] habet ex regionibus Conacant et Oracen et Persidam et terram Romanorum."

92. John K. Wright, *The Geographical Lore of the Time of the Crusades*, American Geographical Society Research Series 15 (New York: American Geographical Society, 1925), pp. 454–455.

93. John K. Wright, "Notes on the Knowledge of Latitudes and Longitudes in the Middle Ages," *Isis* 5 (1923), 88, no. 41.

94. Ibid., no. 52.

95. Scot: "Est etiam planeta potentissimus omnium ad significandum et influendum utrumque scilicet bonum et malum, pacem et guerram" (M, 102ra).

96. Alcabitius: "Si [complectitur Soli] Mars, significat ducatum exercitus et investigationem bellorum." Repeated by Bonatti.

97. Cf. Haly: "Dedit [Sol] Marti suam militiam, et quod dux esset sue militie, quia celum solis est sub celo Martis, et convenit natura et calor suus cum natura et calore ipsius."

98. Scot: "Si Marte [complectitur Sol] significat investigationem bellorum et guerre arsuram occicione" (M, 102rb).

99. Scot: "Quid notificat . . . calorem, deitatem, guerram" (M, 105rv).

100. Alcabitius: "et significat iaculationem iaculorum." Bonatti: "Et habet etiam significare illos qui noverunt bene lanceare lanceas, et iaculare iacula, venationem atque venenationem quae fit per modum venendi, sicut faciunt aliquando aliqui qui venenant sagittas cum quibus occidunt feras." Scot: "Ex magisteriis hominum significat . . . ludibria . . . ut . . . astiludium" (M, 102rb).

101. Bonatti: "Et significat etiam regnum magnum, et omnes alias dignitates laicales tam magnatum quam aliorum."

102. Scot: "Significat patres et magnates, ut papam, imperatorem, reges, et alios barones ut soldanum Babilionie et cetera" (M, 102rb).

103. Scot: "Si Iove [complectitur Sol] significat principatum fidei, ut prelaturam grandem, ut pactum velut esse papa cardinariam [*sic*] factum et cetera" (M, 102rb). Scot's source for this is Alcabitius: "Si [complectitur Soli] Jupiter significat in fide principatum et religionem." Scot stated that the same configuration can also signify simply "religionem" (M, 102rb). See Appendix 2, below, for the conjunction of the Sun and Jupiter.

104. Not to mention Peter of Spain (*Par.* 12.134), who also was a cardinal before his elevation to the papal throne.

105. Isidore, *Etymologiae* 7.13.5.

106. Ibn Ezra: "Viventium autem homo, equi, leones. . . ." The Sun rules, or has his house in, the sign of Leo both by day and by night, according to Ptolemy (*Quad.* 1.17) and the medieval astrologers, e.g., Alcabitius, *Isagogicus* 1.2 (ed. Venice, 1521, fol. 4r).

107. Albumasar: "habet . . . patres et fratres." Ibn Ezra: "De hominis <natura> autem esse eius est . . . patres, fratres, mediocres." *Lib. nov. iud.*: "significat . . . item et fratres mediocres" (B, 211rb).

108. Bonatti: "Sol [est] significator patrum naturaliter. . . . Et est res quam natus diligit prae aliis rebus, praeter fratres de his quae possunt ei accidere ante filios, exceptis predictis 2. post nativitate."

109. Ibn Ezra: "De hominis <natura> autem esse eius est . . . communitatis coniunctio."

110. Scot: "Ex qualitate animi significat portare dulcem amorem propinquis et amicis" (M, 102rb). The *homo Solaris* is "delectabilis et placidus ad societatem" (M, 102va).

111. Scot: "libenter servit alteri quando potest, vel si ad servitium invitaturi et tamen si serviat alteri malum recipit premium, et ideo dicitur quod perdit multa servitia que facit alteri utiliter et bona fide" and "magis est utilis alteri, quam alter sibi" (M, 102va). Scot suggests that the *Solaris* may nonetheless be motivated by ambitious self-interest: "Hic enim homo naturaliter delectatur . . . similiter stare pro vernula domini cum intentione proveniendi ad maiorem gradum honoris, et eligi in dominium ceterorum istae regionis velud est episcopatus, postestarie et cetera" (M, 102va).

112. This appears especially in contrast to Priscian, the other grammarian in the *Comedy* (*Inf.* 15.109); I develop the parallel in *Dante's Swift and Strong*, pp. 27–32.

113. Alcabitius: "significat . . . ex sectis . . . culturam bonam et eis similia." Repeated by Bonatti.

114. Scot: "Ex sectis fidei significat cultum boni actus, ut legalitatem, veritatem, studium placide doctrine, verecundiam laudabilem, magnanimum, et per viam humilitatis subditi se permittit facile convincere" (M, 102rb). Elsewhere Scot explains the connection between humility and the Sun, "cuius condicio est multe varietatis ut sunt signa et ymagines, unde modo ferox est et nocivus quibusdam et aliis et mitis et humilis" (M, 102ra). The *Lib. nov. iud.* associates the Sun with humility in supplications: "significat . . . rursum et quidam vocis interpellant supplicibus humiles atque effabiles petentes" (B, 211rb).

115. Alcabitius: "[Sol] est significator . . . scientiarum et laudum." Scot: "Significatio fame . . . convenienter in omni" (M, 105rv), and "Hic quidem homo . . . affectat habere semper prerogativam laudis et honoris, ut officium ambixaries etc." (M, 102va).

116. Albumaser: "[Sol] habet leges." Scot: "legalitatem" (above, n. 114).

117. *Lib. nov. iud.*: "significat . . . medicos, legem" (B, 211rv).

118. Peter of Spain (Petrus Hispanus Portugalensis), *Tractatus, Called Afterwards Summule logicales*, ed. L. M. de Rijk, [Utrecht] Philosophical Texts and Studies (Assen: Van Gorcum, 1972).

119. De Rijk, p. xxxix: "the *Thesaurus pauperum*, a medical handbook which for centuries was to enjoy a renown [sic] equal to that of his famous manual of logic."

120. R. Stapper, *Papst Johannes XXI. Eine Monographie* (Münster i. W.: Schöningh, 1898), pp. 29–30; de Rijk, pp. xxxix–xlii.

121. *Conv.* 3.11.10, 4.27.8–9. See M. Mattioli, *Dante e la medicina* (Naples: Edizioni scientifiche italiane, 1965), pp. 73–78.

122. Peter of Spain, *Thesaurus pauperum*, pr., in *Practica Jo. Serapionis . . . aliter Breviarium nuncupata* (Lyon: Jacques Myt, 1525), fols. 253r-272r, at fol. 253ra: "In nomine sancte et individue trinitatis, que omnia creavit, que singula dotavit virtutibus propriis, a qua omnis sapientia data est sapientibus et scientia scientibus,

opus supra vires aggredior de ipsius adiutorio confidens qui per nos operatur omnia opera nostra bona sicut per instrumentum, quod opus pauperum thesaurus nominatur, illi hoc opus assignans qui pater pauperum nuncupatur, in quo si attente legatur omnium fere infirmitatum efficaces invenientur medicine et faciles si illum habuerit cooperatorem medicus qui de terra creavit medicinam." I am indebted to my colleague the late Jerry Stannard for a copy of this edition, which he made in the Tübingen University Library.

123. Scot: "Ex magisteriis hominum significat . . . salutem anime" (M, 102rb). Mars and armorers on fol. 101vb.

124. Albumasar: "habet leges, iudicia, magistratus, intelligentias, tum patres et fratres." By Dante's time the classical sense of *magistratus*, which was restricted to government officials, had been broadened to include the academic "degree of master, [or] licence to teach": R. E. Latham, *Revised Medieval Latin Word-List from British and Irish Sources* (London: published for the British Academy by Oxford University Press, 1965), p. 285.

125. Albumasar: "victoria."

126. Scot: "Hic enim planeta semper alta permittit unicuique ac magnifica, ut divitias, dignitatem, honorem, et cetera. Unde facit quemlibet esse beatum in vita sua nisi turbetur ab influencia ceterorum, ut Saturni vel Martis et cetera" (M, 102rb–103va).

127. On the originality of Dante's twofold beatitudes, see E. Gilson, *Dante and Philosophy*, trans. David Moore (New York: Harper & Row, Harper Torchbooks, 1963), pp. 200–224.

128. Alcabitius: "est significator . . . elevationis et perfectionis." Bonatti: "Et est significator . . . elationis et perfectionis."

129. Thus Sapegno: "la nostra persona sarà in uno stato di maggior perfezione (*più grata*)" (p. 962, at *Par.* 14.43–45).

130. Albumasar: "honestas." Alcabitius: "et significat . . . ex qualitate ipsius animi . . . quae sequuntur honestatem, sc. largitatem et gloriam" (Bonatti repeats this). Scot connects the Sun with *honor* or *honestas* seven times, ranging from assertions that the *Solaris* desires, or will get, *honor* to specific examples of the *honores*, e.g., senator or ambassador (M, 102ra–va).

131. *Lib. nov. iud.*: "Solis equidem significatio de regibus sublimes et potentissimos, eorum gloriam et precii ac fortitudinis dignitatem precipue attingit" (B, 211rb).

132. Bonatti: "Et est significator . . . gaudii." Scot: "cuius proprietas est . . . letitia" (M, 102ra); "Que vita eius est . . . leta convenienter et gravis"; "Ars attribuita . . . levius, bona cum gaudio" (M, 104rv); the *homo Solaris* "in facie satis apparet ylaris" (M, 102va).

133. In the same spirit, both Francis and Poverty appear in their union "joyous (*lieti*)" (*Par.* 11.76), and Dominic's father is named "Felice" (12.79; cf. 13.30).

134. *Summa theologiae* I q.45 a.6 ad 2. See also *Enciclopedia dantesca*, 5:872, s.v. "valore."

135. J. A. Mazzeo, *Medieval Cultural Tradition in Dante's "Comedy"* (Ithaca, N.Y.: Cornell University Press, 1960), pp. 56–90.

136. Petrocchi's text does not make theological sense, for it has one person of

the Trinity disposing and signing the other two persons. This interpretation, proposed by Daniello (d. 1565), implies an impossible variation in the love between Father and Son, which according to Catholic theory is eternal and unchangeable: "se lo Spirito Santo (il *caldo amor*) dispone, nell'atto di creare, il Verbo procedente dal Padre . . . ; e *segna*, sugella, l'impronta del Verbo nella creatura, questa aduna in sé il massimo della perfezione" (Sapegno, pp. 954–955, ad loc.). But, as Pietro di Dante perceived, it is God *as a unity* who disposes and signs the material directly ("absque medio") in the special cases of Adam and Christ (ibid.), in contrast to the normal case, in which God operates through the defective intermediary of Nature (*Par.* 13.67–78). Thus the sense requires that all three persons be the subject of "dispone e segna," and accordingly Porena proposed that we read "'l caldo amor, la chiara vista / e [*not* de] la prima virtù"; but Petrocchi rejects this because no manuscript supports the reading, and I would add that the *de* correctly describes the Son's relationship to the Father ("lumen *de* lumine"). There is, however, another possibility: four manuscripts do read "amore" instead of "amor" (Petrocchi, 4:214, at *Par.* 13.79), and hence it is possible that the original read "amor e," some later ones dropping the *e* and the others joining it to *amor*. Thus the sentence would have a compound subject: the "caldo amor" *and* the "chiara vista / de la prima virtù," i.e., all three persons of the Trinity, together disposed and signed the matter of Adam and Christ. Paul Priest does not discuss this problem but assumes on other grounds that the passage describes "the Trinity's *direct* creation of man": *Dante's Incarnation of the Trinity* (Ravenna: Longo, 1982), p. 184.

137. Scot: "Quid notificat . . . calorem, deitatem, guerram" (M, 105rv).

138. Dante, *The Banquet*, trans. Ryan, pp. 174–175.

139. Cf. the more generalized formulation that includes the angels as well: *Par.* 28.106–114.

140. Cf. the Augustinian triad of memory-intelligence-will, the human faculties that endure beyond death and that are both human and divine: *Purg.* 25.79–84 and Singleton ad loc.

Chapter 5: Mars

1. This local patronage is more specific than that of Venus over the whole province of Tuscany, which was based on its hot and humid climate (above, p. 89, n. 108), not to mention that of Mercury over the entire sixth climatic zone, which includes Tuscany (above, p. 63).

2. Scot: "Et cum sit extra temperiem complexionis laudabilis id quod significat" (M, 101va).

3. Haly: "Quando erigitur in circulo suo et separat se ac retrahit a fumositatibus terre et humiditatibus, fortificatur eius calor et siccitas."

4. Haly: "Et quando descendit in circulo suo versus terram et eius fumositates, humectatur et minuitur calor eius." Cf. Ptolemy, *Quad.* 1.19, and John of Seville: "permutatur eius natura causa circuli."

5. For this commonplace doctrine, see e.g., the table of the dignities of the planets given by Alcabitius (ed. Venice, 1521, fol. 3v and 4r).

6. Literary interpretations that see Mars's nature tempered by Venus have been based, not on astrology, but on theories of number and of musical harmony: see Jeffrey T. Schnapp, *The Transfiguration of History at the Center of Dante's "Paradise"* (Princeton, N.J.: Princeton University Press, 1986), pp. 14–18, and Victoria Kirkham, "'Chiuso parlare' in Boccaccio's *Teseida*," *Dante, Petrarch, Boccaccio: Studies in the Italian Trecento in Honor of Charles S. Singleton*, ed. A. S. Bernardo and A. L. Pellegrini, Medieval and Renaissance Texts and Studies 22 (Binghamton, N.Y.: State University of New York at Binghamton, Center for Medieval and Early Renaissance Studies, 1983), pp. 305–351.

7. The vapors in this case are moist exhalations from the sea caused by the rising Sun: see Patrick Boyde, *Dante, Philomythes and Philosopher: Man in the Cosmos* (Cambridge: Cambridge University Press, 1981), pp. 74–81, esp. 81. Mars can also act on dry exhalations: see *Conv.* 2.13.20–24.

8. Ptolemy, *Quad.* 1.4.

9. *Conv.* 2.13.21, trans. Jackson (altered), p. 109; ed. M. Simonelli (Bologna: Pàtron, 1966) p. 61: "<sì come dice Tolomeo nel Quadripartito>, <e>ss<o> Marte dissecca e arde le cose, perché lo suo calore é simile a quello del fuoco; e questo é quello per che esso pare affocato di colore, quando più e quando meno, secondo la spessezza e raritade de li vapori che 'l seguono. . . ." The reference to Ptolemy is a plausible reconstruction suggested by Busnelli-Vandelli (1:203, n. 6). The consensus of MSS reads: "si é che esso asse Marte," but editors who have failed to make sense of "asse" have either suppressed the word (Biscioni) or emended it to read "esso" (Simonelli). It would be both simpler and clearer to read "asse" as the Latinate expression *a se*, "from itself" or "by its own power" (cf. "ab antico," *Inf.* 15.62), and I have adopted this reading in the translation.

10. Singleton, 3.2:172.

11. Stephen Bemrose, *Dante's Angelic Intelligences: Their Importance in the Cosmos and in Pre-Christian Religion*, Letture di pensiero e d'arte (Rome: Edizioni di storia e letteratura, 1983), pp. 21–113.

12. *Summa theologiae* I q.108 a.5 ad 1 (ed. Caramello, p. 512): "*Virtus* autem dupliciter accipi potest. Uno modo, communiter, secundum quod est media inter essentiam et operationem: et sic omnes caelestes spiritus nominantur caelestes virtutes. . . . Alio modo, secundum quod importat quendam excessum fortitudinis: et sic est proprium nomen ordinis. Unde Dionysius dicit, 8 cap. *Cael. Hier.*, quod *nomen Virtutum significat quandam virilem et inconcussam fortitudinem,* primo quidem ad omnes operationes divinas eis convenientes; secundo, ad suscipiendum divina. Et ita significat quod sine aliquo timore aggrediuntur divina quae ad eos pertinent: quod videtur a fortitudinem animi pertinere." Translation in *Basic Writings of Saint Thomas Aquinas,* ed. Anton C. Pegis (New York: Random House, 1945), 1:1001–1003.

13. *Summa theologiae* I q.108 a.6 ad 4 (ed. Caramello): "in nomine Virtutum intelligitur quaedam fortitudo dans efficaciam inferioribus spiritibus ad exequenda divina ministeria." Trans. in Pegis, *Basic Writings,* 1:1008.

14. *Vita nuova* 13.4; see R. Kay, *Dante's Swift and Strong: Essays on "Inferno" XV* (Lawrence, Kan.: Regents Press of Kansas, 1978), p. 187, n. 4).

15. On fortitude: *Ethica Nicomachea* 3.6–9 (1115a–1117b21); Aquinas, *In decem*

libros Ethicorum Aristotelis ad Nicomachum expositio, ed. R. M. Spiazzi, 3rd ed. (Turin: Marietti, 1964), pp. 151–167 (lib. 3, lect. 14–18).

16. Women could also possess *andreia,* though in a way appropriate to their sex: Aristotle, *Politics* 1.13, 1260a22.

17. *Eth. Nic.* 3.6, 1115a33–34, trans. W. D. Ross, *The Works of Aristotle,* vol. 9 (Oxford: Clarendon Press, 1915).

18. *Summa theologiae* II-II q.123 a.3 (mean), a.4 (perils of death), a.5 (war), and a.9 (emergencies).

19. *Summa theologiae* II-II q.123 a.3 resp. (ed. Caramello, p. 581): "ad virtutem fortitudinis pertinet removere impedimentum quod retrahitur voluntas a sequela rationis." The reasons are given earlier in a.1 (p. 557).

20. *Summa theologiae* II-II q.123 a.2 resp. (ed. Caramello, p. 558): "importat firmitatem animi in sustinendis et repellendis his in quibus maxime difficile est firmitatem habere, scilicet in aliquibus periculis gravibus."

21. *Summa theologiae* II-II q.123 a.3–4.

22. *Summa theologiae* II-II q.123 a.5.

23. *Summa theologiae* II-II q.139 a.1.

24. The parts of fortitude are treated in *Summa theologiae* II-II q.128–137.

25. *Summa theologiae* II-II q.128.

26. *Summa theologiae* II-II q.128 resp. and q.129 a.6 (*fiducia* = *magnanimitas*); q.129–133 on magnanimity and its opposing vices.

27. *Summa theologiae* II-II q.129 a.1.

28. *Summa theologiae* II-II q.129 a.3 resp. and ad 2 (ed. Caramello, p. 585): "magnanimus exteriora bona contemnit, inquantum non reputat ea magna bona, pro quibus debeat aliquid indecens facere. Non tamen quantum ad hoc condemnit ea, quin reputet ea utilia ad opus virtutis exequendum."

29. *Summa theologiae* II-II q.133.

30. *Summa theologiae* II-II q.130–132.

31. *Summa theologiae* II-II q.133 a.5.

32. *Summa theologiae* II-II q.129 a.7, q.139 a.1 ad 2.

33. Nonetheless Thomas may well have been the source, since *affani* = *labores.* According to *Summa theologiae* II-II q.139 a.1 ad 2 (ed. Caramello, p. 610): "actus fortitudinis ibi [in patria] est perfrui plena securitate a *laboribus* et malis." For Can Grande's military exploits before 1312, see Singleton ad *Par.* 17.78 (p. 297).

34. Properly speaking, such general recognition is the goal of the magnanimous man (*Summa theologiae* II-II q.129 a.8 resp. and q.132 a.1–2), but magnificence is a species of magnanimity insofar as the former is concerned with doing on a grand scale whatever can be done, whereas the latter more broadly aims at doing anything that can bring due honor (q.134 a.2 ad 2).

35. *Summa theologiae* II-II q.124 a.4.

36. *Summa theologiae* II-II q.139 a.2.

37. *Par.* 17.27: "ché saetta previsa vien più lenta." Cf. *Summa theologiae* II-II q.123 a.9 resp.: "ut Gregorius dicit, in quadam homilia [*in Evang.* 35.1], 'iacula quae praevidentur minus feriunt. . . .'"

38. *Par.* 17.135 is paraphrased in this sense by Sapegno ad loc. (p. 1000); see also *Enciclopedia dantesca,* 1:364.

39. Cf. Kay, *Dante's Swift and Strong*, chap. 6.

40. Ptolemy, *Quad.* 1.4 (above, n. 8); Albumasar: "natura calidus, siccus"; Alcabitius: "operatur calorem et siccitatem"; similarly Haly, John of Seville, Ibn Ezra, Scot (M, 105rv), and Bonatti.

41. John of Seville: "est callidus et siccus absque temperie"; Bonatti: "distemperatam."

42. Scot: "Natura Martis est absque temperamento quia est summe calida et sicca, discors valde ab aliis" (M, 101va).

43. Haly: "Inclinatur Soli amore sui, et defenditur auxilio eius, quoniam Sol exaltatur in domo sua et gubernat eum de calore et siccitate quam recipit ab eodem."

44. Alcabitius: "Leo domus Solis" and accompanying table (ed. 1521, fol. 3v and 4r). The Montecassino commentator, quoted by Sapegno (p. 985 ad *Par.* 16.37), explains how Leo can be said to belong to Mars: "Dicit suum, ratione complexionis eius [Leonis], nam est complexionis calide et sicce sicut Mars." Another, less plausible, explanation is possible, however, since Ptolemy stated that three stars in the constellation Leo, including Regulus, the *cor Leonis*, resembled Mars to some extent in their action (*Quad.* 1.9).

45. Haly: "Debilitatur in signis humidis [*sic*] et aqueis, fortificatur et erigitur natura eius in igneis et aereis signis."

46. Scot: "cuius proprietas est influere . . . siccitatem" (M, 101va).

47. Ptolemy, *Quad.* 2.8 (trans. Robbins, p. 185).

48. Ibn Ezra: "Et eius est corporis qualitas sicca."

49. Scot: "bibo [*sic*], et sepe sitium patiens" (M, 101vb).

50. To be sure, "thirst" occurs in other cantos of *Paradiso*—5 times as a noun (*sete*) and 3 as a verb (*asseta*)—but only here in Mars does thirst seem to be astrologically appropriate.

51. Haly: "est planeta . . . igneus, fervens." Ibn Ezra: "est comburens."

52. Scot: "Operatio in elementiis . . . calorem et arsuram" (M, 105rv); "cuius proprietas est influere arsuram" (101va); "et in signo sue nature, ut Ariete qui est sibi naturalis domus, unus calor eius est arsura vel quasi" (101va); "cuius proprietas est influere . . . combustionem" (101va).

53. Albumasar: "eius est . . . ignitabula exustio." John of Seville: "In die est stella . . . combustionis." Ibn Ezra: "ipse significat . . . ignis combustionem." Scot: "quid notificat . . . combustionem" (M, 105rv), and "ex infirmitatibus significat . . . combustionem, et similia mala sue proprietatis" (101va). Bonatti: "Et cum per se solus fuerit significator, significat . . . combustiones."

54. Alcabitius provides the basic medical principle: "et ex infirmitatibus . . . quicquid fuerit cum inflamatione caloris." Fevers were already mentioned by Ptolemy, *Quad.* 2.8 (trans. Robbins, p. 183); these and red pustules are listed, among other Martian infirmities, by Alcabitius, Ibn Ezra, Scot (M, 101va), and Bonatti. Bonatti inserts impetigo in a list derived from Alcabitius: "Et significat ex infirmitatibus . . . pustulas sanguineas, impetiginem, albaras. . . ."

55. Ptolemy, *Quad.* 2.8, trans. Robbins, p. 183; 1551 ed., pp. 30–31: "Eius autem opera particularia hominibus sunt bellicationes, et guerrae multae inter eiusdem generis viros." Similarly, Scot: "est planeta beliger, et ideo dicitur deus belli" (M, 101rb).

56. Scot: "bella" (M, 105rv); "est . . . planeta bellicosus" (101rb, cf. 101va). Ibn Ezra: "Eius siquidem sunt bellicosi." John of Spain: "In die est stella bellicosorum."

57. Scot: "incipere bellum in campo" (M, 102ra); "item significat scolas doctrine pertinentis ad gueram, ut scruruturam [?], predari, discipare, destruere, inaurare, insurgere, minari, et cetera" (101va).

58. Albumasar: "eius est . . . omne cruentum artificiumque mortiferum."

59. Grandgent jumped to the conclusion—based on the Pilgrim's fragmentary and selective perception—that this is "evidently a triumphal hymn to Christ" (quoted by Singleton ad *Par.* 14.125). Nonetheless the note of victory does sound an authentic Martian theme, for Mars "est planeta . . . victoriosus" (Haly), and "ipsius sunt hominis natura vel habitus . . . victoria" (Ibn Ezra). Cacciaguida claims that in his day Florence went undefeated, since the lily on her standard "non era ad asta mai posto a ritroso" (16.153). Benvenuto explained that victors reverse the standards of the vanquished (*Enciclopedia dantesca,* 1:425).

60. Military service was among the arts ruled by Mars: "Item portare arma in servitio alicuius domini ut potestates terre et capitanei castelli, aut alterius viri qui sit in guerra" (Scot, M, 101ra).

61. The terms "crusade" and "crusader" were not current in Dante's day; equivalents, however, were available, such as "Holy War" and *crucisignatus.*

62. For example, La *"Divina Commedia"* . . . *col commento Scartazziniano,* ed. G. Vandelli, 19th ed. (Milan: Hoepli, 1965) ad *Par.*18.11–51 (p. 769): "combattenti per la Fede"; thus also Sapegno ad 18.31–33 (p. 1003) and *Enciclopedia dantesca,* 3:845. Singleton Englishes this as "warriors for the faith" (ad 18.35–36, p. 305); cf. Musa ad 18.34.

63. Traditional astrology does provide a rationale for the eight heroes. Alcabitius says that Mars "per se significat . . . ducatum exercitus," and Bonatti echoes him. Similarly, Albumasar: "eius [Martis] est . . . reges violenti."

64. Alcabitius: "ex magisteriis habet omne magisterium . . . quod fit per ferrum et ignem, sicut est percussio gladiorum cum martellis." Mars's fiery nature and ruddy color presumably justify respectively his rulership over fire and iron, which almost all our astrologers recognize: fire in Alcabitius, John of Spain, Ibn Ezra, and Scot (M, 101va–b); iron in Albumasar, Alcabitius, John of Spain, Ibn Ezra, and Bonatti. The *Paradiso* does not associate either with Mars.

65. Scot: "Sui [sc. Marti] sit . . . aptatio armorum, ut spate, gladii, lorice, lancee, sagite, et cetera" (M, 101va). Later he varies the list: it is a Martian art "facere loricas, henses, cervileria (*casques*), helmos, iacula, sagitas, lanceas, uncos fer<r>os et cetera armamenta" (M, 101vb–102ra).

66. Although saddles as well as swords can have pommels, "pome" at *Par.* 16.102 is generally taken to refer to the latter: *Enciclopedia dantesca,* 4:592.

67. Another Martian image may occur at *Par.* 16.9, where time is said to diminish the mantle of inherited nobility with its "shears (*le force*)," since Scot says that the arts of Mars include "filing metal instruments": "limare instrumenta metalica ut fibullas et stateras" (M, 101vb).

68. Albumasar: "eius est . . . castra regum"; Ibn Ezra: "et eius sunt castra, turres," and "significat . . . parietes perfodere, hostia frangere."

69. The text names only the castles of Aguglione and Montemurlo; the others are identified by Singleton ad *Par.* 16.62–63, 65, 66 (pp. 273–275).

70. Ptolemy, *Quad.* 2.8: "Mars brings about . . . capture, enslavement" (trans. Robbins, p. 183). Albumasar: "eius est . . . captivitas." Ibn Ezra: "significat et<iam> . . . incarcerare, captivare." *Lib. nov. iud.*: "carcerem" (B, 211rv). Scot: one of the Martian arts is "gubernare malefactores" (M, 102ra).

71. *Lib. nov. iud.*: Mars "significat . . . fugitivos" (B, 211ra).

72. *Enciclopedia dantesca*, Appendice, p. 30: "omnia bona talis non solventis publicentur, vastentur et destruantur, et vastata et destructa remaneant in comuni."

73. Ibn Ezra: "ipse significat . . . sequestationem."

74. Haly: "est planeta . . . destructor" (4ra); "quando est dominus alicuius nativitatis . . . interficit et destruit" (4rb); and "destruit populationes" (4rb). Ptolemy, *Quad.* 1.17: "Mars's destructive and inharmonious quality" (trans. Robbins, p. 81; cf. 2.8). Ibn Ezra: "ipse significat . . . omnem destructionem et confractionem," and "est . . . dissipativus."

75. Ibn Ezra: "Et ipsius sunt hominis natura vel habitus . . . perditiones." Cf. Albumasar: "eius est . . . perditio."

76. See Toynbee-Singleton, pp. 301–302, s.v. "Galigaio" and "Galli"; repeated by Singleton ad *Par.*16.101, 105 (pp. 278–279). See also *Enciclopedia dantesca*, 3:89.

77. In Singleton's notes to *Par.* 16.88–106, 133, I count 19 families that had been "destroyed" in one sense or another.

78. Ptolemy, *Quad.* 2.8 (trans. Robbins, p. 183). Again, Mars causes "violent deaths, especially in the prime of life" (idem). Thus also Albumasar ("eius est . . . pugna cedes") and John of Spain ("est stella . . . mortis ab ense").

79. Ptolemy, *Quad.* 2.8 (trans. Robbins, p. 185).

80. John of Spain: "in die est stella . . . occisionis." Scot: "cuius [Martis] proprietas est influere . . . occisionem" (M, 101va), and "notificat . . . occisiones" (105rv).

81. Albumasar: "eius est . . . contradictio." Ibn Ezra: "et ipsius sunt hominis natura vel habitus . . . contradictiones." Haly: "[Martianus] diligit . . . contrariari alteri leviter" (4ra).

82. Ibn Ezra: "ipse significat . . . contentiones." Albumasar: "eius est . . . dissensiones . . . [et] controversie."

83. Haly: "[Martianus] diligit . . . rixas" (4ra; cf. 4va). Scot: "est [planeta] . . . rixosus" (M, 101rb); "est quidem planeta valde potens in omni significatione mali rixosi et publici" (101va); and "facile movet [Martianus] verba rixe seu dissenssionis" (101vb).

84. Ptolemy, *Quad.* 2.8: Mars "brings about . . . civil faction . . . [and] uprisings (trans. Robbins, p. 183)." Albumasar: "eius est . . . seditiones."

85. Scot: "sepe alteri fal<l>ax et mendax" (M, 101vb); "testimonio alteri est . . . sepe falsidicus" (105rv); "est etiam planeta falsidicus" (101va); and "ex sectis significat illos ex maiori parte promoventur mala facere publice vel privatim, ut mentiendo . . ." (101va). Albumasar: "eius est . . . fallax." John of Spain: "est stella . . . mendacium." Ibn Ezra: "estque . . . augumentativus . . . falsitatum." Bonatti: "significat . . . mendaces."

86. Albumasar: "eius est . . . periurus." Ibn Ezra: "estque periuriorum mul-tiplicativus." Bonatti: "significat . . . periuros."

87. Mars inspires "manifest friendship" (Albumasar: "eius est . . . manifesta amicitia"); hence the pilgrim, who fears he may be "a timid friend (*amico*) to the truth" (*Par.* 17.118), is urged to "make all your vision manifest (*manifesta*)" (128).

88. Scot: "fraudulentus" (M, 101vb). John of Spain: "est stella . . . falsas chartas componentium." Bonatti: "significat . . . falsarios, tam monetae, quam chartarum." *Lib. nov. iud.*: "fraudulentus acusator" (B, 211ra).

89. Scot: "valde est suspitiosus negotiorum in malo et simulator" (M, 101vb).

90. On the fraud, see *Enciclopedia dantesca*, 1:954–955, and sources given by Singleton ad *Purg.* 12.105 (pp. 264–265).

91. Albumasar: "eius est . . . perfidia." John of Spain: Mars "est stella . . . perfidorum."

92. Ibn Ezra: "estque . . . augmentativus . . . accusationum." This tendency can be compounded with Martian falsification to produce a "fraudulentus acusa-tor," according to the *Lib. nov. iud.* (B, 211ra).

93. Haly: "diligit . . . litigia" (4ra). Albumasar: "eius est . . . dissensiones, litigia." John of Spain: "est stella . . . litis." Ibn Ezra: "et ipsius sunt hominis natura vel habitus . . . litigium." Scot: "cuius proprietas est influere . . . litem" (M, 101va) and the Martian knows how "incipere . . . litem in contracta" (102ra).

94. The two lawyers were Baldo di Guglielmo da Aguglione and Fazio dei Morubaldini da Signa (Sapegno ad *Par.* 16.56–57); details in *Enciclopedia dantesca*, 1:498–500 and 3:1043.

95. Thus Singleton ad *Par.* 15.128; a less harsh judgment in *Enciclopedia dan-tesca*, 4:1085–86.

96. Albumasar: "eius est . . . perversi iudices."

97. Ibn Ezra: "in lege prohibita aggreditur," and his first example is "lat-rocinium."

98. Ptolemy, *Quad.* 2.8: "lawlessness . . . robbery and piracy" (trans. Rob-bins, p. 185). Albumasar: "eius est . . . predationes . . . [et] latrocinia." Haly: "est planeta . . . felnus" (4ra), and "eius est latrocinium, furtum, derobare stratas" (4rb). John of Spain: "est stella . . . furum, latronum." Ibn Ezra: "significat . . . eres subripere." Scot: "ex sectis significat . . . furando" (M, 101va), and "stare in convictu predatorum" (102ra). Bonatti: "significat . . . fures . . . [et] latrones diurnos."

99. Singleton ad *Par.* 16.94–95 (p. 277).

100. Ibn Ezra: "ipse significat . . . sanguinem." Albumasar: "eius est . . . omne cruentum."

101. Scot: "Mars naturaliter in persona tenet cistam fellis et humorem eius, in genere epar, cor, venas, renes, et dorsum id est spinale" (M, 101vb). Hence it rules diseases of the blood as well: "est stella . . . infirmitatum a sanguine" (John of Spain).

102. Ptolemy, *Quad.* 2.8: "raising of blood" (trans. Robbins, p. 183). Alcabi-tius: "et per se [Mars] significat . . . effusionem sanguinis" (repeated by Bonatti

and Scot, M, 101rb). Albumasar: "eius est . . . vulnera" and "vulnerum et lesionum causa pluriumque." Alcabitius: "significat . . . vulnerationem" (similarly, Bonatti). John of Spain: "in die est stella . . . vulnerationis."

103. Haly: "totum cor suum exponit in rebus suis agendis" (4rb).

104. *Conv.* 4.22.8: "più ama l'animo che 'l corpo o che altra cosa."

105. Bonatti: "et dixit [Dorotheus] quod significat . . . animi amorem . . . in omnibus rebus."

106. See Kay, *Dante's Swift and Strong*, pp. 199–208. The astrological doctrine of signatures may conceivably play a part in Cacciaguida's concept of a "pure" population (*Par.* 16.51).

107. Albumasar: "eius est . . . omnia contaminans." Scot: "Meliorem graciam habet in extraneis quam in propinquis" (M, 101vb).

108. Albumasar: "eius est . . . corporisque passiones calide."

109. Alcabitius: "natura eius in complexione corporum est colerica." Ibn Ezra: "sua quoque est colericus rubeus." Scot: "significat . . . in humoribus colericum rubeum" (M, 101va); "que infirmitas . . . collerica, calida et sicca" (105rv); and "Mars naturaliter in persona tenet cistam fellis et humorem eius" (101vb). Bonatti: "operatur per naturam suam . . . cholericam." John of Spain: "eius est fel"; he also ascribed another anger-producing organ to Mars: "eius est . . . splen."

110. Ptolemy, *Quad.* 2.8: Mars "brings about . . . the wrath of leaders" (trans. Robbins, p. 183). Albumasar: "eius est . . . gravis ira." Haly: "est planeta . . . iratus" (4ra), and "cito irascitur ira forti" (4rb). John of Spain: "est stella . . . iracundiae." Scot: Mars "reddit etiam gentes sue similitudinis . . . veloces ad iracundiam" (M, 101va); "in ira [Martianus] est clamosus" and "velox ad iram" (101vb). Bonatti: "significat . . . iracundiam."

111. Ibn Ezra: "et ipsius actus sunt cum . . . furore, et rabie," and "morbique eius sunt . . . rabies." Scot: "est planeta . . . furiosus," (M, 101rb), and "ex qualitate animi Mars significat in hominem . . . furorem vie" (101va).

112. Scot: "significat impie et furiose absque modo discretionis" (M, 101va).

113. The Amidei felt "disdegno" towards Buondelmonte (*Par.* 16.137), and canto 17 opens with an intertextual reference to Ovid, *Metam.* 1.756 ("erubit Phaethon *iram*que pudore repressit"), noted by Singleton at *Par.* 17.1 (p. 286).

114. Scot (M, 101va); also Mars "est planeta . . . fortis" (101rb), and "potentia eius est . . . fortis" (105rv). Cf. Albumasar: "eius est . . . vires"; similarly, Ptolemy attributes "violence" to Mars (*Quad.* 2.8, trans. Robbins, p. 183).

115. Above, after n. 36. Alcabitius: "et dixit Dorthius [*sic*] quod . . . significat perseverantium . . . in omnibus rebus" (repeated by Bonatti). Haly: "nec manuum retrahit de faciendo id quod incipit" (4rb). Scot: "ex qualitate animi Mars significat in hominem . . . duritiam" (M, 101va).

116. Albumasar: "eius est . . . effrenis audacia." Alcabitius: "et dixit Dorothius quod . . . significat . . . audaciam . . . in omnibus rebus," and "ex partibus partem audacie" (both repeated by Bonatti). Ibn Ezra: "et eius est facies proterva instabilis." Scot: "est planeta . . . audax" (M, 101rb), which "reddit etiam gentes sue similitudinis audaces in agendis" (101va); *audax* also mentioned at M, 101va, 101vb, and 105rv.

117. Albumasar: "eius est . . . timor ac tremor." Ibn Ezra: "morbi eius sunt . . . timor." Scot: "ex infirmitatibus significat . . . timorem, pavorem" (M, 101va).

118. Scot: "hic enim homo . . . in factis et dictis animosus" (M, 101vb).

119. Albumasar: "eius est . . . elatio magna."

120. According to Alcabitius (and Bonatti, repeating him), Mars signifies "levity (*levitas*)," which may explain why Beatrice "lightens (*disgrava*)" the Pilgrim's burden (*Par.* 18.6). Scot, on the other hand, reports that "in stratera [Mars] est planeta ponderosus" (M, 101rb), though I hesitate to see this reflected in the three uses of *grave* in the Martian cantos: *Par.* 16.36, 17.23, and 17.108.

121. Aquinas, *Summa theologiae* I-II q.84 a.1 in corpore; cf. *Enciclopedia dantesca*, 2:285–286, s.v. "cupidigia" and "cupiditá."

122. Scot: "cito cupit omnia que videt" (M, 101vb). Among the Martian's mental qualities, Scot lists "laxivitatem animi" (M, 101va), i.e., *lascivitatem*, "action without restraint."

123. Alcabitius: "et per se significat . . . invidiam" (this quality is omitted, however, in the 1512 edition). Alcabitius further attributes "maximum invidiam" to a conjunction of Mars with Saturn, and Bonatti repeats this assertion.

124. On the varieties of sloth, see *Enciclopedia dantesca*, 1:26–28, s.v. "accidia."

125. Scot: "valde est suspitiosus negotiorum in malo et simulator" (M, 101vb). Alcabitius takes Mars to signify "negociationem in omnibus rebus," and Bonatti repeats the statement, though the 1491 edition substitutes "negationem" for "negociationem." Scot's assertion probably summarizes Albumasar: "eius est . . . in rerum commutatione consultu reditu, multi murmuris et pene deformis, inverecundus, incestus, spurcus, ingratus."

126. Scot: "prodigus" (M, 101vb, 105rv), "prodigalitatem" (101va), and "largitatem" (101va).

127. Bonatti: "et significat etiam quod comedet natus carnes putridas, et non bene coctas."

128. Scot: "est planeta . . . superbus" (M, 101rb); "facit etiam hominem . . . superbum" (101va); "ex qualitate animi Mars significat in hominem . . . superbiam" (101va); and "moralitas eius est . . . superbia" (105rv). Bonatti: "et dixit [Dorotheus] quod significat . . . superbiam . . . in omnibus rebus" (quoted from Alcabitius); "cum per se solus fuerit significator, significat . . . superbos." John of Spain: "est stella . . . superborum."

129. On the family, see *Enciclopedia dantesca*, 5:776–781. The *Ottimo commento* identified the Uberti with *Par.* 16.109–110 (see Sapegno ad loc.).

130. Bonatti: "dixit Adila: Mars dat homini curuum habere corpus atque crassum."

131. The allusion at *Par.* 17.1–2 to Ovid's tale of Phaëthon includes an intertextual reference to pride: "Phaethon, quem quondam magna loquentem / . . . superbum" (*Metam.* 1.751–752).

132. Albumasar: "eius est . . . forme [*sic*, = fame] et glorie amor." Scot: "cupidus honoris et regiminis" (M, 101vb).

133. Dante touches only obliquely on the related tendency of the proud to be vain and boastful (e.g., *Par.* 16.1–9), perhaps because he stresses this weakness in connection with Mercury. Several astrologers ascribe these failing to Mars, however. Albumasar: "eius est . . . elatio magna, tumiditas, iactantia." Scot: "sensus eius est . . . ingeniosus et vanus" (M, 105rv, cf. 101vb); "vanagloriosus quasi de omni quod habet et facit" (101vb); and "reputat se sapientiorem quam sit ac valentiorem" (101vb).

134. Alcabitius: "et dixit Dorothius quod . . . significat . . . calliditatem . . . in omnibus rebus" (repeated by Bonatti).

135. Scot: "sensus eius est . . . ingeniosus et vanus" (M, 105rv, cf. 101vb).

136. Haly: "est . . . modici intellectus et diminutus sensu" (4rb).

137. Scot: "unde in bonis est simplex vel quasi, et in malis est sapiens vel quasi, et ob hoc recipit multa dampna" (M, 101vb); "facit etiam hominem sagacem in malo exercendo" (M, 101va).

138. According to *Enciclopedia dantesca*, 5:59, "scempia" at *Par.* 17.62 means "dissennato," which corresponds exactly to Haly's "diminutus sensu" (see n. 136, above).

139. Haly: "stultus"; "nescius est et obliviosus . . . nec considerat rerum fines"; and "exaltatio sua est in domo Saturni qui significat . . . gentem stultam."

140. Albumasar: "eius est . . . stulta securitas . . . <in>discretio." The text of the Sessa edition (Venice, 1503) reads "discretio," but the other qualities listed suggest the opposite, which is explicitly given in the *Lib. nov. iud.* as "indiscretus" (B, 211ra).

141. Scot: "significat impie et furiose absque modo discretionis," and "facit etiam hominem . . . impium" (M, 101va).

142. Cf. *Mon.* 2.3.10–17, where Dante traces Aeneas's genealogy in order to show that Rome owed her character to the "patrem romani populi" (§ 6).

143. Scot: "facit etiam hominem . . . inportunum in tollendo et volendo" (M, 101va). Cf. Albumasar: "eius est . . . malignus, temporis incompositus."

144. Albumasar: "eius est . . . varie cogitationis in rebus cogitandis."

145. Scot: "facit etiam hominem . . . loquacem" (M, 101va); "loquax" and "eloquens" (101vb).

146. Cacciaguida's speeches: *Par.* 15.13–30, 46–69, 88–148, 16.34–154, 17.37–99, 124–142, 18.28–36; in indirect discourse, 15.37–39 and 18.37–51. Aquinas's speeches: *Par.* 10.82–138, 11.19–139, and 12.34–142.

147. These references to the "latino" of Aquinas and Cacciaguida need not be taken literally (see *Enciclopedia dantesca*, 3:351) but I see no reason not to. An alternative view of Cacciaguida's Martian eloquence could be developed along the lines indicated by Mark Musa, who observes that "Cacciaguida has in a sense run the gamut of language: from Latin and words the poet could not understand . . . to the use of vulgar proverb here" (ad *Par.* 17.129). Between these two stylistic extremes Musa characterizes Cacciaguida's speech as dignified and archaic in canto 15 (ad 50–53) and as "the genteel vernacular of his own day" in canto 16 (ad 32–33). Yet another possibility is that Dante may have interpreted the loquacious influence of Mars as a general disposition towards speech; at any rate, a variety of speech

phenomena are touched on in the Martian cantos: the language of the heart (*Par.* 14.88–89), baby talk (15.122), an ineffability topos (18.10), and most notably, tongues that are silent rather than loquacious (15.9, 16.45, 16.134, and 17.87)

148. Albumasar: "eius est . . . maledicus." Ibn Ezra: "estque . . . augmentativus maledictionum."

149. Bonatti: "et cum per se solus fuerit significator, significat . . . contumelias." John of Seville: "in die est stella . . . contumeliae." Scot: "cuius proprietas est influere . . . insultus" (M, 101va).

150. John of Seville: "est stella . . . derisorum." Bonatti: "significat . . . derisores."

151. Scot: "dicere dedecus alteri prece alterius" (M, 102ra). Albumasar: "eius est . . . turpiloquia."

152. Scot: "que vita eius est . . . horida sibi et alteri" (M, 105rv).

153. Scot: "ex qualitate animi Mars significat in hominem . . . clamorem" and "ex infirmitatibus significat . . . clamorem" (M, 101va). Haly: "exaltatio sua est in domo Saturni qui significat clamores" (4rb).

154. Alcabitius: "et per se significat . . . feditatem coitus." Bonatti: "significat . . . abundantiam coitus."

155. Scot: "reddit etiam gentes sue similitudinis . . . ad cetera ut et eundem litigan<d>um et luxuriandum," and "est . . . seductor quasi omnium, quia primo blanditur suaviter et postea mordet nocenter" (M, 101va); "violare virginem" is one of his *artes* (102ra).

156. Ibn Ezra: "estque . . . augmentativus . . . lenonie."

157. E.g., by Singleton and by Musa, supported by *Enciclopedia dantesca,* 2:144.

158. Villani, *Croniche fiorentine* 5.38 (text below in n. 231); trans. R. E. Selfe, *Villani's Chronicle* (London: Constable, 1906), p. 121.

159. The episode from the Old French prose romance *Lancelot du Lac* may be read in Paget Toynbee's transcription and translation, "Dante and the Lancelot Romance," *Dante Studies and Researches* (London, 1902; rpt. Port Washington, N.Y.: Kennikat Press, 1971), pp. 1–37, esp. pp. 17 and 30. For divergent interpretations, see the article "Romanzi arturiani," *Enciclopedia dantesca,* 4:1029.

160. Albumasar: "eius est . . . nonunquam aborsus, et causa eiusdem." Alcabitius: "et per se significat . . . casus puerorum, i.e., abortivorum." Ibn Ezra: "et ipse significat . . . fetus in matris utero truncationem et aborsum mulieris immitem." Bonatti: "et si fuerit malli esse, fueritque significator mulieris, abortiet, et aliquando erit ipsa eadem culpabilis illius aborsus."

161. Albumasar: "eius est . . . pregnanti gravis, parturienti inimicus, partui periculosus."

162. That artificially induced abortions were a problem in thirteenth-century Europe can be gathered from John T. Noonan, jr., *Contraception: A History of its Treatment by the Catholic Theologians and Canonists* (Cambridge, Mass.: Belknap Press of Harvard University, 1965; rpt., New York: New American Library, Mentor-Omega Books, 1967): techniques were described, not only by medical writers (Avicenna and Rhazes, p. 249), but by Albertus Magnus (258); canon and civil lawyers

addressed the problem (264–265); actual cases are known (270); and Dante himself may have alluded to the practice in *Purg.* 25 (261–262).

163. Alcabitius: "habet ex etatibus iuventum usque in finem iuventutis"; similarly, Ibn Ezra, Scot, and Bonatti (who defines the age as the years from 22 to 45). Albumasar: "eius est adolescentia."

164. Bonatti: "et ob hoc est Mars naturaliter significator fratrum, quoniam fratres sunt tertium accidens quod accidit nato post conceptionem, scilicet post nativitatem, et quod natura magis diligit inter illa quae possunt ei prius occurrere, sic et Mars est tertius planeta qui est in ordine planetarum, et sequitur Saturnum in ordine ipsorum tertius."

165. Alcabitius: "est significator fratrum." John of Seville: "est stella . . . fratrum." Scot: "est etiam significator fratrum" (M, 101va). Bonatti: "significator fratrum naturaliter." Alcabitius also offers an interpretation at once broader and narrower than his first formulation: "et per se significant . . . fratres medios atque sorores"; cf. Bonatti: "et significat fratres medios." Ibn Ezra: "et ipse significat fratres litigiosos."

166. Scot: "si cum Sole [Mars] significat batituram auri" (M, 101va). Bonatti agrees and gives examples.

167. Scot: "item significant [Mars] scolas doctrine pertinentis [*sic*] ad gueram, ut . . . inaurare," and "ex infirmitatibus significat . . . innaurationem, combustionem, et similia mala sue proprietatis" (M,101va).

168. Ibn Ezra: "eius siquidem sunt . . . expoliatores ferrique artifices."

169. Bonatti: "et si [Marti] iungatur ei Venus, significat opera fabricantium, quae fiunt pro ornamentis mulierum, sicut annuli, monilia, et similia."

170. Scot: "hic quidem homo naturaliter delectatur in arte periculosa vel gravi, fatigabili, vili, ac pauci lucri" (M, 101vb). John of Seville: "habet [Mars] communitatem cum Venere et Mercurio in omni opere manuum."

171. Ibn Ezra: "et ipsius sunt hominis natura vel habitus . . . chorizationes." On the translation, "sing in a choir," see R. E. Latham, *Revised Medieval Latin Word-List from British and Irish Sources* (London: published for the British Academy by Oxford University Press, 1965), p. 85, s.v. "chorizo."

172. E.g., Scot: "Mars duo habet habitacula in celo, scilicet Arietem in die et Scorpionem in nocte" (M, 101vb), and "naturalis domus [Martis] est . . . Aries in die" (105rv).

173. Ibn Ezra: "avium vero astur, et cetere talium que vivunt ex rapina."

174. *The Oxford Classical Dictionary*, ed. N. G. L. Hammond and H. H. Scullard, 2nd ed. (Oxford: Clarendon Press, 1970), p. 651. See also G. Rabuse, *Der kosmische Aufbau der Jenseitsreiche Dantes* (Graz: Böhlaus, 1958), p. 57, n. 46.

175. Al-Biruni, *The Book of Instruction in the Elements of the Art of Astrology*, trans. R. R. Wright (London: Luzac, 1934), whose Arabic text Dante is hardly likely to have known, does assign the wolf to Mars—along with the leopard and the lion! (trans. Wright, § 418, p. 246). Dante could, however, have consulted the *Lib. nov. iud.*, which allots to Mars "porcos, leones, et feras" (B, 211ra); the "feras" appear in al-Biruni as "destructive or mad wild beasts" (p. 246). Cf. Gianni Schicchi and Myrrha, both of whom are destructive pigs in *Inf.* 30.25–46.

176. Alcabitius: "et habet ex coloribus rubedinem"; thus also Bonatti, who attributes the opinion to Alchaiac and Albubeter. Ibn Ezra: "et color aspectus eius intense rubeus existit." Scot: "cuius color est ruffus ut ramum" (M, 101rb; cf. 105rv).

177. In another view, they will redden with blood at the temples: see *Enciclopedia dantesca*, 5:545, s.v. "tempia."

178. Alcabitius: "dixerunt quidam quod habet ex membris . . . venas." Scot: "Mars naturaliter in persona tenet . . . in genere . . . venas" (M, 101vb). Mars also produces facial complexions in various combinations of red, according to Ibn Ezra, Bonatti, and Scot (M, 101vb).

179. Ibn Ezra: "metallorum terre possidet . . . lapidem rubeum omnem."

180. *Lib. nov. iud.*: "margarite marcie sunt potestatis" (B, 211ra).

181. Singleton ad *Par.* 15.22 (p. 252).

182. Ibn Ezra: "Pigmentorum altemdabal et crocus."

183. Scot: "ex coloribus notat ruffum vel album et citrinum" (M, 101va).

184. *Encyclopaedia Brittanica*, 11th ed., 4:952, s.v. "cairngorm."

185. *Enciclopedia dantesca*, 5:653, s.v. "topazio," citing F. Crivelli, "Le Pietre nobili nelle opere di Dante," *Giornale dantesca* 48 (1940), 49–66, and A. Lavasseur, "Les Pierres précieuses dans la *Divine Comédie*," *Revue des études italiennes*, n.s. 4 (1957), 31–100. See also A. Lipinsky, "La Simbologia delle gemme nella *Divina Commedia* e le sue fonti letterarie," in *Atti [del] Congresso nazionale di studi danteschi, Caserta, 1961* (Florence: Olschki, 1962), pp. 127–158.

186. It may well be, as Singleton suggests (ad *Par.* 15.85, pp. 257–258) that Cacciaguida resembled a *heated* topaz, which then turns red; this would be consonant with the other descriptions of the souls in Mars, which stress their redness (14.87, 94; 15.24).

187. Thus *Webster's New International Dictionary of the English Language*, 2nd ed. (Springfield, Mass.: G. and C. Merriam, 1934), p. 57, s.v. "alabaster."

188. Alcabitius: "habet . . . ex saporibus amarum" and "amari sapori" (both repeated by Bonatti). Scot: "significat . . . in saporibus amarum" (M, 101va). John of Seville: "est stella . . . amari saporis."

189. I take it that "the salt taste (*sale*) of another's bread" (*Par.* 17.58–59) does not qualify as bitter.

190. The allusion to Malta (*Par.* 9.54) is decisive: see above, chap. 3, after n. 99.

191. Alfraganus, *Liber de scientia astorum*, trans. Gerard of Cremona, ed. R. Campani as *Il "Libro dell'aggregazione delle stelle"* (Città di Castello: Lapi, 1910), lists places in the third climate, including "regiones Ascemi," which include the "Domus Sanctificationis idest Jerusalem" (pp. 97–98). The translation by John of Seville, ed. F. J. Carmody as Al Farghani, *Differentie scientie astrorum* (Berkeley: n. p., 1943), renders the two passages quoted above as "regiones Assem id est Ierosolimitana regio" and "Beit-al-Macdis id est Domus Sanctificationis siue Domus Sanctificata que est Ierusalem" (diff. 9, nn. 97–108, p. 17). Alcabitius uses Alfraganus's terminology in assigning the region of Jerusalem to Mars: "et dixit Dorothius quod . . . [Mars] habet ex partibus mundi Asce." For the origin of this

regional name, see Campani, ed. cit., p. 97, n. 18. At this point Bonatti, who usually transcribes Alcabitius word for word, paraphrases him: "et habet ex regionibus Hierusalem. . . ."

192. Ibn Ezra: "de climatibus eius [sc. Martis] est tertium, ut Egyptus et Alexandria." For Israel, see above, chap. 4, at n. 87.

193. Against the interpretation offered in the text stands the fact that in Mars Dante displays three heroes associated with the Holy Land: Joshua, Judas Maccabaeus, and the first Christian king of Jerusalem, Godfrey of Bouillon (*Par.* 18.38, 40, 47). Since I am reluctant to assume that Dante was inconsistent, I prefer to interpret these heroes, together with the others who appear with them, as exemplars of martial fortitude in God's service.

194. J. K. Wright, "Notes on the Knowledge of Latitudes and Longitudes in the Middle Ages," *Isis* 5 (1923), 75–98, gives the coordinates of 58 cities from the Marseilles Tables on pp. 87–88. The following fall within the third climate as defined by Alcoarismi: Almedina (no. 17); Algoz (no. 18) = ? Yenbo, the modern port of Medina; Chebil (no. 23), in south-central Asia, = ? Kabul; and Alcazum (no. 47), at the head of the Red Sea, = ? Suez.

195. Scot: "dominatur generaliter contra Saracenos et gentes bellicosas bellatrices" (M, 101vab).

196. Singleton, commentaries ad *Par.* 18.43, 46, 47, 48 (p. 306).

197. Alcabitius: "et dixit Dorthius [*sic*] quod . . . habet ex partibus mundi . . . terras Romanorum usque in occidentem, et terras tuscorum." Bonatti: "et habet ex regionibus Hierusalem et terram Romanorum usque ad occidentem."

198. For suggestive, but not conclusive, evidence that Cacciaguida may have been related to the Elisei family, which various legends traced to a Roman origin, see *Enciclopedia dantesca*, 2:658, s.v. "Elisei."

199. Alcabitius: "et terras tuscorum." For context, see n. 197, above. Both the 1512 and 1521 editions read "tuscorum."

200. Alcabitius: "et dixit Dorothius quod . . . significat . . . mobilitatem . . . in omnibus rebus." On Dorotheus, see *The Oxford Classical Dictionary*, 2nd ed., p. 363.

201. Haly: "sua natura mobilis et mutabilis est, et fit una [tempestas, sc. aestas] vice humidus et alia [sc. hiems] siccus" (4rb). Ibn Ezra: "significat et<iam> motum de loco in locum." Scot: "potentia eius est . . . fortis, tutus, et motor" (M, 105rv).

202. Alcabitius: "et dixit Dorothius quod . . . significat . . . festinationem in omnibus rebus," and "per se significat . . . festinationem" (both repeated by Bonatti).

203. Scot: "ex qualitate animi Mars significat in hominem . . . velocem motum" (M, 101va); "moralitas eius est . . . velocitas" (105rv); and "reddit etiam gentes sue similitudinis . . . veloces ad iracundiam" 101va).

204. Scot: "facit etiam hominem . . . agilem" (M, 101va), and "leviter vadit [homo Martianus] et celere" (101vb).

205. On *avaccio*—from Latin *vivacius*—see Singleton ad *Inf.* 10.116 (p. 159) and ad *Par.* 16.70 (p. 275).

206. Albumasar: "eius est . . . improvisa festinatio."

207. Ibn Ezra: "significant et<iam> . . . percutere." Albumasar: "eius est . . . plage."

208. In comparing the satire of his poem to the wind, "che le più alte cime più percuote" (*Par.* 17.134), Dante may also have in mind Mars's association with destructive winds, mentioned three times by Ptolemy, *Quad.* 2.8.

209. Scot: "Ex infirmitatibus significat . . . percussionem iniuriosam," and "ex sectis significat illos ex maiori parte promoventur mala facere publice vel privatim, ut . . . percutiendo" (M, 101va).

210. Benvenuto da Imola, *Comentum super Dantis Comoediam*, vol. 5 (Florence: Barbèra, 1887), p. 151: "ibat per domum . . . baculo in manu, nunc verberabat famulum, nunc coquum."

211. On natural and violent motion, see *Science in the Middle Ages*, ed. David C. Lindberg (Chicago: University of Chicago Press, 1978), p. 211.

212. Alcabitius: "est significator . . . peregrinationum," which Bonatti repeats, adding "naturaliter." Scot: "et etiam significator . . . peregrinationem" (M, 101va). Bonatti offers a less philosophical explanation than the one I have advanced: he suggests that trips, like Mars, bring many difficulties: "et est significator peregrinationum, quoniam in peregrinationibus accidunt peregrinantibus incommoda multa, et multae angustiae et predationes atque labores impii, et similia, quae assimilantur significatis Martis."

213. Alcabitius: "et per se significant . . . peregrinationem extra patriam." Bonatti: "significat peregrinationes extra terram, et extra patriam suam."

214. For the view that Dante modelled his poem on the travel accounts of medieval pilgrims, see John G. Demaray, *The Invention of Dante's Commedia* (New Haven, Conn.: Yale University Press, 1974).

215. Ibn Ezra: "ipse significat . . . revelationem," and "significat . . . omne detectum pandere."

216. Alcabitius: "si nullus planeta ei complectitur, significat . . . apertionem."

217. Allusions to Dante's exile: *Inf.* 10.79–81, 127–132, 15.61–72, 24.140–151, *Purg.* 8.133–139, 11.139–141.

218. Scot: "hic autem planeta reddit semper alteri quod promittit, scilicet fortunam adversitatis et facit hominem multipliciter infelicem" (M, 101vb). Elsewhere Scot says Mars "est etiam planeta falsidicus, nequam, et infortuna" (101va); Haly simply says that Mars "infortunat" (4rb).

219. Ibn Ezra: "et ipse significat . . . omnem rem iniquam subito emergentem." Albumasar: "eius est . . . cunctique repentini proventus." Cf. Ibn Ezra: "significat et<iam> . . . ingressum in pericula." *Lib. nov. iud.*: "angustiam" (B, 211ra).

220. In causing the rich and the beggars to exchange their respective conditions, Can Grande will perform the function that Virgil assigned to Fortuna (*Inf.* 7.77–81), so this, too, may be taken to be an allusion to fortune.

221. Scot: "est planeta . . . multis nocivus influentia sui" (M, 101rb) and "iniuriosus" (101vb).

222. John of Seville: "est stella . . . malorum." Alcabitius: "est . . . malus."

223. Ibn Ezra: "et omnino malus totus existit, privatus simpliciter bono."

224. Scot: "est etiam planeta falsidicus, nequam, et infortuna" (M, 101va).

225. Albumasar: "eius est . . . maledicus, maleficus, malignus."

226. Scot: "hic enim homo tales habet moralitates quantum . . . est . . . malitiosus . . . odiosus . . . in malefactis est curiosus" (M, 101vb).

227. Ibn Ezra: "estque turpitudinum augmentativus."

228. These frequency figures are based on *A Concordance to the Divine Comedy of Dante Alighieri*, ed. E. H. Wilkins et al. (Cambridge, Mass.: Harvard University Press, 1960).

229. Singleton translates: "how ill for you that you did fly . . . at the promptings of another." I have followed the more precise nuances indicated by the *Enciclopedia dantesca: male* here = "con danno proprio o altrui" or "per sventura" (3:786) and *conforto* = "il consiglio" (2:144). *Male* might also be translated here as "misfortunately," which would accord with Mars's reputation as the "planeta infortuna," but "harmfully" is more specific.

230. Scot: "cito cupit omnia que videt" (M, 101vb). See above, n. 122.

231. Villani, *Croniche fiorentine* 5.38, s. a. 1215: "una donna di casa i Donati il chiamò, biasimandolo della donna ch'egli avea promessa, come non era bella nè sofficiente a lui, e dicendo: io v'avea guardata questa mia figliuola: la quale gli mostrò, e era bellissima; incontamente . . . preso di lei, la promise e isposò a moglie. . . ." Quoted by Toynbee-Singleton, p. 119.

232. Dante's belief that both were native Florentine families rather than immigrants is historically inaccurate: *Enciclopedia dantesca*, 1:209–210, 2:555–557.

233. Singleton, trans. *Par.* 17.62–65 (p. 191). Sapegno (ad loc., p. 996) agrees with him that Dante is the object of ingratitude and impiety. But I translate "si farà contra" in the sense defined in *Enciclopedia dantesca*, 2:802, no. 25.

234. Paget Toynbee, *Dante Alighieri: His Life and Works*, 4th ed. (London, 1910; rpt., New York: Harper & Row, Harper Torchbooks, 1965), p. 90.

235. The two hills are also appropriate in the context of luxurious living, as suburban villas were located on both sites: *Enciclopedia dantesca*, 3:1021.

236. Most likely the "fiorentino e cambia e merca (*Par.* 16.61) is to be identified with Lippo Velluti (fl. 1295), whose family came from Semifonte: *Enciclopedia dantesca*, 5:906–907.

237. The extreme *terminus a quo* for the immigration from Semifonte would be 1198, when Florence acquired the place: *Enciclopedia dantesca*, 5:150.

238. F. Schevill, *Medieval and Renaissance Florence* (New York: Harper & Row, Harper Torchbooks, 1961), 1:134–136; originally titled *History of Florence* (New York: Harcourt, Brace, 1936).

239. Singleton translates *nequizia* as "iniquity" at *Par.* 15.142; the context has suggested "pravità" here and "sentimento perverso" at *Par.* 6.123: *Enciclopedia dantesca*, 4:38–39.

240. Aquinas, *Summa theologiae* I-II q.84 a.1 resp.: "quandam inclinationem naturae corruptae ad bona corruptibilia inordinate appetenda."

241. Scot: "cito cupit omnia que videt" (M, 101vb).

242. Aquinas, *Summa theologiae*, I-II q.84 a.1 resp.: "Videmus enim quod per divitias homo acquirit facultatem perpetrandi quodcumque peccatum, ad adim-

plendi desiderium cuiuscumque peccati: eo quod ad habenda quaecumque temporalia bona, potest homo per pecuniam iuvari; secundum quod dicitur *Eccle.* 10, [19]: 'Pecuniae obediunt omnia.'"

243. *Enciclopedia dantesca*, 2:285–286.

244. The relevant passages have been collected and analyzed by Joan M. Ferrante, *The Political Vision of the "Divine Comedy"* (Princeton, N.J.: Princeton University Press, 1984), pp. 335–366. Ferrante also discerns and stresses a positive side to Dante's financial imagery.

245. Georg Rabuse, *Der kosmische Aufbau der Jenseitsreiche Dantes* (Graz-Cologne, 1958).

246. *Enciclopedia dantesca*, 3:742–743.

247. G. Wissowa, *Religion und Kultus der Römer*, Handbuch der klassischen Altertumswissenschaft, ed. I. von Müller, Band 5, Abt. 4 (Munich, 1902), pp. 131–133, 483–485. See above, n. 174.

Chapter 6: Jupiter

1. Ptolemy, *Quadripartitum* 1.4: Jupiter "heats," and "his heating power is the greater by reason of the underlying spheres" (trans. Robbins, p. 183). Albumasar, John of Seville, and Ibn Ezra: "calidus." Alcabitius: "operatur [Jupiter] calorem." Bonatti: "operatur [Jupiter] per naturam suam, caliditatem." Scot: "Natura eius est . . . calida" (M, 105rv).

2. Ptolemy, *Quad.* 2.8: Jupiter "humidifies" (trans. Robbins, p. 183). Albumasar, John of Seville, and Ibn Ezra: "humidus." Bonatti: "operatur [Jupiter] per naturam suam, . . . humiditatem." Scot: "Natura eius est . . . humida" (M, 105rv).

3. See Scot's tabular list of planetary properties: "Natura eius [sc. Veneris] est . . . tepida et satis humida" (M, 105rv).

4. Alcabitius: "operatur [Iupiter] calorem et humiditatem temperatam." Scot: "Natura Iovis est temperate calida et humida" (M, 101ra)"; Operatio in elementis est . . . calidum et humidum temperate" (M, 105rv); "Operatur quidem in aere calorem et humiditatem temperantiam" (M, 100vb). Ptolemy, *Quad.* 2.8: "sed aër temperabitur" (ed. 1551, p. 30). Haly: "per eius [sc. Iovis] equalitatem, communitatem, et sue complexionis temperiem, estatis calor et frigus hiemis temperatur."

5. Ptolemy, *Quad.* 2.8: "Sed aër temperabitur, eritque salutifer, ac multorum uentorum humidorum terrae fructus augmentabit" (ed. 1551, p. 30). Cf. *Quad.* 1.4: Jupiter "produces fertilizing winds" (trans. Robbins, p. 183). Similar statements occur in Alcabitius, Haly, Bonatti, and Scot (M, 100vb).

6. Haly: "Et quamvis deus secretum sciat, dicunt tamen aliqui sapientes quod creatus et factus est Juppiter de claritate aeris et lumine suo, ac de vento eius limpido et purgato."

7. Scot: "in fabulis poetarum . . . dicitur ab eis quod Iupiter est stella . . . aerea, temperans ventos et alias impressiones" (M, 101ra).

8. On Jupiter's affinity for blood: Alcabitius, Haly, Bonatti, and especially (7 references) Scot.

9. Mount Etna's first major eruption since Roman times occurred in 1169 and the next in 1669: *Encylopaedia Britannica*, 11th ed., 9:852.

10. Ptolemy, *Quad.* 2.8: "salubres erunt maris nauigationes, & fluminum fundationes temperatae" (ed. 1551, p. 30).

11. Cf. *Par.* 20.72: Ripheus now sees more of divine grace than most men, "even though his sight discerns not the bottom." Since the medium is not stated, one cannot be sure whether or not this is a water image.

12. Alcabitius: "Et si complectitur ei [Iovi] luna, significat scientiam dispositionis aquarum et mensure earum necnon terrarum."

13. Alcabitius: "hic aspectus vocatur tetragonus . . . et est aspectus discordie atque medie inimicice" (ed. 1521, 4r). Cf. Appendix 2.

14. See the article "spirito," *Enciclopedia dantesca*, 5:387–390.

15. On the Aristotelian meteorology of winds, see Patrick Boyde, *Dante Philomythes and Philosopher: Man in the Cosmos* (Cambridge: Cambridge University Press, 1981), pp. 76–78.

16. Cf. God, "that serene which is never clouded (*si turba*)," *Par.* 19.64–65. Here and in *Par.* 18.120 Dante, of course, does not mean to be taken literally. Actually, according to Haly, Jupiter's light is brightest in the sign of Taurus, where it was at the ideal date of the *Comedy* (Appendix 2), and it is more or less obscured in other signs.

17. *Convivio* 2.13.25 (trans. Jackson): "muove tra due cieli repugnanti a la sua buona temperanza, sì come quello di Marte e quello di Saturno; onde Tolomeo dice, ne lo allegato libro, che Giove è stella di temperata complessione, in mezzo de la freddura di Saturno e de lo calore di Marte."

18. Ptolemy, *Quad.* 1.4: "Stella Iovis temperatae naturae est. Media enim fertur inter frigificam Saturni et aestuosam Martis." Quoted from *Convivio*, ed. Busnelli-Vandelli, 1:207.

19. Albumasar: "natura [Iovis] . . . temperatus . . . est," i.e., "temperantia." Haly: "Iuppiter est planeta equalitatis . . . quia temperatus est equalis." John of Seville: "est . . . temperate." Ibn Ezra: "equalis comixtionis." Bonatti: "Et operatur per naturam suam . . . temperatam."

20. See the preceding note for the identification of temperance with equality in astrological doctrine.

21. Scot: "Hic quidem planeta . . . facit quemlibet beatum in suo gradu" (M, 101ra); "in fabulis poetarum . . . dicitur ab eis quod Iupiter est stella benedicta." Bonatti: "Et ex partibus habet [Iuppiter] partem beatitudinis et profectus."

22. Trajan and Ripheus at *Par.* 20.100–129, the Indian at 19.67–81.

23. Ptolemy, *Quad.* 2.8: "cuius opus proprium in hominibus . . . generaliter est occasio fortunae" (ed. 1551, p. 30). Alcabitius: "Iupiter [est] fortuna." Haly: "fortuna per aspectum et corporalem coniunctionem." John of Seville: "Iupiter est . . . fortuna." Bonatti: "Dixit Alchabicius, Iupiter est fortuna." Scot: "Est etiam planeta . . . fortunatus" (100vb); "Hic quidem planeta reddit semper, ac promittit alteri prosperam fortunam" (M, 101ra); "[homo Iovinus] est homo fortunatus alteri, et ideo habet bonum incontrum et superadventum unicuique aliquid facienti nuper" (101rb).

24. See "Fortuna," *Enciclopedia dantesca*, 2:983–986; and, for an appreci-

ation of the novelty of Dante's concept of Fortuna, C. S. Lewis, *The Discarded Image* (Cambridge: Cambridge University Press, 1964), pp. 139–140.

25. Two astrologers connect Jupiter with the interpretation of dreams or visions, which is fortune telling of a sort. Albumasar: "visionum interpretatio"; Ibn Ezra: "vultque [homo Iovinus] scire . . . somniorum interpretationes."

26. Sapegno ad *Par.* 18.70 (p. 1006): "*giovial*: vale: «di Giove», e anche «gioioso»: dal significato primario e tecnico dell'aggetivo si desunse assai presto, senza uscire dall'ambito del linguaggio astrologico, quello traslato di «giocondo, lieto». . . ." Singleton (ad loc.) assumed even more: "in 'giovial' there is doubtless a play on the adjective in its more common sense of 'jovial,' since the planet Jove (Jupiter) was thought to make those born under it to be of joyful and merry disposition" (p. 308).

27. A. Forcellini, *Totius Latinitatis lexicon* (Prato: Giachetti, 1842), s.v. "jovialis." Once the term does refer to the star: Macrobius, *Commentarii in Somnium Scipionis* 1.19.25, "Veneria et Iouialis stella"; the other instances simply refer to the god.

28. After Abulmasar, only Scot connects Jupiter with *hilaritas*: "Facit etiam [in homine] . . . faciem yllarem" (M, 101ra); "Ex figuris hominum significat [Iupiter] . . . [hominem] contra quamlibet personam quasi ilarem et facundum" (M, 101ra).

29. Scot: "Et proprietas eius [Iovis] est . . . gaudium corporis, letitie anime" (M, 100vb); "Item significat [Iupiter] . . . gaudium corporis, letitiam anime" (M, 101ra). He does not maintain the distinction, however: the planet itself is "semper letus" (M, 101vb), it can signify "gaudium novum" (M, 100vb), and it makes the life of a native "gaudiosa" (105rv).

30. Ibn Ezra: "facie ridens." Scot: "[homo Iovinus] semper gerit alacrem faciem contra quamlibet personam" (M, 101rb); "est [homo] etiam . . . aliquantulum grata" (M, 101rb).

31. The classical Latin form *iucundus*, which was derived from *iuuo* ("I help"), was altered in medieval Latin to *iocundus* on the false assumption that it was derived from *iocus*.

32. Albumasar: "Jupiter natura . . . dulcis . . . est"; "et ex saporibus habet dulcem." John of Seville: "eius [Iovis] est . . . gustus dulcis." Bonatti: "Et ex saporibus significat saporem dulcem."

33. Scot: "Ex saporibus significat dulcem et suavem, non vini, zuccari, et cetera" (M, 101ra); "Est enim planeta . . . temperate dominationis in unoquoque dulci" (M, 100vb); "Est [homo Iovinus] . . . in respondendo dulcis" (M, 101rb).

34. Ptolemy, *Quad.* 2.8: "[Iupiter] cuius opus proprium in hominibus est . . . augmentum etiam rerum, quibus opus habent homines" (ed. 1551, p. 30; trans. Robbins, p. 183). This is especially true when Jupiter rules alone: "Iupiter autem cum solus fuerit dominus dispositionis, res generaliter augmentabit" (ibid.).

35. Alcabitius: "et substantie significat abundantiam"; repeated by Bonatti.

36. Haly: "Non habetur utilitas nec aliquid bonum in aliquo factorum nec in aliqua rerum nisi per eum." Albumasar: "[homo] officio et sibi et suis utilis." Alcabitius: "et est planeta . . . usus"; Bonatti: "boni usus." John of Seville: "est stella . . . omnis commodi."

37. John of Seville: "eius est virtus crescendi."

38. Ibn Ezra: "Et denotat . . . fructificationem cum ipsius augmento." Albumasar: "fructuosus."

39. The etymon of *fruor, frui* is *frux*, "fruits." For the theological use of *frui*, see *Enciclopedia dantesca*, 3:66, s.v. "frui." Singleton ignores the theological sense of *frui*, which he translates simply as "fruition."

40. Scot: "Sciendo quod si sit victor coniunctionis [cum Saturno vel Marte], significat omne bonum uniquique in suo gradu, ut . . . ubertatem rerum victualium, panis, vini, olei, animalium, crocei, et quasi omnium" (M, 100vb); "Et proprietas eius est nutrimentum" (M, 100vb). Albumasar: "est eius virtus naturalis ac nutritiva."

41. Haly: "Et quando fortis est, felix et firmus in nativitatibus, fortuna et nati nutritio adimpletur." Scot: "Studet [homo Iovinus] vivere delicate cibus et potibus" (M, 101rb).

42. Scot: "Insuper delectatur [homo Iovinus] habere . . . vineta" (M, 101rb); "ubertatem . . . vini" (M, 101vb); "[Iupiter est] significator mobilis substantie et bone conditionis ac pulcre, ut pecunie, grani, vini, cere, lini, bo<m>bacis, piulorum, et cetera" (M, 100vb).

43. Albumasar: "est eius [Iovis] . . . progenies." John of Seville: "est stella filiorum." Ibn Ezra: "Et ipse itidem pueros et puerorum pueros denotat." Scot: "Item significat . . . bonos filios" (M, 101ra).

44. Scot: "Significat [Iupiter] habundanciam substancie utilis, ut pecunie proventum" (M, 101ra); for the primacy of money, see the series quoted in n. 42 above.

45. Scot: "Quid notificat . . . divi, lucrum, honorem" (M, 105rv); "dominatur enim Iupiter super . . . viros nobiles non corpulentos, set divites, honoratos, et sanguineos" (M, 101ra); "Est enim planeta . . . proficuus" (M, 100vb); "Item delectatur [homo Iovinus] . . . velle habere multas divitias rerum mobilium et immobilium, ut pallia, turres, domos honorabiles, pulcra structura, viridaria arborum et herbarum nobilis essende fructu et odore" (M, 101rb).

46. John of Seville: "est stella . . . pecunie."

47. Ibn Ezra: "Quod autem maxime cogitat est acquirere pecuniam." Scot: "Hic quidem homo naturaliter delectatur in arte . . . multum proficua, velut est . . . sedere ad theloneum et ibi cambire monetam" (M, 101rb).

48. *Convivio* 2.13.25 (trans. Ryan): "intra tutte le stelle bianca si mostra, quasi argentata."

49. Ibn Ezra states that Jupiter governs the colors white, green, and yellow, but this is not to say that the planet itself was so colored: "Ex coloribus autem album, viride, citrinum, et equale." Scot says that Jupiter gives humans white skin and "good color in the face" (M, 101ra); Bonatti mentions only the facial color, which is "aureus admixtus albo."

50. Scot: "in colore ut electrum vel cuprum" (M, 100vb); "Color eius est electri vel cupri" (M, 105rv); "in fabulis poetarum . . . dicitur ab eis quod Iupiter est stella . . . alba" (101ra); "Est enim planeta . . . coloratus" (M, 100vb). Jovian merchants like to deal in gold and silver (M, 101rb).

51. *Convivio* 2.13.27 (trans. Ryan): "la Geometria è bianchissima, in quanto è

sanza macula d'errore e certissima per sé e per la sua ancella, che si chiama Perspettiva."

52. Scot: "Hic quidem homo naturaliter delectatur in arte levi, honorabili, placibili, famosa, et multum proficua, velut est . . . ducere mercationem rerum honorabilium, ut . . . gemmas et . . . vit<r>eos [*var.* vitros O]" (M, 101rb).

53. Ibn Ezra: "Et lapis 'latot' appelatus, albus et citrinius saphyrus, et onicinus, cristallus, et omnis lapis albus, nitens, et utilis," and "Ex coloribus autem album, viride, citrinum, et equale; atque omne lucidum luminosum observat."

54. A. Lipinsky takes Dante's *rubinetto* to be the true, dark ruby, which ancient lapidarists referred to as a "live coal" (*carbunculus*); it was supposed to have exceptional occult power because it united in itself the powers of all other gems: "La Simbologia delle gemme nella 'Divina Commedia' e le sue fonti letterarie," *Atti [del] Congresso nazionale di studi danteschi, Caserta, 1961* (Florence: Olschki, 1962), pp. 127–158, at p. 140.

55. Scot: "Delectatur in hornatu pulcrorum vestimentorum et colore nobili, incisione laudabili" (M, 101rb); "Hic quidem homo naturaliter delectatur in arte levi, honorabili, placibili, famosa, et multum proficua, velut est . . . vendere drappariam bonorum pannorum et pulcrorum colorum," and "ducere mercationem rerum honorabilium, ut . . . cinturas, bursas sete, drapos auri, tapetos et cortinas, diversea incisionis" (M, 101rb). See n. 45 above for "pallia," a Jovian form of conspicuous consumption.

56. Scot: "Delectatur . . . laborare cum acu, ut bursas, coopertoria altariorum, cervicalium cunarum puerorum; vella facere dominarum, tripolli bisum purpuram" (M, 101rb).

57. Ibn Ezra: "Vestimentorum quoque pulchra velut coti, omnisque clamis subtilis."

58. Scot: "bombicis" (M, 100vb, 101rb), "sericum" and "sete" (M, 101rb), "lini" (M 100vb), and "frixios" (M, 101rb).

59. Language arguably applicable to textile design and needlework: *guida*, "pattern" (*Par.* 18.110); *distinto* (18.90, 108); *dipinta* (20.102), *dipinge* (18.109); and *ritrar* (19.7).

60. Ibn Ezra: "Avium autem paviones, galline, columbe, et avis quelibet grano fruens hominibus utilis."

61. Scot: "Insuper delectatur [homo Iovinus] habere . . . bestiolas consolationis in domo bone apparentie, ut . . . aviculas in caveis, columbos, pavones, capones, falcones, ancipitres" (M, 101rb); "Item delectatur . . . aucupare."

62. No antecedents for the Bonatti illustration appear in the *Verzeichnis astrologischer und mythologischer illustrierter Handschriften des lateinischen Mittelalters*; indeed, this incomplete survey found Jupiter pictured with an eagle in only three astrological MSS, all fifteenth century (one Italian), and then the presence of Ganymede indicates a mythographic source: vol. 3, *Handschriften in englischen Bibliotheken*, by Fritz Saxl and Hans Meier, ed. Harry Bober (London: Warburg Institute, 1953), p. 52 and plate VII.

63. Haly: "Iuppiter est planeta . . . formose apparentie et composite persone."

64. Thus *The Oxford Latin Dictionary*, ed. P. G. W. Glare (Oxford: Clarendon Press, 1982), s.v. "compositus."

65. Haly: "Juppiter est planeta . . . communitatis." Alcabitius and Bonatti: "et ex operibus . . . participationem." Albumasar: "hominum societates, cohabitatio, contubernium." Ibn Ezra: "Quod autem maxime cogitat est . . . congregare." Oddly enough, the astrologers also perceive an antisocial strain in Jupiter: John of Seville calls it the star "quietis" and "contemplativorum"; Scot says the Jovian is "in societate quietus" (M, 101rb); and the *Lib. nov. iud.* declares that "loca occulta et inhabitata frequentat et diligat" (B, 210va). Dante may be echoing this trait in his allusion to John the Baptist "che volle viver solo" (*Par.* 18.134).

66. Scot: "Sciendo quod si sit [Iupiter] victor coniunctionis [cum Saturno vel Marte], significat omne bonum unicuique in suo gradu, ut . . . concordia in discordantibus" (M, 100vb). Bonatti: "Et habet intueri quando videt aliquos inter se altercantes seu litigantes, et ponere pacem inter eos, et concordiam mittere in eos, et in bonis semper studere."

67. John of Seville: "eius est . . . cor." Ibn Ezra: "nobilitas cordis."

68. *Oxford Latin Dictionary*, s.v. "concors," notes that the musical sense of the term was influenced by the false etymology *con* + *chorda*, "togetherness of strings."

69. Scot: "Item delectatur [homo Iovinus] . . . uti . . . sonitum instrumentorum bene sonantium" (M, 101rb). Alcabitius: "Et si complectitur ei [Iovi] Venus, significat compositionem sonorum et aliarum scientiarum delectabilium"; Bonatti repeats this and adds: "Erit enim natus citharizator, tubilator, et sapiens in instrumentis musicis."

70. *Par.* 20.14, 18, 22, 23, 142–143. The instruments are identified in the *Enciclopedia dantesca* under their several names.

71. *Enciclopedia dantesca*, s.v. "Pegasea" and "Euterpe." Cf. Horace, *Carmina* 1.1.33 ("si neque tibias Euterpe cohibet") and *Anthologia Palatina* 9.504–505. Her instrument is sometimes called a flute.

72. *Par.* 19.13–18, 40–90, 97–148, 20.31–72, 88–138.

73. Albumasar: "sermones" and "gravi sermone." Ibn Ezra: "loqui non modicum affectat." Scot: "Item delectatur [homo] . . . loqui rethorice" (M, 101rb).

74. Scot: "Item delectatur [homo Iovinus] audire . . . gesta antiquorum concionari, et audire concionatores" (M, 101rb).

75. Scot: "Ars attributa: bona, levis, et honorabilis" (M, 105rv); "Hic quidem homo naturaliter delectatur in arte levi, honorabili, placibili, famosa, et multum proficua, velut est docere scientiam litterarum, sicut gramaticam, physicam, leges, astronomiam, naturam, sedere ad theoloneum et ibi cambire monetam, vendere drappariam bonorum, pannorum et pulcrorum colorum, ducere mercationem rerum honorabilium . . ." (M, 101rb); "Ex magisteriis hominum significat [Jupiter] quod natus sub eo utatur et sciat facere ea que pertinent . . . ad scientiam nobilem litterarum, ut legum et decretalium <et> physice" (M, 100vb).

76. Alcabitius: "Et si complectitur ei [Iovi] Mercurius, significat scientiam arithmetice et scribendi, astronomiam quoque et phylosophiam et geometriam."

77. Haly: "In prima facie Tauri est homo scientie iudicandi bonorum et scribendi." Jupiter was almost 3° into the sign of Taurus: see Appendix 2.

78. Haly: "In prima facie Gemini . . . intromittit se de libris scribendo, legendo, sciendo de bonis moribus ac philosophia."

79. R. Kay, "Il giorno della nascita di Dante e la dipartita di Beatrice," *Studi*

americani su Dante, ed. G. C. Alessio and Robert Hollander (Milan: Franco Angeli, 1989), pp. 243–265. In 1265, Jupiter entered the sign of Gemini on 7 June and was in the first face until 30 June: calculated from Bryant Tuckerman, *Planetary, Lunar, and Solar Positions A.D. 2 to A.D. 1649 at Five-Day and Ten-Day Intervals*, Memoirs of the American Philosophical Society, vol. 59 (Philadelphia, 1964), p. 650.

80. Cf. *Par.* 1.48 and Lucan, *Pharsalia* 9.902–905.

81. Alessandro Niccoli glosses *reverendo* as "degno di reverenza": *Enciclopedia dantesca*, 4:899.

82. *Convivio* 4.8.11: "Dico che reverenza non è altro che confessione di debita subiezione per manifesto segno."

83. This conclusion is a commonplace, but here it is anchored more firmly in the context of Dante's thought than before: e.g., S. S. Bernardi in *Enciclopedia dantesca*, 1:339: "l'a[quila], in quanto tradizionale emblema dell'Impero cui Dio ha affidato la giustizia in terra, è simbolo della Giustizia."

84. Cf. Aristotle, *Ethica Nicomachea* 5.2.

85. Albumasar: "Jupiter natura . . . equus est." Haly: "Juppiter est planeta equalitatis."

86. Alcabitius: "et ex qualitate animi significat . . . iustitiam"; repeated by Bonatti and Scot (M, 101ra).

87. Ibn Ezra: "Eius siquidem circa animam esse charitas inexistit, iustitia, pax, fides [etc.]"; "Hominum autem . . . iusti"; "Et denotat . . . sermonem iustitie et equitatis."

88. John of Seville: "est stella . . . iudicum." Albumasar: "iudicia." Haly: "[Homo Iovinus] amat iudicatus, decreta, et iudicia." Ibn Ezra: "Hominum autem iudices." Scot: "Item delectatur esse iudex, advocatus, notarius in officio communis, capellanus prelati, magister in catedra, milex, potestas terre, capitaneus castelli, et esse rector multorum, ut abbas et prior" (M, 101rb); "dominatur enim Iupiter super iudices" (M, 101ra); "dat influentiam discretionis, ut . . . iuste iudicere" (M, 100vb); "in fabulis poetarum . . . dicitur ab eis quod Iupiter est . . . iustus iudex questionis" (M, 101ra). Alcabitius: "et ex magisteriis que pertinent ad legem, ut iusta iudicia iudicare."

89. *Consilium*, or opinion, is closely related to judgment, which is based on it. Thus the well-advised Jovian acts for good and against evil "provido consilio" (Albumasar); similarly, the Eagle is impelled by the concordant "consigli" of its component souls (*Par.* 19.96), and David is rewarded for the artistic judgment ("consiglio") he contributed to the writing of the Psalms (41).

90. Albumasar: "iura, leges." Alcabitius: "et ex magisteriis que pertinent ad legem." Haly: "significat . . . legem"; "amata . . . decreta"; "legalis." Ibn Ezra: "vultque scire leges, iudicia"; "de magisteriis habet illa quae pertinent ad legem." Scot: "Gratia in altero: legalis" (M, 105rv); "delectatur audire leges" (M, 101rb); "ex magisteriis . . . ea que pertinent ad legem, . . . ut legum et decretalium" (M, 100vb); "Hic enim homo tales habet moralitates . . . legaliter procurat alienos actus qui si diu vixerit suo loco et cetera" (M, 101rb), i.e. he administers the affairs of others as legal agent in place of the deceased or the heir.

91. Aquinas, *Summa theologiae* II-II q.57 a.1 resp. and q.58 a.1 resp.

92. A sample of the first ten occurrences of *iustitia* in the Psalms found that the Authorized (King James) Version regularly renders it as "righteousness"; the Revised Standard Version occasionally varies this to "right": Ps. 4.1, 4.6 (5), 7.9 (8), 7.18 (17), 9.9 (8), 14.2 (15.2), 16.15 (17.15), 17.21 (18.20), 17.23 (18.24), 22.3 (23.3). References to AV, when different from the Vulgate, are placed in parentheses.

93. *Convivio* 4.17.6: "L'undecima si è Giustizia, la quale ordina noi ad amare e operare dirittura in tutte cose." Busnelli-Vandelli ad loc. (2:214) distinguish the two senses of *iustitia* in Thomistic terms without noting that one is backed by biblical authority; this is also overlooked by C. Vasoli and D. De Robertis, in *Opere minori*, 1.2 (Milan: Ricciardi, 1988), p. 727 ad loc. Philippe Delhaye, however, recognized the biblical sense of justice as "la rettitudine morale" but deemphasized Dante's use of it: *Enciclopedia dantesca*, 3:233–235, esp. p. 234b.

94. Haly: "significat bonitatem." Scot: "Est etiam planeta . . . cuius natura est bona, et proprietas eius est . . . omnis influentia boni [followed by a list]" (M, 100vb).

95. Scot: "Est enim planeta omni viventi . . . benignus . . . in aspectu pulcher et benignus alteri"; "Est quidem planeta semper potens ad significandum bonum unicuique et non malum umquam" (M, 100vb); "Natura Iovis est temperate calida et humida, id circo iudicatur bona et conveniens unicuique viventium"; "in fabulis poetarum . . . dicitur ab eis quod Iupiter est stella . . . bona significans unicuique" (M, 101ra); "Significatio fame: bonus <et> pius omnibus" (M, 105rv).

96. Haly: "Juppiter est planeta . . . melioramenti"; "significat . . . meliorationem"; "Si debet ostendere rem aliquam bonitatis vel melioramenti, fortificat, affirmat, et verificat eam." Ibn Ezra: "et est planetis melior"; "et denotat . . . omneque augmentum boni."

97. Albumasar: "honestas." Bonatti: "Et significat . . . quicquid ad honestatem pertinet." Scot: "Item significat . . . factum honestum" (M, 101ra); "Hic enim homo tales habet moralitates . . . honestus" (M, 101rb); "Que vita eius est: gaudiosa, honesta" (M, 105rv).

98. Scot: "Significat etiam gratiam incomparabilem, ut . . . virtutum"; "Et proprietas eius [Iovis] est . . . elevatos in virtute conservans" (M, 100vb); "Ex figuris hominum significat . . . [hominem] bone conversationis vita et moribus" (M, 101ra). Alcabitius: "Et dixit Messehalla quod ex hominibus significat . . . bonis moribus."

99. Albumasar: "[homo] malum fugiens et bonum appetens." Alcabitius and Bonatti: "et significat . . . appetitum in bonis." Haly: "precipit et ostendit bonitatem, prohibet et abhorret malum"; "si habet ostendere aliquam rem horrendam vel mali, retrahit et damnat eam ac impedit per se et sua facta cum beneplacito dei." Scot: "Ex qualitate anime significat . . . cito in bono consentimentum" (M, 101ra).

100. Albumasar: "benivolentia" [*sic*]. Scot: "in fabulis poetarum . . . dicitur ab eis quod Iupiter est . . . stella . . . . benivola" (M, 101ra).

101. Scot: "Cito cupidus omnium pulcrorum que videt et audit est [homo Iovinus] audire bona et rationabilia" (M, 101rb). Ibn Ezra: "Et omnino odiet omne quod consuetudine ac ratione carebit."

102. Albumasar and Haly: "intellectus." Alcabitius and Bonatti: "et est planeta . . . intellectus."

103. Alcabitius and Bonatti: "et est planeta sapientiae"; "et significat . . . omne preceptum pulchrum et preciosum." Albumasar: "sana sapientia." Ibn Ezra: "sapientes." Scot: "Item significat . . . preceptum laudabile . . . fructum sapiencie" (M, 101ra).

104. Scot: "Item significat animam rationalem" (M, 101rb).

105. Albumasar: "certitudo." Scot: "Item significat . . . solutionem . . . [et] intellectum perfectum" (M, 101ra). In his tabular presentation of the properties of planets, Scot says of Jupiter, "Sensus eius est: sapiens et sagax." Previously in the table he had attributed the same two properties to Mercury but in reverse order (M, 105ra).

106. Several astrologers note a contrary tendency in Jupiter, which can signify "simplicitatem" (Haly) and can produce "simplices" (Ibn Ezra) and "insipiens" (Bonatti). Dante reflects this property in references to "stolti" (*Par.* 18.102), "salti" (18.135), and those who are made "folle" (19.122).

107. Alcabitius: "et ex partibus habens partem habitudinis profectus" (ed. 1512, fol. 9v). The text, however, is probably corrupt, since Bonatti, who is quoting Alcabitius verbatim, has instead: "habet partem beatitudinis et profectus." The 1521 text of Alcabitius corrects "habens" to "habet" but retains "habitudinis profectus" (ed. 1521, fol. 10r). Still Bonatti was probably right, since when Alcabitius discusses the lots, or *partes*, the same lot is described as "pars beatitudinis et triumphi atque victorie idest partis iouis" (ed. 1521, fol. 20r), which was translated into fifteenth-century English as "blessednesse and triumphe and victorie": J. D. North, *Chaucer's Universe* (New York: Oxford University Press, 1988), p. 527; see pp. 217–220 for an explanation of the casting of *partes*. Nonetheless Dante may have been using the corrupt version of Alcabitius, as his simile of daily progress suggests.

108. Aristotle, *Eth. Nic.* 2.7, 1107b9.

109. Albumasar: "liberalitas." Alcabitius, Bonatti, and Scot (M, 101ra): "ex qualitate animi significat largitatem." Scot: "Moralitas eius est: largitas" (M, 105rv); "Hic enim homo tales habet moralitates quantum est naturaliter largus, i.e., rationaliter servicialis alteri" (M, 101rb).

110. Albumasar: "magnificentia." For the distinction between *liberalitas* and *magnificentia*, see *Eth. Nic.* 4.2, 1121a19–34.

111. Ptolemy, *Quad.* 2.8 (ed. 1551, p. 30): "cuius opus proprium in hominibus est . . . magnanimitas." Scot: "Est [homo Iovinus] etiam . . . magnanimus" (M, 101rb). For the equivalence of *valor* and *magnanimitas*, see *Enciclopedia dantesca*, 5:872.

112. Aristotle, *Eth. Nic.* 2.7, 1108a30–35.

113. Alcabitius, Bonatti, and Scot (M, 101ra): "ex qualitate animi significat . . . verecundiam." Scot, however, later contradicts this assertion ("Est [homo] etiam . . . vanagloriosus") and then qualifies it: "Hic enim homo tales habet moralitates . . . aliquantulum verecundus"; cf. "Est [homo] . . . in petendo servitium verecundus et dubius" (M, 101rb).

114. Albumasar: "patientia." Alcabitius, Bonatti, and Scot (M, 101ra): "significat . . . patientiam." Scot: "Gratia in altero: patientia" (M, 105rv).

115. Aquinas, *Super Epistolam ad Romanos lectura*, lect. 5, ad Rom. 8.25: "proprie patientia importat tolerantiam tribulationum cum quadam aequanimitate"

(ed. R. Cai, 8th ed. [Turin: Marietti, 1953], 1:123). For the Scholastics, *patientia* was not an Aristotelian virtue; instead William of Moerbeke rendered the Greek *praôtê* by *mansuetudo* (*Eth. Nic.* 2.7, 1108a7).

116. Ibn Ezra: "Eius siquidem circa animam esse charitas inexistit." Albumasar: "spes."

117. Alcabitius and Bonatti: "et significat fidem." Ibn Ezra: "Eius siquidem circa animam esse charitas inexistit, iustitia, pax, fides [etc.]." Haly: "fidelis."

118. Scot: "Ex qualitate anime significat . . . amico fidelitatem" (M, 101ra); "Est [homo Iovinus] . . . in custodiendo rem alterius fidelis" and "in altero se multum confidit" (M, 101rb). Albumasar: "depositio fidelis." Scot generalizes: "Significat . . . tractamentum omnis rei que fit fideliter et sine seductione" (M, 101ra). Cf. Alcabitius and Bonatti ("et ex negociis illa que fiunt absque seductione") and Haly ("in dictis et factis suis . . . sine fraude").

119. John of Seville: "est stella . . . fidei expositorum." Albumasar: "vera fides."

120. James of Majorca and James II of Aragon are said to have "cuckolded (*fatte bozze*)" their crowns and birth (*Par.* 19.138), so the marital infidelity is only figurative; but that of Dinaz of Portugal was real enough and may have been Dante's complaint against him: Singleton ad loc. (pp. 327–328).

121. Aquinas, *Summa theologiae* I q.21 a.4. Cf. *Par.* 7.103–105.

122. For a review of the divided interpretation of *pio* at *Par.* 19.13, see *Enciclopedia dantesca*, 4:525.

123. Scot: "Est enim planeta . . . pius omnibus" (M, 101ra); "Significatio fame: bonus, pius omnibus" (M, 105rv); "Est enim planeta omni viventi pius et clemens, misericors, servitialis, et benignus" (M, 100vb); "Gratia in altero: misericordia" (105rv); "Est [homo Iovinus] etiam multum pius, misericors" (M, 101rb); and the planet exercises clemency towards inimical planets (M, 100vb). Haly had ambiguously described the planet as "pietosus" and "pietatis."

124. Scot: "elevans prostratos" (M, 100vb); "condolens alterius miserie" (M, 101ra, 100vb, 101rb); "luctum pauperibus" (M, 100vb); "Ex qualitate anime significat . . . elimosinam" (M, 101ra). Similarly, Haly says that Jupiter "adiuvat pauperes" and that the Jovian is "in dictis et factis suis, boni solatii"; Ibn Ezra: "vultque . . . domibus depopulatis subvenire."

125. Albumasar: "religio." Alcabitius, Bonatti, and Scot (M, 101ra): "significat . . . religionem."

126. Ibn Ezra: "Hominum autem . . . deum colentes." *Lib. nov. iud.*: "religiosos et deum timens" (B, 210va, attributed to Albumasar) and "amatores religiosos" (B, 210vb, al-Kindi).

127. Scot lists "preces rationabiles" as one of the things Jupiter signifies (M, 101ra), but he probably means requests that one man makes to another, because later he says that the Jovian is "in petendo servitium verecundus et dubius" (M, 101rb). Though not named in the text, Pope Gregory I the Great is generally recognized as Trajan's intercessor because the legend of his miraculous salvation first appeared in a life of Gregory (early eighth century), Dante could have known it in many subsequent versions, but the most likely is that in the anonymous *Fiore di filosofi e di molti savi*, ed. A. Cappelli (Bologna: Romagnoli, 1865), pp. 58–61, re-

printed with bibliography in Toynbee-Singleton, 618, s.v. "Traiano." Medieval interpretations of the legend are analyzed by Gordon Whatley, "The Uses of Hagiography: The Legend of Pope Gregory and the Emperor Trajan in the Middle Ages," *Viator* 15 (1984), 25–63 (Dante, pp. 43–50).

128. Alcabitius: "ex sectis pluralitatem et simulationem." Scot: "ex sectis fidei significat pluralitatem maximam et simulationem agendorum." Bonatti quotes Alcabitius and adds: "finget enim ille cuius Iupiter fuerit significator, quando Luna iungitur ei se velle tenere hanc sectam et illam, et neutram bene servabit; nec tamen eius intentio erit mala."

129. Albumansar: "templa." Ibn Ezra: "Et eius sunt . . . locus divini obsequii."

130. For these terms as used by some Franciscans contemporary with Dante, see Charles T. Davis, *Dante and the Idea of Rome* (Oxford: Clarendon Press, 1957), pp. 197–214.

131. Scot: "Item significat . . . victoriam" (M, 101ra). Ibn Ezra: "Quod autem maxime cogitat est . . . in omnibus vincere, dummodo iure obtineat." Albumasar: "Tum patientia deinde vindicta et victoria in omni contentione."

132. I translate this obscure phrase literally; for possible interpretations, see Sapegno ad loc. (p. 1013) and *Enciclopedia dantesca* 5:1046b.

133. Ptolemy, *Quad.* 2.8 (ed. 1551, p. 30): "cuius [Iovis] opus proprium in hominibus est . . . remunerationes, et <regum> praemia, augmenta quoque rerum regalium, fama nominis, atque magnanimitas." I have emended the 1551 text, which reads *regnum* for *regum*, because Ptolemy's Greek did not promise a kingdom but rather "benefits and gifts *from rulers*" (trans. Robbins, p. 183).

134. Ibn Ezra: "bona fama." John of Seville: "est stella . . . famae." See preceding note for Ptolemy.

135. Scot: "Significat etiam gratiam incomparabilem, ut . . . laudem bone vite, famam" (M, 100vb); "Cupit [homo] habere famam inter gentes eorum que agit et sit" (M, 101rb); "Ex figuris hominum significat . . . [hominem] bone artis et laudabilis actus" (M, 101ra). In Scot's system, all the planets indicated some kind of fame; for Jupiter, "Significatio fame: bonus, pius omnibus" (M, 105rv).

136. Ptolemy, *Quad.* 2.8 (ed. 1551, p. 30): "graduum sublimitas." Albumasar: "dignitates." Scot: "Item significat . . . dignitatem" (M, 101ra); "Appetit [homo Iovinus] etiam habere dominium seu dignitatem" (M, 101rb). Unlike most astrologers, Scot laid great stress on Jupiter as a significator of *honor* (mentioned 6 times), which he links with *dignitas* (M, 100vb, twice, e.g., "augmentum honorum et dignitatum"), and which he regards as some sort of official appointment: e.g., "Optinabit [homo] honores plurimos, ut prelaturas ecclesiasticas si fuerit factus clericus, vel dominium regiminis factus laycus" (M, 101rb).

137. *De vulg. eloq.* 2.2.3: "meritorum effectus sive terminus"; cf. *Conv.* 1.2.11 and *Enciclopedia dantesca* 2:443.

138. It is not clear how many Scottish and English kings Dante meant to condemn for the border wars (*Par.* 19.121–123), so they are omitted from my reckoning, but instead both kingdoms are included among the other states along with the kingdom of Navarre (143) and Venice (141).

139. Scot: "in fabulis poetarum . . . dicitur ab eis quod Iupiter est . . . stella multum dominatrix" (M, 101ra).

140. Scot: "Appetit [homo] etiam habere dominium seu dignitatem" (M, 101rb).

141. Albumasar: "principatus"; "regna"; "est eius [Iovis] . . . magnates et prelati." The 1551 edition of Ptolemy's *Quadripartitum* listed "regnum" as a property of Jupiter, but as the text appears to be corrupt at this point (see n. 133 above), it seems better not to assume that this error had already crept into the text Dante would have used.

142. Albumasar: "indulgens veneri." Alcabitius and Bonatti: "et significat . . . abundantiam veneris." Scot: "Item significat . . . humores libidinis habundantes" (M, 101ra); "In carne [homo] est calidus et facile luxuriosus" (M, 101rb).

143. Scot: "Est enim planeta . . . in aspectu pulcher" (M, 100vb); "Est [homo] pulcher receptus" (M, 101rb); "Parissibilitas [= appearance]: pulcher et pinguis" (M, 105rv). Alcabitius: "Ex dixit Messehala quod ex hominibus significat . . . [homo] pulchre stature . . . pulchri corporis." Cf. Albumasar ("forme dignitas") and Haly ("formose apparentie").

144. Scot: "Item delectatur [homo Iovinus] . . . equitare" (M, 101rb). Haly: "In tertia facie [Cancri] diligit venationem," and "In omnibus partibus Leonis est homo venationis." On King Philip's passion for hunting, see Elizabeth A. R. Brown, "The Case of Philip the Fair," *Viator* 19 (1988), 219–246, at pp. 236–237.

145. Ptolemy, *Quad.* 2.8 (ed. 1551, p. 30): "cuius [Iovis] opus proprium in hominibus est . . . corporum et animarum habitudo conveniens." Albumasar: "salubris." Alcabitius and Bonatti: "et ex operibus, salubritatem."

146. Haly: "et minuuntur epidimie."

147. *Summa theologiae* II-II q.57–122, or 66 questions, which are nearly 35% of the 189 in this *pars*.

148. *Summa theologiae* II-II q.80 resp. (religion is a part of justice) and q.81 a.6: "religio praeeminet inter alias virtutes morales."

149. *Summa theologiae* II-II q.81 a.3 resp.: "Ad religionem autem pertinet exhibere reverentiam uni Deo secundum unam rationem, inquantum scilicet est primum principium creationis et gubernationis rerum."

150. E.g., God is celebrated as creator in Ps. 103 (= AV 104), 144 (145), and 146 (147); as ruler of all things in Ps. 71 (72), 95–98 (96–99), 111 (112), and 145 (146).

151. Ps. 103 (104).24: "Quam magnificata sunt opera tua, Domine! omnia in sapientia fecisti: impleta est terra possessione tua."

152. Ps. 97 (98).9b: "venit judicare terram. Judicabit orbem terrarum in iustitia, et populos in aequitate." Cf. 71 (72), 95–96 (96–97), 98 (99), 111 (112), and 145 (146).

153. *Summa theologiae* II-II q.65 a.4 ad 2: "iniuriae illatae in viduas et pupillos magis exaggerantur . . . quia magis opponuntur misericoridae."

154. *Mon.* 3.15.12–13.

155. Augustine, *De civitate Dei* 10.1.3: "More autem vulgi hoc nomen [sc. *pietas*] etiam in operibus misericordiae frequentatur; quod ideo arbitror evenisse quia haec fieri praecipue mandat Deus eaque sibi vel pro sacrificiis vel prae sacrificiis placere testatur." Quoted approvingly in *Summa theologiae* II-II q.101 a.1 ad 2, with a reference to Augustine's further discussion of mercy as piety in *De doctrina Christiana* 30.32 (cited in obj. 2).

156. Especially, Aquinas would presumably add, to God the Father (*Summa theologiae* II-II q.101 a.3 ad 2). Aquinas tries to limit the scope of *pietas* to blood relatives and to country (II-II q.101 a.1), although presently he enlarges it to include first fellow citizens (ad 2) and eventually anyone to whom honor is due (q.122 a.5 ad 2).

157. Thomas Aquinas, *Comentum in quatuor libros sententiarum magistri Petri Lombardi* lib. 4, dist. 15, q. 2, a. 1, qla. 3, contra, and lib. 3, dist. 33, q. 3, a. 4, sol. 4, ad obj. 3 (*Opera omnia*, vol. 7 [Parma, 1858; reprint, New York: Musurgia, 1948], pp. 716, 376). P. Caramello cites these texts to prove that for Thomas mercy as a moral virtue is a part of justice: *Summa theologiae*, vol. 2 (Turin: Marietti, 1962), p. 165, n. 16.

158. *Summa theologiae* II-II q.101 falls within the treatment of the parts of justice, sc. qq.61–120 (see *divisio* at q.57).

159. Astrology may have suggested the choice of Trajan as one who had escaped from the prison of death, for Jupiter "significat etiam gratiam incomparabilem, ut . . . evasionem de carceribus" (Scot, M, 100vb).

160. Sapegno ad loc. (p. 1026) discusses the evidence for Hezekiah's repentance.

161. *Summa theologiae* III q.85 a.3 resp.: "poenitentia, secundum quod est virtus, est pars iustitiae."

162. *Summa theologiae* I q.23 a.8 resp. and q.116 a.3 resp.

163. Aquinas explains the conditions for meritorious prayer: *Summa theologiae* II-II q.83 a.15 resp.

164. *Summa theologiae* II-II q.86 a.1–2. On the classification, see the introductions to questions 80, 81, 82, and 85.

165. *Summa theologiae* II-II q.59 a.2 resp.

166. *Enciclopedia dantesca*, 3:314.

167. *Summa theologiae* II-II q.58 a.5 resp.; a.6 resp.: "iustitia legalis . . . est in principe principaliter, et quasi architectonice; in subditis autem secundario et quasi ministrative."

168. The role of grace needs clarification. The blessed Ripheus is noteworthy for how much he knows of divine grace (*Par.* 20.70–72), and when the Redemption was made known to him, God was proceeding from one grace to another ("di grazia in grazia," 122); but it is not clear whether his love of righteousness was itself the result of grace. Very likely it was, since Aquinas held that *rectitudo* is the result of grace causing the will to love virtue: *In sententiarum*, lib. 4, dist. 17, q. 1, a. 2, sol. 1, ad 3 (*Opera omnia*, Musurgia ed., 7:772).

169. *Summa theologiae* I-II q.55 a.4 ad 4 and II-II q.58 a.1 ad 2.

170. Ibn Ezra: "De climatibus vero eius est secundum."

171. Alfraganus, *Liber de differentie scientie astrorum*, diff. 9, trans. John of Seville (1137), ed. Francis J. Carmody (Berkeley, Calif.: n. p., 1943), p. 16: "Sed 2^m clima incipit ab oriente et uadit super regiones Acin, post hoc uadit super regiones Indie, deinde per regiones Acint; et est in eo ciuitas Almansora id est Adumata. . . ." Carmody's apparatus identifies Acint as al-Hind and Almansora as al-Mansûra. Gerard of Cremona's translation (made before 1175) of the same passage runs: "Et secundum clima incipit ab oriente et transit per regiones Sin et per

regiones Indiae deinde per regione Assind et in ipso est Almansoria . . . ": Alfragano, *Il "Libro dell'aggregazione delle stelle*," ed. Romeo Campani (Città di Castello: Lapi, 1910), p. 95.

172. "Acint" and "Almansora" are identified by Carmody (see previous note). Campani quotes a medieval Arabic manual of cosmography to the effect that Mansûra is surrounded by a branch of the Indus River (idem). Cf. al-Biruni: "The second climate . . . traverses Hindustan north of the Qâmrûn Mountains and contains . . . also cities of Sind like Mansûrah" (trans. Wright, pp. 143–144). For the location of Mansûra, see *An Historical Atlas of Islam*, ed. William C. Brice (Leiden: Brill, 1981). Not on maps of Pakistan, Mansûra probably was on the site of modern Haidarâbâd: *The Encyclopaedia of Islam*, vol. 3 (Leiden: Brill, 1936), p. 257.

173. Ibn Ezra: "Ex gentibus vero babylonico et perses." Alcabitius: "et habet [Jupiter] ex regionibus Alchirath et Babyloniam et Asen et Persidem et Alaormes et Archadiam." Bonatti: "Et ex regionibus habet Alchirat, Babyloniam, Azomi, Persidam, Almaden, Alandes."

174. The Ethiopians (*Par.* 19.109), on the other hand, come from the first climate according to Alfraganus (ed. Campani, p. 94; ed. Carmody, p. 16). Perhaps Dante included a non-Jovian people because Jupiter "est enim planeta . . . pius omnibus, condolens alterius miserie, quare dictur deus *gentium*" (Scot, M, 101ra). Hence, also, "Gentili" (*Par.* 20.104) and "genti" (126).

Chapter 7: Saturn

1. For Saturn in classical mythology and astrology, see R. Klibansky, E. Panofsky, and F. Saxl, *Saturn and Melancholy: Studies in the History of Natural Philosophy, Religion, and Art* (New York: Basic Books, 1964), pp. 133–159.

2. Alcabitius: "et significat gravitatem frigoris et siccitatis." Haly: "natura eius frigida et sicca." John of Seville: "frigidus et siccus." Ibn Ezra: "Saturnus est frigidus et siccus." Bonatti: "Dixit Alchabicius Saturnus . . . operatur frigiditatem et siccitatem distemperatam." Scot: "Naturam Saturni est summe frigida et sicca" (M, 100rb).

3. Ptolemy, *Quad.* 2.8: "Saturnus itaque cum solus fuerit dispositionis dominus, ipse generaliter erit occasio destructionis ex frigore contingentis" (ed. 1551, p. 30).

4. Klibansky et al., *Saturn and Melancholy*, p. 138.

5. Albumasar: "natura frigidus, siccus, nonnunque accidentaliter humidus." Alcabitius: "Et fortassis erit quandoque complexio frigida, humida, ponderosa." John of Seville taught that Saturn, like the Moon, was alternately wet and dry, depending on its closeness to the Sun: "Saturnus . . . cuius complexio permutatur ex positione Solis, ut de Luna diximus, stando in Auge facit siccum, in opposito humidum."

6. See Patrick Boyde, *Dante Philomythes and Philosopher: Man in the Cosmos* (Cambridge: Cambridge University Press, 1981), pp. 78, 321.

7. Commentators usually identify "the burning Lion's breast" with the star Regulus, but, according to Ptolemy, the heat of that star is only moderate: "The sign of Leo as a whole is hot and stifling; but, part by part . . . its middle part [is] temperate" (*Quad.* 2.11, trans. Robbins, p. 203). Cf. *Quad.* 1.9: "Of those [stars] in Leo . . . the bright star upon the heart, called Regulus, [acts] the same as Mars and Jupiter" (trans. Robbins, p. 49), i.e., it is moderately hot. The "Leone ardente" apparently is to be understood as acting as a whole on Saturn, tempering its extreme cold even as Beatrice's beauty is tempered (*Par.* 21.10).

8. Scot: "Natura Saturni est summe frigida et sicca, mala, dura, gravis, nociva, ponderosa, inmobilis quasi, et crudelis, et ideo dicitur deus terre" (M, 100rb).

9. *Mondo* (= "world," cf. Latin *mundus*), which also occurs in these cantos, can refer to the entire universe (*Par.* 21.71: God "governs the world") but can be limited to earth, either explicitly (*Par.* 21.97: "mondo mortal") or implicitly (22.45: paganism "seduced the world").

10. Albumasar: "accidentaliter . . . gravis," and "eius est . . . rerum dimensio et pondus." Alcabitius: "et significat gravitatem frigoris et siccitatis" (repeated by Bonatti), and "fortassis erit quandoque complexio . . . ponderosa." John of Seville: "significat in ruina ponderum." Scot: "Est etiam ponderosus" (M, 100ra), and see n. 8 above.

11. Bonatti: "Saturnus dat hominem esse . . . gravem," and "significat gravitatem corporis." Related effects on humans: "gravis in eundo et movendo" (Haly); "Est etiam homo [Saturninus] . . . in eundo gravis," and "delectatur in arte gravi" (Scot, M, 100va).

12. Ptolemy, *Quad.* 2.8 (ed. 1551, p. 30): "In mari vero diminutiones et augmenta proprie contingent. In fluminibus autem proprie inundationes maximae, et aquarum detrimenta." F. E. Robbins translates the maritime phenomena as "the high and ebb tides of the seas" (p. 181), but the Latin text is susceptible of a more general interpretation. Alcabitius also takes Saturn to signify rivers: "significat . . . fluminum, si fuerit fortunatus."

13. Bonatti: "Et ex magisteriis significat . . . opera aquatica vel quae fiunt prope aquas . . . et . . . aedificationes domorum et maxime domorum religiosorum induentium nigras vestes, si fuerit fortunatus et boni esse."

14. *Enciclopedia dantesca*, 2:964; *The Catholic Encyclopedia*, 6:128.

15. Albumasar: "omneque melancolie genus." Alcabitius: "significat . . . ex complexione corporum melancolicam, et augmentum eius atque distillationem," and "ex infirmitatibus morbos flegmaticos et melancolicos" (the latter repeated by Bonatti). Haly: "assimilatur [planeta] melancolie que gubernatur de omnibus humoribus et nullus de ea." John of Seville: "significat . . . in melancolia." Bonatti: "ex humoribus significat melancholiam." Scot: "Significat . . . melancoliam" (M, 100rb).

16. Scot: Even when weakest, Saturn "suo posse infortunium conservat unicuique, sicut miseriam" (M, 100rb), and "sunt sue [planetae] proprietatis, ut Saturni . . . vitam miserie mentis" (100ra).

17. Ptolemy, *Quad.* 2.8 (ed. 1551, p. 30): "generabit . . . tristitias." Alcabitius: "Etsi fuerit [Saturnus] malus, [homo] erit . . . tristis" (repeated by Bonatti). Haly: "planeta . . . tristitiarum." Scot: "cuius proprietas est . . . omne malum

significare . . . velut . . . tristitiam," and "sunt sue [planetae] proprietatis, ut Saturni . . . tristitiam" (M, 100ra); "In genere est planeta . . . pessimus aliorum, eo quod est . . . semper tristis" (100rb), and "sepe moratur [homo] tristis, multa cogitans et proponens" (100va).

18. Albumasar: "dolor." Ibn Ezra: "denotat . . . dolorem, contristationem."

19. Ibn Ezra: "Et ipse denotat . . . planctum, dolorem, contristationem, lamentationem, conclamationem," and "fletum." Scot: "cuius proprietas est . . . omne malum significare . . . velut . . . lamentationem . . . [et] plantum [= planctum]" (M, 100ra).

20. Bonatti: "Saturnus dat hominem esse . . . nunquam aut vix ridentem." Scot: "[homo] raro ridet, et risus ei <diu multumque *add*. O> differtur, unde raro apparet ylaris" (M, 100va).

21. Perhaps Dante does admit a trace of melancholy into the heaven of Saturn. Sapegno, at least, remarks on the "accenti di severo dolore" in Benedict's speech (ad *Par*. 22.37–39, p. 1049).

22. Alcabitius: "et ex infirmitatibus morbos flegmaticos et melancolicos."

23. Bonatti: "Et ex complexionibus corporum, significat melancholiam, et fortassis erit illa melancholia cum admixtione phlegmatis, et cum ponderositate atque gravedine corporis nati, ita quod non erit levis incessus, nec leviter saliens, nec addiscet natare vel similia quae faciunt ad ostendendum levitatem corporis."

24. Alcabitius: "et significat . . . tarditatem" (repeated by Bonatti). Haly: "tardi intellectus et impedite loquele." Scot: "est stella multum alta et ideo . . . tarda" (M, 100ra); "tardi intellectus" and "tardus in laborando" (100va); "significat etiam . . . perditionem virtutis celeritatis nervorum" (100rb).

25. Saturn could also signify delay: "Significat etiam . . . longas inducias rerum reddendarum" (Scot, M, 100rb).

26. Scot: "Significat . . . lapides" (M, 100rb).

27. Dante previously had associated Saturn and stones in his *rime petrose: Dante's Lyric Poetry*, ed. and trans. by K. Foster and P. Boyde (Oxford: Clarendon Press, 1967), nos. 77–80, esp. "Io son venuto," lines 7–9 (2:261); see also Robert M. Durling, "'Io son venuto': Seneca, Plato, and the Microcosm," *Dante Studies*, 93 (1975), 95–129, at p. 103; this essay is incorporated and elaborated in Robert M. Durling and Ronald L. Martinez, *Time and the Crystal: Studies in Dante's "Rime petrose"* (Berkeley: University of California Press, 1990). Whether the addressee's name was Pietra is a matter of controversy: *Enciclopedia dantesca*, 4:498–499, s.v. "Pietra."

28. Scot: "Hic quidem homo naturaliter delectatur . . . ollas et formas terre componere, ut campane et cetera, ut argillas, tegulas, lateres, fusarolos" (M, 100va).

29. Scot: "Hic quidem homo delectatur . . . volvere molam acuantem aliquod feramentum" (M, 100va). Bonatti: "Et ex magisteriis significat . . . opera aquatica vel quae fiunt prope aquas, sicut sunt molendina, pontes, naves, et similia. . . ." Bonatti clearly has in mind Saturn's affinity for water, but as elsewhere he is willing to mix the properties of the elements: cf. n. 23, above.

30. Circular motion: *Par*. 21.26, 38–39, 137–139, 22.2, 19, 99; spheres and wheels: 21.58, 22.23, 29, 62.

31. The references to the local people and their villages (*Par.* 22.39, 44) are Saturnian. Thus Alcabitius: "et significat . . . populationem terrarum." And Haly: "diligit . . . populare."

32. . Scot: "In genere est planeta . . . pessimus aliorum, eo quod est . . . salvaticus" (M, 100rb). The form *salvaticus* is a variant of *silvaticus*: J. F. Niermeyer, *Mediae Latinitatis lexicon minus* (Leiden: Brill, 1984).

33. Albumasar: "eius est agricultura . . . [et] fundi paratio." Alcabitius: significat cultus agrorum," and "significat de substantia . . . terre cultus." Haly: "diligit . . . plantare [et] seminare." Ibn Ezra: "Eius quoque est terram colere." Bonatti: "Et ex magisteriis significat . . . cultus terrae, scilicet agrorum, plantationes arborum. . . ."

34. Ibn Ezra: "De hominibus eius pars sunt . . . communiter omnes terre laboratores." Scot: "Significat . . . officium rusticanum" (M, 100rb); "Dominatur enim generaliter contra agri cultores" (100rb); badly aspected, Saturn "est pessimum signum in celo . . . ad omnes res mundi et principaliter ad rusticos" (100ra).

35. E.g., "Hic quidem homo delectatur . . . laborare terram, et facere omnem cultum ipsius, veluti ligonizare, vangare, atare, seminare, plantare, carpere ramos de arboribus, herbas colligere et vendere in fasciculis, ac eam eradicare de glebis . . . (Scot, M, 100va).

36. Ibn Ezra: "De locis vero possidet concavitates: putrefactiones, puteos et loca carceris, atque omnem locum obscurum inhabitatum, et cimiteriorum loca."

37. E.g., Scot: "Hic quidem homo delectatur . . . cavare fossa et sepulturas, terram cum cenoveo et zerla foris defere, puteum atteratum evacuare, et fundamentum domus, puteum, et fontem mundare . . ." (M, 100va).

38. Thus Sapegno ad *Par.* 22.76–77 (p. 1052), citing Matt. 21.13, Luc. 19.46, Isa. 56.7, and Jer. 7.11.

39. He is also associated with the so-called "Shepherds' Cave" nearby. For photographs see Leonard von Matt and Stephan Hilpisch, *Saint Benedict*, trans. Ernest Graf (London: Burns & Oates, 1961), plates 45 and 50.

40. Albumasar: "violentia captivitas, cathene, compedes, carceres." Alcabitius: "significat . . . carceres et vincula." John of Seville: "significat . . . in mani<c>a, carcere." Bonatti: "significat carceres duros et asperos." Scot: "cuius proprietas est . . . omne malum significare . . . velut . . . captivitatem, carcerem," and "significat etiam . . . captivos et tristes."

41. Ibn Ezra: "Suum quoque est clima primum. Et hoc est Indorum regio," and "De hominibus eius pars sunt Mauri: Iudei alfalbarbace."

42. Alcabitius first quotes Dorotheus and then gives his own opinion: "Et dixit Dorothius hic . . . habet ex regionibus Ascine et Indiam et omnem terram nigrorum. . . . et habet ex partibus mundi achiud et alchiut et eorum confinia et terras nigrorum et montes eorum."

43. Alfraganus, *Liber de differentie scientie astrorum* 9, trans. John of Sevillle (1137), ed. Francis J. Carmody (Berkeley: n. p., 1943), p. 16: "Deinde abscindit clima Mare Alculçum id est Mare Rubrum et vadit in regiones ethiopum et abscindit Nilum Egypti." Cf. Gerard of Cremona's translation (before 1175): "Deinde secat

clima versus mare Rubrum et transit in regiones Aethiopum et secat Nilum Aegypti": Alfragano, *Il "Libro dell'aggregazione delle stelle,"* ed. Romeo Campani (Città di Castello: Lapi, 1910), p. 94.

44. Elsewhere, in *Convivio* 3.5.12, he refers to the naked Garamantes who inhabit the first climate. The *Lib. nov. iud.* extracts the astrologer Tiberias, who gives Saturn rule over "captivos ethiopie et indos" (B, 210rb).

45. Haly: "non vult societatem"; "stare vult solus et separatus"; "non habet solatium cum aliquo nec aliquis cum eo." Cf. Albumasar: "solitudo." Ibn Ezra: "Et hominis nature vel moris, ipsius pars est . . . solitarium fore, et extraneum ab aliis hominum." Scot: "displicibilis ad societatem alterorum" (M, 100va).

46. I doubt that the Pilgrim's inquiry to Peter Damian—"perché predestinata fosti *sola* / a questo officio tra le tue consorte" (*Par.* 21.77–78)—is relevant to Saturnian solitude, because Damian has been singled out from a group of Saturnians who all share the same propensity.

47. E.g., his *Liber qui appellatur "Dominus vobiscum"* (*Opusculum* 11) 19 and *De suae congregationis institutis* (*Opusc.* 15) 1, ed. J. P. Migne, *Patrologia Latina* 145:246–252, 336–337.

48. Alcabitius: "significat quoque indumenta nigra."

49. Bonatti: "Et habet significare indumenta nigra, et eos qui naturaliter nigris vestibus utuntur tam religiosos seu claustrales, quam alios."

50. Bonatti: "Et ex magisteriis significat . . . aedificationes domorum et maxime domorum religiosorum induentium nigras vestes, si fuerit fortunatus et boni esse."

51. Albumasar: "servi, manicipia." Alcabitius: "et significat . . . servos." John of Seville: "servi." Ibn Ezra: "De hominibus eius pars sunt . . . communiter omnes . . . servi vilipensi." Bonatti: "Et significat . . . servos et eunuchos et viles personas." Scot: "Significat etiam . . . servos et ancillas" (M, 100rb).

52. All quoted in the preceding note. With more tact, Scot says the Saturnian's services are "undistinguished": "est etiam modici servicii" (M, 100va).

53. *Par.* 21.71 is the only occurrence of the form *serva* in Dante's undoubted works, but it does appear in the *Detto d'amore* that has been attributed to him: "Che Povertà tua serva / Non sia" (lines 349–350), which in Contini's literal translation reads: "che Povertà non sia tua domestica." Dante Alighieri, *Opere minori*, vol. 1, pt. 1, ed. D. De Robertis and G. Contini, La Letteratura italiana: Storia e testi, vol. 5, vol. 1, pt. 1 (Milan: Ricciardi, 1984), p. 818.

54. Paulin M. Blecker, "The Civil Rights of the Monk in Roman and Canon Law: The Monk as *Servus*," *American Benedictine Review* 17 (1966), 185–198.

55. For Damian's reforms as prior of Fonte Avellana, *Dizionario degli istituti di perfezione*, ed. G. Pelliccia and G. Rocca, vol. 4 (Rome: Edizioni Paoline, 1977), pp. 123–124.

56. John of Seville: "significat in patre, avo, et veteribus cunctis."

57. Albumasar: "Tum [significat] senex, patres, avi, proavi, eiusque partis parentes." Alcabitius: "et significat . . . patres etiam et avos et fratres maiores," and "est significator patrum." Ibn Ezra: "et ipse denotat patres et avos." Bonatti: "Et significat . . . patres et avos et fratres longaeviores nato," and "est significa-

tor patrum et avorum et omnium ascendentium qui significantur per quartam domum. . . . "

58. Only Scot specifies senior female, as well as male, relatives: "Significat etiam [Saturnus] . . . homines senes, ut avos et proavos, avas et proavas" (M, 100rb).

59. Ptolemy, *Quad.* 2.8: "Opus autem eius particulare est . . . maxime autem in his qui iam in annos ingressi sunt" (ed. 1551, p. 30). Albumasar: "senex." Alcabitius: "et significat . . . initium senectutis si fuerit orientalis, et significat senectutem ultimam si fuerit occidentalis." Haly: "planeta . . . senex magnus fessus," and "Suaque annorum pars est decrepita etas et vite finis." Scot: "principaliter . . . ad senes"; "cuius proprietas est . . . omne malum significare . . . velut . . . senectutem"; "est stella multum alta, et ideo . . . senex"; "senes at<t>ritur"; "Significat etiam . . . homines senes (M, 100ra)."

60. Ptolemy, *Quad.* 2.8: "generabit . . . mortem" (ed. 1551, p. 30). Alcabitius: "significat . . . causas mortis" (repeated by Bonatti). Ibn Ezra: "Et ipse denotat . . . mortem" and "mortuos"; "Et hominis nature vel moris, ipsius pars est . . . mors."

61. *Regula Sancti Benedicti* (= *RB*) 7, ed. Timothy Fry et al., in *RB 1980: The Rule of St. Benedict in Latin and English with Notes* (Collegeville, Minn.: Liturgical Press, 1981). This book conveniently combines de Vogüé's Latin text with an English translation and a condensation of his notes, but for fuller commentary see: *La Règle de saint Benoît*, ed. A. de Vogüé and J. Neufville, Sources chrétiennes 181–186 (Paris: Les Éditions du Cerf, 1971–1972). It is now generally accepted that Benedict derived much of his material from an earlier, longer work, the *Regula Magistri*, but in the following discussion I shall assume the traditional view that Benedict was the sole author of his *Rule*, as Dante believed him to be.

62. Dante's "danno" and "ria" (*Par.* 22.75, 78) echo "damnatio," which Albumasar lists among Saturn's properties; cf. Haly: "plura suorum faciorum magis sunt ad damnum quam utilitatem ipsius." For the translation of "carte" as "pages" rather than "paper," see below, n. 66.

63. Albumasar: "hereditates resque antique." Alcabitius: "significat de substantia res antiquas et durabiles," and "ex magisteriis res antiquas et preciosas." Ezra: "Et ipse denotat . . . res antiquas." Bonatti: "ex magisteriis significat res antiquas et laboriosas et graves et preciosas" when Saturn is fortunate and "res antiquas et viles" when it is not.

64. Haly: "cogitat et inspicit in rebus antiquis."

65. Alcabitius: "significat opus pergameni in quo scribuntur divini libri." Bonatti: "significat operationem chartarum in quibus scribunt libri ecclesiarum et divina verba atque de divinitate tractantia. . . ." Both indications assume that Saturn is aspected by Jupiter, which was the case at the ideal date of the *Commedia* (see Appendix 2); when otherwise aspected, Saturn still signifies some form of leatherwork: e.g., drumheads, sandals, accounts on parchment, tanning.

66. Italian *carta* can, of course, be translated "paper," but "page" or even "document" is also possible. Cf. Latin "*charta*, carta, karta: any *written document*, without regard to material (papyrus or parchment)": Niermeyer, *Mediae Latinitatis lexicon minus*, p. 174. Thus St. Bernard's Cistercian rule is the *Carta caritatis*.

67. Alcabitius: "significat de sectis eam que unitates confitetur, si fuerit for-

tunatus; et si fuerit malus, significat credentiam unitatis cum multa tamen hesita-
tione, idest dubitatione." Bonatti: "de sectis habet significare fidem Iudaicam,
scilicet vetus testamentum, et omnem sectam quae confitetur unitatem."

68. Alcabitius: "ex partibus habens partem fortitudinis et stabilitatis" (repeated by Bonatti), and "Etsi fuerit malus erit . . . stabilis." Albumasar: "amicitia
stabilis." Ibn Ezra: "firmus in suo verbo." Scot: "Natura Saturni est summe . . .
inmobilis quasi," and "In genere est planeta . . . pessimus aliorum, eo quod est . . .
inmobilis proposite oppinionis" (M, 100rb).

69. Alcabitius: "Et significat . . . multitudinem silentii." Scot: "Significat
etiam . . . silentium" (M, 100rb).

70. Ibn Ezra: "sapiens in consciliis [sic] et dei obsequio."

71. Scot: "et stella multum alta et ideo . . . impia" (M, 100ra), and "In genere
est planeta . . . pessimus aliorum, eo quod est . . . inpius" (100ra).

72. Albumasar: "eunuchi." Alcabitius: "et significat . . . eunuchos." Haly:
"pauci usus cum mulieribus," and "sterilis quia nullum habet filium." Scot: "Significat etiam . . . eunuchos" (M, 100rb), and "est . . . castus ratione sue frigiditatis,
id est raro luxuriosus, cuius semen raro concipit nisi sit in eam semen muliebre sibi
quasi contrarium" (100va).

73. Alcabitius: "significat de figuris hominum homine<m> . . . seductor"
(repeated by Bonatti). Scot: "In genere est planeta . . . pessimus aliorum, eo quod
est . . . seductor" (M, 100rb), but "Hic quidem homo non est seductor" (100va).

74. Bonatti: "Et ut multum tales vivunt in labore et angustia et paupertate,
et comedunt mala cibaria et foetida."

75. Albumasar: "labor." Alcabitius: "significat . . . laborem" (repeated by
Bonatti). Ibn Ezra: "Et eius artificium est omne laboriosum plurimum." Scot: "est
stella . . . laboriosa" (M, 100ra).

76. St. Macarius the Elder (Par. 22.49) also made manual labor part of his
daily routine: Singleton, ad loc. (p. 361).

77. RB 4.14, 31.9, 53.15, 55.9, 58.24, 59.title and 7, 66.3.

78. RB 53.15: "Pauperum et peregrinorum maxime susceptioni cura sollicite
exhibeatur, quia in ipsis magis Christus suscipitur" (ed. Fry, p. 258). Benedictine
monks were known for their hospitality, which is a Saturnian trait. Thus Scot:
"Dominatur enim generaliter contra . . . hostiari<o>s, canos . . . et egros hospi-
talium" (M, 100rb). Cf. the echo at Par. 21.129: the Apostles were content to eat at
any place that received them ("ostello"; cf. Latin hospitium).

79. Ibn Ezra: "et ipse denotat . . . paupertatem." Scot: "Saturni paupertatem, tristitiam, et vitam miserie mentis" (M, 100ra); "est stella multum alta, et
ideo . . . nutrix pauperitatis" (100ra); even when weakest, Saturn "tamen suo posse
infortunium conservat unicuique, sicut paupertatem" (100rb); and "Hic quidem
homo naturaliter delectatur in arte . . . que semper pertinet ad paupertatem, et
ipsum tenet in paupertate, ac facit infelicem seu infortunatum, tristem, cogitantem,
et miserum" (100va).

80. According to John of Seville, hardships are a property of Saturn: "est
stella aerumnosorum."

81. Ptolemy, Quad. 2.8: "In terrarum quoque fructibus evenient diminutiones, paucitates, ac detrimenta, et maxime in his, quibus homines opus habent

necessario erunt autem eorum detrimenta . . . ita quod ex hoc quandoque caristia proveniet, cuius occasione morientur homines" (ed. 1551, p. 30). Scot: "cuius proprietas est . . . omne malum significare . . . velut . . . famen, karistiam" (M, 100ra); "Sunt karistie omnium victualium respectu soliti" (100rb); "Est etiam homo pauci cibi et minoris potus" (100va).

82. Alcabitius: "significat de figuris hominum homine<m> macer." Scot: "est stella multum alta, et ideo . . . macra" (M, 100ra).

83. Alcabitius: "Et dixerunt quidam alii quod Saturnus significat . . . stomachum." Bonatti: "Et dixit Albubetri [sic] quod significat . . . stomachum." Scot: "Saturnus naturaliter tenet interiora corporis, ut . . . certam partem stomachi."

84. Albumasar: "accidentaliter . . . vorax." Alcabitius: "Et fortassis erit [homo] . . . multe comestionis." Bonatti: "facit homines multae comestionis." *Comestio* is scholastic Latin for "consuming (a meal)": R. J. Deferrari, *A Latin-English Dictionary of St. Thomas Aquinas* (Boston: St. Paul Editions, 1960).

85. Ibn Ezra: "Eius vero est arborum pars omnis glandium." Latin *glans* signifies "the fruit of any mast-bearing trees, esp. acorn or beechmast" (*Oxford Latin Dictionary*); "mast" is simply a collective term for nuts.

86. Ptolemy, *Quad.* 2.8: "detrimenta per vermes, qui creantur in oleribus" (ed. 1551, p. 30). Haly: "damnificat nutritionem eius [sc. nati]." Ibn Ezra: "De locis vero possidet . . . putrefactiones." Scot: "oleum coagulat, mel inspis<s>at" (M, 100ra). Cf. John of Seville: "significat in putridis tumidis infirmitatibus." Bonatti says Saturn's natives "comedunt mala cibaria et foetida." Albumasar, Alcabitius, and Ibn Ezra also remark on the fetid odors produced by Saturn.

87. Ibn Ezra: "Et hominis nature vel moris, ipsius pars est meditatio."

88. Klibansky et al., *Saturn and Melancholy*, pp. 155–156. Albumasar: "multe cogitationis" and "longa cogitatio." Ibn Ezra: "Eius quidem pars est anime hominis: cogitationis vis" and "longe cogitationis." Scot: "In genere est planeta . . . pessimus aliorum, eo quod est . . . cogitabilis" (M, 100rb), and "sepe moratur tristis, multa cogitans et proponens" (100va).

89. Albumasar: "deliberatio quoque et intellectus." Haly: "non habet agilem intellectum." Scot: "sepe se desperans cogitando istud et illud" (M, 100va). The image of weighing in the balance (*Par.* 21.24) may also be influenced by the Saturnian craft of making "stateras" (100va).

90. Bonatti: "Et significat . . . malas cogitationes." Scot: "cuius proprietas est . . . omne malum significare . . . velut . . . cogitationem" (M, 100ra).

91. Alcabitius: "significat profunditatem consilii." Haly: "profundas habet opiniones." Ibn Ezra: "sapiens in consciliis [sic] et dei obsequio." Bonatti: "Et dixit Albuaz quod si [Saturnus] fuerit boni esse, significat profunditatem scientiae, et consilium bonum et profundum, tale quod vix aut nunquam sciet alius meliorare illud."

92. Gregory the Great, *Dialogi* 2.8 (ed. *Sources chrétiennes*, 260:163).

93. Gregory, *Dialogi* 2.3 (ed. *Sources chrétiennes*, 260:143).

94. Scot: "cuius proprietas est . . . omne malum significare . . . velut . . . discordiam in domesticis" (M, 100ra).

95. Cf. John of Seville: "significat in morsu venenosi animalis."

96. John of Lodi, *Vita B. Petri Damiani*, ed. Migne, *Pat. Lat.* 144:113–146;

also in *Acta sanctorum*, Feb. III (1658), pp. 416–427. The credibility of this source has been convincingly argued by Lester K. Little, "The Personal Development of Peter Damian," *Order and Innovation in the Middle Ages: Essays in Honor of Joseph R. Strayer*, ed. William C. Jordan et al. (Princeton, N.J.: Princeton University Press, 1976), pp. 317–341, 523–528.

97. Sapegno probably exaggerates in saying Peter was "da poverissima famiglia" (p. 1044). John of Lodi, our only source for Peter's early years, says he was "honestis parentibus editus." The family had enough for the brothers to worry about the size of their inheritance. But when Peter was orphaned, a cruel sister-in-law left him to go about barefoot in rags ("pedibus nudis, vestibus ibat incultus"), so, whatever his family's status, he himself lived like the poor. *Vita B. Petri Damiani* 1 (Migne, *Pat. Lat.* 144:115–116).

98. John of Lodi, *Vita B. Petri Damiani* 1 (Migne, *Pat. Lat.* 144:116): "ad porcos pascendos ejicitur."

99. John of Seville: "porci." Ibn Ezra: "De animalibus . . . omne animal magnum turpe, velut sunt porci."

100. This seems a fair inference from his success as a student, teacher, and writer. Cf. John of Lodi, *Vita B. Petri Daminai* 2 (Migne, *Pat. Lat.*, 144:117): "in quibus [studiis liberalibus] scilicet tam docilis tamque industrius est agnitus, ut ipsis suis doctoribus mirabilis haberetur."

101. Alcabitius: "significat de figuris hominum homine<m> . . . callidus, ingeniosus," and "significat . . . ingenia" (both repeated by Bonatti). Ibn Ezra: "Et hominis nature vel moris, ipsius pars est . . . calliditas."

102. John of Lodi, *Vita B. Petri Damiani* 2 (Migne, *Pat. Lat.* 144:117).

103. Haly: "diligit edificare, seminare, plantare, et populare." The operative words of a typical legatine commission (1225) were: "plene legationis officium duximus commitendum, data sibi libera potestate destruendi et evellendi, edificandi atque plantandi, disponendi, ordinandi, statuendi, diffiniendi et faciendi quecumque, secundum datam sibi a Deo prudenciam, viderit facienda." *Layettes du Trésor des chartes*, ed. A. Teulet, vol. 2 (Paris: Plon, 1866), p. 48. On the formula, see Karl Ruess, *Die rechtliche Stellung der päpstlichen Legaten bis Bonifaz VIII*, Görres-Gesellschaft, Sektion für Rechts- und Sozialwissenschaft 13 (Paderborn: Schöningh, 1912), p. 67.

104. At *Par.* 21.122, Petrocchi takes *fu* to be in the first person rather than the third, and accordingly he punctuates it *fu'* (ad loc., p. 354); Singleton translates accordingly. Since all the manuscripts read simply *fu* (except one reading *fu io*), I indicate that the tendentious apostrophe is merely an optional alternative.

105. See the discussion by Arsenio Frugoni (*Enciclopedia dantesca*, 4:490), who concludes that Dante meant to distinguish one Peter from the other. See also *Enciclopedia dantesca*, 4:511.

106. Scot: "Significat etiam . . . rumores falsos" (M, 100rb). Alcabitius and Bonatti note that Saturn makes men suspicious and causes them to whisper; Scot also mentions the suspicious tendency (100rb).

107. Scot: "cuius proprietas est . . . omne malum significare amicis et inimicis" (M, 100ra). Other general statements of Saturn's generally evil nature: Alcabitius: "est . . . malus." Scot: "Est quidem planeta fortis in malo et potens, malum

semper significans et non bonum" (100ra); "est stella multum alta, et ideo . . . conservans malum, vitans bonum" (100ra); "naturam Saturni est summe . . . mala" (100rb)

108. Scot: "Hic quidem homo naturaliter delectatur in arte . . . vile vel infami" (M, 100va). Alcabitius: "et significat . . . res viles et laboriosas si fuerit malus, ut confricationes in balneis, et fullones, et nautas."

109. Ibn Ezra: "Et in nullis rebus eius adest utilitas." Scot: "est stella multum alta, et ideo . . . bonitate vacua" (M, 100ra); cf. "Hic quidem homo [Saturninus] . . . est . . . in bono simplex" (100va).

110. Albumasar: "noxa facinora." Haly: "vilipensus [est homo Saturninus] cum vilipensis." Ibn Ezra: "Cuius quidem utilitas est modica nocumentum vero grande." Scot: "est stella . . . multis nociva" (M, 100ra), and "naturam Saturni est . . . summe nociva" (100rb).

111. Albumasar: "omnisque malitia, iniquitas, et violentia . . . omnisque boni odium et invidia."

112. Cf. *Convivio* 4.28.

113. Scot: "homo saturninus . . . est pessimus ceterorum, nisi sit divinitus" (M, 100vb).

114. Scot: "est stella . . . malivola" (M, 100ra).

115. Bonatti: "Saturnus dat hominem esse . . . turpe."

116. Albumasar: "hereditates resque antique." Alcabitius: "significat . . . almaverith, idest substantias mortuorum" ("quae remanet post ipsos" adds Bonatti); "significat de substantia . . . hereditates"; "significat . . . res . . . hereditatum." Bonatti: "significat res antiquas et durabiles, sicut sunt haereditates quae deveniunt aliunde, et maxime ex mortuis, et praedia quae acquirent ab eo per fas potius quam per nefas." The *praedia* mentioned in the last citation apply to lands donated to the order's endowment (cf. *Par.* 22.79–84) rather than to the *Rule* itself.

117. On the date of *RB* (between 537 and 553), see R. Kay, "Benedict, Justinian, and Donations *Mortis Causa* in the *Regula Magistri*," *Revue Bénédictine* 90 (1980), 169–193, at pp. 188–193. Approved by A. de Vogüé, "Les Dates de Saint Benoît et de sa Règle d'après quelques travaux recents," *Regulae Benedicti studia: Annuarium internationale* 12 (1983), 11–27, at pp. 18–23.

118. Ibn Ezra: "et ipse denotat . . . mutationem." Hence the poet's choice of verbs: "mi trasmutai" and "t'avrebbe trasmutato" (*Par.* 21.21 and 22.10).

119. Ibn Ezra: "Et ipse denotat dissipationem, destructionem." Scot: "cuius proprietas est . . . omne malum significare . . . velut . . . perditionem rerum" (M, 100ra), and "perditiones apparent rerum multis modis" (100rb).

120. Scot: "Significat etiam res antiquas et deformes . . . aflictiones [*sic*] hereditatis alicuius defuncti" (M, 100rb), and "est stella multum alta, et ideo . . . deformis" (100ra). Albumasar similarly assigns people who are physically deformed ("orbi") to Saturn.

121. Scot: "est stella . . . sterilis" (M, 100ra), and "cuius proprietas est . . . omne malum significare . . . velut . . . gravitatem casus superventuri . . . [et] terre sterilitatem" (100ra). Dante also hints darkly of just such a "serious emergency—*gravitatem casus superventuri*" at Fonte Avellana (*Par.* 21.120) and perhaps at the Roman curia as well (22.14–15).

122. Scot: "cuius proprietas est . . . promissi refrenatio . . . [et] deceptionem

in actibus" (M, 100ra); "facile alteri mentitur" (100va); "Est etiam . . . falsidicus" (100ra). Albumasar: "tum fraudes, nequitia doli, proditio . . . perfidia difficilis." Haly: "proditor." Ibn Ezra: "Et omnino ei deceptio inest fixa."

123. John of Seville: "vecordes." Ibn Ezra: "Et eius sunt infirmitates . . . [e.g.,] fatuitas." Scot: "est stella . . . furiosa" (M, 100ra).

124. Ibn Ezra: "Eius quoque est . . . lucrarique ex rebus mortuorum et in omni eo quod est annosum." John of Seville: "Est stella . . . opificis." Scot: "sunt sue [planetae] proprietatis, ut . . . divitias non superfluas, et illas cum lite et multis impedimentis sue conservationis" (M, 100ra).

125. Albumasar: "mercenarii." Scot: "avarus" characterizes both the planet and its native (M, 100rb–va).

126. Albumasar: "accidentaliter . . . tenax," and "eius est . . . fundi paratio, multaque interdum possessio." Scot: "cuius proprietas est retentio" (M, 100ra) and a memory "bone retentionis" (100va).

127. Scot: "beneficiorum que recipit obliviscitur" (M, 100va).

128. Bonatti: "Et habet significare quod accipiet pignora pignorantium se invicem in custodia, sed non curabit multum componere inter ipsos."

129. Albumasar: "regum consules." Alcabitius: "significat . . . eos qui presunt operibus" (repeated by Bonatti).

130. Scot: "Qui si aliqua vice fortunate habeat aliquod domum prosperitatis ad sui honorem et consolationem, ut prelaturam et dominationem super ceteros, illud non recognoscit secundum debitum gracie, et ideo se male gerit in eisdem ac ex maiori parte in omnibus que habeant rationabiliter facere, unde bonum quod ei datur ab alteris perditur, et iam datur potest dici penitus suffocatum ingratitudine, quare dicendum quod homo saturninus, idest natus sub Saturno, est pessimus ceterorum, nisi sit divinitus" (M, 100vb).

131. Both are Saturnian. Scot: "est stella . . . superba" (M, 100ra). On gluttony, see above, n. 84.

132. Ibn Ezra: "Et ipse denotat . . . conclamationem."

133. Haly: "est pauce tollerantie, quia sustinere non potest malum."

134. Albumasar: "ira, nec tamen effrenis." Haly: "longam tenet iram." Ibn Ezra: "Et si Saturnus solus naturam hominis denotabit . . . erit . . . retinens iram."

135. Albumasar: "abhominatio" and "vulgus atque hominum genus infame." Scot: "est stella . . . infamis," and "significat . . . dedecus facturum bonis . . . [et] omne ignominiosum" (M, 100rb).

136. Anthony Bek, bishop of Durham 1283–1311, "bought cloth of the rarest and costliest and made it into horsecloths for his palfreys." His palfreys were the best in the world, and when he visited Rome in 1302, a greedy cardinal tricked the bishop into giving him a matched pair of them. Robertus de Graystanes, *Chronicon*, ed. J. Raine in *Historiae Dunelmensis scriptores tres*, Surtees Society 9 (London: J. B. Nichols and Son, 1839), p. 64.

137. John of Seville: "Est stella . . . coriarii." Ibn Ezra: "De hominibus eius pars sunt . . . communiter omnes . . . corii preparatores." Alcabitius: "significat ex operibus opera coriorum," and "significat opus consutorum coriorum ferarum animalium." Bonatti: "erit naturale officium nati operari coria et facere operationes ex eis."

138. Ptolemy, *Quad*. 2.8: "generabit . . . timores" (ed. 1551, p. 30). Albumasar:

"metus." Haly: the native "timorosus est," and "timorosus in factis et motibus suis." Ibn Ezra: "timorosus et dubitans." Scot: "gentes tristantur timentes mala futuri, mali presumptiose" (M, 100rb), and "est . . . ex facili timidus" (100va).

139. Ptolemy, *Quad.* 2.8: "generabit . . . anxietates" (ed. 1551, p. 30). Albumasar: "dubitatio." Haly: "planeta . . . anxietatum" and "impedite loquele." Bonatti: "Et si fuerit mali esse, significat credulitatem unitatis cum haesitatione seu dubitatione multa."

140. Alcabitius: "significat . . . audaciam" (repeated by Bonatti), and "Etsi fuerit malus erit indiscretus." Bonatti: Et si fuerit Saturnus mali esse, natus indiscretus."

141. Ptolemy, *Quad.* 2.8: "generabit . . . stupores" (ed. 1551, p. 30). Bonatti: "significat . . . mentis afflictionem." Scot: "cuius proprietas est . . . omne malum significare . . . velut . . . obscuritatem intellectum" (M, 100ra), and "significat etiam . . . turbiditatem sensus cuiuslibet animalis" (100rb).

142. Singleton translates "stupore" at *Par.* 22.1 as "amazement," though "awe" would be closer: see Christopher Ryan's translation of *Conv.* 4.25.4–5 (p. 187). According to Dante's definition of *stupore* (ibid.), awe is accompanied by a desire to learn about objects that have amazed or astonished the subject. However, if "Oppresso di stupore" (*Par.* 22.1) intentionally echoes Boethius, *Philosophiae consolationis* 1.2 ("sed te, ut video, stupor oppressit"), docility would not be indicated, but rather incapacity, since the contrast there is between Boethius's former education in philosophy and his present state of stupefaction, i.e., he is "not merely silent, but altogether speechless and dumb" and "suffers only from lethargy (*lethargum*), a sickness common to deluded minds (*inlusarum mentium morbum*)" (trans. S. J. Tester, *The Consolation of Philosophy*, Loeb Classical Library [Cambridge, Mass.: Harvard University Press, 1973], p. 139).

143. Boyde elaborates on the *stupore*-motif: *Dante Philomythes*, pp. 43–51.

144. Albumasar: "malefici . . . omneque magice omnisque maleficii studium postremo longa cogitatio; rarus sermo; altus secretorum intellectus; occulta profundorum atque inexhausta sapientia." Cf. Haly: "facit experientiam ligandi nigromantica et mirabilia."

145. Georg Rabuse pointed out several parallel passages in Macrobius and an especially striking one in Firmicus Maternus: "Saturne et l'échelle de Jacob," *Archives d'histoire doctrinale et littéraire du moyen âge* 45 (1978), 7–31, esp. p. 21. Whether Dante knew these classical astrologers, and especially the latter, still seems to me to be doubtful.

146. Boethius, *Philosophiae consolatio* 1.pr.1.

147. Albumasar: "fures." Ibn Ezra: "De hominibus eius pars sunt . . . communiter omnes . . . fures." Scot: "naturaliter fur et latro" (M, 100va).

148. Alcabitius: "significat de figuris hominum homine<m> . . . recurvus." Scot: "Facit etiam . . . in gula et spallis curvum ante" (M, 100va); "et cum vadit videtur aspicere terram latrocina<li>ter" (100va); "cum vadit maiori parte prospicit terram" (100va).

149. Singleton ad *Par.* 21.26–27 (p. 348).

150. Ptolemy, *Quad.* 2.8: "In eis [*scil.* in mari ac in fluminibus] iter agere difficiliter accidet" (ed. 1551, p. 30). Albumasar: "eius est . . . tum summa et egestas

navigia, longa via et difficilis." Alcabitius: "significat peregrinationes longinquas" (repeated by Bonatti). Ibn Ezra: "et ipse denotat . . . vias longinquas periculis expositas," and "eius sunt infirmitates . . . iterum separatio." Scot: "principaliter ad . . . viatores" (M, 100ra), and "significat etiam . . . perigrinantes longinque" (100rb).

151. Ptolemy, *Quad.* 2.8: "generabit . . . fugas" (ed. 1551, p. 30). Albumasar: "eius est . . . longum exilium."

152. Alcabitius: "qui, cum ambulaverit mergit oculos suos in terram, ponderosus incessu, adiungens pedes." Bonatti amplifies: "qui, cum ambulaverit mergit oculos suos in terra, ponderosus cum ambulat adiungit pedes et habet eos curvos." Ibn Ezra: "cum duritia ambulans."

153. For the importance of *stabilitas loci*, see *RB* 1, 50–51, and 67; also n. 68, above.

154. Alcabitius: "habet ex coloribus nigredinem" ("nigrum," according to Bonatti). Albumasar: "accidentaliter obscurus." Ibn Ezra: "De visibilibus color eius est niger et pulverulentus," and "de locis vero possidet [Saturnus] . . . omnem locum obscurum inhabitatum." Bonatti: "Et dixit Adila, Saturnus dat hominem esse fuscum." Scot: "in colore brunus vel fuscus ut calamita [= storax] vel ferrum" (M, 100ra), and "Saturnus facit hominem . . . carne maculata colore fuscam vel nigram vel croceam aut quasi viridem" (100va).

155. For daws (*pole*), see R. T. Holbrook, "Romanic Lexicographical Miscellanies," *Modern Language Notes* 18 (1903), 42–45, at pp. 44–45.

156. Quoted by Sapegno ad loc. (p. 1038).

157. Ibn Ezra: "Eius siquidem avium sunt omnes corpore magne, quarum cossa existunt longa, ut strutio, aquila, rahien, idest ardea, et omnis avis cuius pertinens est garritus, corvus, nicticorarum, et avis quelibet cuius color niger existit."

Conclusion

1. Mary Carruthers, *The Book of Memory: A Study of Memory in Medieval Culture*, Cambridge Studies in Medieval Literature 10 (Cambridge: Cambridge University Press, 1990).

2. Boccaccio, *Trattatello in laude di Dante*, in his *Opere in versi; Corbaccio; Trattatello in laude di Dante; Prose latine; Epistole*, ed. P. G. Ricci, La Letteratura italiana: Storia e testi 9 (Milan: Ricciardi, 1965), p. 611.

3. Georg Rabuse, *Der kosmische Aufbau der Jenseitsreiche Dantes: Ein Schüssel zur Göttlichen Komödie* (Graz: Böhlaus, 1958).

4. J. D. North, *Chaucer's Universe* (New York: Oxford University Press, 1988).

5. The groundwork for a more precise understanding of Dante's angelology has been laid by Steven Bemrose, *Dante's Angelic Intelligences: Their Importance in the Cosmos and in Pre-Christian Religion*, Letture di Pensiero e d'Arte, 62 (Rome: Edizioni di storia e letteratura, 1983); but for some unanswered questions, see my review in *Speculum* 61 (1986), 384–386.

General Index

Dante and Beatrice appear throughout the work and therefore are not indexed. Similarly, references to astrology and the principal astrologers are indexed only for the Introduction. Each planet is not indexed for the chapter devoted to it, and likewise the principal characters are not indexed for the chapter on the heaven in which they appear. God is not indexed per se, but the Trinity and its persons are. The English text of the notes has been indexed but not the Latin.

Citation Index

University of Pennsylvania Press
MIDDLE AGES SERIES
Edward Peters, General Editor

F. R. P. Akehurst, trans. *The* Coutumes de Beauvaisis *of Philippe de Beaumanoir*. 1992

Peter L. Allen. *The Art of Love: Amatory Fiction from Ovid to the* Romance of the Rose. 1992

David Anderson. *Before the Knight's Tale: Imitation of Classical Epic in Boccaccio's* Teseida. 1988

Benjamin Arnold. *Count and Bishop in Medieval Germany: A Study of Regional Power, 1100–1350.* 1991

Mark C. Bartusis. *The Late Byzantine Army: Arms and Society, 1204–1453.* 1992

J. M. W. Bean. *From Lord to Patron: Lordship in Late Medieval England.* 1990

Uta-Renate Blumenthal. *The Investiture Controversy: Church and Monarchy from the Ninth to the Twelfth Century.* 1988

Daniel Bornstein, trans. *Dino Compagni's* Chronicle *of Florence.* 1986

Maureen Boulton. *The Song in the Story: Lyric Insertions in French Narrative Fiction, 1200–1400.* 1993

Betsy Bowden. *Chaucer Aloud: The Varieties Textual Interpretation.* 1987

James William Brodman. *Ransoming Captives in Crusader Spain: The Order of Merced on the Christian-Islamic Frontier,* 1986

Kevin Brownlee and Sylvia Huot, eds. *Rethinking the* Romance of the Rose*: Text, Image, Reception.* 1992

Matilda Tomaryn Bruckner. *Shaping Romance: Interpretation, Truth, and Closure in Twelfth-Century French Fictions.* 1993

Otto Brunner (Howard Kaminsky and James Van Horn Melton, eds. and trans.). Land *and Lordship: Structures of Governance in Medieval Austria.* 1992

Robert I. Burns, S.J., ed. *Emperor of Culture: Alfonso X the Learned of Castile and His Thirteenth-Century Renaissance.* 1990

David Burr. *Olivi and Franciscan Poverty: The Origins of the* Usus Pauper *Controversy.* 1989

David Burr. *Olivi's Peaceable Kingdom: A Reading of the Apocalypse Commentary.* 1993

Thomas Cable. *The English Alliterative Tradition.* 1991

Anthony K. Cassell and Victoria Kirkham, eds. and trans. *Diana's Hunt/Caccia di Diana: Boccaccio's First Fiction.* 1991

John C. Cavadini. *The Last Christology of the West: Adoptionism in Spain and Gaul, 785–820.* 1993

Brigitte Cazelles. *The Lady as Saint: A Collection of French Hagiographic Romances of the Thirteenth Century.* 1991

Karen Cherewatuk and Ulrike Wiethaus, eds. *Dear Sister: Medieval Women and the Epistolary Genre.* 1993

Anne L. Clark. *Elisabeth of Schönau: A Twelfth-Century Visionary.* 1992

Willene B. Clark and Meradith T. McMunn, eds. *Beasts and Birds of the Middle Ages: The Bestiary and Its Legacy.* 1989

Richard C. Dales. *The Scientific Achievement of the Middle Ages.* 1973

Charles T. Davis. *Dante's Italy and Other Essays.* 1984

Katherine Fisher Drew, trans. *The Burgundian Code.* 1972

Katherine Fisher Drew, trans. *The Laws of the Salian Franks.* 1991

Katherine Fisher Drew, trans. *The Lombard Laws.* 1973

Nancy Edwards. *The Archaeology of Early Medieval Ireland.* 1990

Margaret J. Ehrhart. *The Judgment of the Trojan Prince Paris in Medieval Literature.* 1987

Richard K. Emmerson and Ronald B. Herzman. *The Apocalyptic Imagination in Medieval Literature.* 1992

Theodore Evergates. *Feudal Society in Medieval France: Documents from the County of Champagne.* 1993

Felipe Fernández-Armesto. *Before Columbus: Exploration and Colonization from the Mediterranean to the Atlantic, 1229–1492.* 1987

R. D. Fulk. *A History of Old English Meter.* 1992

Patrick J. Geary. *Aristocracy in Provence: The Rhône Basin at the Dawn of the Carolingian Age.* 1985

Peter Heath. *Allegory and Philosophy in Avicenna (Ibn Sînâ), with a Translation of the Book of the Prophet Muḥammad's Ascent to Heaven.* 1992

J. N. Hillgarth, ed. *Christianity and Paganism, 350–750: The Conversion of Western Europe.* 1986

Richard C. Hoffman. *Land, Liberties, and Lordship in a Late Medieval Countryside: Agrarian Structures and Change in the Duchy of Wrocław.* 1990

Robert Hollander. *Boccaccio's Last Fiction: Il Corbaccio.* 1988

Edward B. Irving, Jr. *Rereading* Beowulf. 1989

C. Stephen Jaeger. *The Origins of Courtliness: Civilizing Trends and the Formation of Courtly Ideals, 939–1210.* 1985

William Chester Jordan. *The French Monarchy and the Jews: From Philip Augustus to the Last Capetians.* 1989

William Chester Jordan. *From Servitude to Freedom: Manumission in the Sénonais in the Thirteenth Century.* 1986

Richard Kay. *Dante's Christian Astrology.* 1994

Ellen E. Kittell. *From Ad Hoc to Routine: A Case Study in Medieval Bureaucracy.* 1991

Alan C. Kors and Edward Peters, eds. *Witchcraft in Europe, 1100–1700: A Documentary History.* 1972

Barbara M. Kreutz. *Before the Normans: Southern Italy in the Ninth and Tenth Centuries.* 1992

E. Ann Matter. *The Voice of My Beloved: The Song of Songs in Western Medieval Christianity*. 1990

María Rosa Menocal. *The Arabic Role in Medieval Literary History*. 1987

A. J. Minnis. *Medieval Theory of Authorship*. 1988

Lawrence Nees. *A Tainted Mantle: Hercules and the Carolingian Court*. 1991

Lynn H. Nelson, trans. *The Chronicle of San Juan de la Peña: A Fourteenth-Century Official History of the Crown of Aragon*. 1991

Charlotte A. Newman. *The Anglo-Norman Nobility in the Reign of Henry I: The Second Generation*. 1988

Joseph F. O'Callaghan. *The Cortez of Castile-León, 1188–1350*. 1989

Joseph F. O'Callaghan. *The Learned King: The Reign of Alfonso X of Castile*. 1993

David M. Olster. *Roman Defeat, Christian Response, and the Literary Construction of the Jew*. 1993

William D. Paden, ed. *The Voice of the Trobairitz: Perspectives on the Women Troubadours*. 1989

Edward Peters. *The Magician, the Witch, and the Law*. 1982

Edward Peters, ed. *Christian Society and the Crusades, 1198–1229: Sources in Translation, including* The Capture of Damietta *by Oliver of Paderborn*. 1971

Edward Peters, ed. *The First Crusade: The* Chronicle of Fulcher of Chartres *and Other Source Materials*. 1971

Edward Peters, ed. *Heresy and Authority in Medieval Europe*. 1980

James M. Powell. *Albertanus of Brescia: The Pursuit of Happiness in the Early Thirteenth Century*. 1992

James M. Powell. *Anatomy of a Crusade, 1213–1221*. 1986

Jean Renart (Patricia Terry and Nancy Vine Durling, trans.). *The Romance of the Rose or Guillaume de Dole*. 1993

Michael Resler, trans. Erec *by Hartmann von Aue*. 1987

Pierre Riché (Michael Idomir Allen, trans.). *The Carolingians: A Family Who Forged Europe*. 1993

Pierre Riché (Jo Ann McNamara, trans.). *Daily Life in the World of Charlemagne*. 1978

Jonathan Riley-Smith. *The First Crusade and the Idea of Crusading*. 1986

Joel T. Rosenthal. *Patriarchy and Families of Privilege in Fifteenth-Century England*. 1991

Teofilo F. Ruiz. *Crisis and Continuity: Land and Town in Medieval Castile*. 1993

Steven D. Sargent, ed. and trans. *On the Threshold of Exact Science: Selected Writings of Anneliese Maier on Late Medieval Natural Philosophy*. 1982

Robin Chapman Stacey. *The Road to Judgment: From Custom to Court in Medieval Ireland and Wales*. 1994

Sarah Stanbury. *Seeing the* Gawain-Poet: Description and the Act of Perception. 1992

Thomas C. Stillinger. *The Song of Troilus: Lyric Authority in the Medieval Book*. 1992

Susan Mosher Stuard. *A State of Deference: Ragusa/Dubrovnik in the Medieval Centuries*. 1992

Susan Mosher Stuard, ed. *Women in Medieval History and Historiography*. 1987

Susan Mosher Stuard, ed. *Women in Medieval Society*. 1976

Jonathan Sumption. *The Hundred Years War: Trial by Battle.* 1992

Ronald E. Surtz. *The Guitar of God: Gender, Power, and Authority in the Visionary World of Mother Juana de la Cruz (1481–1534).* 1990

William H. TeBrake. *A Plague of Insurrection: Popular Politics and Peasant Revolt in Flanders, 1323–1328.* 1993

Patricia Terry, trans. *Poems of the Elder Edda.* 1990

Hugh M. Thomas. *Vassals, Heiresses, Crusaders, and Thugs: The Gentry of Angevin Yorkshire, 1154–1216.* 1993

Frank Tobin. *Meister Eckhart: Thought and Language.* 1986

Ralph V. Turner. *Men Raised from the Dust: Administrative Service and Upward Mobility in Angevin England.* 1988

Harry Turtledove, trans. *The* Chronicle *of Theophanes: An English Translation of* Anni Mundi *6095–6305 (A.D. 602–813).* 1982

Mary F. Wack. *Lovesickness in the Middle Ages: The* Viaticum *and Its Commentaries.* 1990

Benedicta Ward. *Miracles and the Medieval Mind: Theory, Record, and Event, 1000–1215.* 1982

Suzanne Fonay Wemple. *Women in Frankish Society: Marriage and the Cloister, 500–900.* 1981

Jan M. Ziolkowski. *Talking Animals: Medieval Latin Beast Poetry, 750–1150.* 1993

This book has been set in Linotron Galliard. Galliard was designed for Mergenthaler in 1978 by Matthew Carter. Galliard retains many of the features of a sixteenth-century typeface cut by Robert Granjon but has some modifications that give it a more contemporary look.

Printed on acid-free paper.